with faith in the works of words:

the beginnings of reconciliation
in south africa

1985–1995

with faith in the works of words:
the beginnings of reconciliation
in south africa

1985–1995

erik doxtader

Michigan State University Press
East Lansing

David Philip Publishers
Cape Town

Michigan State University Press
1405 S. Harrison Rd., Ste. 25
East Lansing, MI 48823-5245
www.msupress.msu.edu
Printed and Bound in the United States of America.
978-0-87013-851-5

Doxtader, Erik.
With faith in the works of words : the beginnings of reconciliation in South Africa, 1985–1995/Erik Doxtader.
p. cm.
First published: Claremont, South Africa: David Philip Publishers, 2008.
Includes bibliographical references and index.
ISBN 978-0-87013-851-5 (cloth: alk. paper)
1. South Africa. Truth and Reconciliation Commission—History. 2. Reconciliation—Political aspects—
South Africa—History—20th century. 3. Reconciliation—Social aspects—South Africa—History—
20th century. 4. Human rights—South Africa—History—20th century. 5. Apartheid—South Africa.
6. South Africa—Politics and government—1978–1989. 7. South Africa—Politics and government—
1989–1994. 8. South Africa—Race relations—Political aspects—History—20th century. I. Title.

DT1945 .D695 2009
968.06'4—dc22
2008032043

First published in southern Africa by David Philip Publishers
An imprint of New Africa Books (Pty) Ltd

© in text: Erik Doxtader
© in original published edition: New Africa Books (Pty) Ltd

Editor: Arlene Stephenson
Text design and layout: Claudine Willatt-Bate
Proofreader: Helen Hacksley
Indexer: Sandra Cattich
Cover design: Nic Jooste, Comet Design
Cover image: 'Map without Words' by Jenny Parsons

contents

abbreviations vii
preface(s) ix

introduction: the (rhetorical) question of reconciliation
in south africa 1
(dis)placing reconciliation's history, 5 inaugurating words, 11 arguing about
an exceptional past, 18

a footnote (with which to reconcile)? 25

1. the struggle of beginning words: reconciliation in a state
    of emergency 35
    making the "potential" of apartheid's word, 43 by grace or mass action:
    (re)defining the faith and work of reconciliation, 57 between the third force
    and the third way: discerning reconciliation's kairos, 73

2. a middle course between extremes: reconciliation as an art
    of inventing "talk about talk" 85
    different unities in difference: the (non)reconciling terms of afrikaner and anc
    nationalism, 92 making a climate out of a violent situation, 110 trading
    history for words (about words), 126

3. reconciling the sovereign's discourse: constituting the "sufficient
    consensus" of a revolution 140
    codesa's sovereign question, 144 a difficult season of climate changes, 157
    a sufficiently consensual (speech) act of constitution, 175

4. **the opposing questions of beginning: how will the word(s) of reconciliation "deal with the past"? 199**
achieving reconciliation, 203 *the standing of history (making) in transition*, 217 *constituting a vocabulary to deal with the past*, 227

5. **the sacrifices of deliberation: making reconciliation's law 242**
for a model in the middle: speaking to(ward) the act of reconciliation, 247 *composing reconciliation's law of publicity*, 256 *reconciling the difficult sacrifice of a "gift"*, 268

epilogue: the potential of an exceptional beginning 283
reconciling (the) works of words, 285 *making a present for the future's past*, 293

notes 299
bibliography 348
index 364

abbreviations

AAC	All-African Convention	MK	Umkhonto we Sizwe (Spear of the Nation)
AC	Amnesty Committee		
ACDP	African Christian Democratic Party	NEC	National Executive Committee (African National Congress)
ANC	African National Congress	NGO	Non-Governmental Organisation
ANCYL	African National Congress Youth League	NGK	Nederduitse Gereformeerde Kerk (Dutch Reformed Church)
APLA	Azanian People's Liberation Army	NGSK	Nederduitse Gereformeerde Sendingkerk (Dutch Reformed Mission Church)
AVF	Afrikaner Volksfront (Afrikaner Popular Front)	NHK	Nederduitsch Hervormde Kerk
AVU	Afrikaner Volksunie (Afrikaner People's Union)	NIR	National Initiative for Reconciliation
AWB	Afrikaner Weerstandsbeweging (Afrikaner Resistance Movement)	NP	National Party
		NPA	National Peace Accord
AZAPO	Azanian People's Organisation	OAU	Organisation of African Unity
		PAC	Pan Africanist Congress
BC	Black Consciousness	PNUR	Promotion of National Unity and Reconciliation Act
BCM	Black Consciousness Movement	SABC	South African Broadcasting Company
CCB	Civil Cooperation Bureau	SACC	South African Council of Churches
CODESA	Convention for a Democratic South Africa	SACP	South African Communist Party
COSAG	Concerned South Africans Group	SADF	South African Defence Force
COSATU	Congress of South African Trade Unions	SAG	South African Government
		SAIRR	South African Institute of Race Relations
CP	Conservative Party	SAP	South African Police
DP	Democratic Party	SAPA	South African Press Association
EPG	Eminent Persons Group	SPR	States, Provinces, Regions
FA	Freedom Alliance	TEC	Transitional Executive Council
FF	Freedom Front	TRC	Truth and Reconciliation Commission
HRC	Human Rights Commission		
HRVC	Human Rights Violations Committee (TRC)	TVBC	Transkei, Venda, Bophuthatswana and Ciskei "Independent" States
IEC	Independent Electoral Commission		
IFP	Inkatha Freedom Party	UDF	United Democratic Front
KZG	KwaZulu Government	WARC	World Alliance of Reformed Churches
MPNP	Multi-Party Negotiating Process		

preface(s)

i

There have been many beginnings of reconciliation in South Africa. Each has been prefaced with the puzzle of how to begin (again). In the midst of historical division that seems to fate endless violence, how is it possible to weave a unity in difference that can make history? This is a rhetorical question. In the name of a beginning, reconciliation begins with a belief that there are words which hold the potential for all things to become new. Such faith is not easy. Its work comes with no guarantees.

For the very best and the very worst of reasons, reconciliation's words have been used repeatedly to imagine and craft a path between South Africa's past and its future. This book is a history of these difficult words and an argument about how they shaped South Africa's transition from statutory apartheid to non-racial democracy. While concerned to expose and explain some of reconciliation's deeper and more twisted roots, my primary interest is the period between 1985 and 1995. Here, with the onset of a brutal state of emergency, the idea of reconciliation serves both to expose apartheid's crime against humanity and to energise the struggle against it. A bit later, in the name of "negotiated revolution", reconciliation's practice plays a crucial role in turning entrenched justifications for violence into the grounds for productive disagreement and even moments of understanding. Making engaged opponents out of sworn enemies, reconciliation's fragile words come to constitute the potential for politics and a politics of potential.

What then of South Africa's Truth and Reconciliation Commission (TRC)? It seems to me that too much and not enough has been said about this important and wholly controversial body. Many have been tempted to reduce the history of reconciliation in South Africa to the TRC's "unique experiment". Ignoring the very historical sensibility that was used to justify the Commission's efforts, many more rely on a stylised and now rather distorted story to explain its development. As these accounts may not suffice, the latter portion of this book looks behind the TRC and contends that its rationale, formation, and contested mandate can only be understood through a consideration of reconciliation's larger role in the South African transition.

There is an unforgiving quality to reconciliation's various and variable beginnings. This is to say both that reconciliation in South Africa is not always about forgiveness and that there is no assured method for investigating its (prior) gift. In the domain of art far more than science, reconciliation appears to begin with those words that hold the seemingly miraculous capacity to form and fashion human relationships. With this book, I want to suggest that the question of reconciliation's history is nothing less than a call to undertake a rhetorical philosophy of its expression.

ii

Some of the first words that I heard about reconciliation in South Africa were carried over my car radio as I was driving home on an April evening in 1996. At the time, I was paying somewhat less attention to events in South Africa than in the preceding years. In typical public radio form, the report concerned the first hearings convened by the TRC and featured sound bites from Desmond Tutu and snippets of the testimony presented to the Commission by Nyameka Goniwe. Listening with interest to the point of missing my turn-off and also feeling a bit wary, I found myself filtering the exposé through my recent reflections on Hegel's early theological writings and wondering whether reconciliation's role in South Africa's turn from apartheid was an echo of his claim that the need for reconciliation appears in the face of violence that renders life hostile to itself. Following quickly was the question that Hegel deferred: how do words of reconciliation transform human relationships?

Carried by this curiosity, I searched over the next weeks for more specific information about the TRC and its development. Awash in western reportage and dissatisfied with its lack of detail, I happened upon a number of documents from the 1980s, all of which demonstrated in no uncertain terms that the notion and practice of reconciliation had been important and controversial in South Africa for quite some time. In the most basic sense, this book began with the puzzles that followed from the discovery that reconciliation was not so new after all. Originally, I envisaged a volume that worked from early religious debates over reconciliation to the constitutional negotiations that ended statutory apartheid and then through the TRC's attempt to help South Africa "deal with its past". This proved untenable. There was simply too much material and the question of reconciliation's role in the late days of struggle and early years of transition proved more complex than I had first imagined. Wading through boxes at the National Archives in Pretoria, the unsorted transcripts from South Africa's two constitutional conventions revealed layer upon layer of argumentation about reconciliation, a heated debate over how to talk about talk, and then a protracted attempt to speak in ways that would make South Africa anew. So too, three dusty and uncatalogued boxes at Parliament's archive in Cape Town betrayed how this work set the stage for a nearly two-year controversy over the merits of a truth commission and the ways in which this nuanced dispute turned the TRC against that which many have defended as its motivating and founding "compromise".

Among others, these inquiries underscored how the deep optimism inspired by South Africa's transition has its counterpart in reservations about whether reconciliation rests on a naïve idealism or a proselytising desire to spread the good news. Whether proffered by the philosophers, theologians, or politicians, definitive renderings of reconciliation are frequently met with worries about the hidden agendas that lurk within a concept's magic and the costs that accumulate in the shadow of its hope for grace. In short, expressions of interest in reconciliation frequently bring boisterous assent from the choir and muttered rebuke from guardians worried that the flock has been blinded to the timeless virtue of realism. As both of these reactions contain a mixture of truth and dogma, the resulting ambiguity makes it tempting to assume that reconciliation's power is either an unsolvable mystery or an incoherent hope. What the South African case suggests, however, is that reconciliation may be better understood as a form of potential, a kind of transitional power that may or may not come to be (actualised). On this view, the demonstrable risk of reconciliation is that we may wait endlessly on its promise of renewal. At the same time, however, reconciliation may interrupt history and mount a challenge to its precedent. Its potential is a moment between the times that holds out the opportunity for a critique of violence that takes exception to given forms of human (non)interaction and reflects carefully on the sacrifice entailed in their remaking.

Reconciliation's potential does not arise *ex nihilo*. Nor is it explained by vague truisms about "revolutions without victors" or slogans fashioned from Milan Kundera's literature. Along with the increasingly common claim that it is possible to model the "South African experience", this means that there is now a somewhat urgent need to investigate reconciliation's historical depth and the particularities of its performance. Recalling comments by Walter Benjamin, in one of his early theories of criticism, the problem of reconciliation's generalisability enters a cul-de-sac at precisely the point at which it is defined as a procedure for "democratic consolidation" or inflated into the totality of a revolutionary experience. Neither puppet nor metaphysics, reconciliation in South Africa speaks to the ways in which human beings forge "possibilities of understanding". A potential of this sort, as Frantz Fanon suggested, demands that we be "doubly careful" not to mistake a relational good for either a stable product or a fanciful dream.

Tied to these concerns in a certain way, there is one additional matter that must not be left unsaid, although I leave it to those who understand its potential distinction to reflect on whether it too calls for a certain kind of reconciliation, or at least additional work. Without apology, this is a Cape Town book. While it grew in many places – inside and outside South Africa – it ultimately found form under the shadow of the mountain, in a remarkable city that has become a home and which continues to struggle with the history and power of its manifold divisions, on a peninsula where a tremendous human spirit remains haunted by a hedge of bitter almonds that continues to grow.

iii

The appearance of this book has been prefaced by myriad forms of assistance and numerous acts of kindness. In 1999, the project found its footing with the help of a fellowship provided by the Social Science Research Council and the MacArthur Foundation. This generous award afforded the time and resources needed to undertake several years of research. Thereafter, much appreciated support from the University of North Carolina – Chapel Hill and a delightful period at the Institute for Justice and Reconciliation allowed me to extend my time in Cape Town. More recently, several grants from the University of Wisconsin have made it possible for me to spend nearly half of each year in South Africa.

In the early and uncertain days when it is difficult not to wonder whether one is dallying in the midst of folly, Giorgio Agamben, Jay Bernstein, Liz Goodstein, and Bill O'Neill lent reassurance, offered inspiring insights, and took the time for conversations about how to think through and around the concept of reconciliation. As the project took fuller form, a number of people lent a critical ear, shared their perspectives on reconciliation's meaning in South Africa, and provided materials that added crucial substance to my research. In this regard, I am particularly grateful to Karin Alexander, George Bizos, Mary Burton, Maurice Charland, Halton Cheadle, Lynn Clarke, Hugh Corder, Scott Deatherage, John de Gruchy, Andre du Toit, Fanie du Toit,

Carol Esau, Nyameka Goniwe, Felipe Gutterriez, Paul Haupt, Wilmot James, Heinz Klug, Antjie Krog, Karla Leeper, Gordon Mitchell, Laurie Nathan, Reingard Nethersole, Sifiso Ngesi, Amy Ross, Fiona Ross, Nicky Rousseau, Tracey Saunders, Jeremy Sarkin, Tyrone Savage, Graeme Simpson, Britta Sjogren, Jonathan VanAntwerpen, and Rob Walker. The staff at the South African National Archives was incredibly accommodating and helpful in my attempt to trace certain lines of debate at CODESA and the MPNP. So too, the librarians at the University of Cape Town and Parliament were extremely generous, not least as they helped find answers to picky questions and provided documents that shed new light on the TRC's creation. In slightly different form, small portions of chapters one and four appeared in a 2001 essay that was published in *Rhetoric and Public Affairs*. I appreciate Michigan State University Press's permission to use that material here.

I want to express my deep appreciation to the many individuals who had much better things to do and yet still had the generosity of spirit to devote the time and energy for an interview and in many cases a follow-up conversation. All of these exchanges revealed new dimensions to the problem at hand and offered candid if not sometimes difficult perspectives on reconciliation's contested history. In particular, I am grateful to Desmond Tutu for providing a crucial lesson about the limits of analytic thinking and Mac Maharaj for indulging my near endless curiosity about the post-amble of the 1993 interim constitution. Too, I would like to say that the late Dullah Omar offered incredible encouragement and assistance that allowed me to see around a vital corner.

In part and whole, the manuscript was read by a number of people and benefited greatly from their comments. Lectures and talks at the Institut de France, Concordia University–Montreal, the University of Iowa, the University of California–Berkeley, and Baylor University offered the chance for conversation and feedback that proved very helpful in revising certain lines of argument. The members of my seminar on South African reconciliation and transitional politics and the participants in the University of Wisconsin African Studies colloquium helped me to see the missing pieces of the puzzle and how they fit together. Sarah Burgess read closely, considered the details, and asked the very best of questions. Steve Lucas provided invaluable suggestions about how to frame the book's central claims. His efforts, along with the support of Rob Asen, Sue Zaeske, Chris Garlough, and Rob Howard, helped bring the project to a close. At David Philip, Alfred LeMaitre has been the very best of publishers. I have truly appreciated his enthusiasm for the manuscript and am very grateful for his tremendous assistance in getting around the last turn.

Absolute stars, my parents supported this work from the beginning, scoured the shelves at used bookstores for volumes on South African history, clipped newspaper articles, and trusted in my need and then my desire to live so very far away. Despite its cost, Bill Balthrop encouraged the project from start to finish. In a deeply troubling moment, Chris Shannon somehow understood and did so with the greatest of care – thank you. Mark and Jenny Parsons listened sympathetically, helped me to think laterally, and took me well away from the project at precisely the right times.

Several individuals have played an indescribably important role in the writing of this book. With unalloyed generosity, Philippe Salazar welcomed me to Cape Town, helped me to gain my bearings, warned me of the city's allure, and offered a lovely place to work in the Centre for Rhetoric Studies at the University of Cape Town. A scholar in the true sense of the word, Philippe tarried with my arguments, taught me to look for that which "dances on the heads of pins", opened the doors to numerous forums at which I was able to present portions of the manuscript, and inspired me over the course of many long dinners by the sea to sharpen my questions and dig deeper. With a remarkable understanding of reconciliation, Charles Villa-Vicencio lent enormous support for my research, engaged with the project in a way that helped me to learn how to say what I wanted to say, and provided caring encouragement at moments when the project seemed to defy completion. He also offered an incredible gift – the opportunity to step outside the academy in order to consider the problem of reconciliation from a number of other vantage points. As a Research Fellow at the Institute for Justice and Reconciliation, I have benefited immensely from this perspective.

There is always a certain sadness that attends my reading of those usually last lines in which an author seems compelled to apologise for long hours spent at the writing desk and other apparent transgressions. With Sara, things are happily different. Together, the calling of our respective work is linked tightly with the joy of our play; our times of quiet solitude beckon toward and enrich our animated engagements; moments of ordinary life open to adventure and back again. For these sustaining rhythms of love and companionship, I am truly and humbly grateful.

Tamboerskloof
January 2007

this book is dedicated to
Carl Wangsvick, Donn Parson, and the memory of Thomas Farrell

introduction:
the (rhetorical) question
of reconciliation in south africa

*History writes the word "Reconciliation" over all her
quarrels and will surely write it over the unhappy
differences which have agitated us in the past. What
is good in our work is not disposed of in the present,
but can safely appeal to the ear of the future. To that
ear you have appealed; so do we. Who knows but
that there our respective contentions will reach a
friendly settlement which no one foresees to-day.*
General Jan Christian Smuts to Lord Milner, 1905

*[W]e need to remind ourselves that the quest for
reconciliation was the fundamental objective of
the people's struggle, to set up a government based
on the will of the people, and to build a South
Africa which, indeed, belongs to all. The quest for
reconciliation was the spur that gave life to our
difficult negotiations process and the agreements
that emerged from it.*
President Nelson Mandela in Parliament, 1999

Reconciliation begins with a struggle to discern the potential of difficult
words. For a beginning that turns the differences of a quarrel to the
unifying friendship of a settlement, it reaches for those words that write over
but which do not always right the sacrifices that echo as history's wounds.
The efforts of such a disposition hold no assurances of felicity, especially
as reconciliation's power to (re)turn the past's potential depends itself on
a sacrifice, a release of self-certainty in the name of composing words in

common and a calling to abide within that motion of language which holds open an opportunity to make a space for all, including those who have defiled justice with the endless logic of emergency and the violent quest for a sovereign security that is always and yet never to come. In reconciliation's promise of a beginning, there is thus the risk of waiting forever; a deferral in which the becoming of its potential does not or perhaps ought not come to be.

In the aftermath of the Anglo-Boer War, Jan Smuts' hope for reconciliation foundered. Fresh memories of British brutality, disputes over economic inequality, and deep worry about the future of Afrikaner culture were all reasons to delay if not decline the call to create and embrace a "spirit of unity and cooperation". In the midst of these divisions, however, there did appear to be at least one point of agreement: reconciliation's proposed bond was an exclusive one, a hope that the Afrikaner and the British would forge a "racial partnership" in the name of realising the potential of the "great human laboratory" that was South Africa and rendering her a "dear City of God". An anticipation of both apartheid's vocabulary of social engineering and its subsequent rationalisation by the Dutch Reformed Church, this vision of reconciliation figured the vast majority of South Africans as an obstacle to raising the country from the "rut of its past". In the name of making a new South Africa, reconciliation's words of unity were given to writing over one divide by deepening another.

Almost a century later, a prisoner turned president opened Parliament's debate over the work undertaken by the Truth and Reconciliation Commission (TRC) with an argument about reconciliation's considerable and crucial role in the "small miracle" that brought non-racial democracy to South Africa. Defying Camus' claim that "twenty-seven years in prison do not, in fact, produce a very conciliatory form of intelligence", Nelson Mandela first set the Commission aside in order to reflect on the larger question of how reconciliation conditioned the terms of struggle and supported the protracted negotiations that ended statutory apartheid. As its hope "gave life" to a constitutive agreement in the midst of bitter faction, Mandela held that reconciliation was a "spur". A difference made and the making of a difference, it sat and turned between the (false) historical promise of union through the enforcement of separation and a future founded on the creation of unity in diversity.

From Smuts' hope that it would enable a productive forgetting to Mandela's concern for remembering its productivity, reconciliation has long shaped the form and content of South African politics. From myriad pulpits of many faiths, reconciliation has been celebrated as the saving grace of separate development, condemned as a heretical justification for evil, and defended as a means of mobilising the people against the criminalisation of their own humanity. In times of intense struggle, its practice was held up as a way to make peace while standing at the brink of endless violence and dismissed as an unjustified and unjust capitulation. Advocated by individuals and groups who claimed to have little (else) in common, reconciliation provoked and held open the question of how to create a "home for all". From within the midst of the deepest divisions, South Africans have (re)turned to reconciliation repeatedly. With an eye toward beginning again, this gesture has provoked controversy over the potential of reconciliation's generative turn, a power dedicated to (re)constituting the form and content of human relationships.

While there have been many beginnings of reconciliation, their story is not a tale of origins. Nor is it a narrative about the miraculous transcendence of conflict or the remainderless synthesis of incommensurable interests. Much more fragmented, the beginnings of reconciliation in South Africa appear and take form in a public and institutional discourse. Varied and variable, this discourse draws from the tangled language of reconciliation to speak of the possibility for radical change, defines reconciliation as a form of speaking given to cultivating the grounds of understanding from within the midst of violence, and sometimes performs reconciliation's transformative power through a very particular (and contested) form of speech-action. In South Africa, the question of reconciliation's beginnings is the question of how to create the conditions for talk and the ways in which talk can make a difference.

In the name of a beginning, reconciliation's words have mattered. Long before the Truth and Reconciliation Commission became a touchstone of the country's transition, South Africans argued carefully about the meaning of reconciliation and disagreed vehemently about its value. At the intersection of religion, politics, and culture, this debate not only supported but enacted a deep and enabling criticism of separate development, an opposition that aimed less for revolutionary liquidation than the joint creation of constitutive power, a form of collective action in which the historical causes of conflict were (re)figured as an opportunity to open a "middle time" of transition. In the midst of intense violence and standing on the brink of civil war, reconciliation's call(ing) thus countered a silencing *stasis* with the question of whether there was yet time for speech, a moment in which committed enemies were asked to recognise what remained in common, a shared opposition that marked both the limit of apartheid's law and an occasion to create the "sufficient consensus" needed to dismantle its rule.

This book wagers that the history of reconciliation in South Africa is a rhetorical history. It takes seriously the possibility that reconciliation's history appears only as we follow and consider the development of a diverse set of calls, arguments, and deliberations about what reconciliation means, how it works, and why it is important. Focusing largely but not exclusively on the period between 1985 and 1995, the book's first contention is that these exchanges demonstrate the way in which reconciliation preceded, conditioned, and followed the transition from apartheid to constitutional democracy. Showing that the transition was far less the achievement of reconciliation than an event in which reconciliation was used to open a time and space for history-making, the book's second contention is that a rhetorical history sheds substantial light on reconciliation's performative quality, the precise ways in which its characteristic speech constituted a mode of collective action, a form of power that did not transcend conflict but turned articulated rationales for violence toward the potential for productive (dis)agreement.

In South Africa, reconciliation abides within speech that not only contains but constitutes the potential for becoming otherwise in a different way. This may be a discomforting thesis, particularly for those anxious about the dangers of "mere rhetoric" and worried that the appearances of words serve only to mask reality. While it cannot be wished away, it must be said that this chosen phobia has become a convenient way to ignore reconciliation's obvious and immanent connection to speech, a relationship that in no way represents a rhetoric *of* reconciliation but which does mark a fragile and variable creativity, a "coming to terms" that has "made (transitional) sense" from within forms of violence which mark the limit of expression. Certainly, the unfolding of this power requires a cautious reading, one that takes care to appreciate reconciliation's unsteady process and discern how its potential has frequently left those most in need to wait. Indeed, contrary to the view that it can be located solely within the confines of a quasi-juridical body that worked in its name, reconciliation does not have a certain place in South African history. An indication of its calling to a faith in words, this ambiguity extends deeply into reconciliation's meaning and marks the very hinge of its beginnings.

(dis)placing reconciliation's history

South Africa is now an international symbol of reconciliation. A source of tremendous surprise and inspiration in the global community, the transition from apartheid has been taken as evidence of reconciliation's power and a basic indicator of its value for countries struggling to overcome legacies of deep division. Indeed, the form of South Africa's turn to democracy has played a key role in moving the concept of reconciliation from the margin to the centre of debates over how conflict-torn societies can redress the costs of violence, support democratisation, and promote the protection of human rights. More than once, Nelson Mandela has been called abroad to work his reconciling "magic", a form of conflict resolution that has produced tangible success as well as some doubts about the generalisability of the South African experience. In the West, audiences continue to be fascinated by Desmond Tutu's account of South Africa's transformation, a turn that the Archbishop emeritus has frequently cast as a miracle, an unprecedented gift of peace and a moment in which citizens undertook a process of forgiveness that left the world "open mouthed at the revelation of such nobility of spirit".[1] Far and away, however, it is the "unique experiment" that Tutu led which has made the deepest and most lasting impression. Celebrated, investigated, criticised, and increasingly copied, South Africa's Truth and Reconciliation Commission is now very much the *sine qua non* of the country's transition, a body that is increasingly perceived as a lynchpin in the process of ending apartheid and defended as a "central tenet to the reconstruction of South African society".[2]

From a brief discussion of the TRC's formation and subsequent attempt to "promote national unity and reconciliation in a spirit of understanding which transcends the conflicts and divisions of the past", I want to begin this book by suggesting that the tremendous attention paid to the TRC has generated and helped cement an increasingly monolithic perception that the Commission's work represents the instigation, site, and process of reconciliation in South Africa.[3] Coupled to something of an international fetishisation of the TRC, one that has largely overlooked the Commission's intensely controversial development and the question of whether its ambiguous mandate reflected a larger political or cultural interest in a concept that has proven notoriously hard to define, this perception has covered over if not deterred questions about reconciliation's role in the struggle against apartheid as well as the negotiated settlement that culminated in the 1994 election. In other words, the evident move to reduce reconciliation to the terms of the TRC's work begs the question held in Nelson Mandela's 1999 claim that reconciliation was a defining element of the transition: in the years before the Commission took to its stage, how can we begin to see let alone understand the ambiguous nature of reconciliation, the terms of its practice, and the ways in which it shaped South Africa's turn from apartheid?

To fanfare, scepticism, and pointed opposition, the TRC began its public work in April of 1996, nearly two years after Mandela's election. Referred to by some as the "mother of all laws", the Commission's founding legislation created a "juristic person" and charged its three primary committees – Human Rights Violations, Amnesty, and Reparations and Rehabilitation – with a number of complex and conflicting tasks.[4] Initially authorised to work for a mere 18 months, a tenure that was extended and extended again such that parts of the process were not completed until 2003, the TRC was handed a vital and clearly insurmountable task, a set of goals, expectations, and obstacles that both (unduly) raised the hopes of some citizens and made plain that the Commission could indeed promote but not accomplish reconciliation. Reflecting on its charge to "complete as full a picture as possible" of gross violations of human rights, the Commission's 1999 *Final Report* underscored that one of its central aims was to create an understanding of South Africa's history by uncovering the truth of past violence, allowing citizens to recount their experiences, establishing accountability for the crimes of apartheid and the excesses of struggle, restoring the well-being of individuals through a recognition of "untold suffering", allowing admitted perpetrators to "come to terms with their past", preventing amnesia, and taking steps to ensure that the past would not compromise the future.[5]

For its efforts to help South Africa "commence the journey towards a future founded on the recognition of human rights, democracy and peaceful coexistence", the Commission's early work met with substantive praise and also significant criticism.[6] Based largely on her experiences in covering the Commission for SABC radio, Antjie Krog's *Country of My Skull* was one of the first full-length studies to reveal the sheer enormity of the TRC's task, the exhausting and agonising testimony of victims, and the divisions sown inside and outside the Commission by an amnesty process that very few seemed to want. Poetic, stark, and nearly as much a diary as a hermeneutic reading of a complex and quasi-juridical "orgy of alliteration", Krog's work closes with a reflection that says much about why the Commission captured the world's attention even as it was under virtual siege from all sides of the South African political spectrum:

I am filled with an indescribable tenderness toward this commission. With all its mistakes, its arrogance, its racism, its sanctimony, its incompetence, the lying, the failure to get an interim reparation policy off the ground after two years, the showing off – with all of this – it has been so brave, so naively brave in the winds of deceit, rancour, and hate. Against a flood crashing with the weight of a brutalising past on to new usurping politics, the commission has kept alive the idea of a common humanity. Painstakingly it has chiselled a way beyond racism and made space for all of our voices.[7]

Beyond racism? An inhabitable space? With Krog's assessment, some would disagree. In a 1997 essay, Mahmood Mamdani levelled a critique of the Commission, an argument as to why the Commission had forsaken justice and "created a diminished truth" that wrote the vast majority of apartheid's victims out of its version of history.[8] With a similar tone and nearly identical conflation of the difference between the TRC and the legislation that dictated the scope of its activities, Wole Soyinka argued soon after that the Commission's call for truth and forgiveness appeared to misunderstand the priority of reparation and restitution.[9] From a quite a different and decidedly less fair perspective, Anthea Jeffery contended in 1999 that the TRC's work was fatally flawed, a finding that rested heavily on her naïve claim that the Commission's *Final Report* "distorts as much as it discloses the truth".[10]

The debate continues and it is likely to do so well into the future. In the years since the TRC first gathered in a crowded East London community hall to hear testimony, the Commission's work has motivated a voluminous literature, a diverse set of studies that have mustered the resources of myriad academic disciplines. The TRC's operating procedures and organisational politics have been parsed by anthropologists, political scientists, and former members of the Commission; the narrative dynamics and costs of testimony have been scrutinised for their integrity, silences, trauma, and grammar; the amnesty process has been assessed for its fairness and relative contribution to restorative justice, a concept that has joined a host of others used to describe, plot, and assess the work of truth-telling, healing, and nation-building. Increasingly, as TRC-like structures have been created in several other nations, including Sierra Leone and Burundi, and localities such as Greensboro, North Carolina, significant attention has been paid to whether and how the Commission's structure and mandate can be modelled.[11]

While there is little doubt as to its significance (as opposed to its success), the TRC has come to enjoy premier status in accounts of the South African transition. Frequently held up as the focal point of reconciliation, the Commission has provoked inquiry that has largely failed to question the historical, political, and legal roots of the very concept that focused its mandate. With the notable exception of Johnny de Lange, one of the TRC's architects in Parliament, this is partly to say that very few have shown more than a passing interest in the debates that preceded the Commission's formation.[12] In 1999, the TRC itself was accused of this omission by a Member of Parliament who argued in the debate over the Commission's *Final Report* that the body had overlooked its debt to the process of reconciliation that supported South Africa's larger transition:

> The report also does not take into consideration of the so-called miracle
> transformation of South Africa. There is no reference to the miracle
> transformation that took place in this country where previously polarised
> communities have been able to find each other across the divide and
> to bring about change in this country without any violence. I feel the
> TRC would have done all of us a better service. The world admires the
> miracle of South Africa and its leadership, which is not admired by the
> TRC. I think we owe it to ourselves to admire and take note of the fact
> that we are part of history-making in this country.[13]

Did reconciliation precede itself? While this question has been used to suggest that the TRC was an insular and exclusive body, it also draws attention to the fact that many academic analysts and some former members of the Commission have cast its development in a number of perplexing ways and gone to rather elaborate lengths to suggest that reconciliation in South Africa became a significant issue only with the TRC's creation. For instance, the appendix that follows an award-winning reflection on the complexity of forgiveness in South Africa suggests that a "major concern of CODESA was how to deal with the past in a way that would break the cycles of violence, bring about social cohesion, and restore peace. The result was the establishment of the Truth and Reconciliation Commission".[14] Setting aside the apparent confusion between the Convention for a Democratic South Africa (CODESA) and the Multi-Party Negotiating Process (MPNP) that occurred in the wake of the former's failure in 1992, there are a number of reasons to question whether the TRC "resulted" from a process that actively bracketed many of the issues that buttressed calls for the Commission's development. As troublesome, the common perception that the TRC somehow followed necessarily from the negotiations process has obscured the controversy that raged in 1995 over the Commission's rationale and the terms of its founding legislation, a dispute that is crucial not least because of the possibility that many attacks on the reconciliation process are better read as arguments about the law that defined the TRC's agenda and power.[15]

The most common explanation of the TRC's development holds that it grew from a debate over whether South Africa needed a "truth commission", a body akin to those created in Latin America and dedicated to documenting human rights abuses and promoting democratisation.[16] In its *Final Report*, the TRC traces this debate back to Kader Asmal's 1992 claim that South Africa's turn from apartheid would not be well served by Nuremburg-style trials, a position that I discuss in chapter four and which gained momentum when the ANC responded to allegations of human rights violations in its training camps with a call for a truth commission in which all sides of the conflict would participate.[17] Tied closely to the disputes over whether indemnity and amnesty marked a path to successful transition or the short road to an unjust forgetting, the influence of these early calls for a truth commission have been viewed largely through the lens of "compromise", a perspective that has been used to support two different accounts of the TRC's creation. On one side, some analysts have suggested that the TRC grew from a compromise over amnesty, an agreement that balanced the ANC's unwillingness to condone a blanket amnesty with its concern over whether the old regime's security forces would support a new dispensation if it came with the threat of indictment and prosecution. On the other side, a significant contingent has argued that the TRC reflected the "spirit" of compromise which underwrote the constitutional negotiations that took place between 1991 and 1993. Interpreted variously, this spirit has been taken to mean that the Commission was a counterpart to the negotiations process, a body that either extended the latter's efforts or addressed issues that negotiators kept off the table in the name of avoiding paralytic dispute. Tied to a religious debate that I detail in chapter one, it has also been read as evidence that the TRC sprang from "our morality as a people" and reflected a cultural interest in realising a common humanity (ubuntu).[18]

At the centre of nearly every account of the TRC's development is the post-amble of the 1993 interim constitution. Contrary to popular conception, this short text did not mandate the Commission's formation or fate its development. What it did do, at one level, was require Parliament to pass the "mechanisms, criteria and procedures, including tribunals, if any," needed for an amnesty that would serve the nation's "reconciliation and reconstruction" and be "granted in respect of acts, omissions and offences associated with political objectives and committed in the course of the conflicts of the past". In these terms, an explicit and directed concern for reconciliation appeared almost three years before the TRC's legislation was signed into law. This appearance, however, has yet to be investigated in a systematic way. In his work on the TRC, for instance, Richard Wilson contends that the post-amble's "amnesty provisions were the only indispensable and necessary part of the process of 'national unity and reconciliation'" and then argues that "reconciliation was the Trojan horse used to smuggle an unpleasant aspect of the past (that is, impunity) into the present political order, to transform political compromises into transcendental moral principles".[19] Rooted in a casual appeal to something he calls "reconciliation talk" and ignoring a great deal of philosophical reflection on the matter, Wilson's assessment risks the myopic, particularly as it fails to notice that the post-amble does indeed make a set of substantive claims about the larger value of reconciliation, a case that I take up in chapters three and four and which pins the very enablement of the constitution's promise of non-racial democracy on an extra-legal practice of reconciliation, a practice that appeared within and supported the negotiations that produced the constitution itself.

A clear indication that the TRC did not develop *ex nihilo*, the post-amble raises questions about both the Commission's development and the evident interest in reconciliation that preceded its creation. In the aftermath of the 1994 election, why was it sensible and sensical to discuss the need for reconciliation and methods for its promotion? Where and how did reconciliation gain its political and social currency? Who was defending reconciliation as an important political good? How was this case justified and contested? Was it warranted by appeals to South African history or various socio-cultural beliefs? How was the claimed need for reconciliation linked to the larger dynamics and discourses of transition? To the degree that the TRC's creation was tied to the logic and spirit of transition, did reconciliation play a role in either the late struggle against apartheid or the negotiations process that brought it to an end? What did reconciliation mean in these contexts? Was it practised? If so, does it shed any light on the motives, form, or mechanics of the transition, the ways in which South Africans figured and performed a radical form of political change?

As they require displacing the TRC from reconciliation's centre stage, I do not believe that these questions have received the attention that they deserve. Individually and together, they hint that a full understanding of the Commission's development demand inquiry into the large and contested place of reconciliation in South African politics. Equally important, these questions hold open the possibility that reconciliation's significance may have less to do with the TRC than the ways in which reconciliation shaped the form and performed crucial aspects of the transition from apartheid to non-racial democracy. In short, the question of reconciliation's history is the double problem of discerning how reconciliation's practice developed over time and assessing the ways in which it enabled the work of moving the country from past to future.

While such inquiry does not aspire to locate reconciliation's origin or unearth its essential meaning, it does suppose that contemporary strictures against inquiry into the "original" cannot be used as a warrant to ignore or unduly depreciate the experience of making new the moments in which human beings endeavour to compose the means needed to begin again. In South Africa, such work is the very stuff of reconciliation's potential, a calling that has troubled and reconstituted the fabric and movement of human relationships which have been wracked by the violence of separate development, an endless promise of redemptive unity that was always but never to come.

inaugurating words

Few predicted that South Africa would escape civil war. Fewer still anticipated how the country's transition would develop or that Nelson Mandela would take the podium for his inaugural address on the steps of the Union Building in May of 1994 and be heard to announce, "Laat ons die verlede vergeet! Wat verby is, is verby." (Let's forget the past! What's done is done).[20] While surprising to many, this (conditional) gesture was not unprecedented. Well before the election, Mandela made (and retracted) the fragile case for reconciliation as a way to move the country from past to future. So too, many of those eager for political reform and those who were wary of it had called on citizens to embrace (different senses of) reconciliation's sensibility and enter into its practice. From a state of emergency that began the apartheid government's final betrayal of all principles save the violent preservation of its own sovereignty to a moment in which the country sat on the brink of civil war and then to an unlikely process of negotiations that culminated in a new (interim) constitution, the notion of reconciliation has been the subject and object of substantial talk.

This book is an inquiry into how such words have worked and whether they have made a difference. To introduce this idea, I want to turn from the notion that reconciliation has a history to the questions of why this history takes shape in a complex rhetorical practice and how an understanding of this practice provides a way to understand reconciliation's precise contribution to South Africa's turn from apartheid. Prefaced by a brief consideration of reconciliation's characteristic and frustrating ambiguity, my argument here is that the history of reconciliation is held in a host of words that announce, trouble, and constitute the work of history-making. Far more than a law or commission that proceeded in its name, reconciliation took shape with(in) words, a varied set of calls, arguments, and deliberations in which speech about reconciliation defined the contours of its practice and performed its work of (re)turning and (re)figuring the form (and content) of human (inter)action. Found in the midst of violence that appears to breach the very conditions of creative expression, the matter of reconciliation's role in South Africa's transition is the rhetorical question of its unfolding and enfolding capacity to invent the power of speech from within moments of its apparent foreclosure.

Reconciliation is a frustrating concept. In a recent reflection that captures the problem nicely, John de Gruchy observes that engaging with the idea of reconciliation requires entering into play with a "word that is so overloaded with ambiguity in some contexts and so emptied of meaning in others".[21] Leading quickly to Antjie Krog's suggestion that it may be "time to get rid of the word", de Gruchy's assessment points out how the concept of reconciliation frequently seems to float.[22] As it has "gathered a set of possible meanings reflected in the rhetoric of the pulpit, parliament and the press, as well as embodied in literature, art, and popular discourse", reconciliation appears to lack a fixed or singular object. At times, it refers to an open-ended process. At others, it is (an impoverished) shorthand for a particular state of affairs. Lending credence to the dubious idea that it is best conceived as an essentially contested concept, the underlying problem is that reconciliation appears to be a good that actively frustrates efforts to define its constitutive elements. Underscored by Johnny de Lange's admission that he has "not met two people with the same definition of reconciliation", the problem has much to do with Adorno's observation that it is a "concept that means beyond itself" and an idea that "bars its affirmation in a concept".[23] Recalling how the ancient Greek's held it out as a way to transform enmity into (civic) friendship, reconciliation troubles what *is* in the name of transforming into what it *is not,* a process that is difficult to define precisely because it challenges, exceeds, and provisionally (re)constitutes the power of definition.[24] This characteristic ambiguity is compounded by the fact that reconciliation is addressed or given to the transformation of human relationships, those fragile and shifting bonds that join us together and which have meaning only as we come to agree on their terms, dynamics, and value. Appearing and moving between human beings, relationships are difficult to identify as such, particularly as their form varies over time and their formation does not reduce to a set of procedures or rules. For reconciliation, a notion that founders quickly on the dictates of the command, there is thus a crucial sense in which its practice and value hinges on those who hear its calling and find the means to jointly delineate the terms and meaning of its pursuit.

Philosophers, theologians and social theorists have long puzzled over how to define the object of reconciliation and pondered whether the question of its power is a query about the substance of "nothing in particular". Looking broadly across this debate, a literature that I have considered elsewhere and which plays a rather bit part in this book, one finds a recurring and crucial tendency to cast reconciliation as a potential (*dunamis*), a form of power that is more than an abstract possibility and less than something (ever) fully actualised.[25] Following partly on the path of Pauline theology, the young Hegel traced the development of this potential with great care, arguing that reconciliation appears between a "causality of fate" that renders life hostile to itself and the abstract hope of a beautiful (re)union.[26] According to Hegel, reconciliation refuses these equally debilitating forms of violence with the potential of the word (*logos*).[27] Against the unbridled assertion of self-certainty and the infinite deferral of subjectivity, reconciliation holds an opportunity for human beings to oppose the isolation of being with those words that perform the work of (be)coming into a relation of unity in difference. Neither sovereignty nor grace, reconciliation is a (re)turn to the generative power of speech and a potential to speak in ways that (re)constitute relationships.

Echoing this line of philosophical thought and then setting into the South African context, Alex Boraine, the former Vice-Chair of the TRC, has argued that reconciliation entails "speaking the language of potential". Presented as a response to the controversy in South Africa over "what do we mean by reconciliation", this claim can be read in two ways. First, it suggests that reconciliation can be viewed as "an exchange of ideas in a climate of mutual respect and peaceful co-existence".[28] In South Africa, this interpretation has significant precedent. Sensing and claiming to fear endless civil war, Mandela did nothing less than theorise the rhetorical elements of reconciliation when he wrote to P.W. Botha in 1989 and preached to fellow comrades on Robben Island that one key to reconciliation lay in the ability of ANC leaders to relinquish their own language and converse with their oppressors in Afrikaans. Dave Steward, F.W. de Klerk's former Director General, has held that reconciliation is "based on communication", a view that has an important relationship with Kader Asmal's claim that reconciliation has allowed South Africans to recover "the conscience of words" and Dullah Omar's view that reconciliation's work entailed the "move from repression to speech".

Second, the idea that reconciliation involves "speaking the language of potential" suggests that it holds a power to set language into motion, an operation that yields the potential for speech at those moments in which mutual respect and peaceful coexistence cannot (yet) be taken for granted. Put differently, reconciliation struggles to fashion the potential for that speaking which holds the potential to (re)make the grounds for speech. Between 1985 and 1995 in South Africa, this (meta)concern appears within many different calls for reconciliation and widespread discussions about its capacity to figure the time and support the collective work of transition. Viewed alone and over time, these exchanges show that opposed communities and sworn enemies were mutually interested in the idea of reconciliation, able to define, debate, and revise its meaning, and willing to defend the proposition (within limits) that its pursuit could play a substantive role in the design and enactment of political-constitutional reform. Resting partly on an old and heated debate over whether reconciliation was a way to rationalise or overcome (the logic of) separate development, religious and political discussions of reconciliation marked a tentative but shared concern for how to open and sustain a beginning that would both alter the arc of South Africa's history and constitute a peaceful "unity in diversity" out of a conflict that appeared ready to confound if not negate the historical interests of its protagonists. This is not to say that reconciliation's value was universally embraced. A source of significant dispute, many appeals for reconciliation were rejected as disingenuous and strategic attempts to dictate the terms and form of transition. Others were viewed with great suspicion, particularly as they appeared to suggest that justice needed to take a back seat to the pragmatic demands of nation-building.

In South Africa, there is a long history of speaking about reconciliation's potential and an old debate over the potential of speech to enable and enact reconciliation. In a very basic way, this is why the question of reconciliation's history must be grasped as a rhetorical question. Distinct from the hope for a timeless unity, reconciliation's substance *is* the contingent communicative interaction that it constitutes and supports. In many quarters, however, this conclusion signals reconciliation's irrelevance, if not danger. As Aletta Norval notes in the introduction to her study of early apartheid discourse, the linguistic turn in philosophy and critical-cultural studies continues to struggle against what Adorno once referred to as an "allergy to expression", the idea that in order "to understand political phenomena, we need to probe beneath or below their surface to grasp their real, underlying meaning".[29] Going further, Reinhart Koselleck has recently observed that inquiry into the development, expression, and significance of words continues to be hampered by the fact that, "Even where spoken speech or its written equivalents are included in the [historical] representation, linguistic evidence comes under ideological suspicion or is read only instrumentally with pre-given interests and evil intentions in mind."[30] While willing to challenge something of this tendency, particularly in the wake of Hayden White's tropological approach to historiography, Koselleck nevertheless echoes Hans Blumenberg when he maintains that "no speech act is itself the action that it helps prepare, trigger, and enact", and then contends that "A history does not happen without speaking, but it is never identical with it, it cannot be reduced to it."[31]

In a study that resists something of this *cordon sanitaire* between word and deed, while also rallying the possibility that rhetoric contains the capacity to "build and argue ideas", Philippe-Joseph Salazar has shed crucial light on South Africa's larger turn from apartheid, an event in which the country's attempt to found democracy and "find peace within itself" relied heavily on a series of rhetorical processes, varied forms of oratory, and diverse deliberative modes.[32] Far from an adornment, although not without an element of fashion, the rhetorical arts, according to Salazar, contributed to the redefinition and rebuilding of South Africa, particularly as the capacity for deliberation composed a vision of the collective good as well as enacted the commonality needed to imagine the nation yet to come. While Salazar emphasises that these appearances (borne) of speech are not without an ideological dimension, the case also recalls something of Hannah Arendt's defence of public life: in the desire for being in common, there abides a need for (be)coming into relation, a process whereby human beings gather the words needed to "present themselves", fit themselves into a "world of appearances", and occupy that "in-between space" which holds the potential for a shared beginning.[33] With a character that remains small and dealing with "what is in the main contingent", rhetoric's constitutive appearances are thus neither ephemeral nor teleologically necessary. They are relational goods. As such, their study is less an excursion into the transitory than a way to understand how the action of speech comes to constitute the fragile space and unsteady time of transition.[34]

If reconciliation has an immanent connection to rhetorical practices that may yet shed light on the ways in which human relationships are dissolved, brokered, and refigured, the question that follows is how we might begin to locate reconciliation's operativity and assess the precise forms and limits of its power. Initially, there is an extensive record of how South Africans have deliberated and debated about the occasion, dynamics, and value of reconciliation. In some distinction to broad-based public opinion research and local ethnographic inquiry, my attention in this book is directed largely to public, legal, and institutional argumentation about reconciliation. Mostly in English, the predominant language of politics in South Africa (see the "footnote" that follows this introduction), these texts show a variety of forms, demonstrate an explicit concern for reconciliation, and proceed from different assumptions about its nature, practice, and value. From declarations issued by the churches that supported or opposed separate development to transcripts of official and unofficial constitutional negotiations to debates in Parliament and arguments presented to South African courts, some of these materials are well known even as they have not been examined with respect to how they advance arguments about reconciliation or how they argumentatively enact its practice. Others, particularly the transcripts of deliberations at CODESA, the MPNP, and select debates in Parliament, have received almost no critical scrutiny.

As a whole, the texts considered over the course of this study admit to both a diachronic and synchronic reading. Resolved to look both ways, I am thus concerned to examine how interest and argumentation about reconciliation took form over the course of a decade and scrutinise particular moments in which dedicated controversy over reconciliation's (constitutive) words appears to perform and confound its power.[35] Ultimately, the balance is a fine one. This book is not a history of South Africa's transition. It is, however, addressed to a rhetorical record that cannot simply be unhinged from the move toward non-racial democracy, particularly as the terms of this record consistently link reconciliation to the logic of transition. However, this same record also features a set of significant interruptions, points at which appeals for reconciliation appear to unravel history's chronological time in the name of constituting a very precise and powerful transitional logic. At these moments, reconciliation is far less a coherent procedure than a contingent practice, a provisional process in which the potential for a beginning takes shape as standing justifications for violence are recast as reasons for peaceful interaction.

Across these intersecting axes, the task of seeing reconciliation's development and interpreting its dynamics is supported far more (and better) by questions than the strictures of methodology. Recalling Hans-Georg Gadamer's account of hermeneutic inquiry, this means that each of the ensuing chapters begins with a question that appears to both focus and trouble the meaning of a particular set of texts which address the idea and practice of reconciliation.[36] My reply to these questions tends to take shape through what Paul Rabinow has called an "interpretive analytic". A form of hermeneutic inquiry that aims to plot the ways in which reconciliation is a "use of language and operation performed on it", this approach relies on three interlocking ways of reading reconciliation's rhetorical history.[37] First, I devote substantial attention to the expressed grammar of reconciliation and the situations that were defended as occasions to define, enable, and contest the terms of its practice. More than marking instances of its use, this approach offers a view of what Wittgenstein called the "ostensive definition" of reconciliation, a sense of how the concept was invoked in relationship to circumstance, the mechanics of its usage by individuals and institutions, and how this usage was justified and altered over time.[38] Thus, less concerned with what reconciliation *is*, an abstraction that slights the question of how appeals for reconciliation challenge the *given* power of definition, the concern here is how to understand the rules of language that supported speech about reconciliation, the historical precedents that rationalised and complicated its practice, and how reconciliation's subject and object were composed and set into play by a calling toward language – a process of entering into speech that cannot be grasped by those approaches which presuppose that reconciliation is a state of affairs rather than an event that presents the question of what we are doing and able to do with our words.

Second, the history of reconciliation requires close attention to its rhetorical "ways of operating". More than a legacy of its definition, discussion, and advocacy, reconciliation's development includes a number of moments in which its words hold and engender its performance. Thus, contrary to the presumption held by some forms of historiography, I spend significant time considering the operativity of reconciliation's words and plotting how some argumentation about reconciliation constitutes a significant form of action. In this regard, the perspective afforded by speech act theory and tropology offers a way to discern how particular calls for reconciliation disturbed the (given) signs of the times by offering words to an opponent or enemy that had been previously deemed unworthy of conversation, irrational, or evil beyond redemption. Similarly, it is apparent that some argumentation about reconciliation in South Africa served to interrupt historical tradition, name the causes and costs of violence, and (re)constitute norms of dialogue. The close study of these dynamics betrays something about how reconciliation's power hinged on its capacity to compose meta-discourse, a variable form of "talking about talk" in which would-be interlocutors questioned and remade the grounds of common understanding and collective action.

Third, the arguments that serve to define and enable reconciliation also present the question of how it has functioned as the subject and object of discourse. On one side, this concern has led me to grapple with how the language of reconciliation comes to figure its speaking subject and the ways in which reconciliation's promise of subjectivation depends on a sense of potential that demands obedience to a discursive "law" and also challenges the meaning and force of its precedent with an *ethos* that radically decentres the liberal subject. On the other side, the development of reconciliation invites attention to how it became an object of sustained interest and deliberation, along with the ways in which its "appropriate" practice were negotiated and contested over time. Relevant to both the "shift" from a religious to political interpretation of reconciliation that occurred in the late 1980s and reconciliation's subtle but crucial role in the constitutional negotiating process, this "problematisation" of reconciliation provides a way to trace how claims about its necessity were rationalised and challenged.[39]

arguing about an exceptional past

In South Africa, reconciliation appears with(in) speech. With a turn, it composes a potential to speak. And, with another turn, it yields a speaking that endeavours to fashion a relation of unity in difference from within the divisions wrought by violence.

Looking between the onset of the state of the emergency in 1985 to Nelson Mandela's signing of the *Promotion of National Unity and Reconciliation Act* in mid-1995, this book investigates how South African politicians, activists, religious leaders, and citizens have argued about the meaning of reconciliation and the ways in which these arguments have explained, enabled, and contested reconciliation's capacity to turn historical justifications for violence toward norms of dialogue. When was it time to speak of reconciliation? How was reconciliation (best) spoken? What modes of speech realised and challenged its promise?

With these questions, a rhetorical history of reconciliation provides a way to deepen our grasp of the turn from apartheid to constitutional democracy at the same time that it clarifies the diversity of practices that define and perform reconciliation. Such work does not aim either to reduce the South African transition to reconciliation or to broker the suggestion that the end of statutory apartheid produced a state of reconciliation. Instead, my argument at the end of this book is that reconciliation played an *exceptional* role in composing the logic of the transition and that this role took the form of a transitional logic which created an *exception* to history in the name of (re) constituting the potential for history-making. This claim to the exceptional has several dimensions, all of which bear directly on how we might understand and assess reconciliation's power of beginning.

At one level, it means that the concept and practice of reconciliation was used in South Africa to initiate and sustain a critique of violence that challenged the apartheid regime's attempt to govern through an endless state of emergency, a state of exception in which the law exempted itself from itself in order to sustain the terms of sovereign power. Revealing the regime's hypocritical equivocation of justice with the emergency and focusing opposition on the violence embedded in the identitarian logic of separate development, calls for reconciliation were important for the ways in which they turned away from the law's word (precedent) in the name of opening a time for collective struggle dedicated to the work of creating space for transition.

At a second level, my argument about the exceptional quality of reconciliation refers to the precise ways in which reconciliation's words held the time and conditioned the work of transition. As an *occasion* for creating the grounds for non-violent interaction, a process of motivated debate that enacted the potential for *constitutive* forms of dialogue, and a form of public *representation* dedicated to the deliberative redefinition of history's meaning and force, reconciliation in South Africa was not the end of violence but a demonstration of how the threat of endless violence could instil a mutual desire for talk between enemies; it was not a revolutionary promise but the appearance of a present in which to make the time and space for invention;

it was not the miraculous recovery of subjectivity but an expression of its contingent character made in the name of fashioning its relationship to an Other; it was not forgiveness but the occasion for deliberation about what could and could not be forgiven; it was not the achievement of peace but the creation of a commons in which to address the substantive question of what living in peace might actually mean. Evidence of an art of "being-in-between", reconciliation's words interrupted the power of definition in the name of composing a unity in difference that did not amount to synthetic mediation so much as it instantiated a middle voice that tropologically turned historical justifications for violence into shared oppositions that contained the potential for individual and collective (inter)action and productive (dis)agreements.

Finally, reconciliation's potential marks a mode of rhetorical invention that fashions an important if not constitutive exception to itself. Appearing at the limit of language, reconciliation's words performed a turn from the isolating claims of sovereign privilege to a formal-pragmatic mode of deliberation, a process of "sufficient consensus" (making) that both unexcluded the middle in which human beings forge relationships and cultivated an *ethos* of publicity in which the self's interest in identity was relaxed in the name of undertaking identification with others. Yet, this inventional work was not without cost or significant opposition. Standing before the law in the name of its reconstitution and bracketing the dictates of history, reconciliation's work provoked deep controversy over its apparent sacrifice, its call for individuals to set aside the demands of justice in order to compose a bridge between past and future. Thus, faced with the costs of its creative power, the idea and practice of reconciliation was turned against itself, an opposition whereby it (once more) reconstituted the grounds for beginning again, a (re)turn to the contingency of its potential that grounded the contentious case to develop a commission of truth and reconciliation.

These arguments unfold over the course of the following chapters. To begin, I consider how appeals for reconciliation in the mid and late 1980s served similar functions as they appeared in religious debates over how to struggle against apartheid and the proto-talks convened between ANC and government representatives. In both contexts, arguments about reconciliation had very much to do with time, the need to recognise a *stasis* that required combatants to set aside the historical dynamics and interests that appeared ready to fund endless violence. In chapters one and two, I am concerned with this reading of the signs of the times, the ways in which reconciliation was used to delineate an opportunity, a moment of *kairos* that was held out as an occasion for speech in the midst of its apparent impossibility. From a brief consideration of apartheid's early years, chapter one investigates how English-speaking churches opposed theo-political rationales for separate development, particularly the Dutch Reformed Church's claim that apartheid's identitarian logic could be justified on the grounds of a future reconciliation. Tracing this opposition as it moved from a doctrinal to a political debate, the chapter details how apartheid's opponents defined reconciliation as a good for the present. More precisely, religious activists argued that reconciliation was a way to name apartheid's heresy and challenge its identity-based law in the name of forging political identifications that contained the potential for transition. In the 1980s, this interpretation of reconciliation appeared precisely at that moment of struggle when the law's creation was felt to negate the creative power of collective interaction. Within the church's struggle against apartheid, the Word of reconciliation marked a time in which there was a need to begin (again) and opened a time in which words (again) held the potential for political action.

For religious opponents of apartheid, the occasion of reconciliation was a moment of transition, a time to turn from the law's separating and silencing language. In chapter two, I examine how South African political leaders echoed and also selectively borrowed from this case in order to establish the need for drastic change. From an opening reflection on whether historical instantiations of Afrikaner and African nationalism contain a shared commitment to reconciliation, the chapter looks closely at how reconciliation was defined by enemies as a way to "come to terms" in the midst of escalating violence and ungovernability. Concerned with the period from 1987 to late 1990, it plots how reconciliation was used to create the time and space for talk at a moment when the two main protagonists in the South African conflict appeared to have no common ground and little desire to interact. At this turning point, appeals to reconciliation were interpreted as a sign that all South Africans were caught in a common condition, a situation of violence that would end only as each side took steps to create the climate of good faith needed to commence preliminary dialogue about how to negotiate the end of apartheid. In short, the need for and architecture of the "talks about talks" grew from calls for reconciliation. From early and secret talks to the groundbreaking agreements reached after the 1990 release of Nelson Mandela, reconciliation helped justify the decision by each side to set aside their historical justifications for violence. At the risk of appearing to sell out their own causes, this mutual although not always reciprocal release of self-certainty produced less peace than a deliberative forum in which to undertake heated disagreement. In the name of speaking about how to begin negotiations, appeals to reconciliation delineated a shared humanity, constituted a common set of referents, and embodied something of the trust that was needed to tarry about how best to move from apartheid to constitutional democracy.

The occasion of reconciliation was a time for speech. By late 1990, the question that followed from this apparent opportunity was whether talk could enact transition. In chapters three and four, I consider how the practice of reconciliation was used to support the production of such constitutive power. Focusing on the official and unofficial negotiations that occurred between December 1991 and December 1993, chapter three begins by examining the early days of CODESA and the expressed terms of the convention's collapse in June of 1992. Of particular concern is how negotiators were unable to use the good faith created in the talks about talks to support directed argumentation about which party held the sovereign power to author the new constitution. Paying close attention to the convention's opening speeches and some of the minutes from its working groups, the chapter tracks how the ANC and South African government each claimed that the other did not have the standing needed to define the nation's post-apartheid form. Fuelled by intense debate over the 1992 *Further Indemnity Act*, the controversy that led to CODESA's failure prompted a redefinition of standing negotiating procedures and rules for decision-making. Specifically, the MPNP began with extended debate over the nature and value of "sufficient consensus", a formal-pragmatic mode of negotiation. Tracing the development of this idea and how its practice was challenged by those dissatisfied with the MPNP's decisions, the chapter concludes with a consideration of the 1993 decision in *Government of the Self-Governing Territory of KwaZulu vs. Mahlangu and Another*, a judgment that served to set the value of reconciliation before the law.

From the contentious and divisive work at the bargaining table, chapter four turns to the close of the MPNP and its ratification of an interim constitution, a founding text that featured a post-amble which both announced the achievement of reconciliation and urged its continued practice. Defining the latter partly through a mandate for amnesty, the post-amble was a crucial motivation for the debates over reconciliation that followed the election of Nelson Mandela and which quickly came to focus on the question of whether South Africa needed a truth commission. Addressed to early and mid-1994, the chapter devotes significant time to analysing the post-amble's terms, a reading that demonstrates why amnesty played such a troublesome role in the transition and how it was defined as a form of reconciliation that could serve South Africa's fragile new democracy. Looking back to Kader Asmal's 1992 call for a body that could expose the truth of apartheid in a manner that did not require convening Nuremburg-style trials, the chapter then details how the post-amble provoked a pre-election debate about how South Africa was going to "deal with the past". Linked closely to a debate in Parliament over how to fulfil the post-amble's mandate, this discussion lent crucial momentum to the idea of a truth commission, a body that was first theorised through the lens of international human rights doctrine such that it appeared to sit in at least partial opposition to the form of reconciliation advocated by the post-amble. In the early days of democracy, reconciliation's ability to move the country from past to future was thus troubled by the hermeneutic question of how South Africans needed to read and account for the "force" of history. This challenge turned reconciliation's promise against itself, creating an opposition that exposed the need for a form of reconciliation that could grant a (middle) voice to those whom the post-amble claimed to serve.

Addressed to this problem of representation, chapter five investigates the making of reconciliation's controversial law. Focused on the period between late 1994 and mid-1995, the time in which the TRC's mandate was defined and debated, the chapter begins with a close reading of Parliament's deliberations over the first draft of the Commission's authorising legislation, the *Promotion of National Unity and Reconciliation Act*. Supplemented by an extended analysis of the pubic testimony over the bill that was taken by the Joint Portfolio Committee on Justice, the chapter traces how the TRC was initially held out as a "model in the middle", a body that would allow South Africans to stand between past and future in order to recover their voice, hear the experiences of others, and (re)learn the words of democratic politics. This rationale motivated opposition from both ends of the political spectrum. Tracing these objections in Parliament's debate over the Commission's power and the Constitutional Court's complex 1996 ruling that amnesty was a justified violation of victims' rights, the chapter demonstrates that the TRC was ultimately defined and defended as a public good, a structure that would emerge from public debate, hold open and transparent hearings, and provide a crucial thread with which citizens could weave the fabric of non-racial democracy. More precisely, I contend that the Commission's charge to promote reconciliation hinged on its capacity to embody and produce publicity – forms of discourse, disclosure, and deliberation that asked if not required victims and perpetrators of apartheid-era violence to speak in a manner that subverted their own (historical) self-interest. Anathema to liberalism and its traditional commitment to retribution, the ethic of sacrifice embodied in the Commission's charge was rooted in a definition of reconciliation that recalled but also turned the good faith of the MPNP. In the name of dealing with the past and fashioning the grounds for a unity in difference that stood apart from conventional demands for justice, the TRC was charged to promote a form of reconciliation that would enable law by (re)constituting the commons.

In the closing moments of this book, I do not answer the question of whether reconciliation in South Africa "worked". Indeed, as beginnings hold the potential for middles rather than endings, I suggest that this persistent question is very much the wrong question, a problem that turns away from the issue of how reconciliation has worked, usually in the name of a synthetic judgment that reifies the very process that it hopes to explain. The way in which the non-definitive matters is the crucial puzzle, a concern for how the contingent appearances of speech challenge the historical edicts of language and its law. It is between violence and understanding that reconciliation begins its work and finds not the cause but the faith needed to begin again.

a footnote
(with which to reconcile)?

The language of apartheid is a totally necessary
part of its ideology. Without the special words and
phrases that have been created, the ideology would
disappear, because it is not a theory constructed
on the basis of reason, but an expedient developed
to disguise the truth and erected on the basis of
a special language. The opponents of apartheid
are forced into a semantic trap: once you begin
to use the language of apartheid, you have
already accepted something of the premise. Yet
it is impossible to write about South Africa today
without using some of this special, and totally
misleading language.
Hilda Bernstein

by conventional standards, there is a footnote now (over)due. A common if not nearly obligatory feature of inquiries into South African history and politics, this footnote, "the footnote", is a space dedicated to a discussion of how (and sometimes why) an author will name the racial and ethnic identity of South African individuals and groups. In the early phases of conducting research for this book, I began to gather examples of these footnotes and puzzle over the various ways in which they described and defined "who is who" in South Africa. Now with a substantial collection, I have found these notes interesting and perplexing. Beneath their apparent uniformity lies a terministic diversity that speaks to and (re)presents one of reconciliation's central questions, the problem of how to negotiate between the need to name for purposes of reaching common understanding and the violence that attends the name's definition and attribution of (racial) identity.[1]

To begin, consider two rather typical examples of the footnote, one taken from Dan O'Meara's study of Afrikaner nationalism and a second that appears in the early pages of Heribert Adams and Kogila Moodley's attempt to theorise apartheid's reform:

> The racial/ethnic terminology of South Africa is a political minefield.
> In terms of the 1950 Population Registration Act – only repealed in
> 1991 – every individual was classified into one of four racial categories
> at birth or at entry into the country. This classification could only
> subsequently be changed by the state itself. In the apartheid hierarchy
> of racial domination, the position and particular forms of oppression of
> the oppressed "non-white" groups differed. Unfortunately, no analysis
> of South African politics can avoid using these racist categories – whose
> very terms have been deeply contested. Thus, for example, at various
> phases the NP government referred to the African majority as "Natives",
> as "Bantu" or, more recently, as "Blacks". The first two terms were
> always rejected by black activists, while the term "black" was used by the
> Black Consciousness Movement to refer collectively to all three racially
> oppressed groups – Africans, so-called Coloureds and Indians. Except as
> otherwise indicated in the footnotes, I use the term "black" in this more
> inclusive sense, preferring to use the term "African" for those called
> "Blacks" by the apartheid regime. The official category of "Coloured"
> people was likewise regarded as racist by members of this group, most of
> whom refer to themselves as "so-called Coloureds" – and sometimes, in
> a bitter irony, just as "so-calleds". I have retained this clumsy appellation
> as far as possible. Finally, Afrikaans is the mother tongue of millions
> more South Africans than the total number of white "Afrikaners" who
> have given this language such a bad press. A long debate in Afrikaner

---

1   Here, the decision to set race into brackets reflects an argument as to how race and
    the concept of "racial identity" have not always been and need not be the primary
    motivation or locus for reconciliation in South Africa. Indeed, the degree to which
    reconciliation must be wed to the problem of race has been a source of controversy,
    especially with regard to the design and work of the TRC. See Antjie Krog,
    "Anticipating a Different Kind of Future," in *Transcending a Century of Injustice,*
    ed. Charles Villa-Vicencio (Cape Town: Institute for Justice and Reconciliation,
    2000), 128.

nationalist circles has grappled with the status of what General Hertzog once called "brown Afrikaners" – the millions of so-called Coloureds, most of whom are native Afrikaans-speakers. While in the 1990s the National Party suddenly discovered that the so-called Coloureds might be admitted into Afrikaner ranks, I employ the term "Afrikaners" in the sense used by the National Party throughout the vast bulk of its existence – as shorthand to indicate those more correctly designated by the clumsy formulation of white Afrikaans-speakers.[2]

And, Adam and Moodley:

The use of racial and ethnic labels is not meant to reproduce, uncritically, the legal classifications enacted under apartheid. Racial and ethnic groupings are, of course, always socially constructed and therefore contested and ever-changing in their boundaries and meanings. Individual South Africans, like people everywhere, have often identified themselves in terms other than – or contrary to – state imposed classifications. Nevertheless, given the history of South Africa, one cannot avoid using such problematic labels as "Coloureds," for people of mixed historical origins, about 9 percent of the population; "Indians" or "Asians," for descendents of indentured laborers and traders from the Indian subcontinent, now 3 percent of the population; and "Africans" or "blacks," for the Bantu-speaking majority, about 76 percent of the population. In political discourse, "blacks" also refers to members of all three "non-white" groups who are conscious of their discriminated status. The restrictive use of "Africans" for the indigenous majority does not imply that others have not also become Africans through longtime residence and subjective identification, as both the African National Congress, and to a lesser extent, the Pan Africanist Congress recognize.[3]

In these texts, a history of naming is equally its performance. Reflecting on the contours of political, legal, and cultural tradition, each borrows and crafts a language of description, identification, and classification that serves as a basis for reference, a means of identifying individuals, people,

2 Daniel O'Meara, *Forty Lost Years: The Apartheid State and the Politics of the National Party, 1948–1994* (Johannesburg: Ravan Press, 1996), xxi–xxii.

3 Heribert Adam and Kogila Moodley, *The Opening of the Apartheid Mind: Options for the New South Africa* (Berkeley: University of California Press, 1993), 3.

speakers, descendents, activists, populations, majorities, minorities, and South Africans. In O'Meara's note, this awkward invention begins with the terms of apartheid law, a classification system which was both definitive and the object of intense political opposition. With the latter, O'Meara turns the grounds of appellation toward the question of how those "outside" the law have chosen to "refer to themselves", a claim to self-representation that leaves his note to function as an ambivalent statute, an echo of the (state) law that is interrupted by an (en)act(ment) of naming that rests on the grounds of common sense, tradition, and individual interest. Radicalising this ambiguity, Adams and Moodley choose to deploy the "socially constructed" name, a form of signification that has "ever-changing" meaning and which is shaped by the linguistic affiliations and preferences of particular individuals.[4]

In many footnotes, an expression of dissatisfaction attends the naming of racial and ethnic identity, a caveat if not (self) rebuke that recalls Walter Benjamin's claim that the act of naming is a hinge, a creative power that both constitutes and exposes the limit of ethical life.[5] Put differently, the footnote

---

4   In the years since the end of apartheid, many footnotes have taken a similar path, paying greater attention to South Africa's linguistic diversity and the question of how identity formation is supported and complicated by the constitution's recognition of eleven official languages. The issue is an explicit theme in Marijke du Toit's brief study of oral history in South Africa, an essay that includes this footnote: "In order to distinguish between Afrikaans and so called 'Bantu languages' without categorising the former as non-African, I have used the term 'indigenous' African languages. Isi-Lungu shares the same root form with um–lungu or 'white person' in isiZulu and isiXhosa, but specifically refers to the English language. Of course, adopting the word 'indigenous' might itself be problematic in the context of this article, if taken to connote fixed, authentic, and clearly delineated constructions of 'native' knowledge. I leave to readers to deduce the identity politics played out in my choice of terminology" (Marijke du Toit, "Telling Tales: The Politics of Language in Oral Historiography," *South African Historical Journal* 42 (May 2000), 89). As I discuss in chapter one, there is a long history of concern and controversy in South Africa over the relationship between language development and identity formation.

5   In this matter, working toward the claim that the human capacity to name both inaugurates and breaches the ethical, Benjamin wrote, "Name, however, is not only the last utterance of language but also the true call of it. Thus, in the name appears the essential law of language, according to which to express oneself and to address everything else amounts to the same thing" (Walter Benjamin, "On Language as Such and on the Language of Man," *Walter Benjamin: Selected Writings, Volume 1, 1913–1926*, ed. Marcus Bullock (Cambridge: Harvard University Press, 1996), 65).

frequently holds and expresses a fundamental unhappiness, a regret as to how the will to name cannot escape the historical violence of the language on which it depends.[6] While this infelicity is expressed in different ways, its attempted redress frequently involves a quasi-legal denial, a pronouncement that more or less turns the footnote against its own performance of attribution. As one footnote puts it, "Though these categories were used by the apartheid regime to divide and control the population, these are nonetheless labels that South Africans use to refer to themselves. Nothing about our use of these terms should imply approval of anything about apartheid or acceptance of any underlying theory of race."[7] Reflecting on the dangers of following (legal) tradition, Spitz and Chaskalson take the matter a step further when they contend (or confess) that (their own) racial "labels" have the "unfortunate effect of perpetuating the usage of apartheid's racial terminology".[8] Although

---

The underlying question of whether humans name by forgetting the contingency of naming recalls Nietzsche's discussion of concept formation. See Friedrich Nietzsche, "On Truth and Lies in a Nonmoral Sense," in *The Rhetorical Tradition: Readings from Classical Times to the Present*, eds. Patricia Bizzell and Bruce Herzberg (Boston: St. Martin's Press, 1990), 891. See also Deborah Cook, "From the Actual to the Possible: Nonidentity Thinking," *Constellations* 12 (2005): 21–35.

6   For one important discussion of the name's gift and the way in which the name holds (back) its given-ness, see Jacques Derrida, *On the Name*, trans. David Wood (Palo Alto: Stanford University Press, 1995), 68. For an account of how the "mode of address" to an Other bears on the potential for recognition, see Judith Butler, "Giving Account of Oneself," *Diacritics* 31:4 (2001): 22–40.

7   James Gibson and Helen Mcdonald, "Truth – Yes, Reconciliation – Maybe: South Africans Judge the Truth and Reconciliation Process," Research Report (Cape Town: Institute for Justice and Reconciliation, 2001), 3. This problem of complicity is precisely what leads Leonard Thompson (prior to O'Meara) to declare that the task of "identifying human groups" is akin to entering a "terminological minefield" (Leonard Thompson, *The Political Mythology of Apartheid* (New Haven: Yale University Press, 1985), ix; Leonard Thompson, *A History of South Africa* (New Haven: Yale University Press, 1995), xiii).

8   Richard Spitz and Matthew Chaskalson, *The Politics of Transition: A Hidden History of South Africa's Negotiated Settlement* (Johannesburg: Witwatersrand University Press, 2000), 4. For instance, observe how the following "note on terminology" shifts from a language of description to an attribution of being: "Although the term 'nonwhite' is an unfortunate description and justifiably resented by those thus described, I have decided to use this term when it is necessary to distinguish broadly

their position does not come with a theoretical argument about how to measure the force of such repetition, it may be more than a gesture of political correctness, particularly as debate continues in post-apartheid South Africa over how the "complex process of regeneration and rediscovery that is an inevitable aspect of the rebirth of societies" is complicated by allegedly neutral but still very loaded systems of race classification.[9]

Presented as a regrettable necessity, the footnote is also a site of dedicated argumentation. Looking across different notes, it is not uncommon to find pointed disagreement over questions such as whether the struggle against apartheid served to detach the term "black" from specific racial and ethnic identities in the name of denoting all of those oppressed by the regime.[10] More direct, some notes refute how other notes represent particular groups or interpret vernacular forms of self-identification.[11] Such exchanges frequently

---

between white South Africans and those who are Cape Coloured, Asian, or African, instead of having to enumerate 'Africans, Coloured, Indians' every time reference must be made to them together" (Susan Ritner, *Salvation Through Separation: The Role of the Dutch Reformed Church in South Africa in the Formation of Afrikaner Race Ideology* (PhD Diss., Columbia University, 1971), 274). More recently, there has thus been something of a trend to replace the traditional form of the footnote with a larger discussion of subjectivity and subject formation, the ways in which it might be possible to understand the "discursive production of subjects and identities" in relation to historical interest, state power, and public politics. For one example see *Between Unity and Diversity: Essays on Nation-Building in Post-Apartheid South Africa*, ed. Gitanjali Maharaj, (Cape Town: David Philip, 1999), 6.

9 Quoted in Thabo Mbeki, "A Complex Process of Regeneration and Rediscovery," *ANC Today*, 10–16 December 2004. The occasion of Mbeki's remarks were reports that ten years after the official end of apartheid, the South African National Blood Service had destroyed the President's donated blood because he had refused to complete a questionnaire which was used by the Service to assess the "safety" of donated blood based on a system of race profiling (see Sapa, "Apology for Mbeki Blood Slip-up," *Mail and Guardian Online*, 7 December 2004 <www.mg.co.za>). More prominently, the debate over whether to use racial categories has figured centrally in debates over the design and value of affirmative action and Black Economic Empowerment (BEE) initiatives.

10 Thompson also wonders after the problem of how to name those in the struggle, a question that raises the problem of whether and how one can and ought to take sides in the conflict by naming opponents of the regime as "terrorists" or "freedom-fighters" (Thompson, *History*, xiv).

11 The debate between Frank Welsh and Leonard Thompson over whether "Bushman"

circle around the controversial concept of "coloured", a classification that the 1950 *Population Registration Act* held out for those who were deemed "neither white nor black" and which includes many who identify Afrikaans as their first language.[12]

Taking stock of the potentially damaging homogenisation wrought by naming, Tom Lodge has argued in one of his footnotes that a full recognition of the "social cleavages" and bonds within particular groups demands the use of "class related concepts rather than those drawn from the study of ethnicity".[13] A reference to the larger debate over whether apartheid's development is best understood through the lens of race or class, Lodge's point is partly that the footnote's terminological stance may obscure elements of the very history that it endeavours to illumine. In his note, Bernard Magubane makes the case in a more explicit way, refusing the concept of "white South Africans" on the grounds that it unjustifiably accepts the "moral and legal status of white settlers' claim to the South African state" and fails to reveal how the historical assertion of white sovereignty proceeded partly through the attribution and enforcement of subjugating labels such as " 'Kaffirs', 'Natives', 'Bantus', and now 'Blacks' ".[14]

In the footnote, the invention of the name is both a precondition of beginning and a critique of its cost. A means of producing reference and a (potentially) shared orientation, its names are equally a risk of violence, a defining logic that forecloses on the new by replicating that which has already been. Read this way, as the question of how to oppose the future of the name's precedent in the name of constituting the grounds for agency in the present, the footnote expresses if not enacts an occasion for reconciliation, a moment in which to struggle with the necessity and necessary cost of the name, the given forms of language that underwrite the attribution of

---

is to be preferred to San or Khoi or Khoisan is an evident example. Compare Frank Welsh, *South Africa: A Narrative History* (New York: Kodansha International, 1999), xxiii and Thompson, *History*, xii.

12 I discuss the terms and implications of this legislation in chapter one. For additional work on coloured identity, see Gavin Lewis, *Between the Wire and the Wall: A History of South African 'Coloured' Politics* (New York: St. Martins, 1987).

13 Tom Lodge, *Black Politics in South Africa since 1945* (New York: Longman, 1983), ix.

14 Bernard Makhoseze Magubane, *The Political Economy of Race and Class in South Africa* (New York: Monthly Review Press, 1979), xi.

identity and the inventional qualities of speech that harbour the potential for identification. In South Africa, however, the issue is not simply how to move from the former to the latter. Addressed to more than the repetition of a classification system that was created by apartheid and enforced by its statutes, debate over reconciliation circles around the larger problem of how the will to name can be (re)turned to the Word, a law (before the law) of faith given to demonstrating the name's historical contingency, recollecting its forgotten experience, and discerning its potential to constitute relationships of unity in difference.

If the footnote expresses one object of reconciliation, a mode of naming that may need to be(come) otherwise, it also demonstrates why reconciliation is not immune to its own call to throw the name back into language, back into the question of what it means to forge and speak the name. Put differently, those footnotes that recognise South Africa's linguistic diversity and which condition the dynamics of identity formation on the nuances of particular languages, hold the question of whether reconciliation's meaning can be taken for granted. Are the concept's English connotations definitive? Is there a term for reconciliation in South Africa's other ten official languages? How is the word translated? In one or more languages, does it have a sense or sensibility that resists translation?

While these questions deserve extended study, one that I cannot undertake here and which will likely need to involve philological and ethnographic forms of inquiry, it is also true that in the latter years of struggle and early phases of the transition from apartheid, institutional discussion and debate about reconciliation tended to occur in English, the predominant language of politics in South Africa. Reflected in the pages that follow, this presumption does not always reveal the tensions between the term "reconciliation" and its counterparts in the three most widely spoken languages in South Africa.[15] In Afrikaans, for instance, the word "versoening" can connote making peace and the undertaking of atonement for past transgressions. In many contexts, it carries a significant sense of sacrifice, a mode of accommodation or appeasement that has sometimes served to differentiate it from English interpretations of reconciliation, particularly those that set it on the mantle of forgiveness or which function as a call to set aside history's announced duties

---

15 With emphasis on the term's Greek roots, I have traced the etymology of reconciliation elsewhere. See Erik Doxtader, "Reconciliation – A Rhetorical Concept/ion," *Quarterly Journal of Speech* 89 (2003): 267–92.

or obligations. In isiXhosa, the term "uxolelansio" can connote the work of reconciling, an activity that may be geared to settling a quarrel or creating harmony. With a similar meaning, the isiZulu term "ukuhlangana" can also refer to a restoration between enemies.

At a larger level, the question of reconciliation's translatability has shaped debate over whether the concept serves the political-social interests of black South Africans. Writing in 1987, Itumeleng Mosala used the controversy over the *Kairos Document* as an occasion to argue that "white people's understanding of reconciliation, contrary to that of blacks, is based on a cold-blooded exclusion of the history of alienation".[16] Observing how the "racism of 'non-racists'" is often funded by appeals to reconciliation's loving unity, a norm of multiracialism that can erase black experience, Mosala concludes that the meaning(fullness) of reconciliation turns on a refusal of liberalism's empty promise in favour of liberation and socio-economic restoration. More recently, the TRC's "reconciliation-based discourse" has been criticised for legitimising a logic of racial similarity and a non-racial politics of harmony that, according to Grant Farred, has stripped "black resistance of its oppositionality" and condoned a nostalgia in which "black acts of intellectual counter-insurgency are denied their potentiality to effect change".[17] In these terms, as a hope for "publicly getting along", the call for reconciliation may risk a fundamental misreading of the situation in South Africa, particularly with respect to the material inequality wrought by apartheid and its redress. Thus, while he fails to question whether the TRC can or ought to serve as the "representative anecdote" of reconciliation in South Africa, Farred's position is important precisely because it demonstrates the need to consider how the operativity of reconciliation's discourse bears on the potential for effecting change, the ways in which it opens and forecloses an opportunity to

16 Itumeleng Mosala, "The Meaning of Reconciliation: A Black Perspective," *Journal of Theology for Southern Africa* 59 (1987), 19.

17 Grant Farred, "The Black Intellectuals Work is Never Done: A Critique of the Discourse of Reconciliation in South Africa," *Postcolonial Studies* 7 (2004), 122. Much like the approach to reconciliation taken by Wole Soynika that I discuss in the introduction of this volume, Farred's position is both historically sensitive and rooted in a rather unhinged historicism. Foregoing any attempt to question the terms of the transition and how it might have been crafted otherwise, it systematically conflates the work undertaken by the TRC with a much older and varied discourse of reconciliation. The risk of this approach is a self-confounding sense of what it may mean to stand in a relation of productive opposition.

name experience, (re)constitute the identity that abides within the name, and struggle in the name of a unity in difference that may (or may not) render violent relationships otherwise.

In the footnote, the question of reconciliation's rhetorical history appears as the problem of what it means to oppose the law's classification, a precedent and logic of identitarian exclusion that is enabled and sustained by the violence that it promises to overcome. With this opposition, reconciliation is far less a hope for harmony than a fragile potential for human beings to come to terms, a constitutive mode of expression that struggles to discern how the work of naming might inaugurate and proceed within a relation that neither forgets nor romanticises its contingency and its costs. Against the "being" inscribed by the language of the footnote, reconciliation asks whether and how we might yet speak to the matter of becoming.

1

the struggle of beginning words: reconciliation in a state of emergency

Whereas in my opinion it appears that circumstances have arisen in the areas mentioned in the Schedule which seriously threaten the safety of the public and the maintenance of public order; and the ordinary law of the land is inadequate to enable the Government to ensure the safety of the public and to maintain public order, therefore I, in terms of Section 2 (1) of the Public Safety Act, 1953, hereby declare that as from 21 July 1985 a state of emergency exists within the areas mentioned in the Schedule. Given under my hand and the Seal of the Republic of South Africa at Pretoria this Twentieth day of July, One Thousand Nine Hundred and Eighty-five.

P.W. Botha

During January untill June South Africa has spended something like 500 000 in buying weapons for killing and injuring Blacks. Presiden Botha is not worried about us .... Not to say President Botha don'nt know anything about what is happening he know exactly what is going wrong the fact is that he's not the real christian as he said in Durban when [he] was speaking. The reason why I say he is not a Christian is he allow soldiers to kill us but he says he believe in one god.

Shoitto (13 years old)

The tradition of the oppressed teaches us that the "state of emergency" in which we live is not the exception but the rule. We must attain to a conception of history that is in keeping with this insight. Then we shall clearly realize that it is our task to bring about a real state of emergency ...

Walter Benjamin

reconciliation begins in the moment of its apparent foreclosure. With a call to faith, reconciliation's words appear in a state of emergency, a moment in which the sovereign grants the law an exception to itself and creates a zone of indistinction in which absolute authority is assumed with plausible deniability. With its simultaneous sacrifice and sanctification of precedent, the "undecidable" logic of emergency allows the law to speak *as if* it is not the law, a hypocrisy that supports the sovereign's desire to deter the "dangerous experience" of speech with a language of the ban, a prohibition not just of expression but self-definition.[1] While defiance of this silencing containment is taken as proof of its necessity, the enveloping exclusion of emergency does not foreclose the potential (*dunamis*) for things to be(come) otherwise. Against the law's violent relation of non-relation, reconciliation begins with the making of a time that stands in opposition, a moment that challenges law's endless promise of a future peace and struggles for those words of faith which hold the potential for beginning (again) in the present.

In the middle of 1985, the state of emergency in South Africa was both rule and reality. While announcing plans for exceptional reform, the apartheid regime did little more than perform the violence embedded in the founding premise of separate development. Casspirs and Saracens combed the nation's townships, supporting occupations that involved over 30 000 troops. For reasons of sovereignty or no reason at all, the doors of houses and shacks belonging to "terrorists" were broken down in the early hours of morning. The ambushes were less predictable and frequently fatal. Deemed a threat to "national security", thousands of individuals were listed as "prohibited persons" in the *Government Gazette*. Literally a "ban", this largely uncontestable judgment curtailed already limited rights of association, movement, and speech. Inside and outside the jails, indefinite detention was legislated into the fabric of everyday life. Between November 1984 and the end of 1985, over 12 000 individuals were detained by the state. Arrest usually brought interrogation.[2] For some it ended with death by torture. Human beings disappeared. Some were loaded into state aircraft, drugged, and dropped from altitude into the ocean. Memorialised by place and number – the Cradock Four, the Nietverdient Ten, the Kwandeblele Nine – activists were given funerals that gave way to demonstrations that gave way to funerals. The cycle was not interrupted by the state's attempt to ban funerals held out of doors, at which it was illegal for people who could arrive only by vehicle to display flags, banners, or placards while listening to a minister who was prohibited from criticising the government during the service.

In this river of blood, one that was not unrelated to the covenant made on 16 December 1838 by those who laagered their wagons at "Blood River" and prayed that they would triumph in their coming battle with warriors of the

Zulu kingdom, the mid-1980s were a critical time for the liberation struggle.[3] Thirty years after the African National Congress' (ANC) *Freedom Charter* had been signed at Kliptown, the movement was in the midst of developing an "unprecedented organisational sophistication", a capacity that shifted the aim of protest from resistance to the "chaos and transformation" of insurrection.[4] Formed partly in response to the state's passage of the 1983 constitution, the United Democratic Front (UDF) played a crucial role in this reorientation. Calling for the end of "fraudulent reforms", the start of negotiations between government and the "authentic leaders" of opposition movements, and the continuation of a non-violent people's struggle, the UDF gave important form and direction to the masses. Aligned but not always in sync with the ANC, its national efforts included the promotion of civic organisations dedicated to wresting control of townships from state-appointed leaders and the coordination of consumer boycotts, school stay-aways, and labour actions. Such work appeared to change the "balance of power between the South African Government and black opposition".[5] By mid-1985, many sensed this turn. Underscored by the formation of the Congress of South African Trade Unions (COSATU), it marked a moment to create "ungovernability", a time to take physical control of communities and promote the "radicalisation" of black political consciousness.[6] In an interview with American journalists, Nelson Mandela claimed from the confines of prison that "there is no room for peaceful struggle in South Africa". Molly Blackburn, a member of the Progressive Federal Party, argued that "if you are black and living in the Eastern Cape, you can honestly say that you are living in a state of civil war".[7] Such were the signs of the times.

Winter brought an unprecedented rush of political protest, repression, and brutality. Considered today, the speed and intensity of these events is somewhat overwhelming. In late June, the ANC convened a consultative conference in Kabwe, Zambia. Against the backdrop of a South African government raid on Gaborone and mutinies in its own Angolan training camps, the Congress' meeting was a tumultuous affair, complete with generational and ideological rifts that had developed since its last full gathering in 1969.[8] Concerned with the strategy and tactics of struggle, the ANC affirmed its commitment to a "people's war" dedicated to the "seizure of power" and the creation of a non-racial democracy. At least on paper, it repealed a long-standing policy against attacks on soft targets.[9] In the "Call to the People of South Africa" that was issued after the conference, the ANC leadership declared, "The enemy is falling back. Let us turn his retreat into a rout, the rout into collapse, collapse into surrender." By proclamation, it was time to take the fight to where the enemy lived.

State leaders did and did not tell a different story. Closing Parliament on 19 June, President P.W. Botha warned of a "struggle for the soul of South Africa". Without irony, he declared that the country had to be governed by law not force and then promised to equip the military and police with "better means" to maintain order.[10] Turning then to the possibility of an "artificial unitary state based on one man, one vote", Botha raged, "I do not believe in a way in which already acquired stability and Christian civilised norms are dumped on the scrap heap because we are threatened from all sides by Governments and organisations which do not have the welfare and interests of our people at heart but which seek the furthering of their own selfish interests."[11] With the hardest of hearts, the laager was (re)forming. The circle, however, was growing smaller. Several weeks after Botha's address, the Human Sciences Research Council issued a report indicating that the continuation of apartheid was "nothing short of a recipe for escalating race and class conflict".[12] Two days prior, *The Cape Times* managed to editorialise that conditions in the Eastern Cape townships were growing more explosive and noted with naïve if not condescending surprise that faced with conditions which "resemble life under the heel of a foreign occupying force … six-year-old children carry stones in their hands and meeting unaccompanied whites, scream 'voertsek' (be off/fuck off) with corrosive hatred. The people seem to fear the police rather than look to them as protectors."[13] Reported or not, the repression was stark and the conflict was escalating.

In the first week of July, the bodies of Matthew Goniwe, Fort Calata, Sparrow Mkhonto, and Sicelo Mhlaui were found along the road between Port Elizabeth and Cradock.[14] While their families, friends and neighbours believed that they had been assassinated by the state, it would take years to reveal something about the sequence of events that led to the ambush and murder of the Cradock Four.[15] A teacher, principal, husband, and father, Matthew Goniwe was a prominent and popular civic leader in the Cradock community, an activist that many compared to Steve Biko. In the days leading up to the funeral of the four men, the country's townships were wracked by violence. On 19 July, *The Cape Times* offered that President Botha "has no plan at all to restore calm to the country" and then wondered if it was perhaps time for the state to "negotiate black political rights". The next day, some 60 000 people attended the funeral, travelling by all means and modes to pay their last respects and rally against apartheid. While long banned, the flags of the ANC and the South African Communist Party (SACP) were unfurled and flown during the procession. That night, Botha declared a state of emergency in 36 of South Africa's magisterial districts. It was the second such declaration in the country's history, the first coming in the aftermath of the 1960 Sharpeville Massacre.[16] This one would stand for 229 days. Another would follow in 1986, a siege that would last for four years.

Addressing the nation, Botha defended the emergency, claiming that in the midst of "incitement, intimidation, arson, inhuman forms of assault, and even murder", he could "no longer ignore the insistence of all responsible South Africans, especially the majority of the black communities, who ask that conditions are normalised and that they are granted the full protection of law to continue their normal way of life".[17] With the emergency came full indemnity for security forces engaged in "protecting" the country's sovereignty, a near absolute power that allowed all commissioned police officers and military personnel "of or above the rank of lieutenant-colonel" to detain, arrest, and interrogate individuals who were deemed a threat to the "security of the State". It was a time, according to Nicholas Haysom, when the state provided itself with the justification to "operate in the grey areas between an (extended) legality and wanton illegality, to impose order without law".[18] Produced abroad, the ANC's journal *Sechaba* condemned the state of emergency as an excuse for violence and set its immorality within a larger assessment of apartheid: "The apartheid system is cruel. Apartheid is not just separation of people according to races. It is inequality. It is suspicion. It is ignorance of each other, and ignorance of the common interests. It is jealousy. It is hatred – of everything that is not 'mine.' It is bigotry. *It is everything that is inhuman and anti-human.*"[19]

Within the "normality" of curfews, press restrictions, militarisation, and repression, the pace of events did not slow. Frederik van Zyl Slabbert, the leader of the Progressive Federal Party and a man who would soon quit Parliament to undertake efforts that did much to spur political transition, argued that the emergency replaced the promise of reform with a "state of siege". This perception was confirmed when Botha took the stage on 15 August to deliver a speech that altogether failed to cross his heavily promoted "Rubicon". In an address that covered hints of reform and the possibility of negotiations with semi-paranoiac appeals to Afrikaner destiny and the risk of majority domination, the president managed only to fuel opposition to apartheid.[20] As violence increased, thousands more were detained. Reports of torture became more frequent. Hundreds were killed.

The country was building towards *stasis*. In 1985, the forces of the emergency and the power of the people were combining such that the pressures and aspirations of history appeared set to sponsor an endless cycle of violence. On 28 August, the state banned the UDF's largest affiliate, the Congress of South African Students. At some point, it became clear that a substantial number of the Front's national and regional leaders were jailed. As they sought to fill the vacuum, high-ranking members of South African churches suffered increased harassment and detention. In September, a group of activist theologians gathered in Soweto to discuss the crisis and its implications for the struggle against apartheid. Between the false promise of incremental reform and risk of violent revolution, the group was concerned partly with the question of whether the church could or ought to promote a "third way". Many professed scepticism, holding that a neutral path was one of complicity.

After the meeting, the group issued its findings in a short tract entitled the *Kairos Document*. In it, they attacked the state's theological rationale for apartheid and argued that mainstream South African churches could not hope to stand against the regime with a private and passive vision of reconciliation. Attracting substantial attention, the document generated national debate and not insignificant rifts in the religious community. Then a prominent leader in the End Conscription Campaign, Laurie Nathan recalls that there was a widespread feeling of excitement about the text's release. Desmond Tutu, however, declined to sign the document, indicating that he did not think it fair to either the church or the New Testament's rendering of reconciliation.[21] For their part, the government and Dutch Reformed Church (Nederduitse Gereformeerde Kerk – NGK) counselled rejection, arguing respectively that the text was the work of communists and heretics.

In the midst of difficult times, the authors of the *Kairos Document* claimed that reconciliation held the potential for South Africans to end apartheid and begin again. Why? What was it about the moment that revealed reconciliation's need or demonstrated its value? What hope did reconciliation provide to opponents of the regime at a time when speech and action were being dramatically suppressed? Moreover, how exactly was reconciliation to counter and transform a regime that clearly did not want to give way? In what sense was reconciliation a viable and productive mode of struggle? Ten years before the first draft of the Truth and Reconciliation Commission's authorising legislation was tabled in Parliament, the Word of reconciliation was invoked as a way to oppose a state of emergency and energise the struggle for an unprecedented transformation. What does this call to begin say about the time made for reconciliation and what does it betray about reconciliation's capacity to make history?

The *Kairos Document* questioned and called for(th) reconciliation in the name of making South Africa anew. In this chapter, I investigate the premises, terms, and manifold quality of this beginning. Concerned ultimately with how the *kairos* theologians defined the history-making potential of reconciliation, this work first leads backward, to an old theo-political controversy over reconciliation's role in the rise and justification of apartheid. Held out as a vindicating "potential" of separate development, reconciliation was defended by the state-aligned Dutch Reformed Church as a condition yet to come, a future of "unity in diversity" that followed from the logic and law of race classification and division. In the early and middle years of apartheid, this rationalising promise was a lightning rod for those in the South African religious community who opposed the regime and struggled for its reform. Accusing the NGK of heresy, these critics argued over a period of years that apartheid's distorted words of reconciliation had to be (re)turned to the Word. A gift for the present, reconciliation's power could not be delayed without sacrificing law's connection to justice. In 1985, at a moment when the roads of collective action were increasingly blocked by the barricades of emergency, the *Kairos Document* drew from and then radicalised this position, arguing that reconciliation's beginning hinged on the expression of oppression's experience, words that challenged the state's legitimacy and supported the work of (re)making its law. Understood in relation to its antecedents, this case delineated the occasion of reconciliation in South Africa, a moment that held a time of beginning.

This chapter is addressed to how a variety of South African religious institutions argued about the potential of reconciliation to move the country from past to future and the ways in which these calls defined and redefined reconciliation's power to make history. Shedding light on one important aspect of the church's place in the development and struggle against separate development, it begins with a brief consideration of apartheid's early juridical logic and a more detailed discussion of the NGK's 1974 announcement that the system was justified to the degree that it held the potential for a loving unity. Turning then to the question of how this appeal for reconciliation was explicitly and vehemently contested, the chapter's second section examines the English-speaking church's public case against separate development, a position that evolved over the course of the 1960s and '70s from a doctrinal rebuttal to an outright political challenge. Detailing how religious critics of apartheid redefined reconciliation through the congruent lenses of prophetic and Black theology, I then return to the *Kairos Document*. Through a close reading of its critique and reinterpretation of reconciliation, the chapter's final section traces how this controversial text figured the time of reconciliation in the midst of emergency as an opportunity and calling for speech that could oppose apartheid in a transformative way.

Without a definitive beginning, reconciliation was called forth repeatedly by the South African religious community as a way to make time, a transition, for moving the country from old to new. In almost all cases, these arguments stood in marked opposition to the power of definition, particularly as it was embedded in apartheid's identitarian law and embodied by its divisive practice. Thus, at deep odds with the state's logic of destiny and origin, religious appeals shed less light on reconciliation's singular beginning than the complex nature of its occasion. Accordingly, the ultimate contention of this chapter is that the arguments advanced by religious critics of apartheid are important because they detail the kinds of moments or situations that warranted a "call" for reconciliation's practice and they illustrate how the practice of reconciliation was given to making time for the collective (inter)action of struggle. Claiming that it was not for all times, church leaders contended that reconciliation's peculiar if not paradoxical occasion was a moment of potential. Against the endless deferral of apartheid's announced promise, reconciliation was claimed to mark as well as create a messianic present, a moment that interrupted history and troubled the precedent of that (secular) law which precluded history-making. More precisely, in the face of an ontological frustration induced partly by law, reconciliation's beginning was defended as a gift that held the capacity for the oppressed to make new with speech. Against a logic and law of identity that promised human relationships in a time yet to come, religious opponents of the state (re)defined reconciliation as a calling to (re)turn to the memory of a Word that could both trouble and remake the creative power of words. In the name of forging "unity in difference", reconciliation's speech was thus an act of opposition, a mode of speaking dedicated to turning separate development's violence towards the potential for understanding. Its (rhetorical) faith was claimed to hold a capacity for individuals to both read and invent the *signs* of the times, words that set the language of law into motion and troubled its power of definition. The ambiguous terms and actualisation of this potential were problems that exceeded and extended beyond the South African religious debate over reconciliation. As the emergency continued, they appeared again, rhetorical questions about the power of words to constitute the beginning of political transition.

1. making the "potential" of apartheid's word

Before it was defended as an antidote to apartheid, reconciliation was used in powerful quarters to explain and justify the system's potential. From its earliest days, separate development was legitimised partly through a select reading of Christian scripture, an interpretation of the Word that was held up as proof of the need for words of law that defined, classified, and divided human beings on the basis of racial and ethnic identity. Developed over time and tied to the announced premises of Afrikaner nationalism, this power of definition was defended as a path that would lead to a reconciling love in the next life. While it is tempting to dismiss such claims as presumptively incorrect and immoral, this impulse may not serve. The architects and apologists of apartheid did craft a complex set of arguments about its value. At least with respect to the concept and practice of reconciliation, the details of this case need to be understood, especially as they provoked and shaped a set of counter-arguments about separate development's (non)reconciling ends.

In South Africa, reconciliation's beginning is tied to the development and logic of apartheid. Here, I want to demonstrate precisely how reconciliation was used by the NGK to rationalise separate development, a tactic that found its fullest expression in a 1974 NGK document that gathered a significant amount of the church's historical thinking about the "merits" of race classification and concluded that the practice of apartheid contained the *potential* for reconciliation. To fully grasp the significance of this position, it is first necessary to reflect briefly on the nature of colonial segregation in South Africa and the early terms of Afrikaner nationalism. While I will return to the latter in the next chapter, my goal here is simply to contextualise the rise of separate development and offer a substantive glimpse of how nationalists first turned to the law in order to enact the identitarian logic of apartheid. Thus, from a reading of the 1950 *Population Registration Act,* I move to a consideration of how the NGK affirmed the religious-moral legitimacy of this system. In particular, the section traces how the church distanced itself from race-based or "chosen-people" definitions of apartheid with an argument as to how respect for every nation's historical-divine linguistic diversity warranted the practice of parallel development and fulfilled scripture's promise of reconciliation. In the NGK's terms, apartheid's virtue rested in its potential, a capacity to engender a future "unity in diversity". A coming (re)union of human beings, this potential provided a (self-sealing) warrant for separate development's earthly law. It was also a crucial referent for those religious critics who believed that the announced but never present beginning of apartheid's reconciliation was a heretical reason to undertake the work of beginning again.

defining laws of division

Apartheid (apartness) started officially in 1948. It began much earlier, with a set of political-colonial and socio-economic dynamics that emerged not long after Jan van Riebeeck established a refreshment stop for the Dutch East India Trading Company in 1652 and planted his hedge of bitter almonds, the first line in the Cape sand.[22] Early settlers brought a noxious racism. For many, eager to serve their view of God's will, the indigenous peoples appeared "dark, sinister, heathen, shiftless, and unclean – thus conspicuously lacking in the outward signs of grace".[23] In the early years of colonialism, this condescension helped rationalise slavery and territorial expansion, forms of domination that fuelled significant social conflict and a series of bloody frontier wars. In 1795, a second colonial force appeared when the British took control of the Cape from the Dutch. Soon alienated by a Victorian sensibility that brought an end to formal slavery and which appeared to threaten their social status and livelihood, a group of Afrikaners began to question whether the promise of their form of life might lie in the country's interior. Setting off in 1835–36 on the "Great Trek", these *voortrekkers* sought to escape an "alien government" and undertake an inspired quest that challenged one form of colonial power with the (re)production of another.[24]

Between the Brit and the Boer, clashes over sovereignty were tied to disputes over (white) ethnic identity and the so-called "native question". In the wake of the Anglo-Boer War, a conflict that left deep scars on the Afrikaner psyche, the Union created by the 1910 *South Africa Act* grew partly from a call for "conciliation".[25] While leaders disagreed about the possible value of relating English and Afrikaner "streams" of community life, few used the moment to question their basic commitment to racial segregation. A flexible and sophisticated ideology, according to Saul Dubow, segregationist policy took form in a series of laws that culminated with the 1936 *Native Bills*.[26] Seen by proponents as a way to split the difference between the "Scylla of [black] identity and the Charybdis of subordination", the bills had much to do with the growing desire for a unified white nation.[27] Largely eliminating the remaining franchise for blacks, the legislation also gave significant teeth to the 1913 *Native Land Act*. Described by some as the single most devastating law in the history of South Africa and passed a year after the formation of the ANC (known initially as the South African Native Congress), the *Land Act* sought to restrict black land ownership through the creation of "native reserves". Read through the lens of the *Native Bills*, it was a stark indication that the aim of segregation was not separate development but a dominating and strict "differentiation in treatment between black and white".[28] In short, while it may have been the "opening shot in the battle to institutionalise racialised social engineering", segregation's legal development was more a referent than a cause of apartheid.[29]

Segregationist legislation presupposed the existence of a homogenous black population that could be regulated with a single machinery. According to Aletta Norval, this collectivising assumption was a crucial motivation for the government to "invent the category of 'the native'".[30] In these terms, racial domination rested on a complex act of definition, a classification system that figured a mass (black) Other and then set it in strict opposition to an equally monolithic (white) self. This binary, however, did not hold. For one, it ignored basic divisions in a state that was not yet a nation. As divergent interests among whites bred political tension, economic inequality and Afrikaner poverty led some to support strict segregation and others to advocate measures that would limit the "influx of blacks in a manner that preserved the labour supply".[31] In the eyes of many, the "viability" of either approach was undermined as conditions on the reserves appeared to produce only unrest, strikes, and migration to urban centres. What's more, the segregationist's static white-black divide ignored the question of where to "place" those individuals identified as "coloured". Viewed together and coupled to the coming of depression and war, these developments coalesced into a crisis of identity, a situation in which the promise of being South African was not enough for whites to "make sense of their history" and sustain hopes for the future.[32] At some basic level, this near existential disappointment was a crucial spark for the nationalism that fuelled apartheid.

Afrikaner nationalism developed in fits and starts.[33] In its early days, it lacked a clear justification and enjoyed uneven support in many Afrikaner communities. Warning against "monocausal" explanation, Johan Degenaar argues that the rise of nationalist sentiment in South Africa must be read through the lenses of "self-determination, *volk* (and religion), race structure, and power (economic, social and political)".[34] To this list, one can add Dunbar Moodie's observation that in the early 1900s, language was "perceived as one of the taproots of the separate ethnic consciousness of Afrikaner culture".[35]

Formed in the wake of the Boer War, the Afrikaans language movement was indeed an important aspect of the Afrikaner struggle for meaning and place. Motivated by concerns about the perceived inequity of conciliation and the fragmenting effects of urbanisation and political liberalism, the movement was addressed centrally to the question of how to understand, create, and codify the terms of Afrikaner identity.[36] In 1908, future Prime Minister Daniel Malan made the case clearly, explaining both why and how it was necessary for all Afrikaners to take great care with the *taal* (language):

> A living powerful language is born from the soil of the People's heart [*volkshart*] and the People's history [*volksmond*] … Raise the Afrikaans language to a written language, make it the bearer of our culture, our history, our national ideals, and you will raise the People to a feeling of self-respect and to the calling to take a worthier place in world civilisation.[37]

Between the lines, this appeal for the word's bond expressed an ambivalence: Afrikaner nationalism both sought and refused "civilisation". For a people with deep ties to the land, the desire for a certain kind of urbanity and material comfort sat awkwardly with the professed dangers of the "plural world".[38] In the 1930s, depression and drought exacerbated this tension. Unable to sustain themselves in the rural areas, Afrikaners took to the cities, a move that brought a perceived reduction in social standing and set them into direct economic competition with blacks.[39] Coupled with the apparent failure of influx control policies, the result was a moral panic, a fear of *swartgevaar* (black danger) that lent support to the notion that God wished the Afrikaner to face and overcome the "descending horde".[40] In 1942, Malan put the matter plainly, contending that a "sea of barbarism" had not yet washed away the grounds for hope:

> It is through the will of God that the Afrikaner People exists at all. In his wisdom he determined that on the southern point of Africa, the dark continent, a People should be born who would be bearer of Christian culture and civilisation. In his wisdom he surrounded this People by great dangers. He set the People down upon unfruitful soil so that they had to toil and sweat to exist upon the soil … God also willed that the Afrikaans people should be continually threatened by other Peoples.[41]

Malan's call was to cultivate *volksgebondenheid*, a belief in the priority of blood, people, and nation. In the 1930s and '40s, the social and political struggles of the past were taken as proof that the Afrikaner did have a place in the world, one that would appear as each individual came to recognise that they "existed only in and through the nation".[42] A key premise of apartheid, this essential nature of the people (*volkseie*) was an important element in the call for separate development.[43] More precisely, the unity of nation required the simultaneous creation of separation and distance from difference. In its early formulations, this nationalist equation leaned heavily on the premise and promise of history, a sense of the past's potential that was characterised in different ways. For one, the aspirations of the *volk* were explained through a narrative of struggle, trials that spoke to a calling if not a destiny. Expressions of this hope litter the record of early nationalist discourse and were summed up well by H.M. van der Westhuizen when he invoked the Great Trek and implored that "the generations of the Voortrekkers can always continue to exist in us and in our posterity and can grow to fullness if we hold today inexorably to the way which they have shown us".[44] As well, the fate of the Afrikaner was increasingly held to rest on the question of race relations, the ability of the Afrikaner to create and maintain a "national differentiation" in which the "non-white population can have the opportunity to develop according to its own nature, in its own areas, and ultimately, so that it could obtain control over its own affairs". Together, the elements of this case to secure "Africa for the Afrikander" routed the promise of mutuality, freedom, and sovereignty through practices of exclusion, guardianship, and control. Demanding a certain sacrifice, the claimed potential of nationalism rested on the idea that self and group actualisation was historically-divinely determined at the same time as it was contingent on a system that could support the development of singular identity through collective isolation. Little more than a way station, the present was an opportunity to take the past and use it as a map toward the future.

While the door opened with the 1948 election, the National Party's slim victory brought a vision of apartheid that had neither clear form nor majority support from white voters.[45] What did exist was the will and ability to make law. Thus, the so-called "four pillars of apartheid" – Afrikaner hegemony, the regulation of space, labour policy, and social control – were erected in something of a flurry, a process that has led Willem de Klerk to suggest that "never in history have so few legislated so programmatically, thoroughly, and religiously, in such a short time".[46] Indeed, nationalism's potential was first embodied in a series of often bizarrely named laws that sought to weld economic domination, white privilege, and state power. As Parliament rubber-stamped, Malan expressed the racist aim of the system with apparent ease, noting in a letter that colour difference was "merely the physical manifestation of the contrast between two irreconcilable ways of life, between barbarism and civilisation, between overwhelming numerical odds on the one hand and insignificant numbers on the other".[47]

The legal correlate of Malan's position was the 1950 *Population Registration Act*. The root metaphor of apartheid's (legal) identity and a pernicious enactment of its identitarian logic, the legislation was an explicit attempt to attribute racial distinction, create the basis for spatial division, and deter so-called race mixture, the creation of what the 1954 Tomlinson Report called a "new biological entity".[48] While it would be amended numerous times, the first version of the Act declared that "every person whose name is included in the [population] register shall be classified by the Director General as a white person, a coloured person or a Black, as the case may be, and every coloured person and every Black whose name is so included shall be classified ... according to the ethnic or other group to which he belongs". While the operative terms of the Act did not see fit to address the black as "person", its glossary did offer that "'Black' means a person who is, or is generally accepted as, a member of any aboriginal race or tribe in Africa". The "white person" was defined not with a single sentence but a full page, replete with notions about those who were "in appearance obviously a white person" and "not generally accepted as a coloured person".[49] Appearances did indeed matter; decisions about how to classify people were to take into account "habits, education and speech and deportment and demeanour in general". Not revised until 1967, the "coloured person" was left in the Act as a negative remainder – a "person who is not a white person or a Black".[50]

By part or whole, the *Population Registration Act* deployed a legal power of definition to identify, survey, classify, and instrumentalise human being(s).[51] The imprecision of the law's criteria was simply a reason to legislate further, work that set distinction upon distinction in the name of rendering "judgments" about racial and ethnic identity. In this way, disciplined populations were created by petty bureaucrats authorised to make assessments that had direct consequences for political representation, economic opportunity, and freedom of movement on the basis of how they perceived the hue of skin, timbre of voice, thickness of lips, or texture of hair. Legally, such determinations were the very basis for whether individuals had standing before the law. In Achille Mbembe's terms, the legislation betrayed a "mode of government" that rested on the "thesis of non-similarity", an attribution and definition of identity that was used to naturalise and justify inequality. In 1987, Oliver Tambo emphasised the Act's enduring significance when he argued that apartheid's "definition of the black people" meant that the system was "inherently an act of violence".[52]

Coupled with the devastating relocations authorised by the 1952 *Group Areas Act*, the process of population registration meant that a basic element of apartheid was up and running. With it, the nationalist aspiration to constitute the words of identity's unity appeared in a legal architecture that very much reduced personhood to race and ethnicity.[53] Denying individuals an ability to claim a basic sense of self or choose their associations, the Act was both a condensation and assertion of sovereign power, a platform for the government to dominate an "African majority" which it claimed did not exist as such. In the name of the nation, law's promise of "separate freedom" now depended on the (enforced) ability of like to gather with like in order to make good on their historically and God-given potential.[54] As a justification (by division) for apartheid, the cultivation of this potential was held to rest partly on a promise of reconciliation.

the rationalising word(s) of separation

From the language movement to the *Population Registration Act*, the word of apartheid's law appeared to hold that race was the founding distinction. This did not mean, however, that the need for separate development was self-confirming. Both before and after the 1948 election, the announced goals of apartheid led many of its proponents to question and then fashion a case for its underlying morality. A crucial space for this justificatory discourse was the NGK.[55] With close ties to the language movement, the church worked over a period of decades to explain why the (sacred) exclusivity of nationalism held the virtue of separation but not the sin of racism. Backing away from the idea that Afrikaners were a chosen people, the NGK's position rested partly on the claim that separate development was preparation for a reconciliation to come. Developed over a number of years, the church's interpretation of this "unity in diversity" did not fully appear until the early 1970s. Borrowing and reinterpreting a complex debate from the 1930s and '40s about the God-given nature of human identity, the position hinged on a temporal deferral, a claim as to how the reconciliation of difference would appear only in the next life. Banking on the future, the church claimed that apartheid's productive waiting was moral to the degree that its enforcement of separation reflected a historical-divine calling that held the potential for a transcending experience of (re)union.

The NGK's theo-politics of race played an important role in rationalising apartheid.[56] Still, the NGK's own admission that it was "intimately involved in the constitutional development of our country" did not mean that it was the only source of argumentation about the merits of separate development.[57] Over time, its positions were supported, supplemented, and challenged by other bodies, particularly the conservative Afrikaner academic community and the powerful Broederbond.[58] Moreover, the NGK rarely held a singular view of apartheid or consensus as to whether the state was appealing to religious doctrine in an appropriate way. From early discussions of the "native question" to controversy over the exact meaning of separate development, debate over the nature and value of apartheid was intricate, ongoing, and not without limit. While the church of the "National Party at prayer" offered, codified, revised, and sometimes dropped various rationales for apartheid, strenuous internal dissent did lead to the expulsion or withdrawal of prominent church members, some of whom came to play important roles in the struggle against apartheid. In the main, however, the NGK did make a definitive contribution. Its complex "theology in the service of nationalism" offered a rationalising Word to those words of law that defined and enforced the identitarian logic of separate development.[59]

In 1974, the NGK's General Synod approved one of its most comprehensive statements on separate development – *Ras, Volk en Nasie en Volkereverhoudinge in lig van die Skrif* (*Human Relations and the South African Scene in the Light of Scripture*).[60] Starting cautiously, the tract acknowledged the risk in "acquiescing to race relations that do not accord with the Word of God". It concluded with the word of law, embracing the logic of classification propagated by the *Population Registration Act* and claiming that while the church ought not to intervene in matters of state, "the golden rule of sovereignty" meant that "a political system based on the autogenous or separate development of various population groups can be justified from the Bible, but the commandment to love one's neighbour must at all time be the ethical norm towards establishing sound inter-people relations".[61] In between, the church justified apartheid with a series of arguments that moved from definitional claims about human identity to a normative appeal for South Africans to embrace the promise of reconciliation.

In *Human Relations*, the NGK's defence of apartheid turns on two central arguments: racial-ethnic differentiation between human beings is a natural inevitability and God wishes nations to develop in their own time and place. Appealing to scripture, the Synod contended that there is a "unity of mankind in God", a vertical (divine) bond that enabled the horizontal (historical) differentiation of "races and peoples".[62] However, conceding that the concept of race was not well explained in the Bible, the NGK turned to the table of peoples and nations that appears in the Book of Genesis. This tack was an old one, a central thread of Dutch reformed theology that ran back to the work of S.J. du Toit, an early advocate of "people's theology", who argued that the unity of different nations followed directly from the appearance of distinct tongues.[63] Echoing the language movement, the NGK's claim was that scriptural lessons about human speech were not just a rationale but a calling for separate development. In 1943, for instance, the Council of Dutch Reformed Churches argued that "according to the Bible, God actually called nations into existence each with its own language, history, Bible, and church, and that the salvation also for the native tribes in our country has to be sought in a sanctified self-respect and in a God-given national pride".[64] Set next to claims about the dangers of liberalism, cosmopolitanism, and communism, the church's long-standing position was thus that the unity of God's creation marked a divine calling to enact a "progressive ethnic differentiation" which would allow all races to fulfil their own destiny.[65]

In the Word given for words, the NGK found a "principle of differentiation". By 1974, following the arc of its earlier thinking, the NGK turned to the story of Babel in order to buttress its case, arguing that human attempts to unify distinct languages were a sign of arrogance by those who sought only to "make a name for themselves". Put differently, the inventional and synthetic power of the Word was reserved for God; virtuous humility demanded that human beings abide in the distinction enacted by different tongues.[66] This too was an old argument. In 1944, J.D. du Toit had claimed that such division was exemplified by the Great Trek, an event that he set in strict distinction to the sinful effort at Babel.[67] Three years later, the Reverend J.D. Vorster expanded the position, arguing that the dangers of cross-talk represented a deep threat to the future of Afrikanerdom:

…we see that when the tower was being built humanity was still one in all respects. We therefore conclude that God had created the human being in such a way that he has the potential in himself to form races in the same way as the acorn bears the potential to become an acorn tree.

51

Every child bore genetic possibilities which, given the proper isolation and inbreeding, could lead to the birth of a separate race.[68]

With a strict teleology, Vorster's position used the language of potential to establish both the premise and alleged promise of separate development. As given by God, the capacity for self-actualisation was an intrinsic good, a potency that required less choice than the creation of conditions which would allow human beings to grow and flourish. In 1974, the NGK used a similar logic when it offered a "qualified yes" to the question of whether apartheid comported with scripture. Rejecting the idea that Afrikaners were members of a select race, it drew from the "lesson" of Babel to claim that language is the *natural-historical* expression of a complex *divine* interest in differentiation: "The diversity of the races and peoples to which the confusion of tongues contributed, is an aspect of reality which God obviously intended for this dispensation. To deny this fact is to side with the tower builders."[69] If the people were not chosen, however, the crucial question was whether the strict maintenance of difference was an excuse for enforced inequality. The NGK replied in the negative, a conclusion that borrowed (and distorted) more than a little from the work of Abraham Kuyper, an influential Dutch theologian who also once served as Prime Minister of the Netherlands.[70]

Writing in the early 1900s, Kuyper argued that God's creation was organised into "spheres of sovereignty". Regulated by "creation ordinances", these spheres of social, individual, and political life were both an expression of divine law and a "motive of consciousness" to the degree that "there is no life without differentiation and there is no differentiation without difference".[71] Thus, attempts to unite what God made distinct were neither possible nor moral; all human beings had to develop in light of their given potential. Creation's invisible (vertical) unity with God did not deny the diversity of appearance in which "humanity is manifested as differentiated in groups, of races, and nations and of societies of different kinds, and also in unequal individuals".[72] According to Johann Kinghorn, this "cosmological hierarchy headed by God" was the "keystone of the Afrikaner value system".[73] For the NGK, it explained the "necessity" of separate development and set the system on the "moral" claim that all peoples needed space to develop in their own terms, independent and unencumbered by outside influence.

The cultivation of difference was held out by the NGK as the potential of separate development. However, the church denied that this so-called striving to flourish in the light of God was a warrant for racism.[74] In *Human*

Relations, it declared a willingness both to serve a "prophetic, priestly, and kingly function [also] towards the people" and to respect the "intrinsic cultural possessions" that constituted the "identity of each people".[75] This obligation required not a "people's church" but one that allowed every group to give "full expression to their national identity". The distinction was crucial, a hinge with which the NGK turned its rationale for separate development away from race and towards the idea that apartheid was an opportunity for all of God's creatures to realise their unique potential and join a larger unity in Christ. As a calling to transcend the limits of earthly life, the NGK thus claimed that apartheid's differentiation was not *prima facie* evidence of racism:

> When such a country honestly comes to the conclusion that the ethical norms for ordering relationships, i.e. love of one's neighbour and social justice, can best be realised on the basis of parallel development, and if such a conviction is based on factual reasoning, the choice of parallel development can be justified in light of what the Bible teaches.[76]

In this "parallel" logic, love carries a heavy load to the degree that it distinguishes "appropriate" forms of differential development from racist forms of "sinful separation".[77] Carrying love from "individual ethics to relationships between groups and peoples", the church held that all nations were equal (but different) and that "neighbourly love" was not the kind that sought to "transform the neighbour into a replica of oneself but accepts him in his own right as someone created in the image of God and affords him sufficient scope for true self-realisation".[78] On one level, the argument was a circle: separatism was justified by the duty to respect distinction. At another, as it followed from the idea of creation ordinances that maintained spheres of sovereignty, the position reduced love to a function of that law which regulated but did not require (or condone) relations between people. Thus, there was very little intersubjective about this love. The walls that "contained" development were only and always parallel, running side by side across the landscape, through time, and toward future salvation. Between them, marking a sort of divine demilitarized zone on earth, sat a love that amounted to little more than voyeurism, an invitation to peek over the top of the wall and assess whether the "Other population" had the ability to realise its separate if not unequal potential. If so, all the better. If not, the church maintained that society needed to discern whether the shortfall was due to unjust exploitation or the failure of those on the other side of the partition to "accept responsibility for their own development".[79] While the difference, so to speak, was not made clear, the NGK concluded its case by claiming that the just sovereignty of separate development was underwritten by a norm of love that held the promise of reconciliation:

> The message of Holy Scripture must remain the fundamental basis for
> the determination of relationships between people. Because man is
> created in the image of God, the basic concepts and norms for his life are
> love, justice, truth, and peace. These arise from his reconciliation with
> God in Christ, by regeneration and renewal (2 Cor. 5:17). On this basis,
> the faithful are called upon to erect the signposts of the kingdom of God
> even in this dispensation, including the sphere of social relations.[80]

While the terms of the signposts may have been difficult to interpret, they loomed over park benches inscribed with a very clear message: *net blankes* (whites only). The incongruity is telling, a troubling illustration of how the 1974 Synod appealed to the "unity in diversity" of reconciliation in order to support separate development while claiming that it had adequate distance from the state to assess the morality of apartheid's practice. On one side, the unifying power of separation was defended as a reflection as well as a confirmation of nationalism's value; the *volk* were not chosen but implicit in the Word of God that created the (human) words which revealed the truth of diversity. On the other, the need to cultivate and protect difference was defined as a basic condition for existence, one that was beyond accountability except as it fulfilled a calling that led toward salvation. Only in the next life would various peoples confront that which related and united them. In the present, peace and justice followed from the (legal) "ability" of (pre)defined populations to develop in light of creation ordinances that were inscribed into the laws of a state dedicated to defending the necessity of the nation's division. For the future, diversity was the imposed and insulating gift of an identity that was "made moral" by its potential to affect the unification of humanity with itself through God. Holding that equality was an internal-private matter, a question of what one did with and within one's sphere of sovereignty, the church's call for reconciliation was thus a promise of a relationship that could not exist, a ban in which the definition of self amounted to an abstract and self-deferring capacity to forge relationships (only) in a time yet to come.

The NGK's logic of human "relations" provided important fuel for the engines of apartheid. In the uncertainty that attended the Nationalist's 1948 electoral victory, the church was a space in which to mobilise a fragmented *volk* and rally the "pride of identity" that underwrote apartheid's founding legislation. In the sight of God, the virtue of unity in diversity depended on the separation of peoples, the definition and division of human beings based on identities that were claimed to be less about race than the origins of language. The proclaimed good news of the Word was thus that law's words of racial classification fulfilled a divine calling that did not necessarily "choose" one people over another. As such, the logic of the *Population Registration Act* could be differentiated from racism by claiming that the law sought the "loving isolation" that marked the beginning of a (long) road to its own transcendence. Neither here nor there, the alleged power of apartheid's division was the claimed potential of reconciliation's unity.

the endless promise of identity's law

The beginning of separate development involved the creation of a complex identity logic that was justified partly on the grounds of reconciliation. Considered through the terms of the *Population Registration Act*, the NGK's *Human Relations and the South African Scene in Light of Scripture* appealed to the potential for a "unity in diversity" in order to rationalise and defer accountability for separate development's self-sealing "parallel" logic. This is not to say that responsibility for apartheid can be left at the NGK's door or even that its embrace of separate development was a necessary condition for its implementation. Rather, the church's position is an important beginning of reconciliation. As it routed the value of apartheid through an appeal to a future reconciliation, the NGK helped to consolidate the logic of separate development while constituting the reference for a protracted controversy over whether the church had misread Scripture such that the idea of reconciliation needed to be (re)turned to the present in order to serve those who opposed apartheid.

From the fears and aspirations that underwrote nationalism, the rise of apartheid created and demanded a power of definition that sought to locate and divide racial and ethnic identity. On Norval's reading, the system's founding gesture was a "novel form of social division", an "undecidable" identitarian logic that both sustained mythic interpretations of Afrikaner history and justified the separation of race groups. This undecidability appeared over time, a double movement between national and racial distinction such that each was used to legitimise and obscure the violent implications of the other. The fictive unity of an organic *volk* was substantiated by an announced threat of racial mixture that was presented less as a reason for domination than a need for the creation of nations in which all individuals could strive and realise their full potential. The identity logic of separate development thus classified human beings through a system that vacillated between the celebration of (national) difference and enforcement of (racial) exclusion. Its "moral vision of social division" derived the purity of the people from that Other which the people were not. At the same time, the claimed virtue of the nation was its ability to promote individual difference, a promise that could not be realised until the Other was itself divided and separated along ethnic or tribal lines. As these two positions were linked to a theology which held that the potential of identity was predestined while also historically contingent, the classificatory logic of apartheid rested on a deep internal tension, a rift that was crucial to the perpetuation of its power.

Evident in the *Population Registration Act*, apartheid's law of identity constituted the grounds of individual and state sovereignty by operating both inside and outside itself. The claimed historical need of the Afrikaner was also defended as a divine imperative that set justice beyond the grasp of human beings. What linked the two sides of the equation was the idea of "potential". From Malan's defence of the language movement to Vorster's plea to cultivate the Afrikaner "acorn" to the NGK's 1974 claim that reconciliation was (always) yet to come, it is the appeal to potential that welds and then obscures several key premises of separate development. In the face of an endless threat that was composed with a mixture of calling and original sin, apartheid was rationalised with a promise of security in the afterlife. However, this hope required that the present be a moment of sacrifice, a time to create space, "group areas" in which (sovereign) individuals could realise their capacities in the context of their own sovereign (purified) nations, collectives that righted the wrongs of Babel in the name of approaching the Word which would someday reconcile. Blurring if not negating the difference between fate and choice, the declared potential of separate development was not only a "piously disguised form of self-justification", but a form of law that constituted by exception, through a violence that was indemnified by a divine calling which the state appropriated and used to weave the idea of a nation that both preceded itself and was yet to (be)come.[81] From within this plausibly deniable logic, the NGK held that the potential of separate development was the potential for unity in difference. More precisely, apartheid's law of identity was the hope for unity *as* difference, a division in which love was for(ever) the desire to not relate.

Many held fast to this promise. Most did not, seeing all too well how its potential entailed an infinite deferral that legalised racism, economic exploitation, forced removals, political exclusion, degradation, and the systematic violation of human rights. Opposition to this barbarism took many forms. Some of the resistance began with a directed critique of its theology, an inquiry into how it was possible to break through a wall of partition that appeared to shut out much more than reflect the light of God. What could be said about the Word that banned words? How could the nation's sacred history give way to a shared capacity for history-making? What was the potential in the truth of human experience that could challenge the (state) church's understanding of unity in diversity? What did reconciliation mean in the face of apartheid injustice? In different ways and with uneven effects, these questions were grounds on which to struggle against apartheid's repression. In a basic sense, they asked after those words that held a potential in the present to subvert the identity of reconciliation's law.

2. by grace or mass action: (re)defining the faith and work of reconciliation

Two years before events in Soweto changed the face of South African politics, *Human Relations and the South African Scene* made one of the NGK's most systematic cases for apartheid's potential. Drawing from doctrinal arguments about the sovereignty of people(s), the church appealed to *its* Word of a reconciling love in order to condone words of law that enforced difference in the name of a future unity. Before and after its publication, this justification for apartheid provoked response, a challenge that illustrated how apartheid's presuppositions about sovereignty served to "submerge the possibility of discourse" and raised questions as to whether such silence was antithetical to the promise of reconciliation.[82] Thus, while one beginning of reconciliation in South Africa appeared in close connection to the rise of apartheid and the NGK's extended defence of its practice, it began again when religious opponents of separate development (re)defined the concept in the name of subverting the system's claim to embody God's loving Word.

Bound by reservations and then stark opposition to separate development, South African English-speaking churches devoted significant attention to the NGK's claim that racial-ethnic differentiation held the potential for reconciliation. Crucial to understanding the terms of the 1985 debate around the *Kairos Document*, my aim here is to examine the terms of this rebuttal and detail how it moved from a doctrinal dispute over the NGK's reading of

Scripture to the political claim that apartheid's "novel gospel" was not simply error but an occasion to return reconciliation's potential to the present. By the 1970s, the question of reconciliation's power was being theorised along two related tracks. On one side, a number of religious leaders called for the development of a prophetic theology that would expose the false potential of apartheid and delineate the urgent necessity of resistance. On the other, Black Theology drew from the tenets of Black Consciousness to argue that apartheid's law of identity could be thrown off only as the oppressed reflected on their experience in a manner that fashioned exploitative separation into the bonds of collective identification. When read together, these positions turned the NGK's case for the potential of reconciliation against itself in the name of energising struggle. No longer for the future, the power of reconciliation was located between the times, a present in which to craft the terms of history-making. As such, the claimed virtue of reconciliation was its ability to interrupt the logic of separate development, a power that also brought difficult questions about what counted as an appropriate form of resistance. Defended as a way to refuse the isolating identity imposed by apartheid and gather the voices needed for political action, reconciliation thus appeared in the late 1970s to stand in a kind of self-contradiction, a good that vindicated the need for struggle but which did not come with a clear explanation of how it worked or what it would achieve. While figures like Desmond Tutu attempted to redress this dilemma by tying reconciliation to the notion of ubuntu, the task of explaining how to render reconciliation's potential actual was ongoing – a beginning that would find fuller form only in the tumult of the mid-1980s.

debating (the doctrine of) identity's violence

Today, over 70 per cent of all South Africans identify as Christian. In various forms, the faith arrived not long after van Riebeeck, carried by missionaries that spread across the country in order to wage a "battle for sacred power".[83] In his study of the colonial English-speaking churches, Craig Cuthbertson argues that by the early 1800s, it had become "more and more difficult for blacks to distinguish missionaries from the armory of imperial bureaucracy".[84] While debate continues over whether these messengers served only the colonial masters or made some attempt to soften their blows, it is clear that English-speaking churches offered little more than an "ambiguous and qualified" response to colonial racism.[85] While preaching opposition to racially motivated land and labour legislation, their message was directed to congregations that were largely if not strictly segregated. An important rationale for the formation of the African Independent Churches, many of which borrowed from the principles of Ethiopianism to oppose colonialism's religion, this hypocrisy was deeply entrenched, an inertia that was upset but by no means reversed with the rise of Afrikaner nationalism and the 1948 election.[86]

The onset of legislative apartheid provoked negative reaction from many church leaders. Formed in 1936, the Christian Council of South Africa (later renamed the South African Council of Churches – SACC) was at the forefront of this opposition, even as some felt that its criticisms of nationalist policy were more cautious and paternalistic than principled and progressive.[87] In 1952, the Council issued a short tract, "Race – What Does the Bible Say?" Tentative in its tone, the document took rough aim at the NGK's scriptural case for apartheid when it claimed that, "The centre of unity of the Christian church is not race, or religious training, or culture, or social status, or even sex ... It [the church] does not forbid or command the separation or fusion of races."[88] Behind this stance were open questions about whether Scripture could be mustered to support separate development. Asking where and how the Old and New Testaments related race to faith and contending that God's selection of the Jewish people was not the basis for a generalising metaphor, the Council's ultimate suggestion was that context mattered. The point was underscored by its appeal to Paul's teaching that reconciliation beckons a life in common within a "new sphere of moral attainment", a sphere that did not seem to feature in the NGK's interpretation of Kuyper's theology. In other words, the memory of the cross was not a distant hope for unity but the presence of an "at-one-ment" that embraced "all believers" and worked against the "sin of racial pride".[89] Noting its objection to how the NGK was reading Romans 13, the Council went further, claiming that the creation of unity *in* difference was far more consistent with Scripture than a system of apartheid that aimed toward unification *as* division. Thus, as it condoned legislation like the *Population Registration Act*, the NGK's case for separate development came at a significant price:

When the Negro or the Asiatic is treated simply as an instance of a racial type, he is merely representative, not unique as an individual. His personal identity is lost in his racial status and his freedom is restricted by the generalisations about his race. His personality is submerged and he is not respected as a person. Conversely the member of the so-called "superior" race may also lose his individuality in the presence of an exploited people, and be unable to break through to assert his own personal attitude where it stands in contrast with that of his own group. Freedom is lost on both sides of the colour conflict.[90]

The law of racial identity proceeded by exception; it demanded that the self set aside it-self in the name of a legal-juridical generalisation that silenced experience, rationalised the bondage that it claimed to oppose, and severed the bonds of human interaction. While this warning offered a preliminary vocabulary for questioning whether the practice of separate development was consistent with the premises of its declared potential, it neither galvanised public opinion nor explained how critics might productively challenge the state's designs.

Before its time, the significance of the Council's position would be fully grasped only after the state set apartheid's (self) exception into its most violent form – the state of emergency that followed the 1960 Sharpeville massacre, an event in which 67 South Africans were killed as they protested outside a police station against the *dompas* (passbook), the packet of documents that contained the state's evidence of identity and which was used by law enforcement officials to regulate the movement and association of citizens from those "population groups" that were required to carry them at all times. Sponsored largely by the Pan Africanist Congress (PAC), the protest provoked a reaction from government that revealed much about its growing proclivity for violence and the distance that the struggle had yet to travel. For the English-speaking church, the massacre and the state's subsequent repression lent new urgency to the question of whether it was willing to do more than entertain hermeneutic debate over the relative justifications for state policy.[91]

A significant answer appeared in December, following a meeting of the World Council of Churches in Johannesburg. Concerned with growing unrest and the government's apparent affection for violence, the SACC's *Cottesloe Statement* was read widely and in different ways. While some saw it as a stern rebuke of separate development, others lamented that its weak condemnation of the events at Sharpeville was a sign that the church lacked the will needed to challenge the government.[92] Both readings had merit. Addressed to the "complex problems of human relationships" and "united in rejecting all unjust discrimination", the *Cottesloe Statement* began by declaring that, "The church as the body of Christ is a unity and within this unity the natural diversity among men is not annulled but sanctified."[93] However, as this claim was tied to a call for South Africans to recognise and draw from their differences in the name of creating "common fellowship", SACC's apparent objection to apartheid seemed to be retracted when it came time to speak about politics. Holding that all racial groups in South Africa were "indigenous", the Council called for "coloured people" and not the "Bantu" to have "direct representation in Parliament".[94] Similarly, it argued that all citizens deserved the right of free association (a reference to the state's 1949 prohibition of interracial marriage) and life with human dignity, including the ability to own land. But, unable to break from its own colonial presumptions, the tract then expressed "deep concern" over the revival of "heathen tribal customs incompatible with Christian beliefs and practice" and concluded that nationalism had to be respected for purposes of "self-realisation" so long as it did not come at "the expense of others". As the precise threshold of the difference was not explained, the position was not so far from that offered by the state's theologians, some of whom helped write the text and then affixed their name to its bottom line.

The pronouncement that the Cottesloe Consultation was "one of the most significant events in the history of the church in South Africa" may have less to do with the clarity of the resulting text's opposition than the political fallout that it produced.[95] Reading it as a direct challenge, Prime Minister Hendrik Verwoerd demanded that NGK Synods recant their support of the statement and refrain from future participation at gatherings convened for similar purposes.[96] Inside the NGK, Verwoerd's edict had a splintering effect, creating divisions that contributed directly to the formation of the Christian Institute in 1963.[97] Led by Beyers Naudé, the Moderator of the Southern Transvaal Synod who broke ranks after the Cottesloe controversy, the Institute attracted both those from the NGK who opposed its close ties with the state and members of English-speaking churches who believed that their own institutions needed to resist apartheid with greater vigour.[98]

From the beginning, the Christian Institute set the struggle against apartheid in relation to the need for reconciliation. One of its four announced goals was to "act as a group of Christians who wish to help bring about reconciliation between divergent, divided and conflicting groups of different churches and colours in our country". According to Naudé, reconciliation's task was partly to create a "challenge to the powers in the government" in the "name of justice, equality, and freedom".[99] In 1968, the precise terms of this opposition became clearer when the SACC agreed to publish the *Message* to the People of South Africa.[100] Here, the Institute declared that through the crucifixion and resurrection, "men are being reconciled to God and to each other, and that excluding barriers of ancestry, race, nationality, language, and culture have no rightful place in the inclusive brotherhood of Christian disciples". A rebuttal of the NGK's early case for apartheid, particularly as the latter relied on the Kuyperian idea of sovereignty, the message defended reconciliation as a good to be recovered, a practice that could cultivate a "cultural, social (and therefore political), cosmic, and universal" sense of the gospel from separate development's "false faith" in division. Aiming to tear down walls, reconciliation's "real knowledge of Christ" was held out as a power to "shape history" and sustain the promise of righteousness. Thus, in distinction to the Dutch Reformed position, the Institute's claim was that reconciliation's potential had a messianic form. Its power was a gift for the present, a recollection of experience that held an "obligation to assert", a calling for individuals to witness in the "circumstances of time and place in which they find themselves".

Attempting to pull reconciliation back from the future, the *Message* warned of a "situation where a policy of racial separation is being deliberately effected with increasing rigidity" and declared that separate development's plea to "wait for a distant 'heaven' where all problems have been solved", rested on a "novel gospel".[101] This accusation of heresy was also a political claim. To the degree that it set the Word in opposition to the word (of law), apartheid's claimed potential rested on a false and exploitative understanding of identity:

> [W]e are being taught that our racial identity is the final and all-important determining factor in the lives of men. As a result of this faith in racial identity, a tragic insecurity and helplessness afflicts those whose racial classification is in doubt. Without racial identity, it appears that we can do nothing: he who has racial identity has life; he who has not racial identity has not life. This amounts to a denial of the central statements of the Gospel ... It, in practice, severely restricts the ability of Christian brothers to serve and know each other, and even to give each other simple hospitality. It arbitrarily limits the ability of a person to obey the Gospel's command to love his neighbour as himself.[102]

Proposing a love that ran across identity's boundary, the *Message* chided those who undercut "the gifts of the grace of God" and sought to "reject our own humanity as well as the humanity of the other man". The antithesis of reconciliation, apartheid's "identity in dissociation and in distinction", was an unjust repudiation of that which was "already made in Christ". It was both a false law that "exploits difference to generate hostility" and a *hubris* that privileged "natural distinction" over a faith in God's love that beckoned "identity in association". Thus, grasping and rejecting the circular logic of separate development, the *Message* concluded:

> A policy of separate development … calls good evil. It rejects as
> undesirable the good reconciliation and fellowship which God is giving
> to us by his Son. It seeks to limit the limitlessness of God's grace by
> which all men may be accepted in Jesus Christ.[103]

Already present, it was time for reconciliation to turn "hostility into love of the brethren". The power of the Word that remained required the passing away of the "so-called South African way of life" and a confessing "willingness to be made new" that would stand "contrary to some of the customs and laws of this country". Accordingly, it seemed to some that the moment for doctrinal debate was over; the call for reconciliation was now a warrant to question and resist apartheid's legitimacy.

In different ways, the *Cottesloe Statement* and the *Message to the People of South Africa* offered a view of reconciliation that stood in marked contrast to the NGK's interpretation. Each figured the concept as a means of opposing the logic of separate development with a call for those words of love in which the self risked itself in the name of a relationship that defied control by law. In the name of what had been and what could (again) become present, the two positions argued that reconciliation found unity in difference not differentiation. This view challenged the state's (legal) obsession with identity and cast the claimed potential of separate development as a violent ruse, a law that amounted to a "form of resistance to the Holy Spirit". Contrary to the state's claim, apartheid did not reflect God's will. Moreover, as it played the past off the future and back again, the announced promise of separate development marked an occasion and need for action, a mode of reconciliation that turned the claimed potential of the present into a present with potential. The lingering difficulty, however, was whether the faith of reconciliation had a practical form. Cast in opposition to apartheid, how exactly would reconciliation make South Africa new?

a time for reconciliation's potential difference
The *Message to the People of South Africa* formulated a clear line of opposition to apartheid even as it failed to change the state's behaviour or alter the

segregationist practices of many English-speaking churches. Like the *Cottesloe Statement*, what it did do was frame and lend new urgency to a number of basic questions about the church's role in the struggle. First, what was the precise standing of the church to oppose apartheid? At a basic level, rebuttal of NGK doctrine did not address fully the issue of whether it was appropriate for the religious community to use reconciliation as a way to enter the crucible of politics and challenge the state's legitimacy. Second, what forms of opposition could the church advocate? While the *Message's* call for reconciliation argued that South Africans might do well to live "contrary to some customs and rules", it offered little guidance as to just how contrary citizens might be. Together, these questions were an indication that the church's use of reconciliation to criticise separate development frequently appeared to counsel passivity, a need for more "living in accordance" than acting in transformative opposition. If reconciliation was a call to action, how would its interdependent love subvert the violence of identity classification? Did reconciliation condone the use of violence or warrant revolution? If the present really did hold potential, how long would people have to wait for an opportunity to create change?

In the late 1960s and early '70s, these issues were debated frequently in church communities. They were also a reflection of the quandaries facing the larger struggle. Armed with its draconian security legislation – laws that were used to ban the ANC in 1960 and imprison many of its key leaders – the state remained in clear control. Operating from exile, the ANC's Umkhonto we Sizwe (MK) campaigns were noticed but not entirely felt. The masses were most certainly not mobilised.[104] For those in the church, the situation underscored the problem of what to do. The question produced several different replies. For one, the period saw increasing attention paid to the idea of contextual theology, an approach to Scripture that defined the church's work in prophetic terms. Against apartheid's silencing potential, a number of contextual theologians struggled to discern a time for speaking, a *kairos* in which the Word could be (re)turned to voice. Equally important, church leaders considered the matter of what needed to be said, the kinds of words that had the power to turn the word of apartheid's law toward a system of equality. In this matter, Black Theology played an important role, particularly as it drew from the Black Consciousness Movement (BCM) to make the case that individuals needed to recollect and express the terms of everyday experience in the name of locating the individual and collective grounds for struggle. Thus intertwined, prophetic and Black Theology both placed heavy emphasis on reconciliation. With the former claiming that reconciliation opened a time to speak against apartheid's law, the latter defended it as a way for citizens to recover a sense of self that could stand in productive opposition to the identity prescribed by the state. The difficulty, however, was that neither position had a clear explanation of how reconciliation could both subvert and reconstitute identity. For some, the solution to this dilemma appeared in the idea of ubuntu.

The Christian Institute gave clear voice to prophetic theology. Evident in the *Message to the People of South Africa*, it argued that the church could not remain neutral in the struggle or hope to mediate a just solution to the conflict. Heard to echo the ANC's 1961 announcement that it was turning to armed struggle, this view suggested to some that it was time to embrace the "permanent revolution" of God's grace, an idea that was gaining popularity in liberation theology's call for the ministry to discern the historical truth of evil and work in solidarity with the poor and exploited.[105] Reflecting on this work, Albert Nolan argued that it required reading the signs of the times: "The fundamental insight of prophetic theology, then, is the recognition that an *eschaton* or day of reckoning and liberation is near. It is this that turns the present moment into a *kairos* ...."[106] In short, it was time to find the ground for history-making and oppose law's linear logic and precedent in the name of opening a decisive moment, a present that did not reify the past for an abstract future but which constituted its substance through speech that held the potential for action.

One of many from that day, the image of Hector Peterson being carried through the streets of Soweto on June 16, 1976 underscored that it was time to act.[107] In the aftermath of the violence, a growing number of churches drew from the premises of prophetic theology to express and motivate opposition to the state. In 1977, at the Sixth Assembly of the Lutheran World Federation, church representatives issued a brief statement entitled, "Southern Africa: Confessional Integrity". In it, the Assembly called on "white member Churches in Southern Africa to declare that the situation in Southern Africa constituted a *status confessionis*".[108] In these terms, the moment required words that would "publicly and unequivocally reject the existing apartheid system". With both a subjective and objective sense of time, the *status confessionis* thus aimed to interrupt the normal flow of history even as it was underwritten by events that had discernable cause and effect. Writing for the Lutheran Department of Studies, the German theologian, Martin Schloemann, reflected on the South African call. Arguing that a *status confessionis* stands in the face of evil that can be neither ignored nor accommodated and then reaching back to the 1577 Formula of Concord, Schloemann held that the time of confession appeared in the presence of those who were "enemies of God's words". In such a moment, the church was obliged to take extraordinary action against an evident evil:

> It is a situation of persecution and repression, with their open or
> disguised compulsions to establish idolatry, which represents the acute
> threat to the truth that makes us free and to the authentic possibility of
> hearing and living the gospel, and which for the sake of its credibility
> becomes the occasion for a temporary suspension of freedom in dealings
> with specific traditions and structures of religion.[109]

Just below the surface, this call to hear and speak the truth was linked to Bonhoeffer's claim that the time of confession arose when the state compromised the mission of the church. A period when "law and order become excessive", the *status confessionis* was thus a "nominal breaking point", a confessional emergency (*bekenntnisnotstand*) dedicated to resisting the state of emergency that supported the state and sustained its violence.[110] Citing Barth, Schloemann argued that an "indeterminate attitude of political opposition" would not suffice; history had to be (re)turned to God in the name of rejecting false creation and pronouncing a judgment that drew from the Word to energise the faith of struggle:

> It means a situation calling for a decision and a break in the church
> because its essence and its proclamation are at stake, possibly lasting
> in character, and at all events actively perceived with a willingness
> to suffer.[111]

In a *status confessionis*, the Word supported the very speech–action that the law endeavoured to subsume and silence. In its declaration against apartheid, the Lutheran World Federation arrived at the same conclusion, arguing that the time of confession was "not only a matter of words but also of *ethos* and action".[112] The power of faith – the character of speech within the act of confession – stood opposed to the identity of law and the law of its identity. In the time at hand, the "willingness to suffer" was far less an act of submission that an attitude that stood against the (self) certainty of a false creation.

In South Africa, debate over the *status confessionis* had several implications for the church's condemnation of apartheid's "false gospel" and its "theocratic" sleight of hand.[113] First, the call to confession disavowed the "causality" of nationalism. Supplanting *chronos* with a sense of *eschaton* that referred less to the end of time than the time before time's end, religious critics used the confession as a way of countering the state's appeal to national destiny.[114] Second, the faith of confession shed light on the power of reconciliation, particularly as it was being defined in documents like the *Message to the People of South Africa*. In the moment, there was a potential for unity, one that followed less from a common belief in a shared future than an embodied faith in a past sacrifice that figured love as a willingness to reach out to others in the name of understanding. With this *ethos* of self-contingency, the speech-action of confession was a call for that reconciliation which would stand between, break, and bridge the "walls of separation of apartheid".[115]

If they did not appear simultaneously, the heralding of a time to act led to the question of how the Word's speech could make a difference. Aligned closely with contextual theology, this was a central concern of Black Theology, especially as it developed in close connection with the Black Consciousness Movement.[116] According to Nyameko Pityana, Black Consciousness was geared to understanding the forces and systems that were "designed to rob the black man of his soul and dignity".[117]

Founded in 1969 and led by Steve Biko, the South African Students' Organisation's policy manifesto declared that the "basic tenet of Black Consciousness is that the black man must reject all value systems that seek to make him a foreigner in the country of his birth and reduce his basic human dignity".[118] On both interpretations, set against the power that left blacks to be "defined by others", the task of struggle was to develop values that allowed for the recovery and development of experience – "identity, self-awareness, and self-esteem".[119]

In a contribution to a groundbreaking volume that was published by the University Christian Movement and then banned by the state, Biko addressed these goals in a way that shed light on the basic connection between the BCM and Black Theology:

> The philosophy of Black Consciousness therefore expresses group pride and the determination of the Black to rise and attain the envisaged self. Freedom is not the ability to define oneself with one's possibilities held back but only by one's relationship to God and to natural surround-ings. On his own, therefore, the Black Man wishes to explore his surroundings and test his possibilities – in other words to make his freedom real by whatever means he deems necessary. [120]

Concerned to recover the grounds for expression and action, Biko's position was a rejection of the "dialectical" response to racism favoured by some liberal opponents of apartheid. In his terms, only a "feebly defined synthesis" could follow from attempts to set the thesis of apartheid in relation to the antithesis of non-racialism.[121] Thus, Biko implored, "We must realise that prophetic cry of black students: 'Black man, you are on your own!'" At a basic level, this solitude was far less an ideal than evidence of a political-cultural vacuum and a reflection of the "individualistic cold approach to life that is the cornerstone of Anglo-Boer culture". While this characterisation may have accounted less for the anti-liberal *ethos* of Afrikaner nationalism than its persistent conflation of the collective and the communist, Biko did hold that the struggle required the recovery of history in order to restore to the "black man the great importance we used to give to human relations".[122] In terms of religion, this meant that the missionary legacy of Christianity had to be assessed critically in light of the need to "bring God back to the black man and to the truth and reality of his situation".[123]

For many working in the name of Black Theology, religion lacked a human face. If it was to serve the people, the church needed to be a space for the recovery and assertion of an identity that could sustain Black Nationalism.[124] This position however, led some to pause. Was the church intent to become a revolutionary force? In 1977, Allan Boesak devoted substantial attention to this matter in an influential book, *Farewell to Innocence: A Social-Ethical Study of Black Theology and Black Power*. In it, he held that Black Theology was both situational and contextual, a prophetic enterprise that "takes from the past what is good, thereby offering a critique of the present and opening perspectives for the future". Borrowing from a 1973 tract, *Theology in Action*, Boesak claimed that this work proceeded "out of a genuine encounter between God's Word and his world, and moves toward the purpose of challenging and changing the situation through rootedness in, and commitment to a given historical moment".[125] Invoking the need for reconciliation, Boesak held that the task at hand was for oppressed South Africans to develop a sense of identity that neither submitted to nor negated the Other:

> For blacks, authentic humanity means *black* humanity. Blacks know that racial fellowship and reconciliation will never become a reality unless whites learn to accept blacks as black people. This much must be clear: when blacks speak of the affirmation of their blackness, this does not mean a resigned acceptance.[126]

While liberation depended on the formation of identity, this identity was conditioned by a process of reconciliation that worked toward the "wholeness of life". In Boesak's terms, this double power was not a will to counter-domination but a "love in action" that embodied an ethic of equity.[127] Thus, the love of reconciliation was not cheap insofar as it "requires a new image of humanity" and the development of "new structures of society". A call to difficult action, reconciliation marked that moment in which the future promise of "genuine community" did not rule out conflict in the present.[128]

In the early 1980s, Boesak was a popular, powerful, and controversial figure, the moderator of the Nederduitse Gereformeerde Sendingkerk (NGSK) and President of the World Alliance of Reformed Churches (WARC). Moving between pulpit and public stage, he played an important role in the formation of the UDF. In 1982, he stood in Ottawa, Canada and called on WARC to take a "more active role in the struggle against racism" by issuing a broad-based condemnation of apartheid. More precisely, he urged WARC's General Council to declare a *status confessionis* and take punitive measures against white churches that failed to denounce the South African state. Holding out for stronger medicine than that prescribed by the *Message to the People of South Africa*, Boesak argued that racism was a sin which apartheid had entrenched within a "system of domination".[129] Its antidote was the remembrance engendered by a struggle oriented to reconciliation:

> Racism has brought dehumanisation, has undermined black personhood,
> destroyed the human-beingness of those who are called to be the
> children of God. It has caused those who are the image of the living God
> to despise themselves, for they cannot understand why it should be their
> very blackness that calls forth such hatred, such contempt, such wanton,
> terrible violence. Most of all racism denies the liberating, humanising,
> reconciling work of Christ.[130]

In the *Confession of Faith* released after the conference, WARC expelled the NGK and Nederduitsch Hervormde Kerk (NHK) from its ranks and declared apartheid a "pseudo-religious ideology" given to rebuilding the very "walls of partition and enmity" that Christ had broken down. While few were moved by its rebuttal, the NHK responded that the Alliance was politicising the work of Christ and maintained that the "policy of separate development and equal opportunities is not in conflict with Holy Scripture".[131]

Back in South Africa, the counterpart to the WARC declaration was the *Belhar Confession*, a statement that was not officially adopted until 1986 and which declared the existence of a *status confessionis* on the grounds that apartheid was "diversity in despair of reconciliation".[132] The *Confession's* introduction charged the state with heresy and argued that, "The political and ecclesiastical order of South Africa is an order within which irreconcilability has been elevated to a fundamental social principle ...." In direct contradiction to reconciliation, "the main artery of the Christian Gospel", apartheid was always and only false law, a pseudo-ideology that thwarted human community and justice.[133]

While it was deemed "impossible to differ" with its conclusion, the *Belhar Confession's* call to recover reconciliation did not resolve the question of whether its revolutionary power held the risk of making new in a manner that simply replicated the old. This was a larger problem. In a moment of choice without option, the terms of prophetic and Black Theology combined to produce a call for reconciliation that appeared both to oppose and constitute identity. For the present, reconciliation's potential was a (be)coming into relation, an event that refigured individual experience in the name of forging collective identifications that could turn the differentiations of separation toward a unity of difference. Against the heresy of law's emergency, this exceptional potential was a fragile power; synthesis risked a lapse back to the very identitarian logic of the system being opposed. For its faith to work, reconciliation had to stand and pivot between the creation of self-certainty and the creative contingency of collective (inter)action. Found between the times, reconciliation had to un-exclude its middle and proceed in excess of the law of non-contradiction. In at least one important circle, the nature of this peculiar movement was explained through the idea of ubuntu.

The plural form of bantu (person), ubuntu was a key if not also controversial term of Black Theology. With a meaning that is difficult to pinpoint, it variously connotes a group of people, a community, a shared political system or philosophy, and a collective way of life.[134] For some time, the concept has been both romanticised as a utopian tonic and chided as an idea long-borrowed and corrupted by colonial forces interested to either homogenise or tribalise indigenous peoples. Perhaps most frequently, it expresses the idea that "people are people through other people" (*ungamntu ngabanye abantu* or *umntu ngumntu ngabanye abantu*). In 1973, for instance, Bonganjalo Goba traced the idea through the Old and the New Testament's consideration of "corporate personality", arguing that ubuntu was an expression of belongingness and a mode of solidarity. More and perhaps a bit less than a western form of communitarianism, Gobo's view had significant ontological implications. A mode and means of creating time, ubuntu held a sense of kinship in which "everybody is related to everybody else" within a "unique relationship that extends vertically to include the departed and those yet to be born".[135] In a sense, ubuntu bound past and future being such that there was simply no such *thing* as solitary existence. Noting its implications for the nature and definition of human identity, Manas Buthelezi offered a similar position, claiming that ubuntu's potential was a wholeness of life within a present that refused the distinction between past realism and future idealism. On this view, the time of ubuntu was a moment in which to turn the alienation of individual autonomy sponsored by e(x)ternal law toward a recovery of identity *through* communal participation and a love that "suffers selflessly for others".[136]

Appearing to want it both ways, how was ubuntu to navigate between the recovery of identity that was crucial to Black Theology and the need to subvert the state's identitarian law through an ethic of collective belonging and participation? Sitting in the small office that he used during his weekly work sessions at the TRC's central office, Desmond Tutu smiled and leaned back in his chair when I asked him this question. Light-hearted and serious, his reply was that the matter defied strict analysis precisely because the idea of ubuntu holds and performs a movement in which identity takes form in a manner that "is not isolated from others, because that way is death".[137] The importance of the point should not be missed. For a religious leader who devoted significant attention to the promise of Black Theology, ubuntu expressed a form of reconciliation in which the character of struggle is both uncompromising and humane.

In the late '70s and early '80s, Tutu preached and wrote extensively about the connection between ubuntu and reconciliation.[138] Then the Anglican Bishop of Johannesburg and General Secretary of the SACC, he claimed consistently that reconciliation sat "at the heart of the Christian gospel" and was an important element of liberation.[139] Capable of affecting at-one-ment and able to restore friendship, reconciliation's announced power stood in stark contrast to the logic of apartheid and its attempt to turn human relations "upside down".[140] More precisely, Tutu claimed in 1983 that reconciliation entailed the recognition of that diversity which "undergirds and leads to unity and interdependence" and embodied a kenotic form of love that could break down apartheid's "middle wall of partition".[141] With God's outpouring (of) love came the undeserved gift of grace, a basis for the formation of "delicate networks of interdependence".[142] In this position, ubuntu was used to explain how such creativity developed. In the face of apartheid, the standing for humans to form relationships required more collective character than sovereign authority. Part of reconciliation's revealing light, the concept and practice of ubuntu demonstrated that the logic of separate development held a time (that had already been and which remained) to (re)call the potential for collective action.[143] In and for history-making, this remembering movement between identity and identification was a site of practical faith, the opening of a present in which the will to risk one's self for the Other confirmed the self and endowed experience with meaning. In short, ubuntu was a potential for love that developed not from within sovereign spheres but through the memory of a sacrifice that held the Word's gift of words.

holding out for a present

Reconciliation played an important role in the English-speaking church's case against apartheid. Declaring that the *status quo* was untenable, a time of confession that called for things to be (re)made otherwise in a different way, religious leaders first challenged the NGK's interpretation of Scripture by claiming that reconciliation did not justify the identity logic of apartheid law. In the face of state violence and in the name of a relational love, this hermeneutic debate was radicalised in the 1970s and early 1980s. Through the lenses of prophetic and Black Theology, the state's case for separate development was declared a heresy, a falsely "'god-given' context according to the white man in which reconciliation must take place".[144] Decrying apartheid's promise of a "pretty-pretty hereafter", church leaders argued that the occasion of true reconciliation was a *kairos* which returned the grounds for human interaction to the present and opened a moment for words that could support action against an unjust regime. Redefined in the face of its perceived distortion, reconciliation was thus set in distinction to law, a turn that then required religious leaders to explain how reconciliation could both oppose the violence of identity and (re)constitute its power in the name of identifications that would allow human beings to make new in relation.

Permanent or otherwise, reconciliation's revolution did not appear imminent. Perhaps before their time, religious calls for reconciliation made an important case for action, but left unanswered questions about how it might begin. With words to name law's heresy, reconciliation promised a love to overcome violence. However, the signs of the times suggested that this potential was not easily actualised and that it would not come cheap. Inside and outside the church, critics continued to wonder what it meant to undertake a reconciliation that would make new without risking the production of a different novel gospel. Related, calls for reconciliation appeared increasingly distant from the reality of struggle, a gap that led to pointed queries about whether talk of reconciliation was detracting from the work of liberation.[145] Did reconciliation's exceptional power include a justification for undertaking violence against an increasingly repressive state? As this question did not find clear answer in the announced terms of prophetic and Black Theology, debate over what reconciliation might (yet) do continued into the 1980s. The controversy would come to a head only as the state reached back to the precedent set at Sharpeville and declared a state of emergency.

3. between the third force and the third way: discerning reconciliation's *kairos*

In July of 1985, the man who would become one of the TRC's somewhat convenient embodiments of apartheid-era violence assumed command of a covert Special Forces unit known by the name of the farm where it was headquartered – Vlakplaas. For the next several years, Eugene de Kock led this element of the "third force", an organisation that received orders from somewhere near the top, but which remained largely unaccountable for its substantial atrocities.[146] In a basic way, the actions of Vlakplaas operatives were a sign of the government's growing desperation and a tactic to bolster Botha's failing "total strategy". Rapidly losing hearts and minds, facing international sanctions and a collapsing economy, the government was stepping up an undeclared war. Referring to a provision in the *Internal Security Act*, "Section 29" detentions increased. Disappearances and assassinations grew more frequent. At some point, the repression left something of a leadership vacuum in the struggle. With many central figures imprisoned or working in exile, church organisations became "overtly political actors" and "vehicles for promoting the defiance campaign".[147] With this role came state harassment and heated internal debate about the calling of struggle and whether prophetic resistance could include armed action.

The time of reconciliation appeared distant. With the country caught in the state of emergency, reconciliation's potential to turn conflict toward a new beginning was far from given. Framed by the English-speaking church's long-standing attempt to grapple with this problem, the aptly named *Kairos Document* appeared at a crucial moment of struggle and argued that the promise of reconciliation needed to be reinterpreted. Here, my aim is to consider closely the terms and significance of its position. Contending that the *Kairos Document* sheds significant light on the occasion of reconciliation in South Africa, I trace how the document issued a critique of both separate development and the opposition offered by the "mainstream" church in order to radicalise prophetic theology and define reconciliation as a practice that could inspire and invent the words needed to make history in the face of apartheid's violence. Refusing the concept's connotation of a neutral mediation, the *Kairos Document* cast the occasion of reconciliation as a time within the times, a potential in the present that afforded an opportunity for the subjugated to express their experience of oppression and challenge the state's legitimacy with a faith that aimed less for revolution than an *ethos* of identification. As many of these claims had roots in prophetic and Black Theology, the *Kairos Document*'s overall position was not new. What distinguished it, however, was the way in which the text advocated and performed its central argument. Defining reconciliation as a mode of opposition, its words embodied a struggle to turn violence toward platforms for collective interaction. As such, reconciliation was indeed not cheap, especially as its promise for the present depended on its abiding commitment to justice.

The *Kairos Document* appeared in a dramatic and complicated situation. In April of 1985, following a massacre of protestors in the Eastern Cape township of Langa, the SACC issued *A Call to Prayer for the End to Unjust Rule*. Urging citizens to gather on 16 June, the anniversary of the 1976 Soweto protests, the Council did not ask citizens to pray for the reform of apartheid or that its leaders might see the error of their ways. Rather, for the first time, the Council declared: "We now pray that God will replace the present structures of oppression with ones that are just, and remove from power those who persist in defying his laws, installing in their place leaders who will govern with justice and mercy."[148] Divine or otherwise, the times held the *pathos* of revolution.

Reaction to the SACC's call was fast and fierce. The increasingly government-controlled press attacked its position as an illegal and inappropriate embrace of violence. Peter Storey, the President of the Methodist Church, argued that the church had no standing to advocate the removal of state leaders. Ignoring this rebuke, the Western Cape Methodist Synod adopted the call with the proviso that it did not believe that violence was a justified element of struggle. The Western Province Council of Churches went a step further, holding that while the SACC's position was not a call for "violent or anarchic revolution", it was possible that "God's judgment may be that unjust rule in South Africa be ended by violence". In his pastoral letter on the matter, the leader of the Church of the Province of South Africa noted that the turn from a prayer *for* to a prayer *against* the state had "immense" implications. As 16 June approached, representatives of the Catholic Bishops Conference offered a sort of middle ground as it distanced itself from the language of the call while arguing that as the country was facing its "worst crisis", it was time for mourning, repentance, and "making a break with the past and throwing off the shackles of apartheid once and for all". It was time for "new initiatives". It was time for action taken in the name of forgiveness and reconciliation but with a clear understanding that "there can be no peace and no reconciliation without justice".[149] According to the Bishops, it was time for negotiation and prayer that would bring a "speedy end" to apartheid.

Like the 1960 *Cottesloe Statement*, the SACC's call to end unjust rule was held up as a "decisive moment in the church struggle".[150] The assessment had much to do with its exposure of deep splits in the church over what implications followed from the conclusion that apartheid was heresy.[151] In particular, the presumption that the church should maintain neutrality so that it might mediate the conflict fell increasingly under attack, particularly as it seemed to excuse inaction and leave the oppressed to fend for themselves.[152] Poignantly, Frank Chikane, then General Secretary of the SACC, responded that the church had to both mediate and take sides. When confronted with the counter-argument that this would require it to accept the use of violence, he responded that those living in townships did not have the luxury of debate but "time only for responding to the violence of the system".[153] Reasoning more from doctrine, John de Gruchy argued that there was clear biblical support for the church's direct if not violent action against the state.[154] This led many to question how the church might actually participate in the fight. In Charles Villa-Vicencio's terms, the church was confronted with the problem of what counted as "bold history-making interventions against oppression and for the liberation struggle".[155] In short, consensus about apartheid's evil did not provide obvious answers to the question of how to bring about its end.

With the state of emergency declared in July, following the funeral of the Cradock Four, many in the religious community continued to defend a mediating role for the church, a third way which would allow the "two" sides in the conflict to reconcile their differences. In September, the National Initiative for Reconciliation (NIR) saw several hundred religious leaders gather in order to debate the way forward and address the tensions that were dividing the church. Perhaps prophetic but somewhat premature, the conference released a statement that called for the initiation of high-level talks to address the issues of power-sharing and constitutional reform.[156] Shortly thereafter, working under the banner of the Institute for Contextual Theology, a much smaller group of religious leaders and theologians convened in Soweto to undertake the debate that led to the publication of the *Kairos Document*.

Subject to intense scrutiny, the purpose of the *Kairos Document* has been described in many different ways and assessed from a variety of perspectives.[157] Rhetorically, it takes shape in three lines of argument: a declaration of crisis, a critique of state and church, and a "prophetic theology". In the first, "The Moment of Truth", the authors announced their purpose: "the signs of the times" revealed a contradiction that invited action against apartheid. In the midst of a long-standing "silence" about the injustice of apartheid and its violent ways, the theologians claimed, "Now is the KAIROS or moment of truth not only for apartheid but for the Church and all other faiths and religions" (1)*. It is a "favourable time in which God issues a challenge to decisive action" (1). Thus, as a transgression of God's law, the existence of apartheid constituted precisely that *status confessionis* in which every South African needed to discover the betrayal of the state, concede their role in the creation and perpetuation of apartheid, and work to bring about its demise. In the words of the authors, "It is a dangerous time because if this opportunity is missed, and allowed to pass by, the loss for the Church, for the Gospel and for all the people of South Africa will be immeasurable" (1).

Beyond doctrinal or political debate, the moment was an "objective" sign in which the Word of God marked an unbearable contradiction and the necessity of choice without compromise. It was a *kairos*, a time for words that performed not transcendence but opposition to law's oppression. Questioning the power of reconciliation in the face of apartheid, the theologians were thus concerned with the interplay between the time of everyday life and the reserved periods when time exposes the ground for action in the midst of its apparent foreclosure. *Kairos* was thus not simply an opportune time but a moment in which to question the substance of opportunity. It was the appearance and demarcation of a present in which to come to presence, a sign of the times that held the potential to create a time of signs.

---

* Parenthetical numbers refer to page numbers of the *Kairos Document*.

In its second line of argument, the *Kairos Document* delineated the specific contradictions facing all South Africans. Initially, the authors accused government of "misusing theological concepts and biblical texts for its own political purposes" (3). Extending the old doctrinal debate, they challenged the state's reading of Romans 13: 1–7, the New Testament passage that calls on individuals to "obey the governing authorities" that are appointed by God and who serve in his name. The *Kairos* theologians held that this call did not grant the architects of apartheid an "absolute and divine authority" (4). As Paul wrote his letter to the Romans in order to address "a community that had its own particular problems in relation to the state at that time and in those circumstances", (11) it was not applicable to the situation in South Africa. From this bit of contextual theology, the authors found the government guilty of using theology to justify violence. A usurpation of God's Word, dependent on a language of obedience that defied justification, they claimed "state theology is not only heretical, it's blasphemous" (8). The state was a false prophet. Through an evil body of law, it silenced opposition and fractured the covenant of divine justice (7).

What surprised many about the *Kairos Document* was how the South African religious community fared little better than the state. Based on their "superficial and counterproductive" appeals to reconciliation, unnamed churches were condemned for their failure to represent the spiritual and political interests of South Africans (9). Specifically, the document charged that "mainstream" calls for reconciliation preached a tolerance for evil and perpetuated sin. Cast as further proof that South Africans faced a moment of choice, the authors contended that in the present situation, "one side is right and the other wrong". Reconciliation could not mean negotiation or compromise; tolerance beckoned false peace, the perpetuation of evil, and "a total betrayal of all that the Christian faith has ever meant" (10). As the "dominant" South African theology defined reconciliation in terms of personal guilt, it turned a blind eye to structural injustice and bolstered the state's claim that it expressed God's will (12–14).

Apartheid theology rendered justice violent. Religious opposition to the state privatised this contradiction at the expense of political change. In its third line of argument, the *Kairos Document* used these claims to justify a turn to "prophetic theology". In the name of undermining the moral and political fabric of apartheid, this meant that critics of apartheid had an obligation to "know what is happening, analyse what is happening (social analysis) and then interpret what is happening in light of the gospel" (17). A key goal of this interpretive work was the recovery of citizens' lost and denigrated experiences. Echoing the terms of Black Consciousness, the authors concluded that "effective struggle" begins in "our experience of oppression and tyranny, our experience of conflict, crisis and struggle, our experience of trying to be Christians in this situation" (17). Moreover, social analysis revealed that apartheid was a form of tyrannical oppression, not a race war. The state's espoused promise of legal equality was betrayed by its historical commitment to violence (22). This contradiction, the divorce of law from justice, was proof that the South African "regime has no moral legitimacy". It was also taken as an explanation of why God was not neutral in the struggle. A false master that pitted oppressed against oppressor, the state was an enemy of God and the people of South Africa. Still, this "offence against God" was not an "excuse for hatred" (24). Instead, the *Kairos Document* argued that the experience of suffering could be used to re-establish humanity's relationship with God: "At this stage, like Jesus, we must expose this false peace, confront our oppressors and be prepared for the dissension that will follow" (11). More fully, it claimed that this work entailed an act of naming:

> The evil forces we speak of in baptism must be named. We know that these evil forces are in South Africa today. The unity and sharing we profess in our communion services or masses must be named. It is the solidarity of the people inviting all to join in the struggle for God's peace in South Africa. The repentance we preach must be named. It is repentance for our share of the guilt for the suffering and oppression in our country (29).

Opposed to the blasphemous state and private forms of contrition, the fight against apartheid could be energised by speech. This power of naming stood in direct contrast to the NGK's 1974 claim that it was the urge to name that led to the sin of Babel. In fact, the *kairos* theologians claimed that as citizens identified evil and confessed their role in its creation, they would discover the basis for collective action from within a sense of shared guilt. How? By what means would confession empower those who had been victimised?

Against guilt and violence, confession named a past transgression and established a future faith in God's Word. This work promised a "double-justice" to those who had suffered at the hands of the state. At first, *kairos* marked a time of choice that demanded action without compromise. However, it was also a moment when the integrity of the human word was suspect; just action could not be measured by either social or individual standards. In the time *provided*, the integrity of both was doubtful. Opposed to a "cheap" substitute, real reconciliation took inspiration from the "burden of the cross" (18). It began in testimony that remembered an experience of suffering and confessed the offences that each individual had inflicted upon others. Perhaps a form of ubuntu, this speech "does no[t] separate the individual from the social or one's private life from one's public life" (16). Instead, real reconciliation creates relationships between human beings and between humans and God. The double form of this renewal represented the bar of justice. As individuals conceded their transgressions in the name of forgiveness and renounced their certain power over the word (of God), they would find their voice and the grounds of collective action. In such speech, the potential for a better life can only be built in the present.

> We must begin to plan for the future now but above all we must heed
> God's call to action to secure God's future for ourselves in South Africa.
> There is hope. There is hope for all of us. But the road is going to be
> very hard and very painful. The conflict and the struggle will intensify
> in the months and years ahead. That is now inevitable – because of
> the intransigence of the oppressor. But God is with us. We can only
> learn to become the instruments of his peace even unto death. We
> must participate in the cross of Christ if we are to have the hope of
> participating in his resurrection (26).

According to Charles Villa-Vicencio, this claim was addressed to church leaders and citizens who inhabited the "edges of civil society".[158] Its reception, however, was not uniform. Many praised the text's attempt to energise the vocabulary of political resistance. Others panned the document, deriding it as politically dangerous and theologically suspect.[159] The condemnations were grounded in two objections. First, the *Kairos Document* had little to say about how the church could make an effective contribution to the struggle against apartheid; it did not detail the form of the opposition that it advocated. Second, the tract seemed to rest on a contradiction. While encouraging all citizens to confess their transgressions, it also claimed that "no reconciliation is possible in South Africa without justice, without the total dismantling of apartheid" (10). More clearly, the authors appeared to condition the power of forgiveness on the future actions of the state:

> Human beings must also be willing to forgive one another at all times
> even seventy times seven times. But forgiveness will not become a *reality*

with all its healing *effects* until the offender repents. Thus in South Africa
forgiveness will not become an *experienced reality* until the apartheid
regime shows *signs* of repentance (34). (emphases added)

Some readers questioned whether this call made reconciliation contingent on
revolution? Arguably, it did not.[160] As the position distinguished the faithful
attitude of reconciliation from its *outcome*, reconciliation could both precede
and follow the demise of apartheid. If so, the occasion of reconciliation
was a moment of rhetorical invention given to discerning the potential for
collective action from within the midst of violence. A period of urgency and
opportunity, time stands in opposition to both the past and future. In the face
of conflict and systemic injustice, institutional and human norms of progress
are suspect. As the covenant breaks, all times revert to God. The result is a
present, a point of *stasis* in which individuals can move neither forward nor
backward. Lacking a coherent relationship to ourselves, others, or God, the
time is an anxious one. It is a period of ontological frustration in which the
need to act is imposed, sensed, and hindered.

In the *Kairos Document,* the potential of this time appeared as a process
as well as a product of speech. Equally unacceptable, the perpetuation of
apartheid and violent revolution demanded a *turn* to the language of faith.
Through confession and the naming of offences, individuals were called to
concede past mistakes. As this naming process instilled a sense of vulnerability
into the confessor, it was a source of both despair and hope, a marker of
the breakdown and importance of human interaction. Put differently, the
negativity of confession was deemed productive to the degree that it motivated
individuals to build relations with other humans and with God. Recalling the
idea of ubuntu, this speech work was modelled on God's love, a form of
expression that involved an outpouring of self for the Other and an *ethos* that
served as the basis for opposing apartheid.[161] In these terms, the occasion of
reconciliation was a time within the times, a faith in God's Word that crafted
the path to the future out of a painful past, in part by demonstrating that as
the state denigrated justice, it contradicted its own theological premise and
undercut its legitimacy.

At a turning point and a point at which to turn in the fight against
apartheid, the *Kairos Document* defined reconciliation as a rhetorical process
that could begin a time of transition. Initially, the need for reconciliation
appeared when human beings confronted a moment of choice, a time in
which there was not much time. According to the theologians, this instant

developed from the law's false appropriation of God's Word. It was a point when a state of emergency had allowed the law to foreclose on the ability of individuals to endow expression with content. Against this law, a form of oppression that used the ban to erase individual and collective history, and sacrifice present meaning on the altar of future happiness, the *Kairos Document* called on the victims of apartheid to name their experiences in a manner that demonstrated the contradiction between law and justice.

In his important work on Pauline theology, Giorgio Agamben characterises this work as a shift from "doing what the law says" to "saying what the law does". It is a tropological turn in which individuals name themselves "as they are not". With the naming of experience, the oppressed *are not* simply oppressed. They are capable of collective action. This revelation renders the law "inoperative" by inventing a potential for politics in which the meaning of justice is not presupposed but open to question.[162] Put differently, the law's divine façade, a cover that obscures the distinction between law and justice, is challenged by speech that cannot be contained by a state of emergency. This speech is addressed to the contingent in-between of human relationships and opposed to outright revolution. Its "messianic" power rests on what is normally considered to be weakness; the call to name the experience of oppression is partly a call to confession, a form of speech in which the certainty of human identity – the appropriation of God's Word – is supplanted by the faith of identification.[163] In turn, this speech-action opens a present moment in which the task of (re)authoring law takes shape in a process of collective interaction that both discovers and moves between past and future. Performed in the middle voice, as confession that enacts and explains the contingency of human interaction, reconciliation appears as a rhetorical call to make history. In the *Kairos Document*, it was an opportunity to define and enter into the beginning of apartheid's end. The difficulty, however, was whether citizens could render this communicative faith in the word practical. Between revolution and accommodation, the *Kairos Document* did not specify how the communicative faith of reconciliation could find and open the time in which to create the good faith needed to hold open the space for constitution-building.

There was infinite time or no time at all. In the wake of the *Kairos Document*'s call to discern the signs of the times, the state of emergency continued. By the end of 1985, nearly 7000 people had been or were being detained by the state.[164] The declared and "sanctified" potential of separate development appeared to rest increasingly on the logic of the ban, a state of exception in which the "sovereign 'creates and guarantees the situation' that the law needs for its own validity".[165] The word of law was striving to amass the power of all words, a gathering designed to render the present hollow, an endless period of waiting for the past's divine calling to appear in a future (never) to come. For their part, the defenders of this legal architecture held that reconciliation would (yet) justify apartheid's "undecidable" identitarian logic. However, for religious leaders opposed to the heresy of a love without relation, this promise of unity *as* difference marked the very occasion of reconciliation. In the time at hand, there was a *kairos* that held the "non-necessity of the present"; an opportunity to remember how the Word of reconciliation could constitute words of opposition that struggled in the name of a unity *in* difference.[166]

The *Kairos Document*'s (re)definition and call for reconciliation was new and it was not. Its terms were both a reflection and a radicalisation of reconciliation's beginning within the development, justification, and religious opposition to apartheid. It is this extended beginning that merits close scrutiny, particularly given the light that it sheds on reconciliation's occasion, the times in which it has been called to endow words with a history-making potential. Drawing from the Afrikaans language movement and early Dutch Reformed Theology, the NGK relied on reconciliation to claim that separate development was less a form of racism than a means of ensuring that individuals with God-given differences could realise their potential both on earth and in the next life. In the 1960s, this rationalisation for racial classification provoked doctrinal debate and dispute over whether God's Word could be used to condone the law's definition of identity and its ensuing divisions. Later, under the entwined banners of prophetic and Black Theology, apartheid's deferred promise was rejected as heresy, a novel gospel that distorted the meaning of Christ's sacrifice and foreclosed precisely those forms of human relations that reflected and held God's grace. As Soweto underscored the need for resistance in the present, and with the church playing an important leadership role in the struggle, the 1980s brought the question of how reconciliation might create and support concrete political action. Tied to arguments over the relative merits of revolutionary violence, the *Kairos Document* both troubled and redefined the idea of reconciliation. Declaring its importance in the state of emergency, the document held that reconciliation could spur productive opposition to apartheid only as its constitutive confession named the experience of oppression in the face of unjust law.

The beginning of reconciliation is a call to begin with/in words that turn identity toward the (be)coming into relation of identification. This is the crucial point. Considered over time, the religious debate in South Africa over the meaning and value of reconciliation holds important lessons about its occasion, the way in which it opposes and also constitutes the promise of beginnings. In opposition to the logic of separate development, the need and desire for reconciliation appeared in a time outside of time. Its promise took shape in a present that was not simply the intersection of past and future but the problem of their meaning and relationship. Thus, reconciliation began in extraordinary time, a *kairos* in which there was not much time. In this moment, there was a decisive need for choice but a lack of stable ground from which it might be rendered.

In a state of emergency, the historical reasons that support hope and justify action appear self-confounding. There is only something like what Hegel called the "causality of fate", a dynamic in which the declared sufficiency of the past will not suffice for either the present or the future; against the Word, the law's words of precedent hold only violence. Cast as a promise of the "normal", this endless and unaccountable threat marks the occasion of reconciliation. In the words of one commentator, "Reconciliation, in essence, represents a place, the point of encounter where concerns about both the past and the future can meet."[167]

What is this place? How does a time without time yield space? In the extreme case, when caught fully between past and future, what is it that (re)constitutes the capacity to invent shared meaning and make history? At this moment, when the terms of (historical) reference are suspect, reconciliation represents a *topos* of potential, a place for becoming that is equally a coming into place. In the *stasis* that constitutes the desire for reconciliation, history is (re)called in a contingent way, as a reserve of experience that is not yet power. Precedent turns towards play; the commonplace becomes the question of the commons; the subject and object of reconciliation begin to exchange places.

These movements figure prominently in the controversy that attended religious calls for reconciliation in South Africa. Over time, the temporal-spatial horizon of reconciliation was defined as a gift that created the *standing* to make the future through a remembrance but not knowledge of the past. In time, reconciliation was cast as a provisional opposition to the "promise" of a separate (identity-based) development that was always to come. Thus, the occasion of reconciliation not only (re)presented but also called forth the rhetorical question of how to craft a discursive potential for history-making at a moment when history appeared to negate the grounds for speech.[168]

For a beginning, reconciliation opened a time that beckoned a voice that was not its own, speech that called identity to stand *as it was not*. For the present, its words opposed the violence of law in the name of its (re)constitution on the grounds of faith, an intersubjective *ethos* of (inter)action. In this sense, the legacy of the *Kairos Document* is a lesson about how reconciliation marks an exception to the law's exception, a moment in which the task is not to transcend conflict but to fashion words that operate in its midst. Put differently, reconciliation's speech grasped and demonstrated how language "takes place" as time.[169] In 1985, this turn from *stasis* to *status*, the grounds for that speaking which turns language toward motion, did not have clear form even as its idea was increasingly important to those struggling against the regime. In the moment, the occasion of reconciliation was the problem of how to create the potential for talking about talk, a creative potential for the present that would unravel the law's creation by turning a situation of violence into a climate for productive opposition. Thus, reconciliation begins with the rhetorical question of how to stand in the present with words that contain the potential to oppose law's silencing exception and (re)constitute a unity in difference from within the division of endless emergency.

2

a middle course between extremes:
reconciliation as an art
of inventing "talk about talk"

*It is the present situation, the present, I say, that has
baffled my calculations.*
Cicero, Letter to Atticus

*What is important for our situation is that we are
all here.*
Albert Luthuli

South Africa is waiting to become – a hovering society.
Frederick van Zyl Slabbert

*The gravity of the situation does not allow for rhetorical
gestures of any kind.*
Nelson Mandela

reconciliation begins with the question of how to talk about talk in the
midst of violence without end. On 12 June 1986, four months after the
close of the 1985 emergency and four months before the NGK offered a
qualified retraction of its support for apartheid, the government issued a new
and more draconian set of "abnormal laws".[1] To endure for almost exactly
four years, the edicts were a perverse expression of sovereignty, a situation
of exception that led the *South African Journal on Human Rights* to editorialise
that citizens faced the danger of a "psychological acclimatisation" in which
the misrecognition of "abnormality as normality" would "undermine the
chances for struggle and real political change".[2] In the short term, however,
the physical violence grew worse.

Between June and early 1987, some 25 000 people were detained by the state. The Black Sash reported that many were children; youth between 16 and 18 had become a "prime target of State repression". Over the course of the year, 2223 people were killed in political violence, a figure that the Minister of Law and Order refused to convey to Parliament. All the while, Executive Orders designed to "refine" the emergency appeared weekly in the *Government Gazette*, including measures designed to further deter public gatherings and limit the media's ability to report on the scope and motivations of "unrest". Security forces continued to enjoy indemnity, a status that presupposed their good faith and left citizens seeking accountability with the nearly impossible task of proving otherwise. In this situation, as the forces of liberation rallied against a state driven more by a fear of insecurity than legitimacy, many sensed the inevitability of civil war.

The signs of the times portended battle. On one side, President Botha's Total Strategy continued to tack between promises of reform, the escalation of repression, and attempts to ensure South Africa's regional hegemony. Directed largely by the State Security Council, a shadow cabinet charged to combat the liberation's struggle's so-called "total onslaught" and to promulgate economic reforms that would quiesce black citizens, the strategy involved the "militarisation of the state and the politicisation of the military" in the name of promulgating cosmetic changes and ensuring the "continuation of white minority rule" in the face of what F.W. de Klerk would later describe as a "concerted campaign" dedicated to "general revolution".[3] Winning few converts, one apparent effect of the state's efforts was the banishment of "moral, social, religious identity and 'ideological' principle from its own legitimacy discourse".[4]

To this violent devolution, the ANC responded with a call for national and local ungovernability. Both a mode of struggle and its by-product, ungovernability was defended by the ANC in mid-1986 as the key to mobilising "people's power" and sustaining the drive for revolution. According to the National Executive Committee (NEC), "We have reached a point of no return. The historic conditions necessary to ensure the collapse of the apartheid system have taken shape in greater measure than ever before in our history. But much still needs to be done to destroy it once and for all."[5] Much indeed. Sympathetic commentators argued that the ANC's position had been largely overrun by the forces deployed to enforce the state of emergency and, more important, that the means of ungovernability were undermining its ends, a dynamic that was sowing chaos within the movement and making it difficult if not impossible to direct its power.[6]

In late 1986, South Africa was caught between the politico-military violence of the Total Strategy and the revolutionary aspirations of ungovernability. Combined with an economy that sat on the precipice of freefall, it appeared that the country was caught in a situation of stalemate, a condition that led one commentator to argue that the "state and opposition have become entangled in a death embrace".[7] Although others used slightly less dramatic terms, claiming that the forces of apartheid and struggle had entered into a deadlock, checkmate, or violent equilibrium, the point was the same: entrenched in a cycle of violence and counter-violence, neither side appeared ready, willing, or able to move forward or back. With its legitimacy all but exhausted, the state did continue to enjoy an overwhelming military advantage over a liberation movement that had support from masses that lacked the capacity to organise let alone win the decisive final battle. Thus, as the government's announced commitment to preserve national sovereignty collided with the ANC's internationally supported claim that apartheid had to be dismantled in its entirety, the two sides each blamed the other for using violence to short-circuit meaningful reform, the nature of which was also in fundamental dispute. As well, differing interpretations of the situation created divisions within each camp, particularly between those in government who believed that the "political system had become obsolete" and those who still clung to the "promise" of apartheid.[8] Even so, many of the *verligtes* in Botha's cabinet appeared to assume that black political participation was by definition a threat to the survival of the white minority, a position that led the ANC to conclude that government's proposals for reform were a shell game. In short, the situation seemed to portend only endless violence, clashes fed by a fundamental lack of trust, little common ground for talk, and radically different visions of the country's future.[9]

A moment of arrest and an arrested moment, the stalemate was not without a dynamic quality. More than mutual paralysis, the situation marked a *stasis*, a condition that Barbara Cassin has aptly described as a "public illness which, in its extreme phase can be translated as 'language trouble'".[10] In 1986, as conflict overran the ground for talk and both sides confronted the limit of their own expressed rationales for action, this trouble with words appeared to have several dimensions. First, public statements released by the government and the ANC proceeded from an attitude of negation. As the struggle to defend the state or secure liberation was deemed all or nothing, each side saw the other as little more than an obstacle to be overcome.

Second, the divergent means of conflict confounded the idea of victory and complicated the possibility of a ceasefire. The government's superior military forces could win the battle but never the war since mass action made governance impossible even as it could not generate the power needed to assume control of the nation. More subtly, the two sides had little ground on which to build the basis for compromise. As the government was unwilling to barter with "communist terrorists" to the same degree that the exiled leadership of the ANC refused to deal with "authoritarian racists", each was the other's "political monster", an attribution that made it difficult if not impossible to generate trust or create even a thin belief that the enemy was capable of rational interaction or interested to undertake negotiations about how to resolve the conflict. Third, the exercise of force appeared to work at the expense of agency. In the moment, the situation was one in which each side's historical justifications for violence appeared increasingly self-confounding; the state's efforts to shore up its legitimacy served only to deplete it further, while the ANC's call for ungovernability seemed to risk many of the organisation's long-standing socio-political goals.

At the threshold of language, *stasis* held the potential for talk. By early 1987, the myriad voices that would soon compose what one commentator called an "orgy of communication" were starting to speak about the need for words.[11] Meeting in secret, members of the ANC and government emissaries began talking about ways to crack the stalemate.[12] Afrikaner business leaders concerned about the haemorrhaging economy travelled north for discussions with the ANC. As many of apartheid's "petty" laws were taken off the books, including the pass laws and prohibitions against mixed marriage, the National Party (NP) heard prolific and fiery criticism from the right-wing Conservative Party (CP) and continued a sometimes divisive debate about whether to continue incremental reforms or launch bolder initiatives. Leaders of the security forces became increasingly vocal about how political violence defied a military solution. Two of apartheid's most vigilant guardians, the NGK and the Broederbond, announced their reservations about its future, arguing publicly that the pace and scope of reform had to increase. Within the ANC, there was heated debate over whether it was possible to fight and to open negotiations at the same time. No longer on Robben Island but still imprisoned, Nelson Mandela began to ask how to jump-start talks without betraying those to whom he remained loyal. A 1987 statement by the ANC laid down substantive and procedural conditions for such dialogue, all of which were rejected by the government on the grounds that they failed to indicate when the Congress would renounce violence. In response, the ANC argued that such a move would not be forthcoming until such time as it was convinced that the government was willing to negotiate in good faith about how to end apartheid. Reflecting the lack of shared trust in the moment, this appeal to faith was significant. Amidst all the words, many of which seemed to lack an audience, representatives from the Congress and government began to claim that political change required the creation of a *climate* for talks, a process in which both sides demonstrated a sincere interest in dialogue dedicated to enacting change. Measured from the start of the 1986 emergency, this work took four long and bloody years – a period of pre-negotiation that set the stage for a set of talks about talks which then led to the opening, breakdown, and recommencement of the negotiations that ended statutory apartheid.

The difficult process of beginning was crafted with small gestures. Indeed, few saw how the tumult of the 1980s would give way to a negotiated settlement which brought South Africa its first non-racial constitution and set the stage for the April 1994 election. What is not a surprise is that this remarkable turn has motivated a voluminous literature dedicated to the question of *why* South Africa was able to escape its apparent fate of civil war.[13] Pointing variously to the exhaustion of apartheid, economic necessity, international sanctions, the end of the cold war, a moderation of the ANC, and the personalities of F.W. de Klerk and Nelson Mandela, critics concerned to explain the causes of apartheid's end have been somewhat less inclined to explore the question of *how* the terms of a negotiated settlement were created and sustained.

By what means did announced justifications for violence support the development of the "talks about talks" that established the grounds for negotiations given to ending apartheid? As expressed moral commitments to justice and sovereignty, how were these justifications relinquished or transformed in the name of undertaking radical socio-political change? How did the combatants build the good faith needed to overcome mutual suspicion and turn a situation of violence to a climate that was conducive to talking about how to talk? Did the beginning of talks depend on an implicit agreement about the nature of the time in which South Africa was caught? Did this reading of the times work to open space in which to cultivate a kind of "agonistic respect" in which it was possible to argue without fear of violence?[14] How and why was this effort set frequently under the banner of reconciliation?

In 1985, the *Kairos Document* announced an occasion for reconciliation, a fragile opportunity to (re)turn to words that held the potential for a renewal of human relationships and the creation of a just peace. In the years that followed, from within the increasingly cramped confines of the emergency, it became clear that this controversial call had an echo. Focused on the period between 1987 and late 1991, this chapter investigates the ways in which key South African political leaders appealed for reconciliation and defended it as a way to create the words that could lead the country out of an endless cycle of violence. Heard from both sides of the conflict, these proposals for reconciliation were carefully constructed. Not all of them were believed. Many drew bitter rebuke and raised questions about what it meant to capitulate with evil. In any case, the rhetorical form and (rhetorical) content of these calls played an important role in the opening phases of South Africa's transition from apartheid. More precisely, I contend here that advocacy for (and against) reconciliation helped figure the potential for a crucial beginning.

At a moment when words appeared to have no constructive power, committed protagonists used appeals for reconciliation to envision and figure the time and space needed to begin a process of talking about talk. Evolving slowly, this meta-speech developed from the recognition of a shared opposition, the mutual acknowledgement of a situation in which violence thwarted both the ANC and government's historical-ideological aims. Over the course of a nuanced debate, Nelson Mandela and F.W. de Klerk used reconciliation to delineate this state of affairs, arguing variously that the country sat on the brink of a conflict that would come at the expense of all citizens and which demanded a different kind of gift, a willingness to transform justifications for violence into a basis for dialogue. In the late 1980s, this relinquishment of self-interest was not an easy task. It required each side to demonstrate their sincerity, show a willingness to listen, and prove that they had the good faith needed to build a common vocabulary and shared norms of dialogue. In 1990, the obvious, critical, and highly controversial enactment of such a gesture was an indemnity that set aside the state's standing law pertaining to those accused of treason and which helped set the stage for the ANC's suspension of armed struggle against a regime guilty of a crime against humanity. Defended explicitly on the grounds of reconciliation, indemnity helped bracket the force of the past and created a moment in which there was a potential for leaders to argue about how to create the conditions for productive argumentation dedicated to enacting fundamental constitutional reform.

Used to turn a situation of violence into a climate for talking about talk, political calls for reconciliation raise a question that South African religious discourses do not fully answer: Did appeals for reconciliation in the late 1980s have a precedent in the nationalist doctrines proffered by the architects of apartheid and the ANC? Drawing from interviews in which South African political leaders address reconciliation's history, the present chapter begins with this problem, a speculative and necessarily brief investigation of how Afrikaner and ANC nationalism contain *topoi* that represent less an overt commitment to reconciliation than a proto-grammar which contextualises the term's use in the last years of apartheid. In section two, I turn from this discussion to the *stasis* that appeared to grip South Africa between 1986 and early 1990. Focusing on how violence was reinforcing distrust and deterring dialogue between the government and the ANC, the section considers how the two parties recognised the situation as a common condition, a mutual paralysis that constituted a reason to create a climate for negotiations. Evident first in secret meetings and then given public form through repeated calls for reconciliation, this shift from situation to climate was premised on the enactment of good faith, a display of character dedicated to setting the stage for talking about talk. In the chapter's final section, I trace the development of these meetings given to the question of how to negotiate, paying particular attention to how the beginning of dialogue relied on an indemnity that opened space for interaction and tentative debate. Recognising that this turn was necessary to the development of negotiations, I conclude by observing how it was not sufficient. At the end of 1990, after a protracted controversy over how to reduce political violence, the talks about talks confronted the limit of their form – the question of how to create productive disagreement about the terms of a new and non-racial constitution.

In the midst of violence, calls for reconciliation held the potential for talk. The first of two that examine reconciliation's constitutive power, this chapter contends ultimately that political argumentation over reconciliation helped create rhetorical opponents out of enemies that were increasingly at a loss for words. Necessarily, this means that the chapter's work bears directly on the question of beginning that sits at the heart of the English-speaking church's advocacy of reconciliation. This is not to say that religious calls for reconciliation led necessarily to its use in overtly political situations. Rather, blurring the line between religious and civic faith, calls for reconciliation in the mid and late 1980s made the case that within the apparent limit of the word there remained a potential for speech which could constitute action.

In the context of both church and state, this opportunity was couched as a threat of self-negation, an experience that led the (collective) subject to recognise that its self-certainty (identity) and historically-legally validated reasons for action had become a deep threat to the (relational) ends that they claimed to serve. As the moment that Hegel described as the power of life turned hostile, this symbolic death was a call to that faith which made an exception to the laws of identity and historical duty. For the church, this time was a *kairos*, a moment of choice that offered the opportunity to (re)turn to the justice of the divine Word in the name of finding words with which to renew human relationships. In the crucible of politics, this expression of faith took a different form, a symbolic and legal indemnity that opened a space for words given to redefining the terms and relationship between law and justice. Through an enabling exception to law, reconciliation's beginning did not transcend conflict but exposed how violence constituted a common condition, a situation that did not enable compromise so much as motivate aggrieved parties to find and express the words which enacted their respective need to speak, listen, and disagree without fear of retribution. In the midst of a state of emergency, the faith of political reconciliation in South Africa offered the basis to learn and practise constitutive forms of talk.

1. different unities in difference: the (non)reconciling terms of afrikaner and anc nationalism

Why reconciliation? As the concept is not a traditional staple of democratisation theory and to the degree that its practice is not a fully trusted element of secular politics, why was reconciliation invoked and performed by protagonists in South Africa? While powerful, the matter cannot be fully explained by the cases for reconciliation that were advanced by South Africa's churches, particularly as they did not hold the reins of power in either government or the liberation struggle. Were there then historical events or socio-political norms that made the term sensible, meaningful, and appropriate in the late 1980s, a time when the South African Government (SAG) and ANC agreed on little more than their enmity for one another? If appeals to reconciliation in the midst of this *stasis* did not simply appear *ex nihilo*, was there a shared precedent for its value or utility?

When presented with these questions, contemporary South African political leaders have much to say about the historical roots and significance of reconciliation. They do not, however, have definitive answers. Arriving late to his suburban Pretoria home after a meeting to arrange the transport of several elephants to Angola, Roelf Meyer, the NP's former chief negotiator and once rising star, puts it to me that political interest in reconciliation can be traced to the "grief [that] had not been addressed" after the Anglo-Boer War. Going further, he offers that reconciliation afforded a way for political parties to "relax about the future" and then claims that it was an "absolutely necessary" part of South Africa's conflict resolution process.[15] Across the country, in a corner office of the Cape Town building that houses government's executive offices, Father Smangaliso Mkhatshwa, then the Deputy Minister of Education and now Mayor of Tshwane (Pretoria), goes a bit deeper, suggesting that reconciliation grew in South Africa from an existential and a pragmatic need to alter the socio-political conditions that "militate against new forms of relationships". It expresses an "imperative to live together", he argues, and marks a historical concern to "move forward" from within situations of stalemate.[16] In the leafy confines of Cape Town's suburb of Newlands, Alex Boraine, a former Methodist minister and Member of Parliament before resigning to direct an influential NGO and serve as Vice-Chair of the TRC, takes a long view on the matter, contending that reconciliation is "different in the South African context", an idea influenced by African philosophy and a practice that involves acts of "compromise and consensus" dedicated to "coexistence via deliberations".[17] Although he claims that reconciliation is the "wrong term", Constand Viljoen, former leader of the conservative Afrikaner Freedom Front (FF), explained to me in his office at Parliament that "conciliation" grew from the fighting over matters of "group interest and domination".[18] On the other side of the political spectrum, Mac Maharaj, a former member of the ANC's senior leadership, attributed the importance of reconciliation to the country's need for a "bridge" that allowed citizens to move from the brink of civil war to joint reconstruction. Historically, he claims, reconciliation's prominence cannot be divorced from the ANC's long-standing commitment to non-racialism.[19]

While one beginning of reconciliation in South Africa appears in the religious controversy over its meaning and value, these reflections suggest that there may be another – one that lurks in the historical terms, interplay, and clash of the nationalist doctrines that respectively underwrote and challenged apartheid. Difficult to approach, the question of this potential is an important precursor to an investigation of the appeals to reconciliation that appeared in the late 1980s. It is also a line of inquiry that demands care, an abiding concern for the fact that Afrikaner nationalism and its ANC counterpart were tenuous, heterogeneous, and contested ideologies. So too, it is clear that neither the government nor the oft-fragmented ANC defended reconciliation as an explicit means or norm of political action in the middle years of apartheid. Thus, the issue at hand is a subtle one, perhaps too subtle. If reconciliation does have a shared precedent, its form may appear only as we consider what Antjie Krog means when she observes "how little ubuntu communism and Boere socialism differ from another".[20] Both mundane and controversial, Krog's claim suggests that the apartheid state and ANC proffered nationalist visions that shared a set of *topoi*, commonplaces about the nature, form, and power of human (political) relationships. Without overdrawing the coherence or significance of these grounds for argumentation and action, my aim in this section is to discuss, briefly and somewhat derivatively, the ways in which both doctrines developed in reaction to an experience of colonialism and placed heavy emphasis on a (different) sense of communal identity, one that called on citizens to question if not resist liberalism's attachment to the idea of an autonomous and isolated subject. Bound in uneven ways to the power of words, these ideological commitments introduced contradictions into the fabric of Afrikaner and ANC nationalism, (self) oppositions that rendered nationalism's promise contingent on creating the potential for a conceptual and practical "unity in difference". Interpreted in dramatically different ways, this struggle with the excess of (historical) identity represents far less a cause of reconciliation's currency in the 1980s than an almost implicit language game, an experience of the dilemmas of beginning that shed a bit of light on why reconciliation made mutual sense to committed enemies at a moment when very little else did.

in the name of "dit is ons erns"

The nation's purpose was not self-justifying. In 1973, the South African Government published a short tract entitled *Progress through Separate Development*. Addressed primarily to international audiences, the booklet is an apt reminder of how the regime responded to those who rallied against apartheid's injustice. Equally a manifesto and lament, it begins by delineating the problem that so stuck in the craw of an apartheid leadership which believed that it deserved a seat at the "first-world" table: "In the world of today, a nation's right to determine its own destiny is no longer supposed to be a disputed issue."[21] What followed this condemnation of the international community's "hypocrisy" was a predictable defence of apartheid, a case in which nationalist policy was distinguished from a theory of racial superiority and cast as a means of reversing the wounds of colonialism to the degree that it ensured "each of the different black nations in South Africa ... the opportunity to exercise its basic right to determine for itself its own future".[22] Without overt appeals to religion, and supplemented by pictures of productive and autonomous "South African Bantu" striving toward their "states of tomorrow", the document's argumentation proceeded with few warrants, a lack of justification that mimicked the system which it was attempting to rationalise.

Just below the surface of its "great idea", Afrikaner nationalism struggled with its own self-doubt.[23] In 1974, the same year that the NGK issued its *Human Relations and the South African Scene*, this insecurity was evident in an address given by Prime Minister John Vorster to a group of East Rand Rapportryers. Concerned to profess the Afrikaner's calling and promote a national "vocation" still to be made, the speech was directed primarily to the Afrikaner youth who Vorster thought might be worried about a future that "probably looks dark, it looks unpredictable, it looks ugly to you".[24] Citing the spread of communism and attacks on apartheid, Vorster argued that separate development was not only acceptable but a cornerstone of the nation, a system that did not "rob the Blacks amongst us of their national character, to despise what is their own and to humiliate them in that way, to reduce them to persons without roots who see no future for themselves". From this negative confirmation of purpose, Vorster announced the Afrikaner's calling, a purpose without which "nations perish" and one that demanded obedience to three "primary principles". In a "multiracial country", the Prime Minister declared, the Afrikaner needed to "retain political power", "safeguard identity", and cultivate "discipline and order in this world of violence and anarchy".[25] While he claimed that such work did not involve "putting yourself on a throne", Vorster did maintain that South Africa's Christian nationalism afforded Afrikaners the "right to differentiate and therefore to hold your political government in your own hands". Far from a burden, the opportunity at hand was dedicated to a higher purpose:

> The Lord never places responsibilities on people who cannot bear them
> and we were given broad shoulders because the Lord knew in His mercy
> which problems we would meet with in Africa. It is our heritage; we
> have to bear it, we can bear it, and I believe that we shall bear it.[26]

"What does the future hold in store for you?" Vorster's question was meant to answer itself, a non-question such that "in spite of the decisions that are being made at present", the time held the opportunity of a (past) calling, a chance to make the future with the vocation of a "separate development that can be sold to Africa". Thus, apartheid's announced promise was rooted in an inviolable identity, a sovereignty that denied the race consciousness on which it was premised. Put differently, Vorster's calling – the call to an "I" that had to "bear responsibility" – named a self-identical subject supported by the cause of history, an identity linked to and defined by a past collectivity that had to be preserved in a way that carried its "victorious opposition" into the future. As this vision of the nation relied on a timeless moment in which to wait virtuously for law to fulfil its own precedent, opposition to apartheid in the present justified neither the relinquishment of self nor the recognition of an Other.

Nationalism's gift took it-self back. In this respect, Vorster's position was typical, according to W.A. de Klerk. With a calling from which many Afrikaners were always and inevitably alienated, the premises of nationalism held and enacted a "schism in the soul", an incongruity between the nation's collectivising myth and the terms of everyday life, a tension that enabled but also upset the grounds of collective action.[27] Colonised and coloniser, subservient to God's designs and fiercely independent, and dedicated to the creation of civilisation while fearful of the city's dilutions, the "irony of Afrikaner history" on de Klerk's reading is that it proceeded from an almost self-confounding sense of purpose. From early days, the Afrikaners were "estranged in their own country" and "suffering under the rejection of the Anglo-Saxon cities", burdens that made it difficult to decide whether to pursue redress for past wrongs or forge ahead into the future.[28] Who was a real Afrikaner? Did the rise of nationalism demand a *hubris* that undercut its justifying principle? Did the perceived need for separate development both repeat the Afrikaner's own history and fall foul of the fact that so often "history negates man's intentions and dreams"?[29]

These questions continue to provoke. Indeed, contemporary debate over the motives and coherence of Afrikaner nationalism shows little sign of abating, particularly given the apparent desire of historians to synthesise race and class-based accounts of its development. For instance, Paul Rich's study of liberalism in South Africa contends that Afrikaner nationalism was driven less by one motive than a complex mobilisation of "ethnic group consciousness" that served as an "ideological means by which certain class groupings attained the necessary economic basis to be able to launch themselves into an industrial society".[30] Writing in part against Dunbar Moodie's view of the Afrikaner's "civil-religion", Daniel O'Meara has questioned this appeal to ideological power, arguing in his study of *volkskapitalisme* that the standard "organising myths" of nationalism, couched frequently in stories about the rise and development of "Afrikanerdom", risk historicism.[31] In his expansive "biography" of the Afrikaner people, Hermann Giliomee reflects on these different accounts and suggests that the long-standing tension between the Brit and the Afrikaner was a decisive catalyst for nationalism, particularly as it appeared within the country's decision to enter World War Two:

> The crucial turning point was the Afrikaner nationalists' outrage over the country being taken into the World War on a split vote, confirming in their eyes South Africa's continuing subordination to British interests, and the disruption brought about by the war effort. This was the catalyst that enabled the NP to draw together diverse people in a powerful alliance: cultural nationalists seeking cultural autonomy, farmers seeking labour, businessmen seeking investment capital and clients, and workers seeking racial protection and opportunities for training; and all of them seeking to secure Afrikaner political survival and a changed relationship between South Africa and Britain.[32]

Behind this synergy, Giliomee discerns a deep concern for Afrikaans, a call to cultivate language in the name of promoting cultural development and sustaining a coherent "social identity". Paying close attention to the language movement that developed in the early 20th century, he suggests that "At the heart of the Afrikaner nationalist struggle was the attempt to imagine a new national community with its language enjoying parity of esteem with English in the public sphere."[33] Across diverse interpretations of nationalism and amidst a growing desire for economic power that appeared to be threatened by British domination and black urbanisation, the word mattered. More precisely, nationalism's attention to the development of oral and written discourse served both to explain and perform a model of human relationships. The basis of this bond(age) appeared clearly in three basic lines of argument, all of which were central elements of Vorster's 1974 address.

First, nationalist calls for Afrikaner unity were framed partly by an argument from destiny, an appeal that drew from and created a binding collective myth, a shared history that bordered on a sacred mission. While he rejects historiographical attempts to impose the idea of a divine calling onto Afrikaner cultural-political development, Andre du Toit does allow that such "imaginative historical reconstruction[s]" were appropriated by "Afrikaners themselves".[34] As they were tied to the problem of how to "reconcile the demands for white survival and justice", these symbolic condensations of purpose had an oppositional form: the calling of Afrikanerdom expressed a unity with God in the face of tremendous obstacles on earth. Alone on Malan's so-called "dark continent", and victims of a colonial subjugation that was remembered but not always articulated, the problem of who was *truly* an Afrikaner held the question of how best to understand the relationship between birthright, religious destiny, and a culture that could enact the people's "common spiritual possession".[35] The desire for "being oneself", an ability to cultivate a (common) self-identity, thus demanded resistance to both British domination and racial equality (*gelyskstelling*) – dangers that offset post-Boer War appeals for reconciliation with an assertion of independence that underscored the importance of sovereignty as it was manifest in language, community, and national institutions.[36]

Second, the case for Afrikaner nationalism entailed substantial appeals to fear. The announced dangers were both past and future, a risk of falling back into political subjugation and a worry that the people's integrity would be overrun or "diluted" by outside forces. In 1950, for instance, the *Anti-Communism Act* was defended not simply as a way to prevent "disturbances or disorder" but also by the much older and larger concern about the dangers of socio-political "fusion".[37] While it served the state in its attempts to repress liberation movements, the law was also a call to stand watch against the perils of urbanisation, "Anglicisation", and proletariatisation. According to Malan, it was just this threat of the city that risked a "second Blood River", a threat of identity's erasure within the anonymous crowd and a permanent position of economic inferiority.[38] Moreover, the city's diffusive and egalitarian tendencies portended equality and political rights that were seen by some as the "absolute negation of self-determination".[39]

Third, the nationalist agenda was often defined in opposition to political liberalism, particularly as the latter expressed the colonial designs of Westminster, legitimised the unbridled accumulation of wealth, and sanctioned an extension of the franchise.[40] While the liberal tradition found happiness and justice in the works of self-sure individuals, nationalists countered this atomistic conception of identity with appeals to a sense of *volksverbondenheid* in which "the realisation of full human potential came not from individual self-assertion but through identification with and service to the *volk*".[41] While this rejection of the liberal was far from total, especially with respect to matters of economic prosperity and the desire to justify separate development as something more than a system crafted by "mere racists", it was an important indication of nationalism's antipathy to cultural assimilation and the equalisation of political rights.[42]

On a hill outside of the town of Paarl, far enough from Cape Town to demonstrate the difference, the Afrikaans Taal (Language) Monument is an apt testament to the way in which nationalism's call for unity drew from the past to indemnify the future. The only words at the site given to the power of the word appear at the monument's threshold, an unpunctuated phrase, "Dit is ons erns". While it does not really translate, the closest being "This is our seriousness, our character", the expression says a great deal about the monument's symbolism: a collection of statuary, according to the official visitors' guide, intended to suggest that the towering (phallic) mother tongue can cover historical loss and oversee the constitution of that unity in difference which holds the potential for civilisation yet to come.[43] Dwarfing, collecting, and alienating the individual in its courtyard of the word, the monument expresses some of Afrikaner nationalism's key *topoi*, a sign system that moved freely between notions of "otherness" and "difference" such that separate development could be defended as an investment in a (coming) "multiracial" (as division of those who are different) South Africa.[44] In short, nationalism's words proceeded from a faith that rendered history definitive but also open. Altogether evident in the logic of apartheid, the precise difference was left to the maker – the Word of law set in stone.

the difficult promise of a non-racial nation

If Afrikaner nationalism was an ideal in denial, the African National Congress defined its nationalism against the denial of a practical ideal, the political rights and economic equality that were progressively distorted, restricted, and withdrawn by the forces of colonialism, segregation, and separate development. In the early 1970s, as the NGK gathered its doctrinal steam and Prime Minister Vorster rallied Afrikanerdom's youth, Oliver Tambo, the ANC's President and leader in exile, was arguing that it was time to "plan further, to prepare to fight, to fight harder, for the victory which has thus far proved elusive".[45] While Tambo's call was made in the name of a "revolutionary struggle" dedicated to "the transfer of power from the minority to the majority of the people of our country", it rested on a long evolving and contested definition of the struggle's "national character".[46] Not always the voice of the people and frequently fractured on ideological grounds, the Congress' vision was one that endeavoured to walk a fine line between a non-racial "national democratic revolution" given to "destroying [the] existing social and economic relationships", and a "chauvinism or narrow nationalism" that would gather power but risk replacing one elite group with another or cede to calls for blacks to "hurl whites into the sea".[47] From within these tensions, the ANC worked and often laboured to devise the terms of a nationalism that would challenge the "potential" of apartheid with words of unity that were gathered from a manifold set of deep divisions.

At the time of its founding in 1912, the South African Native National Congress (the name was changed in 1925) enjoyed little political power and sought rather modest goals, an agenda that has been described as the work of a "debating chamber" dedicated to advocating "somewhat vaguely for some democratic form of government in which Africans would be fully represented".[48] Dedicated to operating within a colonial system from which it was increasingly excluded, the Congress' early years saw it issuing largely "reactive rights demands" in the wake of segregationist legislation and political exclusion.[49] Such work placed a heavy emphasis on securing channels of political representation and participation, a goal that was evident when the Congress challenged the 1913 *Land Act* as "one-sided and inconsistent with the ideals of fair Government by reason of the disabilities it imposes on the Native people of the Union". While it maintained that the legislation's consolidation of segregation would create "friction and racial antipathies between the blacks and whites", the Congress continued its reformist course through the 1930s, a period in which many felt that it lacked the leadership and message needed to gain significant popular support.[50]

In its early days, the Congress was influenced both by liberalism and Christianity. With the former used to promote the somewhat assimilationist creation of a multiracial "nation within a nation", the latter served a number of influential leaders who defined the Congress' goals in religious terms and argued, for instance, that "the universal acknowledgment of Christ as common Lord and King [would] break down the social, spiritual, and intellectual barriers between the races".[51] Perceived as an antidote to the tribalism proffered by colonial segregationists, religion was held out as a way to build political community, promote a universal sense of human dignity, and resist racist stereotyping.[52] With the coming of war and the coalescing of Afrikaner nationalism, however, this *ethos* grew increasingly suspect to a new generation of Congress members, many of whom were dissatisfied with the pace of reform and interested to debate the merits of other paths toward liberation.

In 1935, an All-African convention was held in opposition to the *Hertzog*

Bills, legislation that threatened the last vestiges of the black franchise and promised the creation of a puppet Natives Representation Council. The convention met in Bloemfontein, where ANC representatives played a central role in the gathering and embraced its call for "the ultimate creation of a South African nation in which, while the various racial groups may develop on their own lines, socially and culturally, they will be bound by the pursuit of common objectives".[53] Yet, the formation of a multiracial South Africa anchored by a non-racial political system presupposed an ability to oppose an increasingly repressive state.[54] This problem of how to invent political power was a growing concern, particularly to Anton Lembede, a young member of the Congress who began to argue in the early 1940s that it was time for the oppressed to stop relying on those who would never fully understand "the African spirit" or accept the call to "go out as apostles to preach the new gospel of Africanism".[55]

Against the rising tide of Afrikaner nationalism, Lembede's basic position was that the time for patient collaboration had passed. Arguing for an organic nation, one that could resist the degradations of city life and overcome a history of exploitation, he challenged Africans to recover their self-image and capacity to direct the liberation struggle. At least initially, Africans would have to go it alone, forsaking multiracial collaboration until they were able to meet other groups on an equal footing. As Gail Gerhart has observed, this interpretation of Africanism did and did not sit in tension with the ANC's larger goal of non-racial politics; it left room to embrace the idea of "Africans for humanity" while maintaining that African nationalists had a duty to "their own moral standards and priorities".[56]

In the 1940s, the ANC Youth League (ANCYL) did much to promote Lembede's call for a "single powerful African national front".[57] Starting partly from the claim that "The fault is not in our stars, but in ourselves that we are underlings", the League envisioned itself as the "intellectual powerhouse" within the Congress, a role that included overseeing an ideological redirection that could energise struggle without compromising the ANC's long-standing commitment to non-racialism.[58] Holding that its task was to guide a strategic shift from "constitutional politics to non-collaboration", ANCYL's position appeared in its 1944 manifesto, a text that owed more than a little to the larger Congress's *African's Claims in South Africa*. A Bill of Rights that drew from the *Atlantic Charter's* declarations about territorial integrity, economic advancement, and the sovereign right of self-government, the authors of *African's Claims* sought "the granting of full citizenship rights such as enjoyed by all Europeans in South Africa" and concluded that peace in South Africa hinged on the "abolition of all enactments which discriminate against the African on grounds of race and colour".[59]

While dismissed by Prime Minister Smuts as "widely impracticable", the ANCYL's manifesto expanded this call for sovereignty, focusing first on the philosophical problem that sat beneath "the conflicting living conditions and outlooks on life which seriously hamper South Africa's progress to nationhood".[60] Without the means to pursue an independent destiny, with neither land nor security, and excluded from the rights and equality that constitute the "common heritage of all Mankind", the League argued that the domination of segregation was "rousing in the African feelings of hatred". Lifting the veneer on state policy, the League concluded that the conflict in South Africa was between "race on one side and ideals on the other". Crucial with respect to its view of human relations, the precise position deserves careful consideration:

> The White man regards the Universe as a gigantic machine hurtling through time and space to its final destruction: individuals in it are but tiny organisms with private lives that lead to private deaths: personal power, success and fame are the absolute measures of values; the things to live for. This outlook on life divides the Universe into a host of individual little entities which cannot help being in constant conflict thereby hastening the approach of the hour of their final destruction. The African, on his side, regards the Universe as one composite whole; an organic entity, progressively driving towards greater harmony and unity whose individual parts exist merely as interdependent aspects of one whole realising their fullest life in the corporate life where communal contentment is the absolute measure of values. His philosophy of life strives towards unity and aggregation; towards greater social responsibility.[61]

While it glossed the difference between Brit and Boer, ignoring the ways in which Afrikaner nationalism recoiled against the terms of an individualistic life, this position was rooted partly in Lembede's appeal to the binding force of an African spirit and partly in the practical problem of how to create a unified front that could sustain the fight for power.

By 1948, ANCYL had refined the idea further, arguing in its *Basic Document* that the ANC's vision was less that of Marcus Garvey's "Africa for Africans" than a militant nationalism that did not discount the "possibility of a compromise by which Africans could admit Europeans to a share of the fruits of Africa".[62] While not wholly accepted, especially by those who were wary of multiracial collaboration and keen to develop a message that would uniquely mobilise the black masses, the ANC's argument appeared to commit it to pursuing the "interracial peace" that might follow from the elimination of "white domination" and not to attacking the "European as human being".[63] In 1953, one of the ANCYL's rising stars echoed the point, arguing that while he was not a racialist, there was increasingly no "middle course" through which to pursue political reform. Thus, according to Nelson Mandela, the state's evident unwillingness to recognise the dignity of blacks justified an "uncompromising and determined mass struggle for the overthrow of fascism and the establishment of democratic forms of government".[64]

With a *Programme of Action* that set "national freedom" in opposition to apartheid and advocated direct confrontation with "differential political institutions", Mandela's position was reflected in the ANC's larger debates in the 1950s over how to crystallise the organisation's goals and fashion the means for their accomplishment. Still insecure about its role as the leading liberation movement, the Congress remained particularly uneasy about the merits of collaboration, a reluctance that appeared in the Youth League's early refusals to enter into alliance with the South African Communist Party. While the antipathy would lessen as some leading members concluded that the two groups had at least a partially congruent interest in liberation, the tension between race and class-based interpretations of the struggle would continue to fester.[65] Thus, as the Congress fretted over whether alliances, like the one formed in 1947 with the South African Indian Congress, were diluting its own agenda and on how to narrow the gap between the urban-centered intelligentsia and citizens in rural areas, the problem of how to define the proper focus of struggle bolstered calls for cohesion within the ANC. This perceived need for internal discipline was underscored in 1955 by ANC President Albert Luthuli, when he worried aloud that Africans were not "accepting fast enough the gospel of service and sacrifice for the general and large good without expecting a personal (and at that immediate) reward; they have not accepted fully the basic truth enshrined in the saying 'No cross, No Crown'".[66]

Initiated in late 1951, the Defiance Campaign was a crucial step on the road to mobilising the masses. While it fell short of its expected goal, the campaign demonstrated the significant role that women were to play in the struggle and underscored that alliances were a necessary if not always comfortable condition for power.[67] With respect to the latter, the ANC helped create the Congress Alliance in 1953, an organisation that served to deepen the ANC's ties with the trade unions.[68] One of the Alliance's first acts was to call for a people's congress dedicated to the creation of a "central document for the non-racial movement".[69] Thus, in June of 1955, some 3000 people gathered in Kliptown. Over the course of several days, delegates debated and negotiated the nature of "inclusive politics".[70] Despite harassment and wholesale arrests by the state, the discussion had important results.[71]

Written at a moment when the government was implementing the last of apartheid's founding legal pillars, the *Freedom Charter* declared that "South Africa belongs to all who live in it, black and white, and [that] no government can justly claim authority unless it is based on the will of all the people".[72] With this call for non-racialism, the *Charter* decried the colonialism that had robbed people of their "birthright to land, liberty, and peace" and urged a struggle against apartheid's "laws and practices". More than a manifesto for liberation and less than a full blueprint for governance, the *Charter* was a call for resistance in the name of creating an opportunity for all citizens to author the law, enjoy equal representation, and reap the rewards of their heritage and labour. With this goal, however, came little practical advice about how to begin. More troubling, as its various goals were not entirely consistent and appeared to depend partly on the apartheid logic of "national groups", the *Charter* spurred controversies that undermined the very unity that it hoped to inspire, a fault line that appeared most fully in 1959, the year in which the Pan Africanist Congress was formed in opposition to the ANC's allegedly weak Africanism and the *Freedom Charter*'s "political bluff".[73]

The *Freedom Charter* also provoked an escalation of state repression. In 1956, some 100 leaders of the Alliance – including Walter Sisulu and Nelson Mandela – were arrested, tried, and then acquitted of treason charges. During his testimony about whether he was intent to overthrow the state, Mandela offered that democracy could be achieved through the gradual reform of apartheid, a process that required talks with the government about how to achieve "universal adult suffrage for Africans".[74] Toward the end of the trial, however, just after the 1960 Sharpeville massacre, Prime Minister Hendrik Verwoerd foreclosed such an option when he banned the ANC and the PAC under the terms of the *Suppression of Communism Act*. In his autobiography, Mandela recalls that the ANC had laid plans to move abroad in the event of such a prohibition, a contingency that required the development of organisational principles that could sustain the Congress' work in light of its inability to hold public meetings. Too, banning brought increasing and controversial talk of upping the ante, escalating the struggle in response to the government's repression. As the Congress met the 1960 celebration of the new republic with a national strike, Mandela argued publicly that, "If the government's reaction is to crush by naked force our non-violent struggle, we will have to reconsider our tactics. In my mind, we are closing a chapter on this question of a non-violent policy."[75] Contrasted with his position at the treason trial, the claim suggested that negotiated reform was no longer a viable option.

The ANC's decision to fight was announced on 16 December 1961, the anniversary of the day on which the *voortrekkers* took their vow to God before the battle at Blood River. Organisationally, the ANC's armed wing, Umkhonto we Sizwe (MK), was understood to be separate but firmly under the control of the ANC's larger political structure, a body that would "carry on the struggle for freedom and democracy by new methods, which are necessary to complement the actions of the established national liberation organisations". In part, this arrangement was designed to protect the ANC's unbanned allies and place controls on the use of violence.[76] Hoping to avert a "desperate state of civil war" and contending that violent sabotage against select targets would place significant pressure on the government, the MK's manifesto argued that the "well-being and happiness" of all people depended on the "overthrow of the Nationalist government".

> The time comes in the life of any nation when there remain only
> two choices: submit or fight. That time has now come to South Africa.
> We shall not submit and we have no choice but to hit back by all means
> within our power in defence of our people, our future and our freedom.
> The government has interpreted the peacefulness of the movement as
> weakness; the people's non-violent policies have been taken as a green
> light for government violence. Refusal to resort to force has been
> interpreted by the government as an invitation to use armed force
> against the people without any fear of reprisals. The methods of
> Umkhonto we Sizwe mark a break with that past.[77]

The times had changed and they had not. While the turn to armed action did alter the "national character" of struggle that so concerned Oliver Tambo in the early 1970s, the MK's formation did not resolve the tensions that sat beneath, energised, and complicated the ANC's overall position – a nationalist agenda whose promise of radical and non-racial transformation faced both conceptual and practical obstacles. In this respect, looking across pre-Youth League definitions of struggle to the MK manifesto, there are three threads of the ANC's nationalism that deserve close attention.

First, the Congress consistently argued for the creation of a weak revolutionary power, a mode of struggle dedicated to ending apartheid and cultivating the potential for non-racial democracy. The form of this potential stood in significant distinction to the promise of Afrikaner nationalism, particularly as the latter depended on a calling that used the present only as a site for translating a sacred history into a future redemption. Refusing this deferral, the ANC maintained that the masses could wait no longer; historical subjugation demanded consciousness-raising that mobilised citizens and exposed the incoherence of apartheid's claim to "progressiveness". In 1958, Luthuli made the point explicitly, claiming that the ANC would not accept the state's vision of "going forward by going back".[78] Later, Mandela said the same when he contended that apartheid's "pseudo-theoretical precepts" served only to trap "black South Africans" in the "entrails of a racist beast".[79] In both arguments, the time for struggle was the present, a time that required a form of collective sacrifice which did not use history as a justification for creating a "purified" future but that served the goal of making South Africa into a "home for all".

Second, the ANC took a complicated if not contradictory stance on the merit of liberalist politics. Practically, the rise of the Youth League saw a growing distrust of liberal political parties, many of which were perceived to embrace reform while remaining complicit in the perpetuation of segregation and then apartheid. Committed to multiracialism, the liberal politician struck a growing number of Congress leaders as a "quisling" that sought to "conserve and entrench the apartheid consciousness of people with its concomitant feelings of 'racial' inferiority and superiority…".[80] Still, this hostility lessened somewhat as the Congress entered the 1950s and began the work of alliance-building, a process that figured the liberal as someone able to reach potentially sympathetic white audiences. At a theoretical level, the premises of liberalism were both condemned for their colonial presumptions and central to the Congress' moral case for resistance.[81] Castigated by A.P. Mda as "spineless" and lacking "dynamic power and a creative drive", liberalistic philosophy spoke less to Lembede's "African spirit" than to the alienated individual caught in the confines of city life.[82] Yet even as the ANCYL's Joe Matthews argued in 1951 that "the possibility of a liberal capitalist democracy in South Africa is exactly nil", the ANC was relying on liberalism's logic if not law in documents like *African's Claims* to delineate the evil of apartheid, justify its own struggle, and explain the premise and promise of non-racial democracy.[83]

Third, the Congress placed heavy emphasis on and also laboured to define the "unity" needed for nationalistic struggle. Indeed, cohesion often appeared in short supply given the divisive debates inside the ANC leadership structure between those committed to a non-racialist nationalism and those wed to more Africanist or class-oriented interpretations of the struggle.[84] While the relation between race domination and class exploitation was addressed somewhat in the *Freedom Charter*, the problem saw the ANC accept much of the SACP's position that South Africa's was a "colonialism of a special type". Connoting a situation in which the colonial power did not operate from or have the option of returning to a foreign shore, this account led some to conclude that the struggle against apartheid was a conflict in which the oppressed shared a kind of interdependence with their oppressors.[85] In any case, the Congress' agenda also raised the question of how to promote ideological cohesion within its own ranks. An urban-based organisation, the ANC was frequently accused of intellectualising its work to the point of leaving the people behind. In 1949, these questions of unity were a central concern at a meeting between officials of the ANC and the All-African Convention (AAC). What is interesting about the discussion is how the question of "unity in the fight against oppression" placed a significant burden on the words of struggle. What did unity mean? How was it explained? Who could define or explain it without compromising its integrity? As "democracy was first a word and then a reality", according to the AAC's Reverend Z.R. Mahakane, the definition of nationalism required words that would mobilise but also give voice to the masses.[86] Thus, while Gerhart suggests that the ANC's commitment to multi- or non-racial unity was evidence of its concern for "cooperation and reconciliation", a key underlying problem for the Congress was whether such spirit could be forged through opposition over unity's form and content.[87]

a tenuous shared premise

Between a Christian national system of institutional racism and a liberation movement dedicated to the creation of a non-racial democratic order, what was there to reconcile? One of apartheid's primary architects, Hendrik Verwoerd's obsessive desire to achieve a pure form of non-relation between "population groups" was predicated on the belief that "mixed development" would lead to the "most terrific clash of interests imaginable". In a 1950 speech to the *Native Representative Council*, the soon to be Prime Minister went further, claiming audaciously that with the implementation of apartheid, "I trust that every Bantu will forget the misunderstandings of the past and choose the road not leading to conflict, but that which leads to peace and happiness for both the separate communities."[88] Not long after, Nelson Mandela declined to forsake memory, arguing on behalf of the ANC that, "No organisation whose interests are identical with those of the toiling masses will advocate conciliation to win its demands."[89] While the Congress was not yet the leading movement for the people's liberation, Mandela's position would echo, appearing quite clearly in the *Kairos Document*'s warning that reconciliation risked passivity and undue accommodation with evil. So too, the depth of the ideological clash between defenders and opponents of apartheid would deepen, leading to a point where each decried the other's evil and took it as proof of an incapacity to engage in reasonable dialogue.

To put the matter bluntly, the rhetorical arcs of Afrikaner and ANC nationalism do not appear to hold an explicit concern for reconciliation. Beyond their significant relationship to Christianity and setting aside post-Boer War appeals for conciliation between the Afrikaner and the British, reconciliation is not an overt feature of either doctrine. Nevertheless, the absence of explicit discussion about reconciliation in the two positions does not rule out the possibility that the development of each was rooted in some basic experience with its practice. While the point must remain speculative, the two ideologies do appear to hold an opposition in common. By this, I do not mean only that each was opposed to the other. Rather, the idea is that the definition and public explanation of each position entailed a certain performance of reconciliation's logic, an internal and external demand to explain and enact unity's standing in relationship to difference.

Far from given, the respective power of Afrikaner and ANC nationalism was not homogenous, static, or uncontested. Both positions changed unevenly over time and each failed to win the support of many who were claimed as immediate constituents. Within these definitional gaps and legitimacy shortfalls, both placed significant weight on the actuality and ideality of the communal. Variously, each argued that human identity takes shape less in the isolated individual than the resources, history, and spirit of community. On one side, Vorster's 1974 call to youth appealed to the spirit of the Afrikaner *volk* as a means of deterring forms of equality that were perceived to risk racial mixture and which recalled the alienating and colonial terms of British liberalism. On the other, the ANCYL's manifesto and Mandela's wonder over whether "oppressed people [can] count on the Liberal Party as an ally", highlighted how the ANC's non-racialism demanded a revolutionary unity that would not "advocate conciliation" so long as it appeared in the guise of the liberalism's love of rational problem-solving and the search for a "middle ground" that smacked of an undue accommodation with evil.[90] Moreover, the perceived threat of tribalism led early ANC leaders, especially Lembede, to invoke a sense of communal-cultural spirit, one that was generally humanist and sometimes more exclusively Africanist.

With their shared concern for the power of the communal to exceed and (re)constitute identity, the two nationalisms took starkly different paths. In the name of cultivating and protecting the sovereign sphere of the *volk*, Afrikaner nationalism refined the logic of racial segregation, creating a call for the self to develop communally in non-relation to an Other for which it was altogether willing to attribute identity. This internal contradiction held (and covered) a deep racism and also supported a vocation in which the trials of the forebears were held up as the basis for redemption, an identity that had the potential to exceed its own isolating but nevertheless inviolable (sacred) law. In contrast, the ANC's post-1950s definitions of nationalism held that non-racial difference was both a prerequisite and an outcome of an individually and politically enabling unity. Thus, while its Afrikaner counterpart used the opposition of separation to define its promise, the Congress struggled to delineate what it was not – a space of opposition that precluded self's collapse to the Other's law. Appealing to human rights doctrine yet wary of its colonial presumptions, the ANC's call for unity was rooted in a sense of collective identification that endeavoured to set identity into motion, a dynamic that aimed to recover sovereignty from the (Other's) future and mark the need if not the necessity of struggle against the law in the name of (re)making it contingent on the needs of the present, a state that had undivided space and place for all of those who were present.

In their respective hopes for unity, the announced terms of Afrikaner and ANC nationalism both appear to confront the limit of the word. From the language movement to the Congress' explicit, reluctant, and implied willingness to enter political dialogue with allies committed to differing agendas and an enemy that it claimed would not be vanquished in the wake of victory, one of the perennial questions for each doctrine was whether words could coalesce into that unity that would make a difference and if the differences held in words could be(come) a basis for unity. For both, the calling of nationalism required the making of words that exposed an untold (and enabling) history and crafting those words that would make history. In Afrikaner nationalism, this work was confounded by apartheid's racism, a form of exploitation that it claimed to reject.[91] For the ANC, the problem was one of collaboration, the creation of alliances that appeared to risk complicity and which later left open the option for dialogue with those that had been named as evil. Thus, each position confronted – in its own way and within its own announced terms – that which it claimed not to be and what it did not want to become. Conceptually and practically, this experience marks nothing less than an occasion of reconciliation, a moment of doctrinal incoherence and potential self-betrayal that marked the limit and need to return to the word. Politically, these tensions over how to craft unity in difference represent a proto-grammar of reconciliation, a set of *topoi* in which there was a call to (re)figure a contradiction into a (productive) opposition. They also offer one explanation of how and why contemporary South African leaders possess a vocabulary of reconciliation that appears to have significant historical grounding.

2. making a climate out of a violent situation

In 1986, the terms of ANC and Afrikaner nationalism held no obvious remedies for a conflict that was set to spiral out of control. Opening Parliament in late January, President Botha admitted that South Africa had outgrown the "outmoded system of apartheid" and that "our nation of minorities" must undertake "further constitutional development to broaden democracy".[92] Calling for negotiations and the use of a National Council to meet "Black aspirations", Botha argued that "evolutionary reform" was the only alternative to "revolutionary chaos" and rule by a "political clique" bent on making a "mockery of liberty". In short, change was necessary but only in a form that did not risk the basic logic of separate development. Speaking on behalf of Nelson and Winnie Mandela in Kuala Lampur shortly after May Day protests that included the largest labour action in South African history, Oliver Tambo offered a simple and direct reply:

> [A] cancer cannot be its own cure. The fanatical racists, who have spent
> more than half a century drawing up the blueprints of the apartheid
> system and transforming those theoretical constructions into the South
> African society we know today, cannot, at the same time, be the agents
> for the abolition of the system.[93]

Between *stasis* and fundamental political change, at a moment when "we have the potential to destroy each other, both of us, both sides", Frederick van Zyl Slabbert argued that the possibility of talk was hindered by an "absence of compromise and the absence of people willing to enter into those compromises".[94] Indeed, this shortfall was reflected in the actions and statements of the ANC and government, protagonists that would concede no common ground and who both claimed that the duplicity of the other rendered meaningful negotiations impossible. At the 1985 Kabwe conference, for instance, the ANC leadership offered to negotiate and called simultaneously for an escalation of the armed struggle. Similarly, the state professed an interest in talks but appeared willing to engage in discussions only with a few "moderate" members of the Congress, a tactic that led early overtures to Nelson Mandela to be read more as an attempt to co-opt and control reforms than an expression of genuine interest in open discussion.

What changed? How did the ANC and NP create the basis for dialogue and debate when neither appeared ready to hear the other? In their account of the transition, Heribert Adam and Kogila Moodley reply to these questions, arguing that 1987 saw the beginning of a "reluctant reconciliation" between the conflict's main protagonists.[95] While echoed widely, this assessment is unsatisfying precisely to the degree that it skirts the question at hand: how did would-be negotiators actually appeal to reconciliation and how did these calls invent a basis for speech? If these questions are left unanswered, the result is that a process that depended heavily on talk appears as a sea change in which talk was merely ornamental. Thus, beginning with an account of why neither side believed that it could speak with the other, I want to consider how arguments about reconciliation were used to identify a "situation" that was then taken as a justification to create a "climate" conducive to negotiation. In the late 1980s, these were precisely the terms used by ANC and government officials. Within a number of different contexts, the claimed need to cultivate a climate for dialogue functioned as a reciprocal demand for each side to demonstrate its good faith. Distrustful of one another's motives and sincerity, concerned that expressed interest in negotiations was merely a tactical manoeuvre, and operating from different if not incommensurable visions of South Africa's future, prominent members of the ANC and NP turned to the language of reconciliation in order to fulfil this prerequisite. Defining the situation as a shared condition, a mutual collapse of the historical justifications for conflict, Nelson Mandela and F.W. de Klerk took centre stage in this process. In 1989 and 1990, both leaders fashioned, presented, and debated the case for reconciliation. In very similar ways, each argued for and enacted the idea that a climate for talk involved acknowledging the untenability of the moment and then risking some of the ideological-legal commitments that were rationalising violence. In the name of reconciliation, this release of self-certainty was a demonstration of good faith, a symbolic gesture that held the potential for beginning a process of talking about talk.

in a moment without words

Between past and future, the present appeared to hold little opportunity for action. At the start of 1986, journalist Stanley Uys argued from London that South Africa appeared poised to enter a "spiral of retaliation and counter-retaliation". With each side hardening their positions, he added that as "irreversible momentums are being created on both sides", the country sat on the brink of a "new and uncontrolled situation". The characterisation was apt. Despite a plea for P.W. Botha to "watch his words", Uys concluded that the "brief moment when government might have been able to talk to the ANC appears to have passed".[96] Soon after, van Zyl Slabbert echoed the diagnosis, declaring that apartheid could not be incrementally reformed and warning that the ANC's vision of liberation had detached itself from reality to the point of becoming a "romantic myth". Concluding that "peaceful change is no longer an option in South Africa", the assessment underscored the presence of *stasis*, a moment that appeared to contain neither space nor motive for words.[97]

By May of 1986, it was increasingly apparent that the government and liberation movement had entered a stage of struggle that was and yet could not be definitive. While some scrambled for a third way, Botha's continued promises of reform rang hollow and did nothing but provoke additional opposition.[98] Not surprisingly, the repeal of the pass laws and *Mixed Marriages Act* failed to prevent a significant rise in the number of indefinite detentions and deaths in police custody. On May Day, an estimated 1.5 million people participated in a national strike and stay-away, an event that was framed partly by Winnie Mandela's declaration that, "Together, hand in hand, with that stick of matches, with our necklace, we shall liberate this country."[99] At another extreme, the Afrikaner Weerstandsbeweging's (AWB) Eugene Terre'Blanche belittled government's strategy, predicted the limits of Afrikaner accommodation, and warned that if the state took the reformist course, "South Africa would suffer the biggest hell-revolution ever".[100] In between, the Mobil Oil Corporation ran advertisements in the nation's newspapers calling for "meaningful dialogue" as an alternative to South Africans undertaking to "march against each other only to find out there can be no winners, only survivors".[101] At the time, the company's call did not appear to have a significant audience.

In the wake of the strike, the ANC's *Sechaba* contended that parts of the country were in a "state of war" and claimed that as the country stood at a "point of no return", it was clearly time to admit that "apartheid cannot be reformed – it must be destroyed". Denouncing government proposals for "power sharing" as a façade for the undue "protection of minorities", the Congress then called on citizens to create further "ungovernability" and undertake "an ever greater escalation of the offensive on all fronts, an offensive based on mass resistance, on an intensified armed struggle and on growing refusal to obey racist authority".[102] As activists strengthened "people's militias" in the name of protecting themselves from state attacks, the government was opening its case at the Delmas treason trial and putting the finishing touches on the *Public Safety Amendment Bill,* a piece of legislation that appeared to allow Minister of Law and Order Louis Le Grange to "impose a virtually permanent state of emergency in any area he wishes without calling it a state of emergency".[103] While a further indication of how the space for speech was collapsing in the name of "order", the exercise was largely moot as the government declared a state of emergency on 12 June in anticipation of protests on the tenth anniversary of Soweto.

The onset of emergency corresponded precisely with the release of the report by the Eminent Persons Group (EPG). Charged first to gain an "accurate reading of the political pulse of the country", the EPG was an international delegation that toured the country, meeting with political, church, and business leaders from all sides of the South African ideological spectrum. Noting how it was "struck by the overwhelming desire in the country for a non-violent negotiated settlement", it concluded that the Botha government showed little genuine interest in reform and appeared far more resolved to continue the process of "government by semantics", a tactic designed to embed apartheid's logic into proposals for black political participation.[104] Warning that "if a major conflagration was to be averted time is running out", the group's report argued that while negotiations were vital, they were also premature without a prior and "major act of reconciliation", one that included the release of political prisoners (especially Mandela), a moratorium on violence, and the development of confidence-building measures designed to "allay suspicion and fear". In the midst of emergency, however, the delegation worried that government was unwilling to entertain such an effort to the degree that it clung to the "self-delusion" that victory could be attained by military force.[105]

Touring in support of international sanctions, Oliver Tambo delineated the Congress's position on negotiations, a stance predicated on the assumption that "we are at war against the apartheid system and its inhumanities".[106] The position was crucial, an explanation of how the Congress characterised the regime and questioned the standing of a "man-eating system" to enter credibly into talks about the abdication of its own power. In speeches delivered in London and Paris, Tambo maintained that the government was motivated solely by "racist principle or avaricious self-interest" such that it sought only the opportunity to employ the "sheer use of terror" to compel obedience and direct talks that were calibrated to produce only those reforms that would strengthen the "apartheid system of white minority domination by force".[107] Within a regime premised on the denial of its own inhumanity, apartheid's leaders were neither "ready for negotiations" nor trustworthy dialogue partners. Before there could be talk, Tambo claimed:

> Pretoria must prove its *bona fides*. It is not possible to negotiate with someone you totally distrust in regard to his aims about negotiation. We will not participate in giving the Pretoria regime the possibility of extending its lease of life by pretending to be negotiating. But it can demonstrate its serious intention to negotiate. Its words do not add up to anything. It is its actions that must speak.[108]

Echoed widely in the Congress, this view meant that negotiations could not be the basis of hope. At best, they were one "mode of struggle" among many. According to NEC member Pallo Jordan, legitimate talks would be those that aimed for the "liquidation of the antagonists as a factor in politics".[109] The apparent extremity of this position reflected the ANC's belief that the government was inherently duplicitous and wed to an ideological hypocrisy that was an enactment and a motive for its evil. At the same time, Jordan's claim underscored the ANC's view that negotiations were meaningless if they did not proceed from a clear and specific agenda. What would the talks be *about* and would they include discussion about the historical injustice of apartheid? As Thabo Mbeki put the matter, talks were a trap if the government was unwilling to make a "commitment to the underlying principles of democracy".[110] Lacking such an agreement, the Congress maintained that it would not cede to government's demand that it renounce

violence. Expressed most fully in the 1987 statement on the "illegitimacy of
the apartheid regime", the ANC argued that the government had no right
to assure its own survival at the cost of democracy that would end a crime
against humanity and open the door for reparation.[111]

Willing and unwilling to talk, the ANC's position on negotiations also
reflected its difficult organisational position. Spread across two continents, the
Congress was walking a tight line, particularly given growing tensions over
whether the internal or the exiled leadership counted as the true representative
of the people.[112] Cutting across the border, MK cadres were reported to fear
a sell-out by their leadership at just the moment when victory was in reach.
In response, pragmatists argued that negotiations could be pursued even as
plans were being laid for the "Battle of Pretoria". This two-track strategy was
defended as a way to keep consistent pressure on the government in light of
its unclear intentions and dismal track record at the negotiating table.[113]

While the ANC saw negotiations with government as a principled
(im)possibility and potentially the road to self-betrayal, the government's
stance was no less complicated. Also in June, the state published *Talking
with the ANC*, a tract that (re)announced the government's willingness to
"negotiate with citizens of South Africa, provided that they do not resort to
violence as a means of attaining their political and other goals".[114] With this
offer extended, the remainder of the document was a full indictment of the
ANC. Sparing no effort to demonstrate the Congress's formal alliance with
the SACP, the government claimed that the ANC was "committed to violent
overthrow of the present system for the purpose of seizing total power for
itself".[115] This allegedly revolutionary agenda was held up as proof that the
ANC was a "terrorist organisation" and intent to obscure that the number
of deaths caused by "black on black violence" far exceeded those killed by
security forces. Returning to the matter of talk, the booklet then claimed that
ANC policy documents proved how the Congress viewed negotiations "not
as a means for achieving mutually acceptable constitutional compromises, but
as a means to achieving total power".[116] In distinction to this "unreasonable"
position, the government presented its normative definition of productive
dialogue:

> Negotiation of necessity implies that participants should accept that
> not all their requirements are likely to be met; it implies a willingness
> to listen, to discuss and seek solutions. But these solutions will result
> from deliberations by South Africans in the interest of South Africans.[117]

Beneath SAG's claimed willingness to enter into the "right" kind of negotiations, there were evident and differing concerns about how to protect Afrikaner interests.[118] While the *verligtes* and *verkramptes* in Botha's cabinet argued about the relative necessity, content, and pace of reform, few appeared to disagree with Stoffel van der Merwe's claim that with respect to any possible negotiations, "The self-determination of each nation or population group over its own affairs and joint responsibility for those affairs which concern all of them will also have to be the central guideline for any further constitutional development."[119] Within this position, however, it remained unclear whether the government sought to prevent majority rule altogether or if it simply wanted to install a procedural or consociational democracy, one that would structurally protect the rights and interests of whites.[120] What was not in question: government wanted to control negotiations from start to finish and it did not want to be held accountable for the "mistakes and errors of previous administrations".[121]

As the government and ANC pressed their respective cases for why the situation contained no basis for dialogue, official and unofficial representatives from both sides were meeting secretly at locations in Africa, Europe, and the United States. A 1985 meeting in Lusaka between South African bankers and ANC leaders was given to the question of whether there was any "common ground" between the two groups, especially with respect to the question of South Africa's economic future.[122] Not long after, members of the Broederbond and the ANC's London leadership met to discuss the general contours of the situation in South Africa. Unwilling to meet officially, cabinet ministers used proxies beginning in 1987, individuals who were charged to discover the ANC's conditions for negotiations and whether it was possible to "cut through the middle" of the conflict.[123]

In this middle sat history, a set of causes and ideological commitments that were increasingly less an inspiration than a liability. In June of 1987, as violence escalated and the economy continued to crumble, a young NGO called the Institute for a Democratic Alternative in South Africa (IDASA) gambled that it was time to openly defy precedent and convene a meeting between high-ranking members of the ANC in exile and a group of mostly Afrikaans-speaking South Africans. Formed a year earlier by van Zyl Slabbert and Alex Boraine, the organisation sought to promote "negotiation politics", a process that Boraine did not differentiate from reconciliation.[124] Convened at a time of "grave political crisis", the gathering's announced agenda was to clarify the obstacles preventing talks between government and the liberation movement.

In the communiqué released after the meeting in Dakar, a document that was soundly condemned by P. W. Botha, delegates expressed their strong desire for a "negotiated resolution of the South African question" and argued that its potential depended on further efforts to dispel the "misunderstandings and fear" that separated the main protagonists. In this respect, the report argued that such obstacles were not insurmountable. Claiming that the meeting had been characterised by "an overwhelming atmosphere that this was part of the process of the South African people making history", it contended that there was a potential for talk and that its development hinged on the willingness of both sides to relinquish a bit of (sacred) ground. In principle and practice, dialogue depended on a certain renouncement of history, a repudiation of the ideological motives and legal precedents that were leading each side to conclude that the other was inhuman, driven exclusively by self-interest, and unable to participate in a rational discussion. Setting this problem in the light of day, the Dakar meeting and its counterparts were thus important precisely for their demonstration that the two sides did have something in common – an attachment to historically informed agendas that appeared no longer to serve their expressed goals. The recognition of this shared (self) opposition was the potential to begin talking. Writing after the meeting, van Zyl Slabbert warned that this potential was only that; the country remained in a "pre-negotiations phase" to the degree that there was not yet the "mood and [the] practical conditions for negotiations".[125] The historical fates of a situation had not yet been turned into the contingent climate needed for actual dialogue.

a climate out of two callings

As the "treasonous" members of the Dakar contingent returned to South Africa and as the government continued to deny that it was using intermediaries to talk with the ANC, the conflict's protagonists began to make a more refined case for negotiations. In October, the ANC noted that while it had "never been opposed to a negotiated settlement … we insist that before any negotiations take place, the apartheid regime would have to demonstrate its seriousness by implementing various measures to create a climate conducive to such negotiations". Included in these conditions was the release of political prisoners, the lifting of the state of emergency and withdrawal of security forces from the townships, and the repeal of all "repressive legislation" that restricted freedom of expression, association, and assembly.[126] A bit more single-minded, the government continued to contend that negotiations could not begin until the ANC renounced violence.

Over the following year, the Congress responded to SAG's demand in a number of discussion documents on negotiations. In them, the ANC claimed that there were increasing international pressures for talks and that the country's deepening economic and political crisis presented Pretoria with the "objective conditions" that justified negotiations. Noting that such moments had appeared before and resulted only in further repression, the ANC also reaffirmed that negotiation was only one part of its larger strategy to "keep the initiative in our hands" and pressure the government to take the steps needed to "create a climate" for talks. Adding a condition, it claimed that the government could not be both a player and a referee in any negotiating process. If dialogue was to occur, the two sides could not meet in the confines of Botha's National Council. Accordingly, the ANC's overall position was that talks would have to be prefaced by discussions about:

> [I]ssues [such] as the aim of any negotiations, the preconditions for
> genuine negotiations, the nature of the mechanisms for negotiation and
> therefore the question of who would sit at the negotiating table, the
> cessation of hostilities by both sides, the possibility of the formation of
> a transitional government, the duration of the negotiations and the role
> of the international community in any negotiated resolution of the South
> African question. Discussion of the whole question of negotiations in
> no way affects, and should not affect, the overall strategic orientation
> of our movement and the tasks that arise from that orientation. Our
> strategic task is the destruction of the apartheid regime and the transfer
> of power to the people. This we seek to achieve through mass political
> action, armed struggle, the international isolation of the apartheid system
> and by ensuring that the ANC plays its proper role as the revolutionary
> vanguard of our struggling people. The issue of negotiations has arisen
> precisely because of the advances we have made on all these fronts which
> have led to the emergence of the crisis of the apartheid system to which
> we have referred. We must continuously intensify our offensive on all
> these fronts with the sole aim of transforming South Africa into a united,
> democratic and non-racial South Africa.[127]

Read with the Communiqué from the Five Freedoms Forum, a declaration issued in early July from Zambia and signed by the ANC and over 100 white South Africans, the Congress's bottom line appeared to be that negotiations could not begin without proto-talks dedicated to defining their appropriate form and specific content.

While the ANC and SAG tarried over the conditions for starting a dialogue, the country's most famous political prisoner was busy refusing P.W. Botha's repeated offers of a conditional release at the same time that he was entering into discussions with select cabinet officials.[128] Transferred to the mainland from the prison on Robben Island in 1982, Mandela was approached by then Minister of Justice Kobie Coetsee to begin informal talks three years later, discussions that were expanded to include several others in 1987. Mandela's own descriptions of being driven around the Cape countryside during these meetings are poignant.[129] After being transferred first to Pollsmoor and then to Victor Verster Prison in late 1988, a facility where he lived in a small house and had significant access to visitors, Mandela undertook to see Botha, writing a letter to the President in early 1989 that led to a meeting in July, after Botha had recovered from a stroke.

Mandela's letter deserves close scrutiny. Focused on how the creation of a "proper climate for negotiations" required parties to go beyond "broadcasting their conditions for negotiations without putting them directly to each other", the letter spoke to the need for a beginning, a moment that could bring "the country's two major political bodies to the negotiating table". According to Mandela, his proposal was the result of a "crisis that has freed me to act", the appearance of a "spectre of a South Africa split into hostile camps; blacks on one side and whites on the other, slaughtering each other". Mandela, however, stood outside the scene, a prison inmate able to address the situation only indirectly, through a letter that expressed both his "open mind" and basic inability to enter into actual negotiations.

Mandela then shifted voice. Speaking for the ANC, he contended that while the Congress had "no vested interest in violence", the state's demand that it renounce the use of force prior to negotiations misunderstood that the struggle was a legitimate form of "self-defence against a morally repugnant system of government". This confusion indicated that the state was not prepared to negotiate; it remained unwilling to surrender "the monopoly of power" and negotiate in "good faith with the acknowledged black leaders". The underlying charge of hypocrisy is difficult to miss, a claim as to how the state had moved outside law, forgetting and forsaking the principles of the freedom fighter that were once vital to the Afrikaner campaigns against British domination. Turning back to the present, Mandela then argued that the "key to the whole situation is a negotiated settlement, and a meeting between the government and the ANC …". At this gathering, Mandela claimed that two "central issues" would need to be discussed:

> [F]irstly, the demand for majority rule in a unitary state; secondly,
> the concern of white South Africa over this demand, as well as the
> insistence of whites on structural guarantees that majority rule will not
> mean domination of the white minority by blacks. The most crucial task
> which will face the government and the ANC will be to reconcile these
> two positions. Such reconciliation will be achieved only if both parties
> are willing to compromise. The organisation will determine precisely
> how negotiations should be conducted. It may well be that this should
> be done at least in two stages. The first, where the organisation and
> the government will work out together the preconditions for a proper
> climate for negotiations …. The second stage would be the actual
> negotiations themselves when the climate is ripe for doing so. Any
> other approach would entail the danger of an irresolvable stalemate.[130]

Here, reconciliation means several things. It is first a kind of logical operation, a calculus for relating interests that appear incommensurable. At a larger level, reconciliation marks the conditions for speech, the path by which violence can give way to dialogue. Between the desire and fear of majority rule, accepting both at face value, there is a need for each party to risk itself, forsaking something of it-self in order to demonstrate sincerity to the other. Mandela's letter enacted this position. It was a call for action from outside the authority to which he was bound and a gesture that expressed a willingness to give of self in order to open the potential for talk.

By August there had been some 30 meetings between different representatives of the ANC and SAG, excluding those with Mandela. As *The Weekly Mail* wondered if the Congress was being unbanned by stealth, it did appear that a turning point had been reached. The parties were meeting face to face and there was an increasing sense that each could "do business" with the other. The *Mail* went public with the story that Mandela had been meeting with Coetsee, a report about which the government declined to comment and the ANC confirmed. Amidst concern over who had gained the most from the Botha-Mandela meeting, the ANC released the *Harare Declaration*. Approved by the Organisation of African Unity (OAU), the declaration lent tacit support for Mandela's calls for negotiations but repeated the standing conditions for their commencement. Addressing the question of how negotiations might work, the Congress contended that parties would need to secure a ceasefire, "negotiate the necessary mechanism for drawing up a new constitution", and undertake the "formation of an interim government" to oversee elections. Despite its claim to the contrary, the proposal left the ball firmly in the state's court.

The Nats (members of the National Party), however, were dealing with other matters. Shortly after his stroke, Botha resigned as leader of the party but stayed on as State President. This unprecedented move led to a brief leadership struggle from which F.W. de Klerk emerged victorious. When Botha made his caustic exit from politics shortly thereafter, attention turned to the new leader, an ambiguous figure who had played bit parts in the Cabinet and was read by many as a conservative. With this estimate Dave Steward disagrees, claiming that de Klerk had voted against Botha's piecemeal reforms because he believed that they were counterproductive in the face of the need for larger change.[131] In the campaign leading up to the September national election, de Klerk appeared to confirm something of this view, particularly as he claimed that apartheid was no longer working. In quick response, critics wondered if he had any views about its morality. A key supporter, Kobie Coetsee thought de Klerk "a man of his time". As it turned out, the new President was a man who could stand in neither past nor future.

On 20 September 1989, de Klerk's inaugural address had much to say about reconciliation. The mandate of the election, he argued, "places us irrevocably on the road to a new South Africa". By the same token, the President contended that the path ahead was not one of revolution: "We accept that time is of the essence and we are committed to visible evolutionary progress in various fields." While the hedge recalled Botha's reluctant reformism, de Klerk went on, citing the need to "turn our words into actions" and pleading for a "new spirit and approach in our fatherland". Claiming that progress had long been hampered by "suspicion and mistrust", the President declined to "argue about cause and effect on this occasion". Instead, he declared that "the time has come for unity within our diversity to take form". While de Klerk signalled that minorities needed protection from the effects of such change, his larger argument was an explicit call for reconciliation:

> Protest regarding past injustice or alleged injustice does not bring us
> closer to solutions either. Nor do unrest and violence. There is but one
> way to peace, to justice for all: That is the way of reconciliation; of
> together seeking mutually acceptable solutions; of together discussing
> what the new South Africa should look like; of constitutional
> negotiations with a view to a permanent understanding ...[132]

The argument was significant and controversial. Perhaps an unprecedented retreat, de Klerk's appeal led some to ask whether he was attempting to deflect attention away from apartheid's crimes. For others, the juxtaposition of reconciliation and violence suggested that the government was finally serious about beginning talks and that it might do so with some measure of good faith. In November, de Klerk challenged the ANC to "come test us, through dialogue and negotiation" and reiterated that he was committed to reform and convinced that attempts by whites to cling to power would only ensure the onset of civil war.[133]

Ensconced in his increasingly crowded house on the grounds of Victor Verster Prison, able to consult with more and more of his advisors and colleagues, Mandela sent de Klerk a letter prior to their meeting in December. In it, Mandela addressed the President's call for reconciliation, debating with him the term's precise meaning and its implications for talks. In a basic way, the letter was nothing less than a rhetorical criticism of de Klerk's inaugural address. To begin, Mandela questioned the government's sincerity, arguing that it had not committed to creating the "proper climate for negotiation" and that, in fact, the "whole approach of the Government to the question of negotiation with the ANC is totally unacceptable, and requires to be (*sic*) drastically changed". Citing de Klerk's "mere rhetoric", Mandela contended that the government's ongoing campaign of violence, including its unwillingness to recognise the ANC as a legitimate political organisation, was inconsistent with its announced agenda: "How does one work for peace and reconciliation under a State of Emergency?" Juxtaposing this question with the precise terms of de Klerk's appeal for reconciliation, Mandela argued:

> By reconciliation, in this context, was understood the situation
> where opponents, and even enemies for that matter, would sink their
> differences and lay down their arms for the purposes of working out a
> peaceful solution, where the injustices and grievances of the past would
> be buried and forgotten and a fresh start made. That is the spirit in which
> the people of South Africa would like to work together for peace.[134]

It would not be long before Mandela found reason to recant this call to forget. In the moment, however, the argument was much more about the demands of the present, the need to convince the government that it did not need to cling to the idea of group rights, and that it was time to meet and work out the "pre-conditions for negotiations".

Over the December holidays, plans were laid to address Mandela's challenge. In his autobiography, de Klerk recalls taking time to think about how to "give practical effect to our strategic framework for constitutional transformation" and undertake a (non-revolutionary) "paradigm shift".[135] On 2 February 1990, opening Parliament without the build-up that had surrounded Botha's 1985 Rubicon address, de Klerk delivered a speech that appeared to set the stage for apartheid's end.[136] Echoing many others, one commentator claimed that the speech was "a final, irreversible turning point in South Africa's history".[137] While the address was a crucial event, the assessment did not fit the particulars; very little was final, given that de Klerk's call for change appeared to rest on government's ability to direct both its means and its ends.

The shortcomings of de Klerk's address were not fully evident in the moment. Mary Burton recalls that the speech left crowds gathered on the Grand Parade for a People's Parliament in a sort of stunned exuberance. To begin, the President addressed the signs of the times, claiming that no citizen could escape the "simple truth" that without a "negotiated understanding" the country faced "growing tension, violence, and conflict". The situation was without a moment of choice: The "season of violence is over. The time for reconstruction and reconciliation has arrived." Holding that there was "no time left for advancing all manner of new conditions that will delay the negotiating process", de Klerk announced his decision to unban the ANC, PAC, and SACP, release 374 political prisoners being held under the emergency regulations, change laws regulating indefinite detention and media coverage of violence, and take the steps required to grant Nelson Mandela an immediate and unconditional release. With this speech-action, the President contended that he had performed the government's good faith and fulfilled the ANC's conditions for creating a climate for talks. Thus, de Klerk concluded, violent struggle was no longer justified and "the time for talking has arrived". There were, however, conditions. While accepting on the government's behalf "the principle of the recognition and protection of the fundamental individual rights which form the constitutional basis of most western democracies", de Klerk argued that the "normalisation of the political process" did not overrule the need to protect the rights of minorities.

For all that it said and did, de Klerk's speech was arguably not the most important of the week. In Parliament, debate over the President's vision was fierce as some wondered if de Klerk was delusional. One prominent critic from the Conservative Party accepted the significance of the speech but reversed its meaning, declaring that "the past few days will go on record in the history of this country as among the most traumatic and humiliating for the White population of South Africa and in particular the Afrikaner people, which regards this part of Africa as its heritage, its fatherland, its all. We are the focal point of our enemies' jubilation."[138] The leader of the official opposition, Andries Treurnicht, was no less worried, claiming that the NP had misread the situation and that its decision to negotiate with "terrorists" marked a "deadly threat" which had "reawakened the tiger in the Afrikaner".[139] While it was not clear who exactly was a threat to whom, Gerrit Viljoen, the Minister of Constitutional Development, responded to the roar with a speech that was equally if not more insightful than de Klerk's.[140]

Noting the pleasure of speaking when "history is being made, as it is now", Viljoen declared that the government's "new South Africa is no mere sweet-sounding rhetoric". The "now new" was a situation in which the "sincerity of our opponents (in the liberation movements) can specifically be tested". According to Viljoen, the test was a "sensible risk" and anything but the road to sure defeat; a turn from "White minority domination to a new situation of Black majority domination" was not "acceptable or feasible", particularly as government was aware that provision of the "full-fledged franchise to the very highest level of government" could not come at the expense of the "justified needs and demands of minorities – in particular those of the White population group". Such interests, he noted, included the rights of language, identity, free enterprise, and meaningful political participation. Nonetheless, as the security forces had advised the government that there was urgent need for a "political solution", Viljoen warned critics that the country stood at the limit of the law. Negotiations were necessary. It was time to enter into what Viljoen's Deputy Minister, Roelf Meyer, called "reconciliation politics". It was time to design the negotiations process and time to assume that "peace in South Africa may not only be achieved by speaking with those people who agree with us".[141] The now new was ready to begin.

the potential of a shared opposition
In the wake of de Klerk's speech, the London-based *Independent* editorialised that while there were no guarantees, conditions appeared to favour the beginning of negotiations. Citing the Eastern European experience, the paper suggested that, "given a degree of sincerity and goodwill, haggling between former enemies over what seem to be irreconcilable differences of power and principle need not necessarily be protracted".[142] Then and now,

the assessment is notable only for its conceptual incoherence. In 1990, it was precisely differences of power and principle that supported those calls for reconciliation which both explained and performed the sincerity and goodwill needed to speak about the initiation of talks. This dynamic is frequently overlooked, particularly given that standard accounts of how negotiations began tend to bracket the question of how each side argued about the appropriate form of negotiations and the conditions under which they were willing to enter into discussions.

Between late 1986 and February 1990, South African political leaders perceived a violent situation and acknowledged that it was a shared reason to appeal for reconciliation in the name of creating a climate of good faith that could support not just talk but speech that held the potential for joint history-making. Thus, understood as a form of "language trouble", the *stasis* that appeared in 1986 was not simply the physical clash of apartheid forces and people's power. It was also composed of multiple historical contradictions, all of which were shaping and sustaining the form of the clash. First, the SAG and the ANC both confronted a moment in which the terms of their expressed justifications for violence became inimical to the goals that they claimed to serve. For the government, the Total Strategy left it caught in an untenable middle, a bad infinity in which reforms were *necessary* but had to be enforced through a state of emergency. Searching for legitimacy, the government faced constituents turned critics as well as a campaign of ungovernability that it could not quell but which it met with a form of violence that demonstrated law's disconnection from justice. With history's calling of the Afrikaner betraying itself, the ANC longed for a revolution, one that it could prosecute but never win. Thus, the Congress's call to render South Africa ungovernable set its tactics into deep tension with its strategy; the path to victory was a conflict that appeared to require the sacrifice of non-racialism. As the battle within the state of emergency escalated toward civil war, the unity of the nation through struggle risked the complete fracture of both.

Second, the shortfall of history's "causes" was also a relational problem, a conflict driven by ideologies that reduced the ground for communication to respective charges of fascist inhumanity and revolutionary terror. Added to this dysfunctional mix were unilateral proclamations about the preconditions, object, and norms of negotiation. Bound to historical positions that had the status of (juridical and ideological) law, the trouble with language was its perpetuation of a situation in which there was no basis for trust and few shared referents between parties. On both sides, the call to negotiate was heard as a request to capitulate to evil. In this way, the *stasis* was a conceptual and rhetorical dilemma within each camp, a collapse of justification and the inability to articulate coherently the grounds for action. Historical, legal, or ideological, the reasons for conflict were warrants for endless violence, the hostility of life raised to the level of total war.

While meetings like the one in Dakar were significant demonstrations that the inhuman Other was human after all, the turn to negotiations was bolstered by public statements that cast the situation as a *shared reason* to create a climate for dialogue. At the limit of cause and necessity, the *stasis* was a (self) opposition held in common. In the 1988 and 1989 debate over whether either side wanted even to consider the idea of negotiations, the recognition of this thin mutuality developed slowly, finding its fullest expression in Nelson Mandela and F.W. de Klerk's detailed appeals for reconciliation. However, this risking of self-certainty transcended exactly nothing. Appeals to reconciliation marked a mutual acknowledgment of the *stasis* and a reciprocal recognition that each side would have to give up something of its historical calling if there was ever to be an occasion to sit down at the negotiating table and argue about how to create meaningful change. Hardly mere rhetoric, the appeals by de Klerk and Mandela were speech acts that performed key elements of the good faith needed to gather just enough trust to sit down and broach the question of how to make history outside the confines of law. While de Klerk's speech of 2 February was far more dramatic, and an indication that it was indeed the government who had to give first, the efforts of both leaders met with praise as well as accusations from powerful quarters that they had sold out their respective constituencies.[143] In any case, the shift from situation to climate was subtle and vital. As they expressed the need and willingness to forget something of the past, arguments about reconciliation opened a slim present in which to talk about the future.

3. trading history for words (about words)

In the midst of an endless conflict, appeals for reconciliation helped open space for "talks about talks", preliminary discussions about the form and substance of constitutional negotiations and, equally important, how to reduce the violence that was continuing to escalate in many parts of the country. Between February 1990 and the start of all-out constitutional negotiations in late 1991, these issues were inseparable. While the ANC pegged the beginning of constitutional reform on the state's demonstration that it would not retaliate against those engaged in mass action, the government continued to demand that the Congress suspend its armed struggle. As each side waited for the other to act, the underlying issue was how to build trust. How could each side forget the offences of the other in the name of talking? How far could good faith be pushed? Could appeals for reconciliation be rendered practical?

Over the course of 19 months, the talks about talk were a crucial step forward. They were not, however, history making. Instead, my contention here is that these meta-discussions cultivated the climate for negotiations partly by exposing the ways in which history was limiting the potential for dialogue. A key result of the talks, the 1990 *Indemnity Act* was an important and controversial means of redressing this problem. Justified on the grounds of reconciliation, the legislation was an important factor in the ANC's decision to suspend armed struggle. More directly, its provision of temporary indemnity from prosecution created a space for negotiations insofar as it allowed wanted or indicted ANC leaders to return from exile and take their place at the table. In this way, the indemnity legislation was a symbolically loaded breach in the rule of law, an exception to the emergency's exception that demonstrated the state's willingness to defy (ideological) precedent in the name of pursuing constitutional reform. From the shared opposition of *stasis* to an indemnity that opened a field of oppositional argumentation, the talks about talk enacted a necessary pivot, a moment in which the potential for reconciling words was set squarely between past and future.

speaking with(in) indemnity

Nelson Mandela was released from prison on 11 February 1990. Nine days after de Klerk's speech to Parliament, the scene at the future President's first public address in nearly 30 years was a festive chaos, due variously to poor planning, a delay in Mandela's release from Victor Verster, and the government's desire to script the event in order to bank credits for its "generosity". Arriving very late to greet an exuberant, tired, and somewhat inebriated crowd gathered on Cape Town's Grand Parade, Mandela's words may not have been fully his own. In an address that resonated with ANC committee-speak, Mandela declared that it was time to create a "climate conducive to a negotiated settlement", praised de Klerk as a "man of integrity", and then set some audiences on edge by contending that the country faced a "decisive moment" in which to "intensify the struggle on all fronts".[144]

It was perhaps not a time for accommodation. While an icon of the struggle, Mandela's position in the ANC was uncertain, especially given that some

Congress members were continuing to express doubts about the wisdom of his decision to negotiate privately with government officials. At a larger level, the tenor of the speech reflected deep concern over de Klerk's claim that any negotiated settlement would have to include substantial but yet unspecified protections for whites. Two days later, the tone did soften. Speaking at a rally in Soweto, Mandela claimed that it was vital to control the struggle amidst the rising tides of violence. Recalling his speech from the dock at the 1964 Rivonia trial, Mandela acknowledged the fear attending his release and urged all members of the struggle to harmonise their words and deeds in the name of demonstrating the good faith need for inclusive change:

> A number of obstacles to the creation of a non-racial democratic South
> Africa remain and need to be tackled. The fears of whites about their
> rights and place in a South Africa they do not control exclusively are an
> obstacle we must understand and address. I stated in 1964 that I and the
> ANC are as opposed to black domination as we are to white domination.
> We must accept however that our statements and declarations alone will
> not be sufficient to allay the fears of white South Africans. We must
> clearly demonstrate our goodwill to our white compatriots and convince
> them by our conduct and arguments that a South Africa without
> apartheid will be a better home for all.[145]

Mandela's position gave public voice to the view of reconciliation that he had detailed in his 1989 letter to Botha. At a basic level, the potential for a negotiated solution hinged on containing violence, creating the common ground needed for dialogue and finding the means needed to define and enable "democratic political practice".[146]

First and foremost, reaction to Mandela's release brought optimism.[147] *The Weekly Mail* hailed his reappearance as a "turning point for the nation". Citing the possibility for national unity and concrete reform, Desmond Tutu lauded de Klerk and suggested that a general amnesty for political prisoners would foster just the sort of goodwill needed to speed the onset of negotiations. Others were less sure. While representatives from the CP decried Mandela's release as a "complete capitulation", the government argued that Mandela was but one important element in the equation. Warning that black domination would thwart reforms geared to the somewhat nebulous "normalisation of political life", de Klerk declared again that his efforts had helped create "a climate for negotiations" and suggested that the ANC had no good reason to put off the start of negotiations.

While the shebeens ran dry in celebration and others hit the bottle in worry over their future lot, Mandela toured the world, meeting with key allies and ANC President Oliver Tambo, who was recovering from a serious stroke. Organisationally, the ANC was less in turmoil than transition. Expectations of Mandela's release had not yet crystallised into a clear plan for how to reintegrate the organisation's most-popular-member-without-a-title. What's more, the Congress' unbanning brought substantial pressure from media, questions about the ANC's vision of negotiated change and how it planned to set up operations in South Africa in order to "re-emerge as a legal, political force".[148] To some extent, these ambiguities suggested that de Klerk did have the upper hand in defining the means and ends of negotiations. In March, the two sides met secretly in London, a gathering that featured significant discussion about the status of those in exile who faced prosecution if they returned home. Shortly thereafter, with the issue far from resolved, the National Intelligence Service smuggled the ANC's Jacob Zuma and Penuell Maduna into the country so that they could serve on a committee charged to design a set of "talks about talks".[149]

With negotiations about the potential to negotiate on the horizon, the problem of violence took centre stage. De Klerk was unrelenting in his call for the ANC to abandon armed struggle. In mid-March, the ANC's Mosiuoa (Terror) Lekota argued that the country's so-called unrest was both an expression of relief over Mandela's release and a means of ensuring that the government kept its word. Steven Friedman, a political scientist and columnist for *The Weekly Mail*, countered that the escalating violence had much to do with the poor organisation of local politics, scepticism amongst youth about a negotiated settlement, and long-brewing tensions between the UDF and ANC.[150] In the weeks that followed, as the nation watched the return of some long-exiled ANC leaders and the tense Namibian independence celebration, clashes between protestors and police grew more fierce. Things were especially bloody in Natal, where Mandela was seen to tour the "valley of death", an area outside of Peitermaritzburg that was wracked regularly by intense clashes between UDF-ANC supporters on one side and members of the Inkatha Freedom Party (IFP) on the other. Taking stock of the situation, Mandela accused the police of inaction and suggested more subtly that they might be working jointly with the IFP.

Police passivity was not necessarily the largest problem. In the wake of the Sebokeng massacre in late March, the ANC condemned the security forces, arguing that "people staging peaceful demonstrations are being shot down in cold blood". Upping the ante, the Congress declared that state-sponsored violence was cause to cancel a scheduled meeting with government officials.[151] The boycott was read by some through a different lens, a view that fed accusations as to how the ANC was not in control of its membership and ill-prepared to begin talks. Mandela characterised the criticism as a shallow tactic and vowed that the Congress would not allow "the government to preach peace on one hand and conduct a war against us on the other".[152] The violence was not, however, limited to the townships. On 12 April, the media reported allegations that ANC forces had tortured several individuals suspected of mutiny in one of its Angolan training camps. While the ANC acknowledged the problem and promised a timely inquiry, critics charged that the Congress was operating with its own double standard.[153] Meanwhile, commentators worried about a "right-wing counter revolution" after a group of Afrikaners stormed an Air Force base and made off with a substantial arms cache. The perceived risk of a backlash was not appeased as the Harms Commission convened to hear testimony about the composition and violent activities of the so-called third force, including the Civil Cooperation Bureau (CCB) and Vlakplaas Unit. In a different venue, a court heard stories about the fatal beating of Stompie Moeketsi by Winnie Mandela's "Football Club".

With myriad forms, violence seemed ubiquitous. Over the course of the year, some 2500 individuals would die in political-related violence.[154] By a kind of sheer necessity, there was progress. On 2 May 1990, just days after Father Michael Lapsley opened a near fatal parcel bomb, 11 members of the ANC met with their NP counterparts at the Groote Schuur Estate outside of Cape Town. *The Weekly Mail* pronounced the gathering "epoch making", an event in which negotiators succeeded in staking the "middle ground" from those on both sides of the political spectrum that opposed talks. After the meeting, Thabo Mbeki reflected, " We were all a bit surprised ... within a matter of minutes, everyone understood that there was no one in the room who had horns – and that in fact, this discussion ought to have taken place years ago." His father, Govan, was more eloquent about the matter, borrowing from the Latin to note that, "From Africa, always something new comes ... Strange things happen." Less enthusiastic, Mandela took the realist's position, suggesting that the new was still contingent on a significant struggle against history:

> This is the first time in 78 years that a truly serious meeting takes
> place between delegations of the ANC and the succession of white

governments that have ruled our country for generations. It indicates
the deadly weight of the terrible tradition of a "dialogue" between
master and servant which we have to overcome.[155]

The Groote Schuur meeting was the first official attempt to talk about talk.
In the name of discerning the conditions needed to open actual negotiations,
the meeting focused heavily on how to end or at least contain violence in
a manner that would allow the government to lift the state of emergency.
As well, the two sides began to compare their visions of transition, an issue
that immediately raised contentious questions about the relative need for an
interim government and the protection of minority rights.

Something was being grown. While it was still early days, the meeting
at Groote Schuur offered tangible hope, especially as it allowed negotiators
a chance to "season our minds" and develop a "political ecology for
negotiations".[156] In the name of a "common commitment toward the
resolution of the existing climate of violence and intimidation" negotiators
agreed to several things, all of which were summed up in the *Groote Schuur
Minute* that was released at the conclusion of the talks. For one, the two
sides pledged to create efficient channels of communication to curb violence.
More important, the *Minute* authorised the formation of a working group
charged to define "political offences" and advise negotiators on "norms and
mechanisms" for the release and indemnification of political prisoners. In the
meantime, the government agreed to consider "temporary immunity from
prosecution" for select members of the ANC.

The terms of the *Minute* paved the way for the 1990 *Indemnity Act*. Signed
on 15 May, the Act's preamble explained the law's rationale: "Whereas for
the sake of reconciliation and for the finding of peaceful solutions it has
now become necessary from time to time to grant temporary immunity
or permanent indemnity against arrest, prosecution, detention, and legal
process ...".[157] For the promotion of "constitutional change in South Africa",
the Act granted de Klerk the power to indemnify those facing charges for
the commission of politically related crimes. Four days after its passage,
38 individuals were named as immune from criminal and civil prosecution
for 90 days. Appearing in the *Government Gazette*, the list featured many
of the ANC's high leadership, including Oliver Tambo, Chris Hani, Mac
Maharaj, Joe Slovo, and Pallo Jordan.

The *Indemnity Act* was not simply the early fruit of preliminary negotiations.
It was also the government's counter to ANC calls for a blanket amnesty, a

proposal that was rejected by Kobie Coetsee in early 1990. Soon enough, the tables would turn. In the moment, however, the government's position was that a limited indemnity would help create space for talk while ensuring that it could keep a measure of control over the process. Nevertheless, the Act was passed only after a fiery debate in Parliament. Amidst loud complaints about how the NP had become the ANC's "useful idiots", the law was attacked for three reasons. First, several claimed that indemnity was a slippery-slope. In this regard, the CP's Pieter Gous argued that "the legislation before us today is merely the beginning of a long process that lies ahead. The next step will be one man, one vote. The next step will be a communist or socialist government. The next step will be the total redistribution of wealth in this country."[158] To some, it appeared that the causes of Afrikaner history still called for vigilant defence. Second, critics argued that the law placed too much power with the executive and questioned how de Klerk would decide who was eligible for indemnity. Did the President have the authority to grant even a temporary reprieve to those accused of murder? Third, the opposition argued that indemnity for "terrorists" served to make "political opponents out of the state". Going further, the CP's Frank Le Roux maintained that "What it boils down to is that one promotes the administration of justice by suspending sound dispensation of justice. This kind of action by the Government hampers effective administration of justice, by which criminal procedure or civil procedure will be pursued in the event of a crime being committed."[159] Taking the position further, one critic complained that the proposed indemnity undermined law solely on the grounds of a "soppy preamble" and an intention to seek "reconciliation with the forces of darkness".[160]

Leaving aside the racist double entendres and paranoid invective, a key part of the opposition's argument was correct: indemnity was helping to *make* political opponents and its provision did raise basic questions about the relationship between law and justice. In the name of negotiations that had the necessarily extra-constitutional function of ending the standing dispensation, indemnity marked a significant precedent, one that would come to have controversial implications over the course of the coming transition. At the start of the talks about talks, however, the Act was defended as a way to ensure that a fragile climate did not devolve back to a violent situation. Precisely, one MP noted that indemnity was not unprecedented and that its use had occurred at other "watershed times in our history".[161] This appeal sat in close relation to Farouk Cassim's claim that it offered a basis for dialogue without the abdication of self-interest:

The Bill does more. Firstly, it demonstrates to all political parties that negotiations are more potent than armed struggle. Secondly, it allows for authoritative leaders in exile to return home, to fill the vacuum, and to establish strict discipline where disorder and mayhem are now rampant. Thirdly, it demonstrates that this Government is serious about negotiations. Fourthly, it will help to normalise political activity in our country, and fifthly, it empowers the State President to keep the momentum of the negotiations going.[162]

Backed by this pragmatic defence, supporters of indemnity offered a response to Le Roux's philosophical-political objection. Quoting Grotius, Raymond Radue contended to fellow parliamentarians that the law of peace follows a forgiving of "the offenders, charges, and damages of war".[163] Similarly but with more detail, the Democratic Party's (DP) Mudene Smuts set amnesty in relation to the "compelling need for political reconciliation" and argued that the "Indemnity Bill introduces a year of grace" into the political situation. This was a key point – amnesty did grant standing to old adversaries. As a "radical gesture of generosity and grace", Smuts thus defended the Bill's exception to law precisely because it "suspends judgment, so that we may learn to live together".[164] Noting that apartheid's law had condoned and carried out atrocities and subverted the "ideals of law and order", she concluded, "We must try to make a new beginning in South Africa, although it is important to realise that a nation cannot be made *de novo*." Perhaps "*ex nihilo*" would have been more apt. At stake in indemnity was the question of what could and could not be carried forward in the name of building a foundation for talk.

Towards the end of the debate over the *Indemnity Act*, the Chairman of the Minister's Council for the House of Delegates, Dr Jagaram Reddy, argued that the legislation deserved support "so that the spirit of reconciliation can become a password in the life of all South Africans, so that reconciliation permeates the hearts and minds of South Africans and so that we can enter into discussion and dialogue in that spirit".[165] The sentiment appeared to be widely shared. Amnesty was the counterpart of reconciliation, an exception to the law that bracketed the force of its precedent in order to create a time and space for dialogue. What's more, the ruling party's willingness to set aside its own law was both an expression of trust and, somewhat cynically, an invitation for "criminals" to demonstrate that they were otherwise. With indemnity, the ground for politics sat between past and future; a present appeared in which it was possible to interact without outright fear of retribution or an ability to dictate the outcome of discussion. As such, indemnity's potential for reconciliation was the (extra)legal correlate of the calls made by Mandela and de Klerk in 1989. It was a symbolic admission that standing (and contested) norms of justice would not suffice and that their suspension offered an opportunity to undertake the task of writing a new constitution. In these terms, indemnity was the discourse-enabling exception to the rule of the emergency.

at the limit of talking about talk

With talk now more than a possibility, negotiators faced questions about how to compose its substance. Except in Natal, the state of emergency was lifted in June. Along with the *Indemnity Act*, its end allowed leaders to talk even as it did little for the thousands that remained in prison and exile, most of whom were waiting for word as to the specific "political offences" that would be covered by the legislation. While the matter was discussed, the government stepped up its case for the ANC to suspend military action, arguing that it was an appropriate (reciprocal) response to indemnity. The ANC refused, claiming that a cessation of struggle would occur only as negotiations made concrete progress. As defined by the Congress, such gains included a firm agreement about who would write the country's new constitution and the need for an interim government. Favouring a quick transition, the government rejected the latter and argued that the constitution needed to be written not by an elected assembly but a body composed of an equal number of representatives from all sides. The government gained some leverage for its position when several ANC leaders – including Mac Maharaj – were arrested and charged with overseeing *Operation Vula*, a plan to smuggle large numbers of weapons into the country in order to dramatically increase attacks on the state. Was the ANC playing both sides off the middle?

In early August of 1990, negotiators met again and issued the *Pretoria Minute*. The agreement was important on several levels. First, it accepted the Groote Schuur working group's finding about the criteria that would determine eligibility for indemnity. Derived largely from the Norgaard Principles, standards that had been devised for the transition in Namibia, they required government to consider the motive of the perpetrator, the context of the offence, the nature of its political objective, and whether its means were proportional to the ends sought.[166] Second, the *Minute* declared that the ANC was "suspending all armed actions with immediate effect". However, the Congress maintained that its cessation of violence rested heavily on the government's efforts to speed up the indemnification of prisoners. Finally, the agreement authorised the formation of a committee charged to explore the possibility of an all-party conference that would take the country to the next stage of reform.

In the months following the Pretoria meeting, hoping that talk about talk would move to talk itself, South Africa sat on edge, able to do little more than make a kind of bloody progress. In late 1990, the NP opened its ranks to all races and the NGK took steps to unify its long segregated congregations. While tangible symbols, the queues to join were usually not long. In the eastern part of the country, thousands were dying in a ferocious conflict that showed little sign of abating. The indemnity process was moving at a painfully slow pace, with only 60 out of several thousand cases resolved by October. Addressing the moment's tension, Steven Friedman argued that if South Africa was to move past deadlock, negotiators had to embrace a spirit of compromise that could get them beyond posturing for control and towards actual discussion about how to write a constitution. In his year-end address to the nation, de Klerk showed few signs of such spirit, arguing that "the time has come for the ANC to decide what they want" and contending that the Congress had "reverted to outdated rhetoric and policies that form the flames of confrontation".[167] To the President's critics, the accusation was a bluster designed to obscure the NP's unwillingness to cede at least some control over the negotiations process.

Good faith was being stretched to its limit. While the talks about talk continued, it was increasingly clear that the parties disagreed deeply about how to define the purpose, form, and procedure of full constitutional negotiations. In February, a year after his most important speech to Parliament, de Klerk announced that the government was strictly opposed to the ANC's "idea of an elected constituent assembly" on the grounds that the "negotiation of a new constitution should be the responsibility of all parties which enjoy proven support and are committed to a peaceful and negotiated solution". Additionally, the President rejected the call for an interim government and proposed that the "time has arrived for a multi-party conference".[168] With respect to the latter, de Klerk urged all South Africans to embrace his "manifesto for the New South Africa", a document that was notable for its clear statement about the need to create a "free and democratic political system". While praising both the manifesto and the President's promise to repeal the legislative pillars of apartheid during the coming year, the

Congress' National Executive condemned de Klerk's "insistence that the minority regime which had no legitimacy in the eyes of the majority of our people, presides over the transition to democracy".[169] Issued in February, the ANC's "Advance to National Democracy" went a step further, claiming that the transition would be a minority-driven façade if it proceeded without an elected constituent assembly and an interim government. Given this risk, the Congress declared that it would continue to view negotiations as one "terrain of intense struggle" among many.

In late summer, dispute over the nature of transition collided with the other problem that was complicating the move to larger negotiations – escalating violence. On 15 April, the ANC ran adverts in several national newspapers claiming that the "success of the peace process" depended on a "mutual trust" which was being undermined by the government's continuing repression in the townships. It also faulted the state for its failure to take action against IFP supporters who were allegedly targeting and killing its members. A week later, the Congress argued that "this wave of violence is the greatest obstacle to the negotiating process" and declared that unless government acted by 9 May to reduce the bloodshed, it would boycott de Klerk's all-party meeting.[170]

This position was, arguably, part of a larger gambit. In its statements, the ANC suggested that de Klerk's meeting was a diversion intended both to cover up the government's failure to speed the release of political prisoners and to create momentum for the unjustified protection of minority rights. Mandela spoke to the latter issue at Pretoria University on 29 March, arguing that "whites are living in a volcano", and addressing the crowd in Afrikaans about the ANC's commitment to non-racial democracy.[171] Two days later, Mandela was more forthright. In a May Day address, he accused government of forgetting that the aim of the struggle was liberation and "not simply to sit down and engage in talks or negotiations". Citing its unwillingness to help reduce violence, Mandela demanded that the state synchronise its talk and action:

> On television screens, the whole nation has seen and heard witnesses testifying to the failure of the police to stop attacks, and in some cases actual involvement. Yet, what action have the authorities taken? The next days, as we come to May 9th are very crucial ones for all South Africans. They will determine whether or not our hopes of moving forward quickly towards the establishment of a non-racial, non-sexist

democratic society in our country are to be dashed even before we have begun to negotiate. Important decisions have to be made and action taken, to establish the bona fides, the sincerity and the true intentions of those who have talked peace and yet unleashed this violence and devastation upon innocent people. Let there be no mistake, no misunderstanding. The gravity of the situation does not allow for rhetorical gestures of any kind.[172]

An indication that talk about talk had not yet opened space for negotiation, Mandela's position signalled that good faith might not be enough to carry the country forward. Along with the need to contain violence, the key question was who would lead the all-party talks. Just prior to its 9 May deadline, the ANC again claimed that de Klerk could not be a player and a referee in the reform process, an argument that appeared to foreclose the Congress's participation at the President's proposed meeting and which motivated church leaders to offer their help in designing an alternative gathering. A week after, Mandela and de Klerk met secretly to take up the question of how to reduce the intense blood-letting that was occurring in the hostels on the reef. Increasingly blunt, Mandela's reaction was that the talks were on a knife-edge and that de Klerk had "no regard for the black man's life".[173] Within a month, just after Mandela was elected ANC President, the charge took on greater significance when it was revealed that the government had trained IFP cadres and provided them with weapons. Dubbed "Inkatha-gate", the scandal lent credibility to the ANC's claim that the transition from apartheid required an interim government.[174]

After several months of unproductive disagreement, the chance to make progress appeared in mid-August. Coupled with the United Nation's commitment to help repatriate exiles, the groups that had offered to convene a "neutral" all-party conference proposed the outlines for the *National Peace Accord* (NPA). Hailed by Laurie Nathan as an "extraordinary and daring experiment in conflict resolution", the Accord created a specific organisational structure to address the problem of violence and was signed by all the major political parties.[175] Employing local and regional "peace committees" and authorising the creation of the Goldstone Commission to investigate the scope and causes of public-political violence, the NPA appeared to set the stage for larger negotiations, especially as it was a step toward "developing a peace culture" and providing evidence that protagonists had the capacity to agree on "norms of political conduct".[176] In this way, the Accord's signing in

September brought to a close the talks about talks. At some level, with yet a long way to go, there was almost trust enough to tarry.

Between 1987 and late 1991, the South African Government and the ANC moved from the "language trouble" of *stasis* to a climate amenable to talking about talk. In considering the significance of this shift, it is important to remember that the turn from violence to dialogue began in secret, with unannounced and plausibly deniable interactions that defied precedent and refused accountability. Perhaps reflecting nationalisms that had long wrestled to understand the secrets of the word's power, there appeared a need for speaking which demonstrated that speech was possible. Not without purpose or even strategy, this was cause enough, especially at a moment when the causes of history appeared only to counsel and condone violence. Then and now, the cost of this gain is a mystery of faith, a marked inability to know fully why words were necessary. More concerned with how this faith of beginning was given public form, my aim in this chapter has been to detail some of the ways in which calls for reconciliation were used to delineate, compose, and justify the potential for speech. In this regard, the process of talking about talk was less about reaching agreement than discerning the basis for a contentious unity from within the midst of deep difference. More precisely, the beginning of reconciliation performed by the talks about talk (re)figured enemies as opponents, a turn that bracketed the past in the name of creating space for future dialogue.

In 1989 and 1990, the secret of talk grew from the appearance of a shared condition. Confronted with a situation in which ideological justifications for action appeared to violently negate their own aims, leaders from both the South African Government and the ANC began to recognise that their mutually untenable position was itself a reason to begin talking. At first, these calls for dialogue were riddled with unspoken agendas and dismissed as the duplicitous designs of tyrants and terrorists. With time and "normalising" contact, the outright refusal of negotiation turned to the question of its preconditions, a problem that saw each side delineate its definition of reasonable and productive interaction. Developed most fully by F.W. de Klerk and Nelson Mandela, these discourses about the conditions for discourse were set within appeals for reconciliation, a process that was claimed to involve the setting aside of historical-legal grievances in the name of creating a climate for productive talk. After the release of Mandela, the two sides waited for the other to offer a sign that it was indeed interested in breaking from the past. This willingness to risk identity, allegiance, and power was defined repeatedly as the need for each party to present a sign of good faith. Backed by the unprecedented meeting at Groote Schuur, the *Indemnity Act* was a crucial and controversial piece of legislation, one that saw the government let go – at least temporarily – of its commitment to law in the name of undertaking reconciliation-oriented discussion. The ANC's subsequent decision to suspend armed struggle – at least temporarily – counted as a reciprocal gesture insofar as its campaigns against the state were tied to the duties embedded in international human rights law. Viewed together, these actions demonstrated that reconciliation and negotiation politics were inextricably tied. From within a shared situation set to escalate out of control, the expressed desire to create a climate for talk involved recognising the common humanity of the enemy and opening a space in which it was possible to undertake meta-discussion about how to define the means and ends of negotiated constitutional change.

The talks about talks both performed and held the potential for reconciliation. At one level, they were a "meeting in the middle" that enacted reconciliation's (non)definitive power, the capacity to craft an opportunity for speech from within the apparent collapse of language. At another level, the onset of talk was just that, an occasion to create the basis for something new; reconciliation's calling contained the potential to make history with words. Its terms marked the beginning of a beginning, a fragile moment bound by the tentative good faith of words. As implied in the Latin, these *bona fides* were a mode and expression of rhetorical character, ones with which leaders set aside their respective laws in the name of constituting and making good on their promise. The power of this *ethos*, however, did not constitute fate. In late 1991, there was dialogue about the conditions for dialogue. While a vast step, this work expressed the formal potential of reconciliation's beginning. The expectations of the new year would bring the question of whether its promise had a substantive component: Could reconciliation move the country from a shared to a productive opposition, a debate given to defining the terms of a new constitution that (re)enacted a unity in difference? With this problem, the law returned, a (re)appearance of sovereignty that would confound, stretch, and then warrant reconciliation's constitutive faith.

3

reconciling the sovereign's discourse: constituting the "sufficient consensus" of a revolution

We declare that there is no unbridgeable gap between unity and diversity.
CODESA Press Release

Differences have been, and differences there will always be.
Frank Mdlalose

All decisions carried through a process of sufficient consensus must be implemented.
Chris Hani

And only if it is possible to think the relation between potentiality and actuality differently – and even to think beyond this relation – will it be possible to think a constituting power wholly released from the sovereign ban.
Giorgio Agamben

reconciliation begins in the creation of a consensus that holds constitutive power before the law. By the end of 1990, the question of how to fashion such agreement marked the limit of meta-dialogue. In practical terms, the problem was articulated well by the Institute for Contextual Theology's *Violence: The New Kairos*, a short tract which argued that optimism was changing to anger as "the talks about talks have not really changed the conditions of life in the townships". High hopes aside, the Institute warned that calls for reconciliation were little more than idle abstractions in situations that compelled "people to plead for arms to defend themselves against attack".[1] The path of the third way was blocked by the violence of more than one third force. On the ground, *stasis* was a continuing form of life. Now or perhaps never, it was time for the good faith of talk to make a difference.

Between the end of 1991 and the beginning of 1994, South African political leaders negotiated and fought over how to define, design, and create a constitution that would take South Africa beyond apartheid. From the start of CODESA to its near "blood on floor" breakdown and to the slow process of gathering the pieces and opening the MPNP, the process of making good on the talks about talks proved more difficult than many had first imagined. Stretching good faith, the work of constitution-making brought problems that raised the temperature of an already delicate climate.[2] Could negotiators learn to argue and disagree with one another in a productive manner? Who had the authority to define the form and terms of a new constitution? Would it contain a provision for power-sharing or include explicit "minority rights"? Did the process of writing the new constitution require or portend an amnesty for those who ordered and carried out apartheid's crimes? To whom was the constitutional negotiations process accountable? Did constitution-making require or break the rule of law that it aimed to make new?

Held up as the definitive start of the transition from apartheid, South Africa's constitutional negotiations have attracted significant attention and commentary, particularly from those interested in the dynamics of regime change and democratisation. Indeed, a variety of conceptual lenses have been used to understand what happened over the course of South Africa's "negotiated revolution", including rational choice analysis of individual and group decision-making; institutional-structural accounts of how the South African business and international political community supported change; bargaining studies concerned with the way in which elite pacts served to demobilise civil society and stabilise the reform process; and interpersonal accounts of how key leaders broke from prescribed positions in order to forge transformative relationships with their counterparts.[3] For some, however, these approaches have proven unsatisfying to the degree that they rely on theoretical perspectives which assume the existence of precisely those goods that must be created within the process of transition. Following David Howarth and Donald Horowitz's argument that the operation of a transition cannot be cogently explained by the political values that may only (or not) follow from it, this dilemma has motivated inquiry into the actual dynamics of the South Africa constitutional negotiations in the name of understanding precisely how these interactions composed the turn from apartheid to non-racial democracy.[4] With few exceptions, however, these investigations have focused on the substantive dimensions of the talks – the content of the decisions made and the policies that they produced. While important, this tack has relegated questions about the *form* of the negotiations to the back bench, a dismissal that has made it quite difficult to understand precisely how the negotiations process performed the work of constitution-making.[5]

Constitutions are both actions and objects. Revolutionary in Hannah Arendt's sense of creating the "foundation of freedom" that they then contain, constitutions are deeply rhetorical events.[6] The making of a constitution, or the act of (re)founding, turns heavily on the invention and exchange of constitutive words, a set of speech acts that define and enable a "terminological calculus" of human relations.[7] The precise status, operativity, and power of these words is a long-standing puzzle, one that appears in Rousseau's wonder as to whether (and how) an act of governance must necessarily precede the formation of government. Between the *pouvoir constituant* and *pouvoir constitué*, at the threshold of turning from the old in the name of making anew, the authority to define constitutively is not a given.[8] Both an ethical and a pragmatic problem, the exercise of the definitional power that marks the creativity and creation of a constitution has the potential to unravel the "democratic" dispensation which it calls into being. Among others, Jürgen Habermas has taken this problem of justification to mean that the "founding fiction" of constitution-making must be scrutinised for its formal-pragmatic integrity and assessed for whether the communicative action of constitutive power carries across time in a way that invites and holds open opportunities for citizens to re-author law in the future.[9]

Over the course of two arduous years, negotiators from many of South Africa's political parties struggled to find, craft, and agree on the words needed to perform the work of constitution. More precisely, they argued and sometimes battled over who could speak constitutively, how to define norms of deliberative decision-making, and the ways in which fundamental disagreements were best transformed into the collective political action of founding a (relatively) new South Africa. In this chapter, I examine how appeals to reconciliation played a central role in the development and (non)resolution of these explicitly rhetorical problems. While many have suggested that the *outcome* of the negotiations process was the achievement of a reconciliation, my contention here is that reconciliation also operated *within* the negotiations as a form of constitutive power, a mode of interaction that underwrote significant and controversial decisions about the kinds of words that were necessary to promote and perform the "sufficient consensus" needed to constitute a beginning.

In the South African transition, reconciliation was an explicit reason to (re)constitute the nation *and* a constitutive means of expression. To develop this position, I begin with the period between December 1991 and September 1992, paying particular attention to the opening of CODESA. Focused on the speeches delivered at the convention's first plenary and several of the debates that occurred in its working groups, the chapter first details the clash that followed the turn from the talks about talks to constitutional negotiations. Evident in the harsh exchange between F.W. de Klerk and Nelson Mandela, the controversy over how to define the forum's purpose and power was rooted in the question of sovereignty, the problem of whether reform had to proceed through the existing sovereign state's law or if the nation's future rested in the sovereign power of the people. Much more than a matter of principle, disagreement over this issue demonstrated that the task of enabling CODESA's constitutive power hinged on a capacity to advance definitional arguments that the ANC and NP each claimed for itself. Thus, the grounds for talking and the potential for productive negotiation began to collapse, a devolution that I trace in section two. Here, considering the period between June and September 1992, my concern is how disagreements over where to locate the sovereign were embedded in disputes over violence, power-sharing, and who would author the post-apartheid constitution. Looking closely at how the ANC and SAG vied for leverage and control of the reform process, I consider how appeals for reconciliation were used to recast the stakes and form of negotiations in the wake of CODESA's breakdown. Tied to a series of agreements that saw both sides return to a process of meta-dialogue and which demonstrated that progress at the negotiating table demanded more than historical self-interest, I suggest that the productive quality of CODESA's failure was its ability to force the question of how negotiators were going to fashion and agree on rules of argumentation; the ways in which they would oppose one another's positions in the name of enacting constitutive power. In section three, I consider this shift as it appeared in the first half of the MPNP. Tracing the definition and codification of a decision-making process called sufficient consensus, the section focuses on how negotiators fashioned a formal-pragmatic mode of constitutive power that rested on appeals to reconciliation and produced serious legal dispute over whether and how the constitution-making process was accountable to the rule of law.

The development and controversial practice of sufficient consensus was not a minor feature of the negotiations process. Far more than decorative, this speech betrays how negotiating parties fashioned the terms and norms of debate that guided and performed the work of constitution. It also provides a clear view of reconciliation's central role in South Africa's negotiated revolution. During the MPNP, calls for reconciliation demonstrated the need for sufficient consensus by explaining how its characteristic argumentation could fulfil the promise of unity in difference that had been created within the talks about talks. Neither transcendent nor revolutionary, sufficient consensus held the transformative action of reconciliation's speech, a form of talk that involved standing against the silencing precedents of sovereign law in the name of enacting a rhetorical faith, a power to define with(in) relation. This act of transition, however, was not without remainder. In the closing months of the constitution-making process, reconciliation's apparent cost was the difficult question of how to carry and redress the historical injustice that it had set aside in the name of constituting a present for the future.

1. codesa's sovereign question

The talks about talks created the potential for negotiations that would bring a new constitution and begin South Africa's transition to democracy. By late 1991, the question was how to render this potential actual. The first formal opportunity to reply came with the opening of the Convention for a Democratic South Africa, an event that demonstrated in no uncertain terms that the high hopes of meta-dialogue had obscured a difficult set of problems. With ambiguous and competing agendas, delegates arrived at the Convention only to find that they disagreed fundamentally about both the means and ends of constitution-making. From its first days, members of CODESA thus began to argue over the purpose, procedures, and status of their negotiations. These definitional disputes held the seeds of deadlock, a paralysis that led van Zyl Slabbert to lament that CODESA was little more than a "debating society".[10] Was it? Did its words betray why the forum was ultimately unable to undertake the speech needed to support action? Was its (lack of) debate the sign of a productive failure?

Transcripts from the beginning of CODESA reveal intense discord about who had the standing to define the transition, what role the state would play in it, and whether certain kinds of negotiating strategies were evidence of one or another party's desire to strip the other of the authority needed to (re)constitute the nation. Here I contend that these arguments are evidence of the fact that the potential for transition that appeared at the start of CODESA was deeply complicated by controversy over the location, meaning, and allocation of sovereignty. As delegates took to their seats, uncertainty about the form and content of the negotiations led directly to the question of how to balance the existing state's constituted power and the need to compose a constituting power that opposed (the) standing (of) state law in the name of making it anew. The elephant on the plenary's stage, the "sovereign" at CODESA was thus both a sign system and a structural mode of power, a symbolic operator that destabilised the grounds of speaking, constrained speech's power to constitute, and exceeded (sacrificed) the capacity of negotiators to speak in relation.[11] Less an opportunity for debate than a demonstration of its limit, the problem of sovereignty did contribute directly to CODESA's failure. It also held a crucial lesson about the need to cultivate reconciliation's productive opposition, a form of joint power that could both dissolve and (re)make sovereign law.

worries about word power

The Holiday Inn at the Johannesburg Airport is predictably if not painfully ordinary. The lobby's architecture, colour scheme, and mediocre coffee make it difficult to determine whether one is in South Africa or Davenport, Iowa. The stale air and worn carpet are reminders of just how many travellers have trudged through the front door. And yet this hotel has an extraordinary history. During the years of struggle, some members of the liberation movement used the facility to plot strategy. So, too, various units of the government's third force convened in its rooms for clandestine consultations and operations planning. In the 1980's, according to their amnesty applications, members of the Civil Cooperation Bureau (CCB) were especially fond of the place. A few years later, the facility quartered many of those who were working to negotiate and write South Africa's interim constitution. While perhaps fanciful, it is difficult not to wonder if more than a few of the bar's napkins were used to sketch out ideas for a Bill of Rights. There really should be a plaque in the lobby.

Some kinds of revolutions start in the most banal of settings. On 29 November 1991, 60 delegates from many but not all of South Africa's political parties converged on the hotel for "talks that will simply set the terms" for the first meeting of CODESA. There was nothing simple about the meeting. Following the ups and downs of the talks about talks, it aimed to heal the splits that were motivating certain parties to resist negotiations and shed light on the causes of continuing violence, particularly in KwaZulu-Natal. The gathering was also charged to hammer out a *Declaration of Intent*, principles that would guide negotiators in their efforts to move South Africa from apartheid to democracy. Speaking to the high hopes that attended the gathering, *The Weekly Mail* wrote: "What we're in line for is intense horse-trading – of walk-outs, sell-outs, poses and postures, of new best friends and fresh antagonisms, breakdowns, start-ups, optimism, pessimism, pockets of peace, waves of violence – and in the end, perhaps, lasting agreement."[12] In the meeting halls and corridors of a shabby chain hotel that has housed more political activity than anyone will ever know, it appeared to many that negotiators were preparing themselves for the difficult "last mile" of the walk to freedom.

The early days of CODESA were indeed more difficult than not. No matter how optimistic, negotiators faced significant obstacles, some of which would not be resolved until just days before the 1994 election. For one, escalating violence was leading some to conclude that the promise of the *National Peace Accord* was being squandered in bureaucratic wrangles that left local communities powerless to stop the slaughter. On the reef outside Johannesburg, hostel killings were common if not daily events. The media ran article after article about how SAG was supporting the IFP, a relationship that was feeding the violence between members of Inkatha and the ANC. The state's denials of the alliance appeared on an equally regular basis.

Inside the meeting rooms, negotiators stood on equally unstable political ground. The value of structured talks appeared to mean very different things to different parties. Few agreed on how the transition would occur, whether the country would be ruled for a time by an interim government, and who exactly would be charged to write South Africa's first democratic constitution.[13] Beneath these issues sat controversies over principles of participation and representation. The IFP, PAC, and Azanian People's Organisation (AZAPO), along with several far right-wing groups, all contended that the ANC and NP were preparing to dominate the process by relying on closed bilateral meetings to make substantive decisions about South Africa's political future. The NP continued to face the charge that it sought to be both a player in the process and its referee. After national strikes in November, the ANC was castigated for using "people's power" at its convenience and reserving mass action for moments when it was frustrated with the government's position.[14] At the same time, public opinion surveys indicated that citizens had high expectations for the talks, hopes that were fed by rather wild media speculation about when an election might occur as well as by announcements from the main political parties about the need to move swiftly toward a "new South Africa". Hindsight would indicate that idealism was running roughshod over reality.

Despite all the problems and amidst renewed boycott threats, the November meeting did count as progress. Parties agreed on the name for their forum and plotted the agenda for its opening session in late December. Too, the meeting helped resolve the Convention's organisational structure, a format in which the work of a plenary body was to be supported by working groups tasked to define and resolve specific constitutional and transitional issues.[15] Within this framework, negotiators agreed to make decisions consensually and, in the event of significant disagreement, to rely on the benchmark of something called "sufficient consensus". Unsure of its definition and whether it would be applied fairly, some wondered and worried after this standard. Of those concerned that the negotiations "process would determine [its] content", few were assured by the ANC's Cyril Ramaphosa when he noted that sufficient consensus meant what the ANC and the NP said it meant.[16]

With ground rules in place, the first plenary session of CODESA was called to order on the morning of 20 December 1991. Its participants gathered amidst troubles that cast significant doubt on what the two-day meeting could accomplish. Inside the World Trade Centre at Kempton Park, the nearly 300 delegates represented some 19 "political parties, political organisations, administrations and the South African Government". Notably absent were the PAC, AZAPO, the CP, and the AWB. The IFP came to the proceedings and pressed for the forum to allow the participation of the Zulu King Goodwill Zwelithini. Led by Mangosuthu Buthelezi, Inkatha had been much in the news. In the week prior to the plenary, several national newspapers ran prominent articles that offered new evidence as to how the IFP had "received massive injections of money and paramilitary training from South African Defence Force Military Intelligence front organisations".[17] The disclosures contradicted F.W. de Klerk's claim that all such ties had been severed.

Inside and outside the meeting hall, delegates and citizens continued to wonder about CODESA's actual purpose.[18] Nominally, the "convention" in CODESA seemed to presuppose precisely what remained in question: What would the forum do? Members of the CP charged that it was a dangerous supra-parliamentary exercise and a deep threat to the integrity of the state. Doing little to counter perceptions about the government's desire to build

147

and then stand on both sides of the fence, Constitutional Development and Planning Minister, Gerrit Viljoen, contended that the body's decisions would have no legal force and that its delegates were duty bound to implement its agreements.[19] For its part, the ANC argued that CODESA's purpose was to create a framework for an interim government, one that would guide the country through an election of those who would write the country's new constitution. Viewed together, these diverging perspectives were telling. While the Convention's *Declaration of Intent* tasked delegates "to set in motion the process of drawing up and establishing a constitution", the major players held exclusive definitions of constitution-making. Certain of their own standing, the ANC and NP were bound by the view that the other did not have the moral or political legitimacy to make definitive arguments about the form or substance of change. In short, the power of CODESA to make history rested heavily on the contested questions of who could speak, how they could speak, and who was obliged to listen.

At CODESA's first plenary meeting, the addresses given by select representatives "contained" the moment's ambiguity. Of those who even broached the substantive, most set their discussion of how or what to negotiate within an epideictic praise of the gathering. Nelson Mandela, for instance, opened his address with a reflection on the meaning of the occasion, arguing that "Today will be indelibly imprinted in the history of our country" and that the convention "represents the historical opportunity to translate that yearning [for peace and democracy] into reality". Speaking to the tension between the two positions, Mandela claimed that CODESA marked the "commencement of the transition", a moment in which democracy was neither present nor preventable. Thus, there was potential, a moment to "lay the basis for the elimination of racial and apartheid domination" and "reach consensus on the definition of democracy". According to Mandela, the success of such work hinged on an understanding of what CODESA could and could not do:

> Even absolute consensus during the life of CODESA will still leave
> an apartheid constitution in place. We need to [be] reminded that
> this very constitution was declared null and void by the UN Security
> Council in 1983. The invalidation of the prevailing constitution is the
> most persuasive argument in support of the view that the incumbent
> government is unsuited to the task of overseeing the transition to
> democracy [and] must now compel it to make way for an interim

constitution of national unity to supervise the transition. This is the only cogent outflow from our deliberations at CODESA. The consensus which we arrive at will certainly have far-reaching implications for the birth of a new nationhood. None of us could be satisfied with circumstances where the consensus struck at this [CODESA] is not translated into full legal force.[20]

Complicated, Mandela's suggestion was that the decisions of CODESA would have to be binding in law even as that law was an illegitimate element of an apartheid regime that had no standing to shape the terms of the transition. The law had to remain but only to support talk that would re-make it through a process that was "owned and supported by the majority of South Africans". In Mandela's terms, the "law and order" of the "jackboot" had to give way, opening the door for "free political activity" and opening the cells of political prisoners with an "amnesty before Christmas". Set in a present for the future, CODESA's beginning was thus a time in which "each one of us is to unshackle ourselves from the past and build anew". According to Mandela, consensus was vital but did not diminish the fact that the sovereignty of the people had to trump the sovereign apartheid state.

A number of so-called third parties at CODESA appeared to be in basic but not complete agreement with Mandela's interpretation of the convention's task. While echoing the ANC's call for the people to prevail, Lucas Mangope, the President of Bophuthatswana, reminded delegates at the plenary that his was a "sovereign and independent country" – a product of apartheid – and a nation that could not be casually dismantled at CODESA.[21] Complaining about the exclusion of the "Zulu nation" from the proceedings, the IFP's Frank Mdlalose warned that negotiations for a new South Africa would succeed only if the country was able to avoid the "evil of centralisation" and preserve the sovereign power of regional governments.[22] Calling on the country to stand against and overcome "centuries of wrong", the DP's Zach de Beer also urged CODESA to produce a constitution that would limit government's scope and power.[23]

By prior agreement, F.W. de Klerk was scheduled to give the last speech at the plenary. Speaking on behalf of the government, the President opened by noting that delegates to CODESA stood on the "threshold of a new South Africa". This characterisation of the moment was somewhat different from Mandela's. With the transition not yet begun, it was time to join forces and overcome the problem of "mutual distrust and suspicion". More on the defensive than not, de Klerk denied the government's interest in being "both a player and referee" and claimed that it was willing to undertake negotiations about "amending the constitution of the Republic to make an interim power-sharing model possible on a democratic basis". This offer was heavily coded. According to de Klerk, CODESA's task was to "institute expeditiously, as a first phase, a government that is broadly representative of the total population". Given the perceived risk of unbridled majority rule, he maintained that the constitution-writing process had to begin with a guarantee of white representation and an assurance that decisions taken at CODESA would be "adopted by Parliament after a mandate has been obtained by means of a referendum". Claiming that the need for change could not lead to the "circumvention or suspension of the present Constitution", de Klerk argued that:

> Government must, after proper elections, be composed in terms
> of the Constitution of the day. Unconstitutional government cannot
> be accepted in a country which is sovereign, independent, and whose
> sovereignty and independence are recognised by the total international
> community.[24]

In direct clash with Mandela's claim that the state's constitution was illegitimate both inside and outside the country, the President was asserting the necessity and right of the state to play a central role in designing the new South Africa – the constituted power did and would remain sovereign. Addressing Mandela's claim that the government had no standing to issue demands or define the constitution-writing process, de Klerk upped the ante, arguing that any such "deep seated policy differences" could not and would not be resolved until such time as the ANC stopped questioning the government's motives from the "two stools" on which the Congress sat. This time borrowing from Mandela, the President's charge was about credibility, a claim as to why the ANC's refusal to abandon the armed struggle meant that it "cannot be trusted completely" and an argument as to how its commitment to violence disqualified it from entering into "binding, legitimate, reliable and credible peaceful agreements".[25] Without question, de Klerk's position was that the ANC's criticism of the government was hypocritical.

Mandela raged back. In an unscheduled address, charge was met with countercharge: de Klerk's position was an attack from a "discredited regime", one that took account of the "White minority" but not the "population of South Africa".[26] Moreover, Mandela claimed that the government's position was an attempt to "impose conditions" on a political process that was itself initiated by the "pressure of the people inside the country". This mass power, he argued, had to continue, especially given the government's ongoing role in political violence and indications that de Klerk was someone who "has sometimes very little idea of what democracy means". As the armed struggle was insurance against the NP's "double agenda" and a regime that had broken its word more times than not, the demobilisation of the MK was contingent on demonstrable progress in the negotiating hall. Otherwise, Mandela claimed, "You are asking us to commit suicide." In concluding, he noted that while the ANC was prepared to work with precisely those who had "created misery beyond words", the state President "cannot talk to us in that language".

Between de Klerk and Mandela, the divide was not simply how to relate different definitions of the transition but equally a dispute over who had the credibility to define South Africa's future and a deep distrust about whether certain "defining" speech acts were veiled forms of violence. In short, the opening of CODESA demonstrated that the hopes created by the talks about talks were not self-actualising. At the close of the two-day plenary session, a somewhat chastened de Klerk observed that the start of CODESA's deliberations had put the "country finally on the road to realise its tremendous potential". The Chair of the meeting, Justice Ismail Mohamed, was a bit more precise about the matter, observing that "yesterday we began an uncertain but politically exciting leap into the future by consciously agreeing to explore, to identify and to debate and to articulate our dreams for a new and free South Africa". This was indeed the difficulty; the potential for change was fraught with opposition about how to make the new in relation to the old. While the creation of a climate for negotiations had put history to the side, using indemnity to bracket the legal precedent that deterred interaction, CODESA brought the past back, raising the question of whether and how it would shape the substantive terms of the transition. The potential of the moment was embodied in the issue of whose definition of change would carry the day and at what cost.

At the plenary, there were several levels to the debate over how to define and enact CODESA's power. First, many of the central players came to the table with different visions of the transition. As the creation of a "new" South Africa represented both an opportunity and a threat, a central problem was how to define the form of this beginning, a task that raised the question of whether breaking from the past was a vital way to clear ground or a dangerous assault on the nation's foundation. On either view, history's role in defining the nature of the transition was contentious precisely because it was linked to deeper questions about subjugation and survival. For many, legacies of segregation and apartheid represented nothing but pain and an attempted genocide. For others, however, this past was held up as a vital source of culture and a testament to power in the face of adversity. Not simply a matter of black and white, the issue was whether there was a duty to define the transition against the past or an obligation to build change from or at least in relationship to it.

Second, negotiators had competing views about how to define CODESA's power. For the ANC, the danger of CODESA's potential was an endless transition, a forum that gave undue power to the minority, delayed elections, and subverted the process of constitution-writing. For the Nats, its perceived risk was chaos and domination, a transition that wrote whites out of politics and undermined the rule of law. Together, the problem was that preliminary dialogue had not addressed the force or status of CODESA's decisions and their relation to a rule of law that was both sacred and scheduled for sacrifice.

Third, the opening days of CODESA illustrated that parties were unsure if not distrustful of how others were justifying their interpretation of a successful convention. The issue was closely linked to the problem of history. While the ANC and NP were clearly the dominant players, all parties contended publicly that the process needed to work in a representative way. But this implied different things to different groups. Some took it to mean that the process had to address the interests of all citizens, others that it ought to focus on the needs of the long disenfranchised majority. Both positions left the NP to worry and claim that a representative forum was needed to prevent outright majoritarianism. This issue was also not black and white. Many of the so-called third parties argued that ANC-NP bilateralism left them out in the cold and promised to thwart transparency. Some of these same groups, however, allied themselves with the ANC on the issue of political prisoners, arguing that their release was critical to the creation of an atmosphere that supported free political participation.

The opening salvos at CODESA were not simply substantive disagreements about matters of policy. Between the lines, delegates were contesting who had the standing to define the forum's purpose, power and procedure. Whose vision of the transition would win out? How would the process of talk shape its actual power? What was a comprehensible, fair, and productive way to talk and make decisions? These questions were a central element of the exchange between Mandela and de Klerk at the plenary. In their respective positions, each contested the other's ability to define the process and outcome of constitution-making; the existence of a principled agreement about the need for change was necessary but no longer sufficient to ensure progress. Thus, they disagreed about how to disagree, and circled around the problem of how to differentiate productive opposition from clash which fuelled fears that the transition would culminate in the violence that would follow from either no substantive change or outright revolution. The talks about talks had left this question to the side, forgoing the issue of how to debate and make decisions over contested issues in favour of establishing a larger agreement about the need to negotiate for a new constitution. At CODESA, this issue could no longer be bracketed.

a beginning without speaking
It was time to confront the questions that were provoking arguments about how to argue. Did the South African Government have the requisite legitimacy to make claims about how the new constitution needed to preserve and respect the state's sovereignty? Was the ANC's refusal to disarm an indication of its insincerity, one that cut against the credibility of its proposals? Did National Party demands for power-sharing demean those who suffered under apartheid? Was the ANC advocating a revolutionary act when it publicly argued that the new constitution should be written by an elected body? Which initiatives really represented the will of the people? With the beginning of CODESA, each of these matters was an indication that the substantive terms of a new constitution could not be dirempted from the formal qualities of the negotiations. Procedures for debate would have to be devised. Much more than a conduit for ideas, the words of constitution-making had to be assessed in terms of whether and how they could sponsor action.

CODESA was a debating society or perhaps a prototype for one. In part, this is to say that the question of how to enable constitutive argumentation and the problem of how to define productive ways of disagreeing did not go unrecognised. Most directly, the matter was addressed in discussions about how delegates would make decisions and ratify agreements. At the pre-convention meeting, negotiators had agreed to strive for consensus but held open the option that decisions could be taken on the basis of sufficient consensus. Subsequently, this procedure was written into CODESA's standing rules:

(1) Every delegation shall, when called by the Chair to express its position on a proposal or matter before the meeting, have such position stated by the leader of the delegation or spokesperson appointed by the leader of the delegation. (2) Agreement will be arrived at by consensus. (3) Agreement by Sufficient Consensus will have been reached when consensus is of such a nature that the work of the Convention can move forward effectively. (4) Disagreeing participants shall have the right to record their objections or dissent. (5) When disagreement exists, the Chair will allow parties to consult amongst each other and with their principals before recording any position.[27]

While it acknowledged the necessity and inevitability of dissent, this process lacked much procedure. The rules said little about how to assess the "sufficiency" of a consensus, how a ruling of such might foreclose debate, and what it meant for the talks to move "effectively" forward.

In January of 1992, the IFP expressed the beginning of what would turn out to be a much larger dissatisfaction with sufficient consensus when it wrote, "A climate for free political participation can only exist where it is made abundantly clear that all participants are given free reign to express their views, aspirations, misgivings, and fears without being nudged or coached with preconceived positions."[28] This position was submitted to CODESA's Working Group One, a body tasked to negotiate about ways of ending violence, stabilising the political process, granting indemnity to political prisoners, and "dealing with the past", a phrase that was tied directly to the need for reconciliation. At one point, the group's work was deemed necessary to enable other working groups and crucial for an "internal solution" to the transition puzzle.[29] In any case, the minutes of the group's early meetings suggest that it debated about how to define the key terms of its charge and was left feeling somewhat "directionless" and "without guidance" about what to do. In this respect, it received a submission from the government which hinted that part of the group's inability to communicate was rooted in the very history with which it was supposed to "deal":

For the last three decades, the political life of South Africans was dominated by, on the one hand, suppression, and, on the other hand, the outrages of a so-called liberation struggle. This has to a large degree prevented the development of a political culture characterised by a democratic attitude, tolerance and persuasion.[30]

The lack of these goods was evident when it came time to address the question of indemnity. Here, significant disagreement existed over how to define a "political prisoner" and what bearing their release would have on "completing the reconciliation process". Within the working group, ANC and NP delegates seemed to distrust each other's positions, with the former accusing the latter of "holding back" and blocking the process with red tape. In one of its submissions to the group, the SACP suggested that the government had persistently refused to provide reasons for its failure to resolve the matter. Congruent with concerns about how the prisoner issue was vital to "confidence in the [negotiating] process", this charge fed claims about the government's desire to "pander to the wishes (or the perceived wishes) of its white constituency" and how it sought to place "its own political future far above the future of the country and need for reconciliation".[31] The counter charge was that the transition could not come at the expense of justice. Viewed together, the two sides of the controversy were a basic indication of how the group could not agree on the meaning of its mandate, how to resolve its disagreements, and what difference their work might make in the larger negotiations process.

As negotiators in working groups mulled over how to argue about policy, it became increasingly clear that CODESA's deliberative structure was ill-equipped to resolve disputes over how to conduct productive debate. While some fared better than others, the documentary record suggests that many working groups laboured under a kind of *akrasia*, a breakdown in the capacity to jointly define how speech could be used to design and justify action. In some cases, efforts to actualise reconciliation's potential were hamstrung by uncertainty over whether reconciliation was a process or a state of affairs. Likewise, the debates showed how concepts like "new South Africa" could generate dispute about the historical basis or validity conditions for speech, the relative sincerity and truthfulness that sat beneath various ideas for structuring the transition. This problem was exacerbated by clash over who could credibly (without hypocrisy) define the terms of transition, and complicated even further by disputes about whether various parties were opposing and arguing with one another in a useful way. Provoking fears of deception, strategic manipulation, and even violence, the vagaries of sufficient consensus did not speak sufficiently to the problem of how to differentiate productive and unproductive disagreement.

As it began to fail, CODESA revealed an important lesson as to how the potential for reconciliation did not fate its actuality. Before the convention, the call for reconciliation grew from within an experience of *stasis*. As violence was seen to confound action, neither side could actualise its historical purpose. The mutual experience of this paralysis underscored that historical justifications for violence both represented and needed to be turned toward an "opposition in common". This was the potential of reconciliation, a present moment to talk about how the (self) confounding historical causes of deep division contained a referent for talking about ways to make the future. At the opening of CODESA, however, this potential grew more complicated. The shared opposition that funded the talks about talks continued to back the need for negotiations but did not seem to contribute to their progress. Evident in the plenary debate and discussions within some working groups, the question became less about how to move from violence to opposition than about the ways in which oppositional forms of argument could yield substantive agreements. On the surface, this problem appeared as negotiators offered very different visions of the duration of the transition, the composition of the constituent assembly, and the nature of post-apartheid democracy. However, these substantive disagreements hinged on the underlying fact that negotiators expressed distrust of how their counterparts were speaking and also disputed the procedures used to ratify decisions. In practice, articulated visions of constitution-making were read variously as insincere, hypocritical, and deceptive attempts to grab power. For some groups, the ambiguous threshold of a sufficient consensus deepened the problem, raising questions about whether the transition would occur around but not with them.

Deeper still, negotiators appeared caught in a circle. Disagreements over whether parties were negotiating sincerely and appropriately illustrated the extent to which the convention's process and content overlapped. Arguments that endeavoured to explain the terms of a new constitution carried a certain performative power, an ability to divide past from future and to set precedents for whether and how history would underwrite the move from old to new. Put differently, CODESA's early work betrayed that claims about how to write the constitution had a potentially constitutive effect, a capacity to define who would and would not belong in the nation to come. With this dynamic came a paradox: meaningful negotiations demanded definitional arguments about how the transition would proceed and what the constitution would do even as these claims were ruled out of order to the degree that they appeared to constitute the very transition that had (yet) to be made. Thus, the opposition in common that had energised talk before CODESA was now something quite different. It was a marker of distrust that kept parties from defining productive modes of disagreement as well as a definitive indication of why the transition could either not start or never end.

From the very beginning and for want of a beginning, negotiators at CODESA did not agree on how to begin. More precisely, CODESA was a beginning in which definitions of South Africa's transition were challenged as strategic, unfair, and inappropriate attempts to undermine taken-for-granted but competing understandings of sovereignty. At the plenary, de Klerk seemed unable to bear that "unconstitutional" speech of constitution-making which might come at the expense of the nation's sovereignty. In turn, Mandela spoke of the popular will, appealing for the constitutive assertion of the sovereign public subjugated by apartheid. Both talked of the need to respect the autonomy of the individual; the sovereignty of the subject/citizen that both required and challenged the power of the legal sovereign. At a basic level, these claims troubled reconciliation's announced promise. Rooted in disputes over the power to define, the capacity to delineate what is and will be, the problem recalled how the NGK appealed to "spheres of sovereignty" in order to appropriate the divine Word and justify separate development, and the way in which the English-speaking church challenged this interpretation in the name of creating space for words that would overcome law. As in the past, CODESA brought with it the question of how to find and legitimise words of beginning, words that did not negate sovereignty but turned it toward the task of its own (re)constitution. The question that required and stalled debate was whether to surpass the sovereign while maintaining its power, or if it was better to maintain power while surpassing sovereignty. In the months after the plenary, each side attempted to fashion a definitive reply and thus begged the question itself. The potential for reconciliation would thus remain at a distance, contingent on the invention of words that could turn and move between constituted and constitutive forms of power.

2. a difficult season of climate changes

The commencement of CODESA brought vexing questions.[32] Beneath the policy issues, disputes over how to define the constitution-making process confounded CODESA's future precisely because they troubled the communicative ends and means of its negotiations. Evident in the plenary's sparring and the early meetings of working groups, the rules and outcomes of talk became suspect as each side's expressed definition of change was perceived by the other as an attempt to grab or preserve control. While a vital piece of the constitutional puzzle, definitional argumentation did not yield the space for productive opposition as much as it fostered opposing sides, each of which appeared committed to overcoming the other. Meanwhile, as negotiators worked at Kempton Park, the NP and the ANC both lobbied outside CODESA in an effort to demonstrate that they were the party which had the historical standing and political authority to define the terms of the new South Africa. While it took decidedly different forms, each side's attempt to occupy the ground for definitive definitional argument was read by the other as an attempt to dictate the terms of the transition. Negotiations thus faltered as talk was increasingly perceived as a conduit for violence. Tied to bloody battles across the country and the yet undecided fate of many political prisoners, the situation came to resemble the *stasis* that existed in the months leading up to the talks about talks. This time, however, the important difference was that negotiators were concerned less with defining the capacity for talk than at odds over how to establish its legitimate power.

The climate was cooling, a turn toward freezing that would prove difficult to redress. Between January and November 1992, South Africans witnessed a remarkable set of events: deadlock at CODESA, the outright breakdown of negotiations, a winter of mass action, and the signing of a controversial memorandum of understanding that opened the door to new talks. Over the course of 11 months, as each side struggled to cast itself as *the* constituted power, the generative connection between word and deed seemed everywhere but then nowhere and then back again. Here, I want to trace these developments in order to suggest that CODESA's fate turned partly on the unwillingness and inability of negotiators to distinguish between the power of oppositional argumentation to generate the potential for agreement, and forms of speech that used opposition to accumulate power at the expense of interaction. Plotting this apparent failure of reconciliation, the section then turns to how negotiators reconstructed the grounds for talk. At a point that is difficult to locate with any precision, key parties turned away from their commitment to oppose one another and began extended discussion about how to create and enact a jointly held mode of constitutive power.

This shift is subtle and important. By the middle of August, as the integrity of both the ANC and the NP's position was being called into significant question, there was a notable change in the tenor and characterisation of talks. Tied to a series of bilateral meetings, continued discussion over the merits of amnesty, and concessions from both sides, negotiators began to focus less on reconciling divisive proposals for power-sharing and more on the way in which reconciliation could support talks in which parties would share the power of constitution. Evident in Mandela's characterisation of the constitution-making process, reconciliation came to connote a willingness to "stand in contradiction", a need to find the grounds for progress from within the negativity of the negotiations process instead of remaining in a cycle that led each side to reject the other's proposals because they were perceived to come at the expense of their respective interests. Consistent with this interpretation, one of the crucial things that happened during the long winter of 1992 was that the ANC and NP came to hold that they would again have to risk something of their own historical position if there were to be negotiations that allowed for argumentation about how to move forward.

the opposition of breakdown, withdrawal, and understanding
On the same day that CODESA's working groups were scheduled to begin their negotiations, F.W. de Klerk took the podium at Parliament. Compared with the tone of his groundbreaking speech two years earlier, the President's tenor in late January of 1992 revealed a basic ambivalence. Declaring that "we are experiencing a decisive period in our history", de Klerk argued that "all South Africans now have to reconcile themselves once and for all" to the fact that there "will be born a new constitutional order". Perhaps less celebratory than determined, the claim was addressed partly to those among the President's constituents who were expressing a fear of change and growing anxious over whether the government was getting ready to capitulate.[33] At a deeper level, the speech raised the question of whether de Klerk was himself willing to take the leap of faith that he was advocating. A discomforting echo of P.W. Botha's 1985 Rubicon address, the President announced the coming of the new by insisting on the preservation of the old. Arguing that CODESA was "not and should not be an institution of authority", he claimed that South Africa's transition would be an open-ended affair and that the move to universal suffrage would be "subject to Parliamentary control", ratified by popular referendum, and bound by "principles of power-sharing".[34] In short, the sovereign was set to remain such. The turn to democracy hinged on the creation of a transitional government that was "broadly representative of the whole population" but only insofar as it preserved some of apartheid's most basic interests.[35]

Gathered on Cape Town's Grand Parade for the ANC's "People's Parliament", protestors decried the President's speech, arguing that his appeal for power-sharing betrayed the government's desire for a "system designed to maintain white power, behind a complicated charade of democracy".[36] The

ANC's National Executive Council was blunter, claiming that the speech was a demeaning demonstration of the government's "insensitivity, uncaring attitude, and complacency towards the plight of millions of people whose lives have been ruined by apartheid". While agreeing that self-determination was crucial, the NEC argued that those in the struggle had no obligation to place their trust in the vision of a "discredited constitutional authority". Refusing the regime's "lessons in democracy", and its call for an exclusive (white) referendum, it went on to claim that "the way in which President de Klerk links self-determination to constitutionally enforced power-sharing with a built-in white minority veto undermines the very principle he purports to uphold".[37] Citing moral principle and the international community's condemnation of apartheid, the ANC's claim was rather simple: the sovereign is not the sovereign.

While the lines may have been drawn, the ensuing weeks demonstrated that they were not always clear. Shortly after de Klerk's address, Mandela seemed to deviate somewhat from the NEC's position when he indicated a willingness to consider "other options" for ensuring the protection of minorities.[38] Inside its alliance, the ANC was also facing criticism from labour leaders concerned about whether it was adequately prepared to bargain for economic equality. From the wings, the PAC continued to denounce the "monster called CODESA", arguing that the government and its violence was slowing the formation of a constituent assembly.[39] Such doubts about the speed and efficacy of talks were also apparent within the confines of the working groups. While Mandela and de Klerk were away to receive the UNESCO Peace Prize, the NP tabled a proposal that called for the creation of an interim government which would guide the country through an indefinite transitional period. The terms of the proposal represented a sort of conditional compromise. This quality was evident in the NP's desire for the creation of a bicameral constituent assembly, the upper house of which seemed to have the power to issue a minority veto of the final constitution. While the ANC considered the idea, liberal parties urged that the negotiating process be slowed so that all voices could be heard and options considered. In a certain sense, the brakes did come on after Minster Stoffel van der Merwe's claim that what the nation really needed to do was "forget the past".[40] The argument cut both ways, an affront to those who continued to endure apartheid and worrisome to those who were fretting about whether de Klerk was preparing to sell the soul of Afrikaner nationalism.

The question of de Klerk's support loomed increasingly large. Having promised that the end of apartheid would occur only with the approval of his constituents, and stung by an election loss to the CP in Potchefstrom, the President undertook what one commentator called an "audacious gamble", announcing that eligible voters would go to the polls in mid-March to vote on the question of constitutional change. The motivation for the referendum was understood in different ways. Some saw it as an attempt by the NP to scare voters with a threat of *wit gevaar* (white danger), the possibility that failed negotiations would lead an "organised hallucination" – the CP – back into power and return the country to high apartheid. Others sensed a power grab, an attempt by de Klerk to co-opt the CP while also undermining the ANC's bargaining leverage. Whatever the reason, de Klerk clung dearly to an argument from history – the idea that voters had to approve such radical change because "all South Africans have experience of domination".[41] Deeply opposed to an exclusive vote and worried that it would solidify support for a minority veto, the ANC was left in an awkward position. A de Klerk loss would complicate if not end talks. Ultimately, combining principle and pragmatism, it urged voters to pass the referendum but defined it as a vote for the larger CODESA process.

While de Klerk campaigned on the "koeksuster trail", CODESA negotiators continued to "whittle at the constitutional mountain". Documents leaked in early March suggested the existence of an agreement over the ANC's plan for a two-stage transition, a process that would begin with Parliament's passage of a constitutional amendment authorising the creation of an interim government. After the disclosure, Finance Minister Barend du Plessis underscored that necessary consensus had not been reached and that negotiators would continue to "talk and talk until we all agree".[42] The motivation for such effort seemed to decrease somewhat after the referendum. Claiming a "landslide victory", de Klerk argued that his 37 percentage point victory marked "the birthday of the real new South Africa", and carried with it a "powerful message of reconciliation, a powerful reaching out for justice". Making many cringe, he continued, "What started out as idealism in the quest for justice – because that was the starting point of the policy of separate development – could not attain justice for all South Africans and therefore it has to be abandoned and replaced by the only viable policy that can work in this country and that is power-sharing, co-operation in the building of one nation in one undivided South Africa."[43] The President felt his mandate and apparently no regrets.

De Klerk had run his campaign partly on the promise that he had the power to make the ANC accept his vision of the transition. In the weeks after the poll, this appeared to motivate a change in negotiating style. Stepping up pressure, de Klerk vehemently condemned the ANC's failure to disband the MK even as there were continuing reports that his own security forces were funding a "pocket civil war".[44] While several media outlets reported that an "interim government is weeks away", the incongruity increased tensions at the bargaining table and deepened splits between a number of political parties. Working Group One continued to struggle with the question of how to enhance the climate for political participation. In Working Group Three, ANC and NP negotiators continued to tread water on the question of how actually to implement a transitional government. The Congress's proposal that CODESA should appoint a transitional executive council was rejected by the NP on the grounds that it would lead to "two governments". This objection was not followed by a clear counterproposal on the nature of interim executive power, a gap that led the ANC to again charge that the government was trying to be both player and referee.[45]

The plenary session known as CODESA II was scheduled for mid-May. While many hoped that the country sat on the "the brink of a historic reconciliation", plans for the gathering were upset by deep disagreements over the procedures that would be used to approve a constitution. The matter turned heavily on the question of ratification percentages. Fearing majority domination, the NP held that an elected constituent assembly would have to pass the constitution by a 75 per cent majority. Given predictions about the outcome of the election, the ANC feared that this margin would lead to a significant delay if not a minority veto. The day before the plenary, the NP backed down and then didn't, agreeing to a two-thirds margin for all matters except those to do with the Bill of Rights and then proposing a Senate that would represent minorities and pass the constitution by the same two-thirds margin.[46] The ANC saw the latter as the backdoor to a veto. It countered with a proposal that appeared intended to create deadlock: the ANC would agree to the Nat's revised ratification percentages with the provision that if the constitution had not been passed after six months, a national referendum would be held, at which point only a simple majority would be needed for adoption.[47] The government could not agree. The talks were frozen.

CODESA II came and went, mostly a formality and an occasion to plan additional meetings. In the ensuing weeks, negotiators made little apparent headway, continuing to disagree about the ratification question and the larger matter of power-sharing.[48] On 15 May, the ANC warned that a failure to reach agreement on these questions would jeopardise all other CODESA agreements.[49] The threat was motivated partly by continuing dissatisfaction with the government's approach to the release of political prisoners and the escalation of violence. Reflecting on the Congress's selective withdrawal from the *National Peace Accord*, *The Weekly Mail* suggested that while the ANC had approached CODESA by oscillating between the "politics of protest and conciliation" its increasing dissatisfaction was motivating a turn to mass action and a militant form of "people's power".[50]

In his address to the CODESA II plenary, Mandela had hinted at just this shift. Asking "How long can we, who claim to be leaders of our people, sit here, talk eloquently, spin out complicated formulas and enjoy the applause while the country sinks deeper and deeper into crisis", he argued that it was time "not to play politics" but to undertake a "radical departure" and make good on the people's "duty to engage in struggle". At base, the position was addressed to the problem and potential of opposition. Demanding over and over to know "who is opposed" to the democratic creation of a constituent assembly, Mandela went further, calling on the government to bridge the divide between its word and deed: "The time has come that you truly cross the Rubicon ... Whether you are genuine about change will be judged not by what you say but what you do."[51] Echoed in Prague a week later, Mandela had set the problem of how to create a form of productive opposition back on the table.[52] The question was not about how to conclude an agreement but whether there was even potential for constructive disagreement.

After CODESA II, the ANC issued a set of strict conditions for its continued participation in the negotiations, left the matter on the government's stoep, and prepared to call its people to the streets. At the same time and across the country, Kader Asmal, a professor of law and NEC member, took time away from Working Group One to deliver his inaugural address at the University of the Western Cape. The argument was an important one; a case for why South Africans should forgo Nuremberg-style trials in favour of a post-transition truth commission. It would take some time, however, before the proposal's spirit resonated (I address the terms of the lecture in chapter four). In the moment, it appeared to shed little light on how negotiators could resolve their differences back in Kempton Park.

In part, CODESA II had not succeeded because participants could not find the common ground needed to reach consensus, especially around the question of "what democracy means".[53] Reflecting on the government's involvement in "Infogate" and "Inkathagate", Chris Hani wondered whether "now is the time for exit gate". The jest was a serious one. Many sensed that the government's approach to the talks was sheer tactics, a perception that was fed by claims about de Klerk's post-referendum confusion of "hegemony in white politics with a broader national dominance".[54] For its part, the ANC's disinclination to talk was read by some as evidence of a legitimacy shortfall, a gap between the leadership and grassroots supporters who were increasingly concerned that the Congress was conceding too much too fast. Within the tripartite alliance, frustration at the table was giving new life to the "Leipzig option".[55] In no small measure, this desire for revolution was being fed by the NP's continuing demand for a transition that guaranteed post-apartheid power-sharing. At a structural level, the inability to resolve this issue suggested to some that CODESA had been poorly designed. The forum was too big and too public, deterring the very sorts of close talks that were needed to resolve the deepest divisions.[56] Thus, the signs of the times were mostly storm clouds on the horizon. The negativity of the talks was increasingly read as each side's expressed desire to negate the interests of the other. In light of escalating violence, neither side perceived the other as capable of advancing a sincere and representative argument about how to move from past to future. There seemed to be everything and yet very little left to talk about.

It was perhaps violence that marked the official end of CODESA. On the night of 17 June, some forty residents of the Boipatong township were slaughtered in a massacre carried out by IFP cadres from a nearby hostel. In the aftermath, furious at the government for its inaction, Mandela's "patience snapped".[57] Having followed a contentious NEC meeting, at which the ANC leadership concluded that the government must accede to its terms or face mass action, the massacre was read as definitive evidence that talks could not continue. On 21 June, Mandela suspended the ANC's participation in all negotiations and claimed that the process was "completely in tatters". According to Pallo Jordan, then the ANC's Publicity Director, the "democracy talks" were off because "We are back in the Sharpeville days. The gulf between the oppressor and the oppressed has become unbreachable."[58] Indeed, recalling the 1960s, the NEC issued a "Call to the People of South Africa", a tract which argued that while the country stood on the "brink of disaster", the problem was not simply a "crisis of the negotiations process" but the larger question of whether there "is to be democratic change, or white minority veto powers". Rejecting the latter, it issued 14 "demands on the regime", including the termination of all covert military activity, the elimination of hostels, the control of cultural weapons, the release of remaining political prisoners, and a demonstrated willingness to create a "democratically elected and sovereign Constituent Assembly to draft and adopt a new constitution".[59] While the NEC urged the people toward "unity and disciplined struggle", de Klerk gave a televised address in which he denied government's involvement in violence and claimed that it was not turning a blind eye to the problem. Going further, the President contended that the ANC was using the massacre to precipitate an "artificial crisis" in the name of sabotaging still viable negotiations and generating support for the "seizure of power".[60]

While de Klerk declared that the country was at a crossroads and that "we must not let the country become ungovernable", the obvious question was whether the time had come for Mandela's referendum. On 26 June, Mandela undertook to explain precisely why the ANC had opted out of the negotiations, arguing that the only thing artificial about the situation was the government's good faith at the table: "[T]he NP government has been pursuing the path of embracing the shell of a democratic South Africa while seeking to ensure that it is not democratic in content." At heart, Mandela's speech was an argument about the nature and need for reconciliation. Explicitly citing his 1989 letter to de Klerk in which he claimed that the task at hand was to reconcile the need for majority rule with the fears of domination, Mandela brought the case forward:

> There can be no movement forward as long as you seek to reconcile
> the two issues I have outlined through any form of minority veto. Such
> solutions may well address white concerns, but they are guaranteed to
> leave majority concerns frustrated. This is a recipe for in-built instability
> and makes peace unrealisable. For as long as the NP government insists
> on a minority veto in whatever form, the negotiations deadlock will
> remain unresolved.[61]

Reconciliation was also relevant to the violence embodied by Boipatong. Compared to three years earlier, Mandela no longer appeared willing to define reconciliation as a setting aside or overlooking of the past:

> At the root of the violence is apartheid and its legacy. All religions
> recognise that reconciliation requires confession and repentance. I have
> avoided imposing such requirements in the hope that you and your
> government would reach that recognition on your own. We believe that

> your failure to acknowledge and recognise the centrality of apartheid with regard to the issue of violence can no longer be ignored. This is particularly so because the NP government persists in attributing the carnage in the black townships to black political rivalry.[62]

Apartheid's unrecognised legacy was precisely the cause of government recalcitrance at the table, the motive for its attempt at "subverting the sovereignty of the Constituent Assembly, subjecting it to the veto of a second house and ensuring that a minority in the Constituent Assembly shall be able to frustrate an overwhelming majority". In view of the situation, Mandela claimed that negotiations were still only one means of struggle and that organised mass action appeared to be a legitimate and necessary means of deterring government-sponsored violence.

In a letter with no less than five appendices, de Klerk replied to Mandela's charges on 2 July, arguing that the NEC's demands were a duplicitous attempt to "justify the abortion of the negotiation process". Denying the government's role in political violence, the President charged that a "cabal with close links to the SACP and COSATU" was propagating insurrection that posed "serious threats to the stability and safety of the whole of South African society". Turning to the impasse at CODESA, he contended that the ANC was intent to distract the country from the priority of "negotiation and reconciliation", talk that had promise but which had been witness to the use of "extremely coercive negotiation tactics" and strategic threats which served only to undermine the possibility of mutual trust. Furthermore, de Klerk castigated the ANC's overall position as naïve, a "sudden plunge, virtually without preparation, into simple majoritarianism". With very little in the way of reply to Mandela's arguments about reconciliation, de Klerk left open the possibility of peaceful negotiations while underscoring his view that "modern democracy goes beyond the mere identification of the majority: it is equally concerned with the protection of minorities against possible excesses of the majority".[63]

Mandela responded two days later and then again on 9 July. Seeing no value in "meeting him [de Klerk] at this stage", he argued in the first statement that the government had ignored, misconstrued, and distorted the ANC's position. More directly, Mandela chastised the President for his threatening tone and apparent desire for "endless negotiations and discussions".[64] The letter that followed was more substantive, particularly as it addressed de Klerk's argument about the ANC's allegedly naïve view of transition.

Methodically, Mandela argued that tangential issues had clouded the larger picture: the "heart of the crisis" is "the question of the constitution-making body". As the ANC's road to democracy ran through an elected, single-chamber assembly that took decisions by a two-thirds majority and included mechanisms for breaking deadlock, the choice was then left to de Klerk: "The composition and function of this sovereign body is the acid test of your commitment to democracy."[65] To Mandela, the question of interim governance was specious if the government did not make good on the pledge that it made when it signed CODESA's *Declaration of Intent.*

Contrary to one popular view, Mandela and de Klerk did much more during the winter of 1992 than simply trade insults. Rather, the record of their "talks about not talking" betrays that the language needed both to describe and to perform transition was complicating negotiations over its substance. Put differently, the exchange shows each leader reflecting poignantly on how the other was speaking and how this speech was making it more not less difficult to identify the issues that prevented progress. Specifically, de Klerk and Mandela argued over how to use and justify the rhetorical power of definition, those forms of speech that served to delineate the terms of transition and codify the process of constitution-writing. Both contended that they were being sincere in the face of the other's duplicitous strategy. In this respect, the important question is less who was right but how the disagreement was rooted in the underlying warrants of their positions. As at CODESA I, de Klerk placed heavy emphasis on the sovereignty of the South African state while Mandela relied on a sense of sovereignty that was largely derived from the rights of the people as defined by international norms of democracy. Understood this way, the issue of violence was not simply who was or was not responsible for Boipatong and the hundreds of other deaths that were occurring around the country. It was also deeply tied to the question of who would take the "unjustified" step of ceding to the violence that had to attend the nation's founding, the cost that followed the act of constitution. Unspoken but rather obvious, it was this sacrifice that sat at the heart of Mandela's appeal for reconciliation.

indemnity's (mis)understanding

In late July, *The Weekly Mail* editorialised that the negotiations were in their "deepest quagmire". It was a moment when the ANC's attention was elsewhere, concerned with the national stay-away planned for 3 and 4 August. The Congress claimed that the protest was vital to (re)creating the conditions for negotiations, an argument that harkened back to the months prior to the *Groote Schuur Minute*. However, such potential had not appeared during a series of mass protests staged in early July. Then, efforts by COSATU to negotiate a national industrial shutdown had broken down, leading to bitter recriminations and further popular protest. Police arrests ran into the thousands and the situation in the townships had spurred the UN to ask whether its intervention would help stabilise the situation. While Cyrus Vance arrived in the country for a series of extended meetings about how to restart the talks, the larger question was what Mandela wanted to accomplish with the upcoming Campaign for Peace and Democracy.

There was no clear answer. On one side, it appeared that mass action was designed to solidify internal support for the ANC, particularly from those vocal sceptics claiming that the Congress did not have the will of the people in mind or the power to bring the government into line.[66] On the other, the campaign was addressed to external audiences, particularly those in the international community who were pressuring the ANC to resume negotiations and claiming that mass action was only starving South Africa's already weak economy.[67] This criticism fed NP charges that mass action was doing more harm than good. What the government's case may have ignored was the possibility that mass action stood between outright rebellion and negotiations, a "middle course" that prevented outright civil war but also generated incentives for talk.[68]

As millions stayed away by taking to the streets, the campaign lent Mandela leverage. In the ensuing weeks, the ANC proposed the resumption of bilateral talks between the two men who were beginning to take centre stage as lead negotiators, Cyril Ramaphosa from the ANC and the NP's Roelf Meyer. While such meetings had been occurring for some time in secret, the Congress suggested that these publicly sanctioned meetings focus on violence reduction, the expeditious release of political prisoners, the clashes in the hostels, and the need to restrict public displays of cultural weapons.[69]

As the constitutional issues were put temporarily on the back burner, however, another kind of violence gathered significant attention. In late August, the Skweyiya Commission released a report on the conditions and alleged human rights abuse in the MK's training camps outside of the country. The news was disturbing even as critics charged that the Commission was composed of ANC sycophants. Most notably, the report demonstrated something of a contradiction between the ANC's expressed commitment to international law and the "violence for the sake of violence" that had occurred in detention camps such as Quatro (Angola) and the Revolutionary Council (Zambia). Citing a litany of human rights abuses – torture, forced labour, indefinite detention, forced confession – the Commission noted that many of its findings were well known before it began its investigation, in part because a number of high-ranking ANC leaders had "openly admitted that abuses occurred in the camps". While making no claim that the demonstrable abuses were in any way equivalent to the violence perpetrated by the South African regime, the Commission concluded that the problem would persist without decisive action. To this end, it argued that, "At a time when there are serious allegations of abuse perpetuated by high-ranking State officials, we believe that the ANC could set an example by initiating its own investigation into the allegations of disappearance and death. This could, in our view, signify a new direction for the protection of human rights in South Africa."[70] With respect to the need for truth, the ANC was not the only one on a rhetorical limb. Appointed after the signing of the *National Peace Accord*, the Goldstone Commission was making inroads into the nature and extent of third force activity, especially with respect to the state's training and arming of Inkatha. At the same time, de Klerk faced mounting pressure to reopen the inquiry into the role of government forces and cabinet-level ministers in the death of Matthew Goniwe and the other members of the Cradock Four.[71]

Concerns over who was accountable for violence corresponded with renewed debate over what role amnesty would play in the transition. At the end of August, it was reported that Minster of Justice Kobie Coetsee had proposed to link the release of additional political prisoners with the provisioning of a general amnesty.[72] While Coetsee denied making the proposal, the issue was clearly on the table. This time, compared to those taken during the talks about talks, the positions were reversed. Now opposed to a general amnesty, the ANC released a statement which argued that the "question of political prisoners cannot be muddied with the amnesty issue" and contended that government did not have the "competence to grant such an amnesty" since the matter could only be taken up by an interim government that could promulgate amnesty legislation that contributed to an "understanding of the past". In the ANC's terms:

If a general amnesty simply sweeps all the misdeeds under the carpet, the clamour for justice will only increase from all those who have been harmed. The truth has to be revealed, and the judicial process completed, to help ensure a democratic future for South Africa.[73]

Some members of the South African media echoed this position, arguing that the government had no right to forgive itself and that the country could not "bury history or eradicate painful memories by decree". *The Weekly Mail* opined, "A blanket amnesty can get negotiations going, but the reconciliation it allows for is as thin as the ice on a lake in winter. Come spring the currents that have continued to flow under the surface will rise to the top again."[74] A month later, it would advocate the formation of a truth commission as an alternative.[75] In the moment, however, the debate was complicating the resolution of the prisoner issue, one of the key conditions for the ANC's re-entry into negotiations. On 28 August, the Congress ran an advert in national newspapers with a list of 380 prisoners who were still awaiting release. While the government claimed that the number was inflated by half, the real sticking point appeared to be the indemnity applications of Robert McBride, Mzondeleli Nondula, and Mthetheleli Mncube, each of whom was on death row for killings that the government deemed to be outside the scope of the legitimate political activity that constituted grounds for indemnity.

As the indemnity-amnesty issue was being discussed, bilateral talks and mass action continued simultaneously. On 7 September, the equation changed. It is difficult to know whose bargaining position was shaken more by the loss of 28 lives at the hands of Ciskei soldiers who shot at a group of protestors after they broke through a fence in order to take their message from the outskirts to the centre of Bisho. In any case, the massacre was a clear signal of the struggle's continued resolve and an indication that mass action was difficult to control and not always with a clear purpose. What was also apparent was that the day's events were read by both sides as a reason to increase the pace of talks.[76] Shortly thereafter, fed by a sense that bilateral meetings had made progress toward fulfilling the ANC's three key demands – prisoner release, reducing hostel violence, and limiting use of cultural weapons – a summit was scheduled.

On 26 September, Mandela and de Klerk returned to the World Trade Centre to sign a *Record of Understanding*. The agreement was a significant breakthrough, particularly as it appeared to signal a rough consensus on the procedure for writing a new constitution. Precisely, the memorandum announced that:

> The Government and the ANC agreed that there is a need for a
> democratic constitution assembly/constitution-making body and that for
> such a body to be democratic it must: be democratically elected; draft

and adopt the new constitution, implying that it should sit as a single chamber; be bound only by agreed constitutional principles; have a fixed time frame; have adequate deadlock breaking mechanisms; function democratically, i.e. arrive at its decisions democratically with certain agreed to majorities; and be elected within an agreed predetermined time period. Within the framework of these principles, detail would have to be worked out in the negotiation process.[77]

Did the ANC win? Did the NP give in? These were the questions of the day. Answers were mixed. At some level, it was clear that de Klerk had ceded significant ground with respect to the mechanics and outcome of the transition. In his autobiography, however, he denies this, arguing that mass action had not influenced his bargaining position and that most of the *Record*'s provisions were simply carried over from CODESA.[78] Speaking to Parliament and treading rather carefully, de Klerk suggested that the agreement ensured progress in a manner that did not foreclose the possibility of a power-sharing arrangement. For the ANC, it was apparent that they had let go of some demands pertaining to security and violence alleviation in order to restart the negotiations process. In fact, this was perhaps the most important gain, the creation of a "process alliance" that opened the door to the creation of a new and "more businesslike" negotiating forum.[79] Not everyone, however, wanted to step inside. Bitterly disappointed that the NP had fled its side, the IFP withdrew from the talks with what one commentator called "one of the most carefully drafted tantrums in history".

While the climate had stabilised, the horizon at Kempton Park held the promise of some additional storms. The *Record of Understanding* was preceded by an agreement for the phased release of some 150 political prisoners. In early October, de Klerk announced that the process would require Parliament to pass new legislation: the *Further Indemnity Act*. The bill was nothing if not expansive, allowing for the pardon of all politically motivated crimes through a secret process overseen by a group of presidentially-appointed judges. Critics cried "star chamber" and argued that the government was preparing the means to grant itself amnesty. As the security force leadership (many of whom had lobbied the President for such protection) applauded the move, de Klerk argued that the measure was both necessary given that those set for release were not eligible for such under the criteria of standing legislation, and a desirable way to "clean the slate in all directions" and "promote reconciliation and peaceful solutions".[80] In direct response, the ANC reiterated its position that prisoner release was distinct from the question of amnesty and, signalling its growing electoral confidence, it warned that the law "will last as long as Apartheid has breath through Nationalist rule and no longer".[81]

Although the parliamentary debate over indemnity had much of the heat that it did in 1990, now it was set against the backdrop of seemingly inevitable change. Thus, the issue was less whether to reconcile than if the bill would promote reconciliation. In this regard, Kobie Coetsee began what was both an important and somewhat pointless discussion by arguing that the *Further Indemnity Act* did not portend a general amnesty but served only as a "supplement" to the existing legal procedures used to release political prisoners. Unconvinced by the state's claim that indemnity was a way to speed the reconciliation process, the CP argued that the bill placed too much power in the executive's hands and ignored statistics indicating that indemnity did little to lessen political violence. Speaking for the Labour Party, Luwellyn Landers took a different tack, arguing that the bill's breadth and secrecy provisions would actually cut against the creation of reconciliation and accountability:

> The truth must be complete, and the truth about past crimes must be officially proclaimed and publicly exposed. There can be no reconciliation until the South African public knows who the perpetrators of past deeds are, what crimes they committed, and on whose orders those crimes were committed. This Bill does not provide for full and public disclosure.[82]

The momentum for this argument was growing. In only a partial rebuttal, the Afrikaner Volksunie's (AVU) Christiaan de Jager argued that the promised reconciliation was about mending fences not only with the ANC but also between "my people, the Afrikaners".[83] Noting the ANC's promise to treat the law as a "nullity", Jan Momberg argued that the bill was nothing more than "cheap reconciliation", an attempt to escape the risks and responsibilities of healing.[84]

Across the different aisles and chambers of Parliament, few agreed that a "further indemnity" would advance the aims of reconciliation. Using the President's Council, de Klerk overrode Parliament's veto and implemented it anyway. With respect to coming negotiations, the significance of the Act was different from its 1990 counterpart. The issue now was not about bracketing the past in the name of creating a climate, but a concern to guarantee power in the wake of a new future; amnesty was one way to counter constituent fears of post-transition domination. Thus, the *Further Indemnity Act* smacked of expediency, especially when its terms were set next to Eugene de Kock's admission that part of the state's "third force" was continuing its dirty tricks campaign. After its "passage", the legislation left de Klerk to walk the tight line of assuring supporters that they would not be prosecuted on the grounds of a law that the ANC steadfastly promised to repeal.

Backed by the *Record of Understanding* and the *Further Indemnity Act*, the negotiations process took an important turn. Almost a year after the opening of CODESA, it was time once again to talk about the constitutive power of talk. Attention to this matter was explicit. In November, Joe Slovo published a short essay in the *African Communist* entitled "Negotiations: What Room for Compromise?" In it, the leader of the SACP argued that struggle forces needed to admit their vulnerability, the fact that they were and were not going to be dealing with a "defeated enemy". If so, Slovo claimed, "a degree of compromise will be unavoidable" and more controversially, desirable. Specifically, he suggested that the ANC-led alliance consider embracing both a "sunset clause in the new constitution which would provide for compulsory power-sharing for a fixed number of years" and a general amnesty for those who "will disclose in full those activities for which they require an amnesty".[85] Together, these "retreats from previously held positions" could jumpstart negotiations without "hampering real democratic advance".

Slovo's position generated significant controversy. In response, Pallo Jordan warned that the proposal allowed de Klerk to continue his strategy of standing on both sides of the fence. Leaving little doubt about his view of the proposed sunset clauses, Jordan concluded: "A national liberation movement that does that is not riding into the sunset, it would be building its own funeral pyre."[86] It was, however, another set of voices that prevailed. In mid-November, the ANC released "Negotiations: A Strategic Perspective". Accepting a great deal of Slovo's logic and some of his policy proposals, the Congress concluded that a counter-revolutionary approach to the struggle only served to feed the regime's power and that the course of the transition would likely require discussion of sunset clauses as well as amnesty. A week later, de Klerk drew from this concession to reframe his view of power-sharing and further distance it from the idea of a minority veto. Read together, it appeared that disagreement was now less an obstacle to talks than a reason for their onset.

What happened between the great expectations of CODESA and its breakdown, between one leader's referendum and another's mass action, between the burials after Boipatong and Bisho, between the closed-door bilaterals and the public achievement of a tangible "record" of understanding? Before CODESA, the potential for reconciliation appeared less as a promise of future harmony than a time in which to build a present from a common experience of violence. At the opening plenary, this moment was elusive as parties struggled to agree on how to define and argue about the power of talk to enact a process of constitution-making. Negotiators had learned to turn violence toward opposition but not how opposition could be used to fund agreement. Now returned, after having been bracketed during the talks about talks, history played a significant role in this shortfall. More precisely, historically justified visions of sovereignty exceeded and collapsed the potential for discourse. Between the NP's referendum and the ANC's mass action, each side used different appeals to the sovereign in order to evidence their claim as to how the other did not have the legal standing, democratic vision, or moral integrity needed to define the form and content of transition. Respectively, the existing state and the figure of the people backed claims about who represented the constituted power authorised to exceed the law in the name of setting it into motion.

Nelson Mandela's appeal to reconciliation in July challenged this logic, allowing a bit of bright light into the double-helix laager of non-negotiation. There was a higher law, a law before the law. This prior and present law was not of history but for it. It was one that demanded faith, a belief that the potential to create had to proceed in the face of the risk that attended creation. The necessary violence of making the new thus had to develop from a position of vulnerability, from talk that transgressed history's causes and remained open to using dispute as a basis for agreements that would compose the constitution-writing process. Indeed, in the days and weeks leading up to and following the *Record of Understanding*, the NP and ANC both subtly backed away from their own announced historical positions about the "necessary" form of change and allowed for the possibility that the transition required the release of that power which was already constituted and being used to turn opposition back toward *stasis* instead of forward into a process of constitution-making. In the form of the *Further Indemnity Act*, amnesty both helped and complicated this shift, opening a moment in which the force of law was (again) held at bay and raising questions about whether the faith of transition came at the expense of history's truth. The latter was a debate still in its infancy. More important at the time, it appeared by the end of November that the problem of how to overcome constituted power had been turned toward the question of how to create a mode of constitutive power. Potential was ready to be(come). In the mysterious "matter" of transition, the question now was less "if" (a permissive sovereign) than "how" (sovereignty's permission).

3. a sufficiently consensual (speech) act of constitution

At CODESA, appeals to sovereignty were heard as violent threats to usurp the power of constitution-making. The mass action that followed the convention's breakdown underscored the problem, an indication that both sides were vying for the legal-historical standing needed to author a new (or not so new) dispensation. At some level, the clash was typical, a practical confirmation of Walter Benjamin's claim that the critique and escape from law's violence demands a kind of talk that sets law aside in order to create power within the confines of a "conference", a deliberative forum that eschews the means and ends of contracts, provides no juridical sanction for lying, and affords the time for parties to "reconcile their interests peacefully without involving the legal system".[87] By the same token, Benjamin notes that such space cannot be filled with revolutionary agendas or transcending aspirations. Its words of reconciliation devolve to hypocrisy if they misrecognise that the power to create peace hinges on the deployment of constitutive power, a making of law that cannot escape the violence which attends its creation.

In early 1993, negotiators began to build on CODESA's productive failure to create deliberative norms that could support disagreement over how to make South Africa new. Here, I consider one of the more important attempts to define and perform such constitutive power. Focused on a set of discussions that took place during the first half of a constitutional convention without an official name, this section examines how negotiators at the Multi-Party Negotiating Process defined, performed, and disputed the theory and practice of "sufficient consensus".[88] Between March and September of 1993, sufficient consensus played a crucial role in the process of constitution-making. Held up as a "home-grown" invention, it was designed and defended as a way to ensure fairness, participation, and the development of productive opposition at the negotiating table. It was also a source of divisive controversy, an idea that defied clear definition and a mode of decision-making which left some parties to complain bitterly about their exclusion from the talks.

The "resolution" of this controversy demonstrated the necessity of what appeared intolerable at CODESA, a spirit of reconciliation that sustained constitution-making through an explicit exception if not opposition to the (sovereign) rule of law. Thus, at the beginning of the MPNP, the decision to use sufficient consensus endowed appeals for reconciliation with a practical form. Underwritten by a spirit of good faith and an agreement to seek progress over self-interest, sufficient consensus was a formal-pragmatic mode of communication, one that was defended as being an intrinsic and organic element of the negotiating process. Before the law, the ambiguous procedures that composed the use of sufficient consensus relied on a shared sense of political honour. At the bargaining table, this *ethos* reflected the negotiators' commitment to reconciliation and also enacted reconciliation's productive opposition, a refusal of law's sovereign edict in the name of creating bonds of mutual identification.

defining consensus sufficiently

The light of early summer brought new hope and revealed winter's scars on the landscape. On 8 January 1993, the anniversary of the notorious *Land Act* and the ANC's formation, the Congress's NEC issued a direct but notably softer rendition of its vision for the transition. Arguing that there that could be no "reconciliation without acknowledgment" of the past, the Council reiterated its dissatisfaction with the *Further Indemnity Act* and added that "to create the new, we will have to start from the heritage of a society torn apart and driven by hatred and division". In the same spirit of remembrance, it recalled the *Freedom Charter*'s principle of non-racialism and reaffirmed the ANC's overarching commitment to a South Africa in which all citizens "learn to treat our languages, cultures and religions with equal respect and dignity". To this end, the Council acknowledged that the ANC had to "prepare ourselves to govern" – work that demanded significant organisational change and required the standing government to embrace the development of a centralised democracy backed by an "entrenched" Bill of Rights.[89]

Opening Parliament on 29 January, de Klerk announced, "It will be to no avail to expect miracles or to sit around and complain." Echoing the NEC's tone, the President embraced the year's "new spirit" and declared that the country was close to reaching a "broad consensus" for the terms of political change. According to the President, the bottom line was clear:

> Every South African is facing a choice: Either to support constitutional change and everything which is reasonably required for its success; or retire to the laager and prepare for an armed and bloody struggle. The

simple truth is that a devastating war will ensue if negotiation does not succeed.[90]

Addressed mostly to his traditional constituents and the deeply alienated far right, de Klerk's claim recast the stakes of what it meant to fear transition. To his counterparts at the table, there was a different message: the government was committed to change and aware that "something dramatic is beginning to happen". But, there was also worry about the President's claim that "certain important actors" had a proclivity for turning to "malicious aggression at the expense of constructive criticism". With respect to the coming talks, however, the President appeared to give a bit of ground, arguing less for a specific form of transition than a reconciliation rooted in a "regional dispensation, based on federal principles and recognition of our cultural and linguistic diversity".[91] A rather clear enthymeme, the call for federalism indicated that the issue of minority rights protection was still important and still not settled.

Bilateral talks continued through the turn of the year. In early February, the ANC and NP filled in a key part of the puzzle, agreeing very tentatively that the country would be governed for no more than five years by a Government of National Unity that would operate on the basis of consensus and oversee the production of the new constitution.[92] While a crucial step forward, the agreement did not assure the resumption of multilateral talks. For one, the IFP continued to balk, arguing that the ratification percentages envisaged for the constitution-writing process would ensure its marginalisation. At a larger level, negotiators faced standing disagreements about what protections to include in the Bill of Rights, which apartheid laws needed to be repealed, and how the new dispensation would conceive and enforce the separation of governmental power.[93] At base, all of these issues rested on the creation of a forum that embodied a "new style of political conduct", a form of negotiating and decision-making that took care with the fact that "the state would be shaped by decisions about the constitution".[94] In early 1993, this perceived link between the form and substance of negotiations led directly to the problem that had so bedevilled CODESA: What did sufficient consensus mean and how was it best measured?

Following the February agreement, plans were laid for a preliminary all-party meeting. Echoing the NP, the ANC's Carl Niehaus claimed, "We are ready to get back to CODESA." As it set aside the key question of whether any of CODESA's architecture or agreements could be used to support a new round of talks, the sentiment was perhaps more optimistic than accurate.[95] On

5 March, a group called the MPNP Facilitating Committee met to consider a draft version of a *Declaration of Intent* to commence negotiations. An important signal, the *Declaration* was seen as a precondition to new multilateral talks and as a way of demonstrating to anxious citizens that the parties were committed to making progress that was now long overdue. Joe Slovo made the latter point well, observing that "we are not just talking to ourselves we are talking to the country". The problem, however, was that both kinds of speech were sending mixed signals.

Almost immediately, members of the committee began to disagree about whether to debate the *Declaration of Intent*'s appropriate terms or if it was first necessary to arrive at a "decision about the decision-making process" that was presupposed by such debate.[96] Was it better to take up a substantive issue in the name of discerning points of difference or was it preferable to establish the rules of engagement in order to prevent expressed differences from devolving to deeper conflicts? Claiming to fear a moment when "we won't be able to decide how to decide", Pravin Gordhan observed that the problem represented a difficult conceptual puzzle: "I believe that we must actually confront the reality that we will have to learn to co-operate somewhere along the line and the decision-making processes and in it's (*sic*) definition it is also going to require cooperation."[97]*

Once again, it was time for meta-talk. With little common ground to define the meaning of common ground, negotiators were back to the problem of how to define and make a sufficient consensus. Suggesting that procedure needed to precede substance, or casting the former as the latter, the ANC's Cyril Ramaphosa delineated the context of the problem and offered a functional interpretation of how sufficient consensus could be used to underwrite the committee's deliberative decision-making:

> Everybody agrees so there is no problem, now if we were to adopt this resolution on the basis of general consensus, we wouldn't have any problem, but obviously you cannot always agree, even in a family, in a committee of an organisation, there comes a time when you don't agree. Generally in our committees, executive committees and so forth decisions are taken by general consensus but sometimes you don't

---

* At the MPNP, the remarks of speakers were transcribed with greater and lesser clarity. In this chapter, the quotations from the MPNP's proceedings are reproduced precisely as they appear in the existing record.

agree. So you then have to develop a method of taking decisions. It will be instructive to state here that [in] negotiations that have preceded this meeting, we did decide that we will take decisions on the basis of sufficient consensus. But what does sufficient consensus mean? Sufficient consensus means that there is an absence of general consensus, so you then say is there sufficient consensus for us to take this decision or that decision. But it also means that once you arrive at sufficient consensus you are essentially saying there is sufficient consensus for us to take this decision and to go on despite the disagreement the reservation that people may be expressing. So, in the process we are involved in, we would need to say what does sufficient consensus mean. I would say that sufficient consensus should mean if for instance the process is able to [go] on because we are involved in the process. If the process can go on, with the support of those who support a proposal, we should say there is sufficient consensus to go on.[98]

A burr since the opening days of CODESA, when Ramaphosa himself had cast sufficient consensus as a form of power politics, this negative and somewhat circular definition quickly gave way to a larger debate. Soon to be at the centre of the storm around its use, Pravin Gordhan addressed the PAC's claim that Ramaphosa's view of sufficient consensus defied objective or even rigorous application. Expanding the concept, Gordhan argued:

Can I speak just briefly from my own experience and that is that in addition to saying that sufficient consensus means that the process goes on, I think we need to accept that there's a quantitative and qualitative element related to it. And secondly, there's a contextual element to it [uuh] tied to the quality. Let me explain what I mean. In the first instance quantitative means what's the numbers looking like. And sometimes that's sufficient to say there is sufficient consensus. Yet at other times, more often than not we have to look that at the quality of the decision we are taking, the quality of the consensus that we actually have and whether that will time the process forward and you can't attach numbers to it and then reinforced by my third point, which is that it depends on the contexts in which you are going to judge on this matter. It depends on what is the kind of position you are taking, what is the kind of issue that you are debating and with what's the next step that you are likely to go into.[99]

The question of how to "move forward" in the face of opposition to a particular decision or policy remained the weak link in the chain. A number of committee members argued that Gordhan's criteria allowed the major parties to dominate the proceedings and use their votes to push the country into transition. Ramaphosa answered this objection in a way that begged its question, claiming that all gathered had publicly committed themselves to enacting fundamental political change and that while it could be "very subjective", sufficient consensus was important precisely so that "the process of transforming our country can go on".[100] While the DP's Colin Eglin agreed that there was a "common purpose" that stabilised the decision-making process, the PAC representative, Benny Alexander, countered that such principles would do little to prevent negotiations from lurching from potential breakdown to potential breakdown. However, a speaker not identified in the transcripts observed that this was correct only if parties failed to accept that some issues would entail judgments rooted in "mood and feeling". The point was echoed by a speaker who noted, in a sort of Rawlsian way, that one key to the process was the ability of negotiators to consider the merits of particular proposals independent of the group or "personalities" that advanced them.[101]

Debate over the relative necessity of sufficient consensus did not convince the PAC that it would or could be applied fairly. Toward the end of the meeting, Alexander reported, "We are not yet happy that we don't have clear defined boundaries for discretion in regards to contextual qualitative and quantitative aspects of the issues before us so that the Chairperson's must have and the house must be clear on this matter."[102] Would parties have a "right" to appeal rulings as to the existence or lack of sufficient consensus? Noting that "because consensus means sufficient consensus is a bit of a tautology", and that since it was an "invention of the South African negotiating culture", the IFP representative, Joe Matthews, argued that the process made no clear allowance for what to do in the face of a deadlock rooted in principle, an objection to a ruling of sufficient consensus that would compel a party to withdraw from the negotiations if its opposition was dismissed or bracketed in the name of moving forward. This problem was met with the suggestion that the overall negotiations might work conditionally such that no single decision at the forum would be final until it had been gathered into a package and ratified by the MPNP's plenary body. More important at the time, however, a number of committee members argued that the viability and power of sufficient consensus had less to do with its strict definition than the attitude that backed its use. The Bophuthatswana representative, Rowan Cronje, summed up this concern for *ethos* when he noted, "[T]he search for consensus and sufficient consensus goes beyond the methodology. It goes to the climate in which we need, the attitude in which need, I think we all realise one way or another our country is desperately in need of a solution … if we are serious we will have to compromise and every party every delegation organisation are saying by participating in the process I will have to give up some of my views."[103] The process would have to proceed on faith. In the name of change, the constitutive power of the negotiations would depend more on a spirit than the rule of law.

Ultimately, the Facilitating Committee came to a sufficient if not outright consensus about the use of sufficient consensus in the negotiating process. This decision was significant. In the days leading up to the MPNP, the issue confronting negotiators was how to agree on the means that would be used to regulate talks, resolve disagreement, and ratify a binding declaration to negotiate for a new constitution. Formal and pragmatic, sufficient consensus appeared to be a viable solution to these problems. It both depended on an ethical commitment to defer self-interest in favour of advancing the constitution-writing process and held a sort of strategic ambiguity that allowed room for negotiators to engage in vigorous opposition without fear of collapsing the larger talks. A way to conduct discourse and a means of adjudicating debate, sufficient consensus was less a procedure than a constellation of concepts – consensus, compromise, and opposition. In this way, it was not simply a way of making the constitution but a performance of constitutive speech. In an uncertain time, without singular or certain grounds for judgment, and still wary of the blurry line that separated violence and power, sufficient consensus offered a way for negotiators to "make it up as they went along". In the name of the new, it was a way to actualise the potential to constitute, a means of inventing that which could not be defined by law but which was given to its creation.

arguing about the (in)sufficiency of practice
The Multi-Party Negotiating Process convened on 1 April 1993. Nine days later, on Good Friday, Chris Hani was assassinated. With the death of the popular SACP leader, the nation did not merely sit on edge; it was one. At the funeral, Desmond Tutu delivered a powerful eulogy, an oration that commemorated Hani's vital and various roles in the fight against apartheid in a way that underscored the stakes of the moment. Asking for and performing

faith in the midst of loss, the Archbishop was emphatic: "We are marching to victory." He said it over and over and over, struggling to turn a deeply shaken hope into a tangible promise that could be taken and fulfilled by bereaved, angry, and nervous citizens.[104] Emphasising the difficulty of the task, *The Weekly Mail* reported that it was a day when the "country first glanced into the abyss" and quoted an activist to say, "The people are shattered into a thousand pieces, everyone is just running with his own little piece of hatred." In a gesture that the *Mail* called both crucial and a serious threat to "their collective political lives", the ANC leadership said and demonstrated otherwise. Faced with renewed and increasingly loud calls to set the struggle on a more radical path, it pleaded for calm, unity, and discipline in the name of making good on Hani's sacrifice.[105] The talks would indeed go on. So would the pain. On 24 April, Oliver Tambo suffered a fatal stroke. In the space of two weeks, the country had lost two of its greatest.

Before Hani's assassination, the multiparty process had accomplished important work. At a series of preliminary meetings, negotiators devised the forum's structure and ratified its *Declaration of Intent*. Organisationally, the MPNP was designed with CODESA's failure in mind. This time, things needed to be smaller, more efficient, and further from the public's pressurising eye. With a five-tiered and progressively more exclusive structure, the MPNP was composed of a Plenary Body, Negotiating Forum, Negotiating Council, and a Planning Committee that included a powerful three-person body known only as the "subcommittee".[106] CODESA's working groups were replaced by seven Technical Committees, small groups that were to operate from a very specific premise: "Technical Committees are not fora for negotiating substantive issues. They are instruments of the Negotiating Council in order to produce systematic documentation to facilitate discussion in the Negotiating Council."[107] Charged then to discern and plot "middle ground", the Technical Committees were concerned to find *topoi* for arguments, points of commonality and disagreement that could be used and refashioned in order to keep the negotiations moving.

Without the enthusiastic tone of its CODESA counterpart, the MPNP's *Declaration of Intent* cut right to the chase. It called for the resumption of all-party talks that would "reach agreements on binding constitutional principles", take steps to implement these agreements in a timely manner, and schedule an election for no later than April 1994. In supporting documentation, the Negotiating Council held that decisions taken at CODESA would be treated as "points of reference, and not as binding agreements".[108] Drawing partly from the earlier suggestion in the Facilitating Committee, it also resolved that while the negotiations process would "involve reaching agreement on a number of key elements", these decisions would take effect only as parties had a "clear understanding of the package of agreements which would constitute the key elements of the transition process". Designed to avoid "suspicion and fears" about the premature implementation of particular decisions, policies that carried the risk of fating the form of the transition, this protocol introduced a conditional quality into the work of creating a constitutive power.[109] Allowing negotiators the freedom to accept sufficiently consensual agreements based on the knowledge that they could be revisited, it also created the option to "pigeon-hole" controversial issues until such time as they could be resolved on the basis of other established decisions.

With the *Declaration*, the Council passed a set of standing rules for the negotiating process. Reflecting discussion in the Facilitating Committee, the guidelines specified that agreements would be taken by general consensus or "if general consensus cannot be achieved, the method of sufficient consensus will be used". The rules authorised the Chair of each meeting to determine the existence or lack of sufficient consensus but also noted that disagreeing parties who considered themselves "materially affected" by such rulings would have opportunities to record their objections, leave meetings to consult with principals, and request the formation of technical committees to investigate the matter in dispute. While expected to work in the "spirit of cooperation" needed to keep the process going forward, the rules did note that dissenting parties could challenge rulings from the Chair about whether there was or was not sufficient consensus.[110] As negotiators set to work, it would take only a month for the ambiguity of this position to develop into a deep fault line.

While tensions outside the negotiating hall increased with the creation of the Afrikaner Volksfront (AVF) by a "committee of Generals", the Technical Committee on Constitutional Issues reported in mid-May that there was significant disagreement over how actually to write the new constitution.[111] A clear echo of CODESA, the dispute involved old questions about who would author the document and if it was desirable to maintain legal continuity during the transition.[112] Added to the mix was a continuing debate over the degree to which the constitution would embody federalist principles. With the IFP and NP arguing for checks that would ensure significant regional and provincial autonomy, the pace of talks slowed. In the light of public pressure, this lag appeared to concern the Negotiating Council. The minutes of its 3 June meeting record that it is "vital to inject confidence in the negotiating process" and that the "the setting of a date for the elections will send a ray of hope and optimism throughout the country".[113] To this end, the Council recommended that the election be scheduled for 27 April 1994 but that in order to "maximise consensus" a decision on the matter would not be taken until its next meeting.

The question of when citizens would vote quickly became the focal point of a controversy over whether sufficient consensus was a fair and fairly applied means of making decisions. On 15 June, the Negotiating Council met to undertake further debate on the election's date. Central on the agenda was a memorandum submitted by Ben Ngubane on behalf of the KwaZulu Government (KZG). In it, Ngubane argued that the Council's proposal risked breaching the integrity of the negotiations:

> It is unreasonable to set an election date when we do not know what type of stages and phases need to precede the election and what the purposes and functions of that election are going to be in the process of constitutional development of our country. Differently put, are we going to vote for the election of a Constituent Assembly or for the empowerment of a federal legislature after member states have already been established .... We feel the obligation to warn all participants that the KZG has reached the end of its road in tolerating the manipulation of this process which is steamrolling through the real issues of our society preventing full awareness and full debate on the possible alternatives.[114]

Rooted in strong opposition to the creation of a centralised government and a desire for a single-phase transition, Ngubane's position put back on the table the problem of how (well) negotiators were talking to one another. For one, it was accompanied by a resolution that called for deferring the decision on an election date so that the Technical Committee on Constitutional Issues could undertake a study into other models for the design of the constitution and an implementation "process which relies on ground up democracy building sub-processes to support the creation of SPRs". Moreover, the KZG declared that until its resolution was passed and such inquiry undertaken, it was "no longer willing to provide its consensus for any further decisions taken by this Negotiating Council" and committed to "challenge any ruling of the chair determining that sufficient consensus had been achieved in spite of KZG opposition".[115]

The KZG's resolution failed by sufficient consensus. What happened next was crucial. After the Chair's ruling, the transcripts of the meeting indicate that several parties exercised their "right" to leave the chamber in order to consult with their principals regarding their opposition to the ruling. During their absence, a motion to recommend formally that the Negotiating Forum approve an election date of 27 April was placed on the table and passed, again by sufficient consensus. Three days later, citing the Planning Committee's claim that it recognised "unhappiness" with sufficient consensus even as it had no knowledge of specific objections, the Council reconvened to discuss the issue of sufficient consensus as it pertained to the MPNP's "standards and management of debate". At the meeting, the IFP's Walter Felgate cast the election date decision as an egregious violation of the standing rules. More precisely, he argued that sufficient consensus had been replaced by blatant "head counting" and was compromised by a suspect decision in which a Chair had ruled in the absence of representatives from some eight different parties:

> The point I'm trying to Mr. Chair is that procedures for handling
> difficult issues are not clear enough, they don't exist in the standing
> rules, there is no prudence built into them to guide the chair and the
> question of special quorums for special interpretations of consensus are
> being made. We have taken legal advice and the legal advice in short
> says that the words, the interpretation in the clauses of such vague and
> ambiguous nature that you could not even seek a ruling of a court on
> the interpretation of them ...[116]

While the claim was oddly prophetic, several responses were made to Felgate's argument, all of which suggested that the IFP and KZG were forgetting the Facilitating Committee's deliberations in March. Joe Slovo argued that since all parties, including the IFP, had helped develop and then committed themselves to the use of sufficient consensus, there was no reason to suspend or revise the MPNP's standing rules. Questioning the IFP's appeal to law, the NP's Leon Wessels argued that the forum was in the midst of "developing a true South African concept which is true to our circumstances" and that legal interpretations of the forum's work could not come at the expense of a "command of our own process". Others reiterated the need to understand sufficient consensus through a spirit of compromise and cautioned that if there was one, the problem was not in "the validity, clarity, or the complexity of the rules" but in their application. Ultimately, Pravin Gordhan offered the most nuanced formulation of the question, a lengthy but important argument about what it meant to apply and perform sufficient consensus:

I think that the issue that we are dealing here is really not a technical or a legal issue. In many ways, it's a political issue and I completely agree with Mr. Jacobs that consensus is not majority. Consensus is where, happily all of us are able to say that we have no reservations whatsoever on a particular decision and we go ahead with that. We also have to face the reality that not all of us are going to agree with each other all the time and we have [to] find a mechanism which caters for that eventuality in order that we have progress in the proceedings of this Council. Now progress is important because the prime purpose of our existence here as Council is that we need to negotiate, but we can't go on negotiating endlessly as well. We need to produce results in order that we develop confidence in the negotiating process and in the capacity of this Council to deliver what it claims it can deliver: a *constitutional making process* in whatever way we design that ultimately. Now in that light, I think we are dealing with two perceptions which I think we must take equal cognisance of. The one perception is that a so-called majority is crowding out a minority and for that reason we need to look at what we mean by sufficient consensus, so that [there] isn't a unfair overwhelming process going on of so-called minorities, whether that minority is 3, 4, 5 whatever the case might be, depending on the issue. The second perception can best be called the filibustering perception, that there are perhaps attempts to delay processes, obstruct processes, etc. So, in whatever decision-making process we want to evolve through the mechanisms that are being proposed, both those processes need to be dealt with and both these processes need to be catered for. If the perception is left that the only reason we want to revisit sufficient consensus is to provide mechanisms for delays or obstructions, and I'm saying perceptions, I'm not saying that's a reality then I think that we are going to get the cooperation of all people concerned. If the quest is for fairer more equitable way of taking decisions, of ensuring maximum consensus, not total consensus of ensuring we have mechanisms available so that we bridge the gaps between different people in a genuine way then certainly that quest needs to be gone into. But fundamentally, we've all got to come to an understanding that we are reaching a point where we've got to become decisive about the substantive issues at one level or another, we've got to find mechanisms … to say that where are we going to meet each other in relation to substantive issues, one of them being self-determination for example, because clearly black

and white or one and two has distant propositions are not going to
be accepted by either party. But, we've got to find some grey zone in
which we can meet that colour, the intensity of the grey zone in which
can meet that colour, the intensity of the grey is of course going to be
the subject of debate and discussion. I think that also needs to exercise
the minds of the members of the Council. When are we going to reach
a point where we begin to say that we are ready to make the decisive
substantive compromises that are necessary in order to take the process
forward? I believe that some parties already believe that they have done
so. They've made a significant number of compromises, gestures, and
points of accommodation in order to cater for certain concerns. Others
might not think [so], that again needs to be discussed and the belief is
that others need to apply themselves to that particular question. In a
way, the issue is not only the decision-making process, whilst it is [an]
important issue to refine, but the other issue is how to find the bridges
of the different views that we have here.[117]

The grey zone. In 1985 and 1986, this phrase had been used to characterise
the state of emergency, the law's self-conflation of itself in the name of
preserving its own violent power. Now, this space represented a mode of
constitutive power, a capacity to stand inside and outside law's violence in
the name of making it otherwise.

In Gordhan's position, the speech-action of constituting law was political
work that had to proceed outside legal boundaries and precedents. The
validity of decision-making was contingent not on rule of law but on how
well it made and supported the background consensus needed to write the
constitution and define a plan for the transition to democracy. Too, it followed
closely that sufficient consensus was itself a creature of the compromises
that would be codified in the constitution; procedure was less important
than the process. Without certain benchmarks for success, the negotiations
required the creation and maintenance of a reflexive relation between
issues on the agenda and the methods for reaching agreement. Accordingly,
sufficient consensus was not only a way of judging the outcomes of debate
but a norm regulating how debate should occur. The process of talking about
constitution-making was also the beginning of its performance. The question,
however, was whether and how the power of this performativity was coming
at the expense of the expression that it claimed to promote and value.

While the Council resolved not to suspend or amend the standing rules pertaining to sufficient consensus, it did call for the creation of an ad hoc committee to study the issue. It was unclear, however, whether the committee's charge was to redefine the standing rules' definition of sufficient consensus or assess whether the rules had been applied incorrectly. The minutes from its first meeting, on 24 June, show the committee taking the second path, undertaking discussion about the perception that sufficient consensus was not "effective or inclusive enough". More precisely, the committee devoted the bulk of its time to the question of whether shortfalls in the process were due to the work of individuals who were chairing crucial meetings but lacked a "feel" for making the appropriate decision or facilitating discussion in a manner that maximised opportunities for consensus.[118]

A month later, the committee met again. As before, it resolved not to recommend a change in the standing rules. It also decided that references to the potentially divisive "quality of chairs" issue should be eliminated from its report to the Council. In place of this issue, the committee debated and agreed to several relatively minor changes in the practice and application of sufficient consensus, namely, chairs should increase discussion time, devote more attention to weighing the reasons for and against particular proposals, and refer particularly contentious issues to technical committees for further consideration. Many of these ideas were included in the committee's final report, a document which also argued that the increasing use of "head counting" to establish sufficient consensus needed to be replaced by a consideration of the nature of the issue, the parties for and against the question, the gravity of the opposition or support, and whether objecting parties were sincere in their objections or seeking to obstruct progress. Beneath all of these small repairs, the group emphasised that the underlying "spirit" of the talks were just as important if not more so than the objectivity of their rules.[119]

While the Ad Hoc Committee on Sufficient Consensus was deliberating, other bodies intervened in the negotiating process. On 25 June, the AWB and several other right-wing groups converged for a demonstration turned rampage through the World Trade Centre. A week later, before the Ad Hoc Committee had released its report, the Negotiating Forum met to take up the question of whether it "should now confirm the date for the election as the 27 April 1994".[120] As it raised the issue of the election's actual purpose, the matter was presented along with a resolution that called for the Technical Committee on Constitutional Issues to "draft a Constitution for the transition" that included provisions for a legislature and national government, a proportionally representative constitution-making body, and a set of constitutional principles that would guide the latter's work.[121]

Advocates for setting the election date argued that it would send a crucial indication to "people on the ground" about when they would be "granted independence from a colonial power".[122] The opposition countered, claiming that given the limited progress of the negotiations, fixing the date amounted to little more than having a "cherry without a cake" of an actual constitution. Maintaining that it "presupposes a unitary state while the form of the state in the present process has definitely not been resolved", a CP representative, Tom Langley, argued that the resolution would promote electioneering, incite tension, and risk violence.[123] Delegates from the Ciskei, Bophuthatswana, the PAC, and the IFP also opposed the resolution, arguing that the question of when to vote remained secondary to the yet unresolved "form of the state". Reciting the controversial sequence of events on 15 June, the IFP's Joe Matthew's argued further that the entire question was out of order since the Council had violated its own rules of sufficient consensus when it undertook the "adoption of the original resolution".[124] In reply, Joe Slovo and Leon Wessels reflected the ANC and NP's increasing unity as they each argued that the purpose of the election was to establish a constitution-making body. On this view, the future form of South Africa's new government could only be taken up after citizens had gone to the polls.

After extended debate and the failure of several counter-resolutions, the Chair of the meeting, Pravin Gordhan, asked delegates to "raise your hands" in order to indicate support for the election date resolution. He then declared that there was sufficient consensus on the issue, a ruling that was immediately challenged by the CP's Frank Le Roux on the grounds that Gordhan had resorted to simple majoritarianism instead of weighing different positions and assessing the overall sufficiency of the consensus. In response, Gordhan argued that his ruling had considered the context of the debate and that it had much to do with the fact that the Council had given significant time to the question in the preceding weeks, allowing a number of opportunities for parties to express their positions and resolve their disagreements. This explanation seemed to ignore the IFP's objection that the Council had run roughshod over procedure. Too, Fanie Jacobs questioned why agreement in the Negotiating Council implied that there was or had to be agreement in its governing body, the Negotiating Forum. Gordhan replied that the two bodies overlapped. Dismissing Joe Slovo's claim that the opposition was engaged in a counterproductive filibuster, the Ciskei's Mickey Webb argued that Gordhan's ruling "could be challenged in Court" and suggested that such a route was perhaps the only remaining option. He then asked that his constituency's "total opposition" be recorded in the minutes and declared that it would not be bound to the decision.[125] In response, Gordhan offered the lunch break as a chance for parties to rethink their positions and consult further. Upon resumption of the meeting, he declared, "I must with deep regret and with every respect for the diversity of views that we have had and for the right of the various people to actually articulate those views, now formally declare sufficient consensus on the resolution before the house."[126] In the name of transition, it was difficult to tell whether it was the rule or the spirit of sufficient consensus that had prevailed.

Shortly after the Negotiating Forum declared that there was sufficient consensus for an election date, the IFP withdrew from the MPNP. Many claimed that it was sour grapes and yet another illustration of Inkatha's insincere approach to the negotiations. Along with threats about its willingness to undertake mass action and civil war, none of which were particularly clear, the party's representatives argued on their way out the door that the agreement of 16 out of 24 parties had never been and never would be evidence of sufficient consensus. In this respect, the IFP was part of a larger contingent that was dissatisfied with MPNP negotiations. Formed at the behest of Buthelezi in the wake of the September 1992 *Record of Understanding*, the Concerned South Africans Group (COSAG) announced its withdrawal from the negotiations. Thus, the controversy was not over. It was time for the contested law of constitution-making to come before the law. Had the power of sufficient consensus turned into the violent imposition of (sovereign) will? Had the Negotiating Council and Forum misused its process and misapplied its procedure to the point where dominant parties were able to manipulate the MPNP's deliberations? The dispute around the election date led directly to these questions, at least for those who were still adamant that the MPNP needed to explore options for a non-centralised government. A year after mass action had punctuated the end of CODESA, the matter was taken not to the streets but to a Transvaal Provincial courtroom.

In mid-winter, shortly after its withdrawal from the MPNP, the KwaZulu Government filed suit against several key figures in the negotiations process, including Pravin Gordhan. In it, they claimed that sufficient consensus was a hopelessly vague means of regulating negotiations and contended that it had effectively excluded them from the MPNP's work. In the days after its filing, the IFP's Farouk Cassim used a televised interview to frame the suit almost exclusively in the terms of power. Questioning both the MPNP's power to ignore the IFP's material interests and its use of sufficient consensus to overrule questions, ideas, and objections about the form of the interim government, Cassim countered with a call for transparency:

> Our point is that we want this being made visible, thing being made manifest, bring it in front of us, let us see whether we have a basis on which to negotiate. If we are going to be just steamrolled, it is going to be a process driven only by those who are seeking to maintain power not to curb power, not to control power, then I think we have a right to stand back and see what is going to come up …[127]

While it suggested that the IFP was willing to rejoin the talks and back-pedalled on claims about the risks of civil war, Cassim's position made clear that the appearances generated by sufficient consensus had, for Inkatha, become an obstacle to the constitution of a "totally democratic package that threatens no one".

The KZG's claims were developed more fully in the heads of argument submitted to the court. Its principle objection: sufficient consensus was unacceptably "vague and ambiguous" because it was "not capable of being applied fairly in a process where widest possible consensus is sought".[128] This claim challenged both the standing and the accepted definition of sufficient consensus. Speaking then to its practice, the KZG contended that it was a "rule of procedure" that aimed to make good on the "right of all parties at the MPNP to put forward for negotiation their propositions for a new constitutional dispensation in South Africa", a right that had been severely curtailed in the Council's meeting of 15 June. In support of this position, the applicants pointed to Section Four of the MPNP standing rules, the provisions that defined the purpose and procedures for establishing sufficient consensus. Further, they claimed that the Council's failure to enforce these rules had eliminated the "whole basis" for their participation in the process. The KZG did not, however, explain how a standing rule could be both ambiguous to the point of being impossible to apply and applied in an unfair manner.

The merits of the grievance presupposed standing. Could the MPNP be sued? Did the KZG have a demonstrable substantive interest? With respect to the former, the applicants argued that the MPNP could be named as respondent because it was sponsored by the existing South African Government. Citing the existence of "firm and realistic expectations" for an agreement that would be implemented by Parliament, the KZG argued that the MPNP represented nothing less than a "public authority" which was governed by rules that conferred specific "rights and obligations". In regard to the second question, it argued that the MPNP's process of decision-making had compromised the process of state formation by prohibiting the IFP and other parties from making a case for decentralised government. Without this opportunity, these groups were assured of having little or no political power in the aftermath of the transition. Thus, as the right to participate in the talks that constituted the transition was abridged, the KZG claimed that the process of constitution-making fell under the rule of law.

The heads of argument submitted by the respondents challenged the coherence and validity of this conclusion. In his submission, Pravin Gordhan claimed that the applicants had no *locus standi*, in part because the cited parties in the suit did not represent a tribunal that could be named by the law for purposes of litigation. The MPNP was not legally containable. What's more, Gordhan argued that the process did not follow from or express any intention to form a contract. Entirely voluntary, the negotiations required and hinged on "a moral and political commitment to the process but did not intend to create rights and obligations" enforceable in law.[129]

What's more, the MPNP had yet to actually do anything. Its agreements were all conditional on the creation and ratification of a final package, something that appeared to be some months away. Thus, the status of the negotiations sat outside the law, taking shape through a process that the latter could not and ought not regulate. On this point, the precise terms of the respondent's claim proved crucial:

> Those participating in the multi-party negotiations process do so not by way of compulsion, but by way of a moral and political commitment to ensure a peaceful transition to democratic rule in South Africa. Their purpose is to negotiate a constitutional settlement. This is therefore a political process. The sanctions for not negotiating and coming to a settlement are political and economic. They were never intended to be legally binding and, I submit, not capable of being legally enforced. *No parties are legally bound by any decision taken or agreement reached, they do no more than bind themselves in honour to respect of the democratic consensus.*[130]

The MPNP's negotiations did not have standing in law because they rested on a civil-political compact given to the creation of a constitutive power that would allow citizens to (re)enter law's fold and author its terms. In short, the good faith of honour had precedent over the juridical structures of the existing state, a body of law that was in the midst of being dismantled.[131]

On 9 September, the court made its ruling, finding against the applicants with costs. The decision rested heavily on the KZG's inability to demonstrate its standing. In this respect, the court held that there no was compelling evidence of an intention to negotiate that signalled the creation of a "binding contract". The MPNP had created no "existing, future or contingent right or obligation", and thus the court concluded that it had "no jurisdiction". More specifically, skirting the question of what "contingent" meant in relation to the negotiations promised future "package", the court cited dictum from a prior case in order to explain why the goal and rules of sufficient consensus did not represent the basis for contract:

> The absence of consensus may render an ostensible contract void,
> but it does not follow that whenever two or more persons are in
> agreement they contract with each other. Many legal situations arise in
> which consensus was a *sine qua non* to validity but cannot be said to be
> contractual.[132]

Establishing that talk at the table did not constitute a legal relation, the court continued:

> From the averments in the founding affidavit one recognises a process by
> participating parties to negotiate a transition to a democratic dispensation
> in South Africa. One understands that those participating in the process
> do so not by way of compulsion, but because they recognise the
> existence of a moral and political commitment to endeavour to ensure a
> peaceful solution to diverse claims, contentions, disputes, and attitudes.
> The mere fact that participants set up structures and rules relative to
> the negotiating process does not vest that which they are doing with
> the quality of an enforceable agreement. It was certainly necessary for
> orderly debate and the achievement of solutions that mechanisms should
> be created to facilitate that process, but that is as it goes. It means no
> more than that they devised a *modus vivendi* to facilitate the negotiating
> process ... We would add however that it would seem to us that it
> would be inappropriate to interfere in the course of a political process
> which is still far from concluded. This also renders it unnecessary for
> us to decide whether there has been strict compliance with the rules of
> procedure, a matter which is at least debatable. Having said that, we can
> only emphasise the need for debate and that the continuing participation

of parties appears to be the only method to achieve an end to which all parties profess to aspire.[133]

Gordhan's argument had proven decisive. In the court's view, the form and rules of talk given to constitution-making were bound by a law of honour that was prior to the law and which literally and metaphorically could not come before it. Sufficient consensus was without dependence on precedent. Its definition and practice was a constitutive power that was prior to, between, and an outcome of the sovereign's constitution. It was also an extra-constitutional enactment of constitution-making. Inside and outside the law, the form of its power hinged on the "validity" of good faith, a willingness not so much to compromise (respective laws) but to undertake the work of constitution in opposition (to law). In this exception *for* law, the process turned toward and attempted to overcome the law's exception *to* law. It dis-placed the sovereign that used law to unite opposites and close discourse in order to open a time for talk in which the shared difference of opposition could yield a transition (not transcendence) to the constitutive power of sovereignty.

The challenge to sufficient consensus did not suspend its use. While the KZG's objections were being filed and adjudicated by the Transvaal Court, the larger but nevertheless fractured MPNP continued to work. Part of the forum's momentum may well have been due to the absence of those sympathetic to the suit, a departure that appeared to further solidify the bilateral channel between the ANC and NP. In late June and early July, the Negotiating Council voted by sufficient consensus to charge the Technical Committee on Constitutional Issues to draft the text of a new constitution.[134] In a sense, the decision was the counterpart of the election date decision, an agreement that the constitution-making process would occur in two stages with the forum drafting an interim constitution and an elected assembly writing the final document in light of specific constitutional principles developed by MPNP negotiators. Of the eventual 34 principles, 27 were drafted and accepted on 2 July. In the aftermath, with the transition now in view, the MPNP's work took on a measure of normalcy, turning to the precise fixtures of the interim constitution and the mechanisms needed to devolve the standing dispensation. Controversy would return in the spring, however, as negotiators confronted the questions of how to get boycotting parties back into the fold and whether the end of apartheid would bring an exception for its crimes.

From the high hopes of the talks about talk and the opening of CODESA to the breakdown of negotiations and their slow recommencement, South African's witnessed a process that appeared to turn the potential for constitution-making toward its actuality. Here I have attempted to trace an important aspect of this fraught and fragile turn, a shift that involved contentious and frequently bitter disagreement about the meaning of democracy, the legitimacy of the forums charged to negotiate the end of apartheid, the means needed to write a constitution, and the problem of whether the new would be obligated to share its power with the old. In a basic way, the task of constitution presented negotiators with the question of who had the capacity to enact the "legitimate violence" of beginning, the standing to assume the mantle of the sovereign in the name of defining the constitutive power needed for its redefinition. The plenary at CODESA exposed the depth of this problem, revealing that the task of constitution hinged significantly on the rhetorical question of how to reconcile the formal and substantive elements of the process, a linkage which required negotiators to define norms of debate and decision-making that could support if not perform the work of constitution-writing. Beyond the experience of the talks about talks, this work required agreement about who had the standing to advance definitional claims about the country's future, whether such vision served the interests of history, and how the rhetorical constitution of power would afford opportunities for its (representative) distribution. Elusive at first, solutions to these problems required negotiators to refigure disputes over the power of discourse toward the invention of shared discursive power. A formal-pragmatic mode of talk, sufficient consensus played a multifaceted role in this turn toward constitution-making.

First, the procedure and practice of sufficient consensus facilitated a "productive opposition" between negotiators. Motivated by the nearly paralysing disputes over who could advance definitive claims about the nature of the new South Africa, sufficient consensus supported and enacted a kind of constitutive clash. When coupled with the idea that delegates would not ratify their decisions until they comprised a complete package, its norms of debate and rules about the conditions under which speech could justify action allowed parties to search for common ground in the midst of proposals that otherwise appeared to negate one another. Encouraging this constructive negativity, sufficient consensus helped turn appeals to sovereign privilege that were being heard as violent attempts to control the outcome of the negotiating process to oppositional arguments that were warranted partly by the need to make progress toward the agreed upon goal of writing a new constitution. This redefinition of stumbling blocks was not simply a call to reinterpret the issues in question. It was also a moment in which parties were charged to recall the founding spirit of the talks in the name of giving up something of their own definitional power. Thus, the manifold practice of sufficient consensus entailed speech acts – "I speak in the name of creating sufficient consensus" and "I declare that sufficient consensus has been created" – that composed and performed the terms of constitutive power in opposition to divisive claims about how the rights of a contested sovereign contained the power to define the form and content of the proceedings.

Second, the controversy that attended the use of sufficient consensus demonstrated that constitutive power defied strict accountability. Before the law, what *was* a sufficient consensus apart from the desires of the negotiation's two primary players? No one could really say. In some sense, this was the (paradoxical) point, the creation of a form of talk in which definitions of the transition could be advanced and accepted on a provisional, non-definitive basis. But, this meant that the process had no precedent. Its practice did not rest on legally valid rules or carry a binding effect that allowed aggrieved parties to seek concrete redress in the wake of real or perceived deviations from procedure. Rather, the norms of discussion and decision-making shifted over time and in relation to context. The process was indeed made as it went along. In certain situations, decisions about whether to allow debate to continue and whether there was a sufficient consensus relied not on strict assessments of who was making the most coherent and forceful argument but on an evaluation of what was needed for the constitution-making process to succeed. This meant that the concept of sufficient consensus contained an important strategic element. Over and over, rulings were premised both on the MPNP's *Declaration of Intent* – the document in which all parties agreed that transition was (historically) necessary – *and* on the fact that particular rulings were conditional on the creation and ratification of a package that was still in the making. Thus, the key end of the negotiations was given but that end could be challenged substantively only in the future. In the present, objections to the principle of sufficient consensus were ineffective precisely because they had no referent on which to cling. The oft-repeated claim that sufficient consensus implied a need for parties to give ground embodied this dynamic, deflecting criticism by obscuring the basis for objections to either particular styles of debate or individual rulings about the existence of "sufficient" agreement. In this sense, the task at hand was not the sort of compromise that proceeded from or prefigured a binding contract. Instead, recalling Benjamin, the productive opposition of sufficient consensus stood in distinction to law, a means of interaction that made an exception to the transgressions of its own rule by claiming that law could not (yet) contain or bind the constitutive honour that backed the work of constitution-making. The consequences of this invention were left for the future, a time that would appear only as the present was enabled in distinction to the deep divisions of the past.

Third, sufficient consensus both followed from and enacted reconciliation. Providing a means to transform disagreements that risked violence to oppositions which counted toward the creation of unity in difference, sufficient consensus was underwritten by a call for faith in the constitutive power of words. Drawing from the potential for beginning anew that appeared during the talks about talks, appeals for reconciliation in the wake of CODESA's failure and during the run-up to the MPNP indicated that the actualisation of such potential demanded less transcendence (or revolutionary force) than a dedicated willingness to stand in contradiction, to find the standing for creation in the midst of self and mutual opposition. Thus, one crucial lesson of CODESA's breakdown was that reconciliation's potential contained the terms of its own negation. In the months that followed, renewed debate about the meaning of reconciliation, including the controversy provoked by the *Further Indemnity Act*, suggested that its power turned on a move from law to *logos*, a tenuous shift in which the sovereign's closure of discourse was opposed by speech that exceeded and then set its words into motion. Put differently, the idea of reconciliation that sat beneath, helped enable, and was performed by sufficient consensus was a call for parties to forge a constitutive *relation* by speaking in non-relation to the rule of law, a set of historical precedents that had little place for the faith or honour needed to invent the terms of a beginning.

Not yet present, the new would arrive with a significant remainder. While it helped explain and perform the operations of constitutive power, the reconciling talk of sufficient consensus did not account for another set of appeals to reconciliation; an argument that was gaining momentum and which recalled the *Kairos Document*'s argument that reconciliation entailed a commitment to justice. Were the fruits of constitutive power to come at the expense of the past? Would transition depend on the old to sustain the new? Did it need to? These questions were at the heart of Kader Asmal's important reflections on the role of justice in transition, a justice that demanded less retribution than truth-telling and a collective recognition of apartheid's horrific costs. Issued in the last months of CODESA, Asmal's concern for how South Africa would deal with the past was an explicit but frequently deferred question at the MPNP. Concerned with the problem of how to dissolve apartheid without forsaking (legal) stability and struggling to agree on the merits and potential necessity of a blanket amnesty, reconciliation's talk was not sufficient. The time of transition was fast approaching – a "middle time" in which reconciliation's constitutive opposition would be called to stand in opposition to itself in the name of bridging the divide between the present's past and future.

4

the opposing questions of beginning: how will the word(s) of reconciliation "deal with the past"?

There is a lot of forgetting to do in South Africa.
Nadine Gordimer

Build the future in the present.
Trevor Manuel

The next stage is beginning.
Roelf Meyer

For the original act by which the body politic is united does not determine what it shall do to preserve itself.
Jean-Jacques Rousseau

Reconciliation begins from the limit of its achievement. On 17 November 1993, MPNP delegates gathered in what is now a casino to approve the interim constitution that ended statutory apartheid, delineated the path to South Africa's first democratic elections, and set out the principles by which an elected constituent assembly would write the country's "final" constitution. That night, a few months from becoming President, Nelson Mandela took the stage and reflected on the MPNP's accomplishment:

> We have reached the end of an era. We are at the beginning of a
> new era. Whereas apartheid deprived millions of our people of their
> citizenship, we are restoring that citizenship. Whereas apartheid sought
> to fragment our country, we are re-uniting our country. The central
> theme of the Constitution of Transition is the unity of our country and

people. This constitution recognises the diversity of our people. Gone will be the days when one language dominated. Gone will be the days when one religion was elevated to a position of privilege over other religions. Gone will be the days when one culture was elevated to a position of superiority and others denigrated and denied.[1]

These words were not idle. Moving in a particular and peculiar way, Mandela's address spoke to how the good and difficult faith of talk had produced a new time and a new place. Yet, what was this moment? Where was this space? Still to pass from past to future and waiting to enter a unified democratic South Africa, Mandela could only speak to what "will be", the future progressive quality of a transition still in the making.

The time and grammar of transition is neither simple nor straightforward. In the *Parmenides*, Plato's Socrates described the "instant" of transition as a moment that is "no time at all" but which contains the (infinite) potential for "unity's" change from becoming to being. Kenneth Burke's depiction of dialectical transformation teaches a similar lesson, underscoring Marx's claim that transitions entail a play of ideal talk and pragmatic confusion.[2] Rilke observed that transitions are a place "where we cannot remain standing". And yet they are moments in which we are also stranded; transitions trouble meaning, blur vision, and render the ground for action unstable; at the limit of time, they incite and contain a struggle between the times, between what has been, what is, and what is yet to be.

This is crucial. In transition, we stand and move within a middle. The onset of its experience brings the problem of how to play between the possibilities of creation and the imperatives of history. In practice, between transformation and tradition, the discourse of transition is at odds with its invention, a tension that beckons a middle voice and a form of subjectivity that craves but cannot fully establish sovereignty. A "magical moment", reflects a Cape Town art teacher, a time of unbridled expectation, persistent patience, and quiet reflection. At its most powerful, a *jetztzeit* (now-time) torn and turning between spontaneity and stability, transition holds the question of how to relate the exhilaration of bringing forth something new on earth and the abiding anxiety that creation is never without cost.[3] In the ambiguous fullness of its "middle time," transitions hold and ask after the double-edged problem of making and acting with words.[4]

In late 1993 and early 1994, many were beginning to question the past in the name of moving to the future. What was the (stable) ground for action?

Before the law, the MPNP's work was without precedent, an exception that appeared ready to extend amnesty to those who committed crimes in the name of protecting an illegal regime. Was law without standing? Did any of its precedent remain? More abstractly but no less important, what was the status of (just) cause, the causes of the past to which many continued to cling, and the precise causes of a so-called "negotiated revolution" that appeared simultaneously to lack and carry revolutionary effect? How did the country get here? What had been (com)promised, brought forward, or lost in the MPNP's work? At a threshold that appeared to stretch the limit of non-contradiction, what place remained for historical identity in a time dedicated to cultivating a sense of identification that would render South Africa new? In various ways, all of these problems had deep implications for the idea, practice, and attainment of reconciliation. Fundamentally, each was a question as to how South Africa was going to turn from past to future in the name of beginning to live within (the law of) unity in difference.

A "now document" that both enacted and opened the door to transition, the interim constitution gave its last words to defining reconciliation, announcing its achievement, and calling on citizens to undertake its practice.[5] In this chapter, I am concerned with the invention of these words and two significant debates in which they were questioned and troubled. Focused on the period between August 1993 and the first few months of 1994, the chapter begins by considering the anxious close of the MPNP and the issue that its delegates could not resolve: amnesty. Tracing the context of the dispute over whether the advent of democracy would bring an exception for those guilty of apartheid's crimes and the excesses of struggle, I follow the amnesty issue through the MPNP's last months to the writing of the interim constitution's post-amble, a short text that was written in December and which mandated amnesty in the name of reconciliation. While hailed by at least one of its authors as the achievement of a "founding" reconciliation, the terms of the post-amble were soon called into question when Parliament convened to ratify the interim constitution, a gathering that provoked debate over whether the new dispensation degraded Afrikaner history and desecrated its sacred calling. Plotting the terms of this controversy and examining precisely how the National Party claimed to embody tradition while simultaneously arguing that reconciliation required South Africa to close the book on the past and move forward, I then turn to a second debate, one convened in the confines of civil society and given to the question of whether and how the country was going to "deal with its past" – a legacy that threatened to haunt if its wounds were not fully exposed, acknowledged, and redressed.

The invention of reconciliation's beginning held the question of whether it was time to begin again. In this chapter, I argue that the constitution of reconciliation at the MPNP opened a transition in which reconciliation's constitutive power was set in opposition to itself and called to account for the cost of its creation. In late 1993 and early 1994, this challenge took several forms. For one, it was a central feature of the interim constitution's post-amble, a text that announced South Africa's achievement of reconciliation but then troubled this production by calling on citizens to undertake a process of reconciliation in the name of enabling the larger constitution's promise of democratic peace. Thus, the post-amble enacted reconciliation's potential while simultaneously questioning its limit. This double movement followed partly from its claim that a law-constitutive reconciliation demanded amnesty, an exception that extended the MPNP's work and also provoked significant worry as to whether the new was fated to leave the old behind. Voiced by individuals and groups with dramatically different interests, this concern underscored that South Africans did not have a shared vision of what the country owed to the past and provoked bitter argumentation over whether the MPNP's constitutive logic was dangerous, a process that stood before the law without an obligation to honour the principle of accountability that was embedded in its precedent.[6] Symbolised in the post-amble, the MPNP's reconciliation thus motivated a diverse set of calls to remember, a debate that turned on whether South Africa had fully accounted for the costs attached to reconciliation's inventional power. Taken up in Parliament as well as civil society, this problem of what was being unduly left behind in the midst of transition was itself a crucial beginning. In it there was an opportunity to initiate systematic discussion about the body most fully associated with reconciliation in South Africa – the Truth and Reconciliation Commission.

Across the annals of popular, critical, and official history, it is widely accepted that the TRC followed from the MPNP and that it did so by the force of the latter's "necessity" or by virtue of its "compromise".[7] Held to explain the TRC's development and used to reinforce the presupposition that reconciliation in South Africa began with the Commission, these two positions obscure far more than they reveal.[8] Moving from the post-amble to the debates over how its call for reconciliation figured a need to "deal with the past", I contend here that while the TRC had formative roots in the emergence and resolution of the amnesty question, the Commission was much less an extension of the MPNP's so-called spirit of compromise than the product of argumentation as to how this spirit was necessarily compromised to the degree that it bracketed histories which were deemed crucial to South Africa's future. The advantage of this interpretation is two-fold. First, it sheds the common but factually incorrect claim that the post-amble mandated the formation of the TRC. Second, it provides a clearer view of the vital but also awkward relationship between the MPNP and the TRC. While it is not entirely incorrect to suggest that these bodies relied on two different senses of reconciliation, such an interpretation risks obscuring how the contingent creation of reconciliation at the negotiating table was one that exceeded but did not escape law and the way in which proposals for the TRC both mimicked and resisted this dynamic when they argued that South Africa needed simultaneously to transcend the past and (re)turn to precisely that history which negotiators had bracketed in the name of making progress, a legacy that was a cause of division as well as the repository of a liberal and liberating identity. While in tension with a significant thread of South Africa's history, this appeal for identity's constitutive memory marked the beginning of the TRC as a call to "come to terms", a demand and duty to find the words of reconciliation that would underwrite the (transitional) power of citizens to enter, find standing, and author the nation's law.

1. achieving reconciliation

At the end of July 1993, the St James Church massacre in Cape Town's suburb of Kenilworth was condemned by the ANC as a "barbaric and vicious" attack, one that left 11 dead at the hands of PAC-aligned gunmen. It was also read as evidence that consensus for the pace and form of political change was far from sufficient. In the wake of Inkatha's challenge at Kempton Park, negotiators worked in technical committees to produce drafts of an interim constitution and the principles that would guide the transition and regulate the drafting of a full and final constitution in the years after the election.[9] Provoking unrest from the right-wing, this progress motivated debate over amnesty, particularly the government's claim that the "indemnity process should be replaced by an agreed general amnesty".[10] In fact, the problems were linked. While opposed by the ANC, the government's case for a broad indemnity was of increasing interest to military and paramilitary leaders who were beginning to wonder if the end of apartheid would see them standing in the dock if not the gallows.

With debate, deferral, and then a last minute resolution of the amnesty question, the end of the MPNP was tumultuous and not entirely successful.

Here, I want to consider the last controversial months of the MPNP's work and a crucial event that took place some three weeks after its Negotiating Forum gathered and ratified the interim constitution. Tracing the spring's debate over whether the ANC-NP bilateral channel was bringing South Africa a new dispensation at the expense of those committed to the perceived comforts of an Afrikaner *volkstaat* (people's state) or at least significantly entrenched regional government, I turn to the rather mysterious writing of the interim constitution's post-amble, a founding text that was never approved by the MPNP, even as it "resolved" the amnesty issue and announced if not performed the achievement of reconciliation. Paying particularly close attention to the post-amble's terms, I contend that its constitution of reconciliation was equally the presentation of a hermeneutic question, a query as to whether the MPNP's exceptional spirit required citizens to recall and read the past in the name of both enacting and opposing reconciliation's generative power.

reconciliation's last (divisive) mile

With negotiators making steady and frequently contentious progress on the constitution's form and content, mid-winter brought difficult questions about the involvement of the ANC and government in the gross violation of human rights. At the end of August, a year after the Skweyiya Commission had found evidence of significant violence and human rights abuses in ANC training camps, the Congress's Motsuenyane Commission released a report which confirmed the existence of serious problems and urged their immediate redress. Taking little time to respond, the ANC's National Executive acknowledged that violations had occurred, accepted "collective accountability", and expressed "regret and apology for each and every transgression". But, the NEC noted, neither the Commission nor any of its predecessors had revealed "a pattern of systematic abuses". Contending that the violence within the MK paled in comparison to the crimes of apartheid, the NEC read the report as a reason to open "a national discourse on the human rights violations of the past" and undertake a "full investigation of the abuses that have occurred under the apartheid system". Claiming that it would demonstrate the country's "commitment to fostering a human rights culture and a spirit of reconciliation for the future", the Council also contended that such work was impossible given the terms of the *Further Indemnity Act*, the state's self-serving attempt to "expunge from the record systematic murder, torture, dirty tricks of every vile sort and the most gross violations of the sovereignty of the neighbouring states". Arguing that accountability for violence could not occur within such a framework, the NEC concluded:

We accordingly call for an establishment of a Commission of Truth, similar to bodies established in a number of countries in recent years to deal with the past. The purpose of such a Commission will be to investigate all the violations of human rights – killings, disappearances, torture as ill-treatment – from all quarters. This will not be a Nuremburg Tribunal. Its role will be to identify all abuses of human rights and their perpetrators, to propose a future code of conduct for all public servants, to ensure appropriate compensation to the victims and to work out the best basis for reconciliation. In addition, it will provide the moral basis for justice and for preventing any repetition of abuses in the future.[11]

Reaction to the ANC's proposal took a variety of forms and tones. General Bantu Holomisa, the leader of the Transkei, applauded the Congress for its "maturity to face the music".[12] The Human Rights Commission (HRC), however, was less sure. In an extended commentary on the matter, it wondered whether the ANC was actually willing to "practice what it preaches" and argued that the Congress appeared to be "exonerating itself through a comparison with the appalling human rights record of the present South African government" and creating a "norm of impunity" by taking collective responsibility for crimes that demanded case-by-case accountability. While amenable to the idea of a truth commission, the HRC cautioned that the value of such a body hinged on the willingness of all parties to undertake a full disclosure of human rights abuses and ensure their timely redress.[13] Speaking for the government, Kobie Coetsee appeared wary of these conditions when he claimed that a commission of truth was "not a proper response" to the abuses. Turning to the ANC's charge that the state's appeals for amnesty were disingenuous, he contended that it was time to "clear the slate and close the book on the past" and then admonished the Congress not to blame the government for violence but to accept the fact that, "We now need to be even-handed as far as our forces and civil servants are concerned, many who believed that they were also fighting a just war against terrorists."[14]

There was more to the government's interest in amnesty than its somewhat new found concern to balance the scales of justice. Created by the 1990 *National Peace Accord*, the Commission of Inquiry Regarding the Prevention of Public Violence and Intimidation was in the last phases of its work, an effort that put a fine point on the state's role in human rights violations. Led by Judge Richard Goldstone, the Commission's interim findings suggested that third force activity had not been curtailed with F.W. de Klerk's dismissal of several security force leaders in late 1992. Indeed, it appeared that government forces were still pursuing their dirty tricks campaign, funding Inkatha, and helping paramilitary groups to secure weapons.[15] With progress at the constitutional negotiating table signalling that transition was nearly inevitable, these allegations underscored the potential value of amnesty for state officials. As well, it suggested to some that indemnity from future prosecution might appease right-wing groups, many of whom had substantive ties with both the SAP and SADF. With the June occupation of the World Trade Centre still a fresh memory, the problem of post-election backlash was dramatised when Abrie Oosthuizen, a ranking member of the CP in the Orange Free State, warned that "should the government dare to enforce ANC/Communist Rule in the Free Sate, it would lead to bloody civil war".[16]

While concerned about accounting for the past and ensuring the country's future stability, the ANC appeared most intent on managing the present. In early September, Mandela claimed, "The message of the ANC is one of reconciliation, not of retribution." When set with the NEC's refusal to consider a general amnesty, this position sent a mixed signal, one that reflected the difficulties involved in discerning who was threatened by the end of apartheid, whether they had any actual power, and if calls to account for past violence were provoking their mobilisation. In any case, Mandela noted that "South Africans should never forget the crimes committed in their name. We, however, know that we must forgive."[17] With these ambiguous terms, Mandela was deferring the question of amnesty in the name of keeping negotiations on track.

At the table, difficult progress was being made in an increasingly bilateral manner. In mid-September, Parliament passed legislation authorising the creation of a Transitional Executive Council (TEC), a body charged to help govern the country and maintain the continuity of law in the run-up to the election. Giving significant power to the ANC prior to their expected victory at the polls and roundly condemned by the CP, the TEC also lent "new urgency" to the talks, underscoring that the Congress and NP had yet to reach agreements on the crucial issues of federalist autonomy for regions, the terms of executive power, and the organisation of the judiciary.[18] In October, following the conclusion of an agreement over a set of fundamental constitutional rights, the NP and ANC took to the bush, meeting in game lodges for intense bilaterals designed to preserve the transition's schedule, "ward off a challenge by the right wing", and prevent the sorts of deadlock that would "plunge the country back into the dark post-CODESA days".[19] Formally, these negotiations indicated that sufficient consensus was still the order of the day, a means of decision-making that was characterised by a somewhat sceptical press as a way to "produce clever political answers for a great divergence of constituency interests even within the two main parties".[20] By early November, the process paid dividends when the Negotiating Council agreed that the country would be run by a Government of National Unity in the wake of the election, accepted a proposal to divide the country into nine regions, and scrapped the legislation that had created and sustained the "independent" states of Transkei, Venda, Bophuthatswana and Ciskei.

While encouraging to most, the speed and perceived exclusivity of the decision-making process consolidated opposition to the negotiations, criticism which betrayed that the federalism question was far from resolved. An escalation of the June controversy over the fixing of an election date, the problem had been brewing for some time. In September, General Constand Viljoen warned that the negotiations process was pushing the "Afrikaner nation into a corner" and then contended that the government and the ANC's approach to federalism was creating a "dangerous situation" in which some right-wing groups were massing for what he believed would be a disastrous civil war.[21] Several weeks later, the Concerned South Africans Group dissolved and then re-formed as the Freedom Alliance (FA), a group composed largely of representatives from the CP, IFP, and AVF, along with the leaders of Ciskei and Bophuthatswana. At its founding meeting, the Alliance declared that it was withdrawing from the Negotiating Council in order to undertake talks with both the government and the ANC about the idea "that member states of a new South Africa should be primarily responsible for the provision of government for the people and by the people".[22]

At base, still deeply worried about the loss of autonomy that would attend the creation of a centralised state, the "fragile alliance" sought structural guarantees about the devolution of federal power, an assurance that variously included the creation of a *volkstaat* and laws which assured "maximum self-determination" for particular regions like the Inkatha-controlled KwaZulu-Natal. Addressed at meetings convened in late October and early November, the NP and ANC expressed interest in negotiations over these issues but argued that the alliance was late to the party and naïve in thinking that they could bully their way to regional independence. Frustrated, Alliance leaders announced on 7 November that they would not participate in the election if their demands were not met. The threat provoked Mandela: "We are people committed to peace. But at the end of the day, when we lose our patience, the right-wing will be crushed."[23] Perhaps telling, the rebuke came just days after AWB leader Eugene Terre'Blanche was convicted for public violence.

The MPNP's Negotiating Forum was scheduled to convene on 17 November to approve the interim constitution. In the 48 hours prior to the meeting, the meeting's observers, participants and opponents each took pains to detail their view of the history-making event. Speaking for the Defence Force, Intelligence Chief "Joffel" van der Westhuizen claimed that the military favoured a negotiated settlement and was committed to serving its civilian master. Warning political leaders to stop their "war-talk", the General declared that "Peace is in the hands of the political leaders, not of military and para-military forces acting in accordance with divergent political leadership".[24] Meanwhile, select residents in some 20 Transvaal towns rejected their imminent incorporation into the new state and demanded that they be ceded a "Boere-Afrikaner" homeland. While this call was congruent with one of its goals, the Freedom Alliance expressed its hope that ongoing negotiations would result in an "all-inclusive solution" which would afford a "constructive start to the new South Africa" and not one based on "division, enmity, and tension".[25]

Struggling to find their own unity in difference, the ANC and government negotiating teams worked deep into the night and behind closed doors to reach a sufficient consensus on a "six-pack" of issues, all of which were deemed crucial to the success of the plenary. The parties announced their success in the morning. Specifically, the two sides agreed that Cabinet's decisions would be taken "in a manner which gives consideration to the consensus-seeking spirit underlying the concept of a government of national unity". As well, they devised a means to entrench regional boundaries and powers, created deadlock-breaking mechanisms for the ratification of the final constitution, and adopted a single ballot paper for the election of national and provincial legislatures.[26] While both the Congress and the NP gave something up for these agreements, their presentation to the Negotiating Council led representatives from other parties to claim that the exclusivity of the decision-making process was "close to a disgrace" and a "farce of what we set out to do".[27] Again in the chair, Pravin Gordhan found that there was sufficient consensus to include the "six-pack" in the interim constitution which was to be taken up the next day by the full Negotiating Forum.

In the end, the MPNP's last meeting may have enacted "consensus by exhaustion".[28] Scrambling to the last moment and concluding its work at 3:30 in the morning, the Negotiating Forum approved the interim constitution. Held up as a creature of compromise by many delegates, the document authorised the formation of a 400-member National Assembly and a 90-member Senate, along with an Executive composed of a President, Deputy Presidents and a somewhat nebulous notion of national unity. Anchored by a set of inviolable constitutional principles that were to be the benchmarks for the Constitutional Court's assessment of the final text which was to be written within two years of the election, the interim constitution was non-racial, progressive, and included protections for a host of civil and social rights.[29]

Reaction to the interim constitution's approval was predictably mixed. Judge Ismael Mohamed declared that the multiparty process had set the country on the "last mile towards our freedom". While Mandela called on all South Africans to "join hands and march into the future", the media seemed to hear him say different things, quoting him in one report to say that the central theme of the constitution was the recognition of "diversity" and then claiming in another that the future President thought that the text's primary theme was "unity". Given the nature of the moment, the incongruity was apt.

Soon to be relegated to a proverbial back bench, F.W. de Klerk declared that "South Africa will never be the same again". Recalling the terms of his 1990 campaign, he then suggested that "Today we have set the seal on that part of my vision". Fours days later, the President did and did not turn to the other side of the accountability coin when he argued in Parliament that the constitution "rid this country of an albatross which we have had around our necks for 300 years, namely the fact that we did not have a fair or just system inclusive of all the people in this country". With this rather crude deflection of apartheid's particular legacy, de Klerk congratulated his National Party for its efforts and contended that "If we had written it [the constitution] on our own, it would have been better". Then, setting a bit of his *hubris* aside, he noted that South Africa's turn towards a "regstaat – a constitutional state" meant that the challenge ahead was "to make reconciliation work".[30]

Such an effort was not at the top of the right-wing's to-do list. Outside the jovial negotiating hall, CP leader Ferdie Hartzenberg was reported to say that "up to half the South African population would not be able to identify with the agreements reached at the multiparty negotiations".[31] Speaking in

Pretoria, Constand Viljoen was heard to claim that "constitutions meant nothing and power everything". Decrying the Freedom Alliance's exclusion from the negotiating process, the General went further, arguing that South Africa stood at the "brink of war" and needed to consider seriously whether and how it was going to meet the Freedom Alliance's demands for regional autonomy.[32] Speaking for Bophuthatswana, Rowan Cronje contended that the Negotiating Council had no legal power to reincorporate the homeland and that it too would continue to press the case for self-determination.[33]

Several days later, Mandela replied at length to the threats that sat just beneath these objections to the new constitution:

> The African National Congress is aware that certain sectors of the
> ultra right-wing are preparing for war. They have already stockpiled
> considerable quantities of arms in certain rural areas. Instead of taking
> decisive steps to curb these threats, President F W de Klerk plays petty
> party politics and attacks the ANC. It is evident that the NP government
> is a lame duck government and entirely incapable of dealing with
> this threat. The ANC calls on all democrats, black and white, to join
> hands and to work together to isolate all of those who want to foster
> racial hatred and violence. I have had a number of meetings with
> the leadership of the Afrikaner Volksfront, including Gen. Constand
> Viljoen and Dr. Ferdie Hartzenberg. Today I want to repeat my call to
> them to stop making inciting and racist statements, and to assist me to
> prevent war and bloodshed. If they do so they will show real courage
> and provide responsible leadership to their people. However, if they try
> to lead their people into a race war they will commit a terrible crime
> against them. The ANC who fought for over thirty years a liberation
> war against apartheid oppression, knows that war is a terrible thing.
> We are trying everything within our means to avoid war. But if the
> ultra right-wing tries to unleash a civil war they will be crushed by the
> democratic forces. Then the leadership of the Afrikaner Volksfront will
> have to take responsibility for the blood of their own people that will
> be shed.[34]

At some level, it appeared that the government's military agreed. According to Lieutenant-General Pierre Steyn, the military's second-in-command, the threats of right-wing backlash were exaggerated. Moreover, he claimed that while some SADF forces might align with the right, a "head-on" conflict was not in the cards.[35] While this claim was echoed by Jan van Eck's contention in

Parliament that security forces would not swim against the widely supported tide of political change, the assurance seemed to beg a question that the MPNP had consistently if not conscientiously deferred.

the forethought of a post-amble

The beginning of the transition was not complete. Aside from the issues that continued to separate the ANC and NP from the Freedom Alliance, the Negotiating Forum's approval of the interim constitution did nothing to resolve the controversy over whether the advent of democracy would bring amnesty. With Parliament soon to convene for a ratification debate over the interim constitution, and clear signs from both the military and human rights communities that they were concerned if not restless about the matter, time for further discussion appeared to be running short. Thus, 20 days *after* the Negotiating Forum's historic vote, the amnesty question was taken out of its long closed "pigeon-hole" and (temporarily) answered in a mere and mysterious 298 words, four short paragraphs that garnered almost no public attention at the time they were written.[36] Known variously as the postscript, epilogue, and post-amble of the interim constitution, this reply was far from an afterthought.[37]

With a complex narrative and argument, the post-amble's terms deserve close and careful scrutiny. Following from the threats that were made in the closing weeks of the MPNP, the post-amble marked an achievement of reconciliation and issued a call for its practice, a process of reconciliation that was both congruent with and opposed to the way in which negotiators had bracketed history in the name of moving from past to future. In this respect, the text was curious if not paradoxical. Proposing that the indemnity – which had helped support the talks about talks as well as the negotiations process – needed to be extended and figured into a reconciling form of amnesty that would enable the constitution's promise, the post-amble also troubled this very same logic by suggesting that the transition to democracy hinged on the ability of citizens to recollect and recognise the country's violent past.

As a whole, 7 December was a remarkably eventful day, replete with the TEC's first official meeting, a call by the Human Rights Commission for the creation of a truth commission, an occupation of Fort Schanskop by a right-wing group calling itself the Boer Commando, an apparent disagreement between Inkatha leadership and its parliamentary caucus over whether the IFP should participate in the election, and a breakdown in talks between government officials and the Freedom Alliance. Late that evening at Kempton

Park, Mac Maharaj and Fanie van der Merwe were charged not just to discuss the matter of amnesty but to resolve it. Comprising two-thirds of the "Sub-Committee" that had been appointed to help coordinate the MPNP and work behind its scenes to troubleshoot problems, the high-ranking member of the ANC met with his NP counterpart during a break in the talks convened to resolve the "leftover" pieces of the negotiations.[38] According to Maharaj, the pair did not have "explicit instructions" as to how to deal with the amnesty issue. They were concerned, he says, simply to move the "process forward", unaware that the fruits of their labour would become the "last words" of the interim constitution. Lacking a secretary, Maharaj recalls that van der Merwe transcribed. They "talked, wrote a sentence or two, played with a word, and then wrote some more". The key sticking point was the difference between "amnesty may be granted" and "amnesty shall be granted".[39] Agreeing to the latter, a decision that Maharaj did not consider problematic, the pair went back to their principals. With little time for discussion, the ANC contingent of Maharaj, Cyril Ramaphosa and Joe Slovo walked the short distance to the NP offices, where the paragraph-soon-post-amble was read and approved.

It should be said that this account of the post-amble's authorship is not without competitors. There are at least two high-ranking members of the ANC who claim that the post-amble was written at their kitchen table. As well, a former member of President Thabo Mbeki's Cabinet has indicated that a substantial portion of the post-amble was written at his request by a prominent Afrikaner novelist and literary critic.[40] In any event, it is clear that the text was the explicit product of the ANC–NP bilateral channel and never approved by the MPNP's larger Negotiating Council. When I asked Maharaj why he and van der Merwe turned to the idea of reconciliation when writing the post-amble, his reply was simply, "It is reconciliation." The post-amble marked a "fundamental change", a decisive moment in which South Africa "averted a race war" by inclusively creating a non-racial state.[41]

There was indeed a "rose in the cross of the present".[42] Both the limit of sufficient consensus and its fullest expression, the post-amble performed reconciliation's beginning. From within an experience and remembrance of (endless) violence, its words opened a time in which there was space to undertake meta-discourse addressed to the problem of how enemies could speak about ways of creating unity from within the midst of stark historical differences. The first hint of this potential appeared in the post-amble's opening clause:

This constitution provides a historic bridge between the past of a deeply divided society, characterised by strife, conflict, untold suffering and injustice, and a future grounded on the recognition of human rights, democracy, and peaceful coexistence and development opportunities for all South Africans, irrespective of colour, race, class, belief or sex.[43]

With a burden of closure, a post-amble brings a perspective that encapsulates the motive and purpose of the constitution that it sums. To this end, the opening of the post-amble employs a voice that is both within and without the text to which it refers. This movement is evidence that South Africa stands between the times. Looking back, there is deep division. It is a history that the post-amble does not abbreviate as "separateness". Rather, recalling the "four pillars" of Afrikaner nationalism – hegemony, regulation of space, labour control, and social surveillance – and echoing the ANC's 1955 *Freedom Charter*, it stands in direct contrast with a system of law that took every conceivable step to *not* work irrespective of "colour, race, class, belief and sex", and which had significant roots in the divine promise that separate development would bring reconciliation, if only in the next life.

From the power that appears on the constitution's "historic bridge", the post-amble's opening calls for(th) and stands between the silencing history of apartheid and the future expression of its "untold" memory. Embodying and reflecting the constituted power of transition, it thus asks the question of what *necessarily* has to follow apartheid and how it might be created. With its call for South Africa to stand before and trouble the law of its own (identitarian) past, the post-amble's second clause is addressed to precisely this problem:

The pursuit of national unity, the well-being of all South African citizens and peace require reconciliation between the people of South Africa and the reconstruction of society. The adoption of this constitution lays the secure foundation for the people of South Africa to transcend the divisions and strife of the past, which generated gross violations of human rights, the transgression of humanitarian principles in violent conflicts and a legacy of hatred, fear, guilt and revenge. These can now be addressed on the basis that there is a need for understanding not for vengeance, a need for reparation but not retaliation, a need for ubuntu but not victimisation.

The constitution's bridge is a "secure foundation" for the dynamic "address" of reconciliation. A governing (freedom) charter, it holds the potential for speech that can "transcend", expression which will turn and (re)make the character (*ethos*) of human interaction. But, this founding (of) law is itself dependent on such work. In other words, the constitution's promise is contingent on the willingness and ability of the constituted "people" to speak before the law with constitutive effect. Thus, the (new) law of the (new) land concedes that the law is not without limit. With this acknowledgment, the post-amble recollects a reason why the making and operation of constitutional law must proceed in opposition to its historical form. A crucial feature of its call for reconciliation, the post-amble is an invocation to remember apartheid's propensity to counter the emergence of law with a state of emergency, the inhumanity of the "ban" that was so much a fact of apartheid, the outward sign of a system that sustained itself by "exception" – a near permanent grey zone that was used to secure its sovereignty, silence speech, and warrant the perpetration of gross human rights violations on the grounds of combating endless danger and securing normality.

What then is required "to transcend the divisions and strife of the past"? The post-amble does not counsel negation of law but the productive negativity of reconciliation, a form of speech that stands before and challenges the law in the name of its (re)constitution. The rule of law must be made through extended exchange that establishes the standing of citizens to speak in a manner that allows participation in its authorship.[44] Explaining the "requirement" for reconciliation, this work demands opposition, a (re)invention of the relationship between law and morality *through* a demonstration that the law's identity is not its own, insufficient to declare an exception to itself. But, the post-amble also attributes this (inter)dependence to citizens. Under the sign of ubuntu, the identity of the individual sits squarely between its own (self) sufficiency and its radical debt to the Other. Abiding in a middle, a space that the post-amble opens and performs, the potential to transcend deep division is the question of how words turn relations of negation into relationships of constitutive opposition.

The (law's) past marks a need and basis for reconciliation. Yet, its offences are actionable, grounds for invoking the (retributive) force of standing domestic and international jurisprudence. Among other things, this means that the post-amble's call for reconciliation sits in opposition to the protections delineated in the larger (interim) constitution. This tension appears clearly when the post-amble's third clause defines reconciliation partly through a mandate for amnesty:

In order to advance such reconciliation and reconstruction, amnesty shall be granted in all respect of acts, omissions and offences associated with political objectives and committed in the course of the conflicts of the past. To this end, Parliament under this constitution shall adopt a law determining a firm cut-off date which shall be a date after 8 October 1990 and before 6 December 1993, and providing for the mechanisms, criteria and procedures, including tribunals, if any, through which such amnesty shall be dealt with at any time after the law has been passed.

In the name of reconciliation, the post-amble's call for amnesty functions as an extra-constitutional mandate, a non-constitutional practice, and a constitutional norm. It delineates what is needed to enable the constitution: the future guarantee of equal rights, political participation and justice depends – temporally and conceptually – on the revelation and exposure of the past. To this "end", amnesty is held (out) as law constitutive, a way to (re)establish the conditions under which the force of law can operate and claim to embody justice.[45] However, very much against the logic of the constitution to which it is attached, this founding (of) law entails a self-exception. Holding that amnesty is a necessary exception to law and that the creation of law's necessity demands amnesty, the post-amble appears to abridge rights in the name of a reconciliation that will allow their future expression.

Declaring the need for amnesty while recalling the violence inherent in such exceptions, the post-amble calls on the law to act as if it is not the law. As the terms and objects of judgment cannot be assumed in the wake of apartheid, the public assumption of history must proceed in the name of their definition. The law must be set and stand in self-opposition, a position that serves to render it non-external to those for whom it claims to work. Thus, the process of amnesty is the uncomfortable gift of a time in which the violence of the past appears to fund not revenge but shared oppositions, the power to gather together and make good again. This opposition is the ancient and immanent connection between amnesty and reconciliation.[46] For reconciliation, the law of amnesty is both an exception to the law, a law of general application that bears substantial similarity to the juridical logic involved in declaring a state of emergency, *and* an exception to the law's sovereignty, a break in (the breaking in of) precedent that interrupts the past's silencing continuity in order to recall and expose its connection to evil. In the post-amble, the law of amnesty embodies the memory of what apartheid law never did: give itself up for those that it claimed as constituents.[47] This gift (of a debt) is reflected in the post-amble's final passage, a clause in which a rather traditional request for divine blessing is equally a reminder that the law of reconciliation may not be so far from a certain (rhetorical) law of faith; that is, the inevitability of the contingency that attends the power to make with words:

> With this constitution and these commitments we, the people of South Africa, open a new chapter in the history of our country. Nkosi sikelel' iAfrika. God seën Suid-Afrika. Morena boloka sechaba sa heso. May God bless our country. Mudzimu fhatutshedza Afrika. Hosi katekisa Afrika.

The post-amble's constitution is both a bridging of history and a bridge on which history can be made. Between chapters, without definitive ending and supported by the faith of an interim constitution composed with 11 official languages – a poignant counterpart to the worries over the tower of Babel that motivated NGK theologians to erect the walls of separate development – it stands between the referent of old writings and the potential of a new vocabulary. Inside and outside the "now document" that it sums and opposes, the post-amble's (coming to) terms open and mark the difficult work of the present, the constitution of a defining moment of transition and a transitional time that troubles the constituted grounds of definition.

From the controversial but generative power of sufficient consensus to the exclusive bargaining in the MPNP's last days, the post-amble was an exceptional accomplishment and a creature of exception. Standing before the law, it (re)collected law's violence in the name of (re)turning it toward justice and it mandated an amnesty that set aside justice's precedent in the name of reconciliation. At the time that it was written, very little attention was paid to the post-amble's elegant prose and awkward logic. Today, however, its founding terms are widely celebrated and defended as a necessary culmination of the spirit that sustained the MPNP's work. Usually referring to the threat of military and paramilitary violence in the run-up to the election, this claim to necessity is difficult to assess. Were the leaders of the security forces acting in a manner that contradicted their announced support for transition?[48] A Member of Parliament in 2000, Constand Viljoen replied to me that, "I know of no coup plan."[49] If so, why did the ANC give ground on amnesty? Time pressure may be one answer. The *appearance* of armed opposition may be another. A third may have to do with a desire to minimise the risk of a legitimacy crisis that followed from the Motsuenyane Commission's report.

Alternatively, the post-amble's call for amnesty in the name of reconciliation may have been important for its argument that the interim constitution was a necessary but not sufficient condition for the transition to democracy. This is not just to point out that the interim constitution was "interim". Both achieving and calling for reconciliation, the post-amble's words enabled the constitution, conditioned its power on an understanding and movement from the past to the future, and performed the idea that the constitution's law was not the (sole) repository of justice. In this way, the post-amble posed the very question of necessity, the problem of how history was to figure (into) South Africa's new beginning.

The post-amble was not the final word. Its performance of a beginning was equally an opposition to it, an expression of the need to begin again. As a hinge that appeared to exceed the law of non-contradiction, the post-amble constituted a political subjectivity that was called to move between the recovery of identity from within the history of apartheid's identitarian violence and the creativity of identifications given to the "people's" unity in difference. Incongruously, it claimed that amnesty was a means to initiate this movement. In the name of reconciliation, amnesty's promise was the risk of an impunity that highlighted the need for speech about the appropriate meaning, form, and precedential value of law's binding words. More precisely, the logic of the post-amble held an unspoken hermeneutic question: In the midst of transition, how was South Africa to read the past, understand the way in which it had been distorted by apartheid, and resolve what role the past had to play in the making of democracy's present and future?

2. the standing of history (making) in transition

Announcing a time of transition, the post-amble's amnesty extended as well as opposed the MPNP's generative logic, the idea that the work of constitution could proceed by bracketing the past and taking exception to the law's precedent. In this way, the post-amble raised and played with the question of history, the problems of how to establish the meaning of the past in the present and whether remembrance was important for the future. Just ten days after the post-amble was written, these questions were the subject of heated debate as Parliament convened in a joint session to ratify the interim constitution and resolve whether it was time to approve its own dissolution. Across the three houses that had been created by racial distinction in the 1983 constitution, MP's wasted little time in taking up the issues that followed from the post-amble's achievement of reconciliation: What was the historical cost of transition? Was the post-amble's transitional bridge a way to leave the past behind or carry it into the future? Did the unity of reconciliation's beginning demand forgetting or did it require finding space to respectfully remember a diversity of tradition?

Parliament's debate over the interim constitution is easily overlooked. With the NP in firm control, there was little doubt that the legislation would pass, an inevitability that makes it possible to assume that the discussion was simply a last chance for a recalcitrant CP to rave about the "injustice" of apartheid's end. Without excluding this aspect of the proceedings, my aim here is to suggest that the debate has a much deeper and richer meaning. The enactment of the legal continuity that characterised the South African transition, the debate focused less on the post-amble's mandate for amnesty than the problem of history that sat beneath it. More precisely, across three lines of argument, supporters and critics of the interim constitution asked questions and offered arguments as to how the cost of reconciliation's achievement at the MPNP was a history that endowed political-cultural life with its meaning. Sitting between those who lamented their betrayal and those who announced their guilt for apartheid, the NP responded to the issue by arguing that it was prepared to close history's book and also embody its lessons. Unable to resolve the tension in this position, it retreated to the claim that reconciliation's achievement was not (yet) perfect and that its remaining promise would not come cheap.

Parliament convened on 17 December 1993 to take up the *Constitution of the Republic of South Africa Bill*. Allotted 1500 minutes, a period that ultimately allowed for "142 turns to speak", the debate's stage was set by several important events. Days before, with protestors writing to the selection committee to ask that it reconsider the State President's award, Nelson Mandela and F.W. de Klerk arrived in Oslo to receive the Nobel Peace Prize.[50] While the latter conceded that apartheid "led to injustice", he also claimed that a fresh start was at hand, a spirit that allowed him and Mandela to "stand together". Appearing rather unsure of his company, Mandela claimed that it was "time to speak of the future of our country" and recognise that "we should live together as a common nation with a common destiny".[51] In an interview on Norwegian television, however, he looked back, noting that the ANC's decision to pursue the "path of negotiation and reconciliation" did not mitigate the fact that the South African Government was composed largely of "political criminals".[52]

Back home, the question of the past was also producing substantial tension as Constand Viljoen claimed that the Boer Commando's occupation of Fort Schanskop was "only preparation for the real thing", and the AWB's Terre'Blanche invoked the possibility of another Blood River to "rectify the betrayal at Kempton Park".[53] More dramatic and symbolically-charged were the celebrations that took place on 16 December, the anniversary of the Vow and the founding of the MK. While tens of thousands gathered at the Voortrekker Monument, Viljoen stood on the banks of the Ncome (Blood) River, urging a negotiated solution to the Afrikaner's demands and then proclaiming that the *voortrekker*'s vow would be reaffirmed to God, "If you give us victory over the darkness, in a peaceful way or not."[54] In Soweto, Mandela celebrated the MK's success in prosecuting the struggle and declared that it had achieved victory to the degree that the country stood on "the threshold of an epochal transition into a new democratic order".[55] Altogether, with some longing to go back and others set to move forward, the early days of transition were far more schizophrenic than reconciling.

As history was being invoked and performed to dramatically different ends, Parliament convened the following day to consider the interim constitution. Roelf Meyer opened the debate, contending that the bill marked the "dawn of a new era" which brought South Africa a "step closer to reconciliation".[56] Then, making an effort that de Klerk had not, the Minister of Constitutional Development and the NP's chief negotiator claimed that on the road to becoming a "new nation":

> We have moved away from apartheid. We, who were responsible for apartheid, are now saying that we want to leave that wrong behind. We are saying that we are sorry. We are also saying, however, that we are now determined to rectify what went wrong.[57]

Underscoring that the success of such work was not a given, Meyer then set the legislation under the sign of ubuntu and contended:

> Once it is promulgated as the Constitution of the Republic of South Africa, it will stand the test of time only if its underlying philosophy becomes the hallmark of the whole of South African society.[58]

For some gathered in the chamber, the test at hand was to resist the signs of the times. Speaking shortly after Meyer, the CP's Daniel du Plessis endeavoured to turn the tables when he drew from antiquity to argue that the post-amble in the interim constitution was appropriate given the tragedy that it summed and enacted. Against the post-amble's claim that the constitution was a bridge on which to conduct the work of reconciliation, du Plessis warned:

Anyone who believes that this constitution will be the bridge between the past of a deeply divided community and a future of peaceful coexistence is seeing a mirage. Such a person suffers from hallucinations in that he sees something which does not, in fact, exist. Never in the history of this country has the chasm between people been wider. Never in the history of the world has it been clearer than it is now that ethnic differences and ethnic divisions require that any bridge which attempts to cross this divide, is built in such a way these realities are taken into account.[59]

What was missing in the "new" South Africa, according to du Plessis, was a recognition of the fact that Afrikaners needed to "govern ourselves, so that we can serve the Triune God in peace and so that we can contribute to the salvation of other peoples".[60] Together, with Meyer's claim that the interim constitution promised the "establishment of a sovereign and democratic constitutional state, equality between men and women and people of all races", du Plessis' argument held the key terms and questions of Parliament's debate, a dispute that unfolded along three intersecting axes.[61]

First, Parliament's debate called into question the act and power of constitution. Reflected in arguments about the meaning of the legislation under consideration and the nature of the time that it bequeathed to South Africa, the CP offered the most hard-line and consistent position. Through and through, it argued that the interim constitution was an undue imposition on South African citizens and held that it amounted to nothing less than the NP's outright betrayal of its own constituency. Speaking immediately after Meyer's opening case, Ferdi Hartzenburg, the CP's leader of the Official Opposition, claimed that time had not been allotted for close study of the legislation. Then he rejected it, arguing that the interim constitution lacked the consent of the people, exceeded the mandate of de Klerk's 1990 referendum, and made no provision for regional autonomy or a *volkstaat*. The latter was crucial, an argument about the need for self-determination and a claim as to how the constitution's cost was the "total capitulation of the NP to the ANC-SACP" and a form of governance that "negates both of those chief elements in the Afrikaner people's history – its faith and its freedom".[62] Moreover, according to the Freedom Front's Pieter Mulder, the agreements that supported the constitution were suspect, the product of a misused process of sufficient consensus that culminated in an agreement which had no more merit than the "war-treaty" of Versailles.[63] Echoing the point,

Cornelius Mulder claimed that the Constitution was only "autochthonous and home-grown to a section of the NP and the ANC". At a deeper level, others contended, its development marked not a miracle but a heresy, a moment in which "the descendents of devout Huguenots are building a new Babel" and an act in which "the God of the Bible is despised and receives no recognition".[64]

While the CP and its allies lashed out at the promise and movement of the post-amble, supporters of the interim constitution rebutted the criticism with several lines of argument, which when taken together held an interesting tension. Following the arc of Meyer's position, the constitution was defended by his NP colleagues as a "new beginning" that was "replacing a dinosaur" and which signalled the "birth of a new democratic South Africa".[65] More deeply, Kassavan Padayachy, a member of the Solidarity Party in the House of Delegates, attempted to turn the CP's arguments back by delineating what he claimed was the very "essence" of the constitution:

> It is a constitution of give and take, a constitution of compromise, a constitution that clearly proves beyond a shadow of a doubt that the pen is, and always will be, mightier than the sword. If people are willing to sit down and speak to each other, then miracles can be performed. I am confident that what we are experiencing here today is nothing short of a miracle created by God himself as a reward to all South Africans, the vast majority of whom, as a nation, have always been God-fearing.[66]

While this spirit of compromise was invoked by a significant number of speakers, its precise result or outcome was cast variously. On the one hand, the work of constitution-building was defined as a transitional event, the opening of a space between past and future, a time of opportunity, and a "beginning not an end". In short, according to the DP's Colin Eglin, the constitution was "unashamedly transitional", a path more than a destination and a basis for learning the work of nation-building.[67] On the other hand, the constitution's compromises were held up as transformative, a completed event that was frequently likened to a miracle and cast as the "burying of apartheid" and the healing of South Africa's "political rift".[68] What is interesting, however, is that NP representatives consistently vacillated between these positions, claiming at various points in the debate that the constitution was the beginning of a bridge-building process that "has only just started" *and* a definitive creation and/or ending that was nothing less than South Africa's successful crossing of the "final Rubicon". Viewed together, the tension between these accounts of the interim constitution's "accomplishment" held the question of whether and how it was making history.

Did the interim constitution "break from the past and give South Africans an opportunity to create a new future", show a "total disregard for the history of the Afrikaner people", or demonstrate that "while it is not good to live in the past, it is absolutely necessary to remember it so that one will not repeat the wrongs of the past in the future"?[69] These questions composed the second axis of Parliament's debate. Here, the crucial issue was whether the turn from apartheid was a fulfilment, (revolutionary) negation, or unprecedented opportunity to understand South Africa's history. The difference between these positions was substantial. For those keen to remind the NP that "history did not start in 1990" with de Klerk's 2 February address, the interim constitution was defended as a basis to remember that "our past is one of oppression, suppression and genocide".[70] Speaking for the ANC-aligned Labour Party, Michael Hendrickse put the matter bluntly, arguing that the time of transition was decidedly not one for forgetting:

> It is only people who have not suffered, have warped their consciences and who have sold their souls that can talk lightly of living in the past … This interim constitution is a start, a move toward the realisation of the hopes and dreams of millions of South Africans, namely to live as free men and women in the country of their birth. We do not want to live in the past, but do not dare tell me that I must simply forget what the Nats and all the White supremacists did. The oppressed never need to be converted to democracy. It is the NP which needs to be converted.[71]

A poignant explanation of the post-amble's claim that the constitution was not self-actualising, this position also called into question how the past was to shape the future. Contesting its lack of conversion, the NP's basic reply was that history represented less an enduring legacy than a reason to oversee reform in the name of ending an apartheid system that had not worked. Congruent with Gerald Morkel's claim that the constitution was a way of "closing this book and forgetting about apartheid", Frederik van Heerden skirted the moral dimensions of apartheid's end and argued that, "With this legislation the Afrikaner people's constitutional calling is fulfilled … A new South Africa is already here."[72] Citing both Winston Churchill and Adlai Stevenson, Abraham Williams, the Minister of Sport, added that the future would be lost in quarrels over the past, and then made bold to say that the NP's leadership in the constitution-making process had "stopped the revolution".[73]

In this claim to have prevented the ANC's "onslaught", there did appear to be a history that mattered to the Nats. With many choosing not to echo Meyer's apology, party members frequently avoided responsibility for the past, chastised conservatives for their war-mongering and myopic views of history, and then argued (implicitly and explicitly) that the NP was dedicated to never forgetting the immaturity, innate duplicity, and historical designs of the ANC. Made frequently and with substantial belligerence, this position was the basis for the NP's claim that it had always and would continue to embody the country's cherished political values. In this regard, claiming that "rhetoric is not going to help us much", Minster of Population Development, Jakobus Rabie, appeared quite ready to perform more of the historical violence that attended his post when he claimed:

> I cannot help but grab the ANC-SACP-COSATU-SANCO-LPSA concoction by the throat. If there is any organisation which contradicts itself on this transitional constitution, it is the ANC with its self-throttling tentacles, bloodsuckers as it were. The organisation is the symbolisation of a many-headed dragon which is being sent in a different bestial direction by each head. In polyglot confusion this dragon-like leadership propounds various nation-destroying standpoints. In respect of the transitional constitution, this specifically proves that the ANC is not a monolithic organisation but a conglomeration of renegade surrogates, each with its own hidden and dangerous agenda. Such a monstrous organisation cannot be trusted with the future of South Africa in any way.[74]

Charitably, this position was a tidy balm for those who believed that the NP had capitulated and was getting ready to leave the political stage to the ANC. Less charitably, it was evidence that the party wanted to remain both player and referee, a body that could claim to serve the will of all South Africans while remaining firmly in control of the country and its transition.

Across the aisle, the CP saw nothing but betrayal in the Nat's rendition of Afrikaner self-interest. Singularly committed to history as a basis for morality and a "workable way of life", the conservatives turned to a page in the past, offering up a theo-poetic rehearsal of Afrikaner nationalism's "true" calling. Following Wynand van Wyk's claim that the NP had callously disregarded the "volk" and forgotten the Boer in the Afrikaner, the Freedom Front's Joseph Chiolé argued that the constitution's promise of "equality and freedom" paved the way for the "domination of the world by the New World Order".[75]

At base, this position was an extreme rendition of the CP's argument that the interim constitution subverted the will of God by supplanting a divinely sanctioned covenant of self-determination with the false idol of non-Christian national sovereignty. Given the NGK's repudiation of apartheid, the standing and authenticity of this calling was set primarily in the hands and words of a politician, former Prime Minister Malan, and a poet, N.P. van Wyk Louw, the figure crucial to the early 20th century language movement.[76] Armed with these warrants, the CP maintained consistently that the government had broken its sacred vows to God and its people, a turn that constituted sin, promised punishment, and justified a struggle to ensure that the Afrikaner was not (re)colonised by an "alien" government.[77] Conceding that he was making "war-talk", Stephanus Jacobs went the next step and swore a new vow:

> All of us must choose … We have chosen to oppose this draft
> constitution, because we have chosen to oppose the subjugation of our
> people, in favour of the freedom our people … I have unequivocally
> chosen the freedom of my people – the Boere-Afrikaner people. We
> say today, on the strength of the history of our people, that the struggle
> our forefathers began, will rage on until we have perished or conquered.
> That is the oath of the CP caucus of 1993.[78]

While representative of the CP's dismay, Jacob's position obscured something of its larger position, namely that the demands of God and history could be accommodated if the new dispensation made provision for a *volkstaat*. Thus, like their NP opponents, the conservatives appeared willing to use the transition as an occasion to play both sides off the middle.

Following closely from the dispute over the past's relation to the present and future, the third axis of Parliament's debate circled around the meaning and value of reconciliation. Citing the success of the MPNP's "sufficient consensus amongst its twenty-odd political parties", a member of the House of Delegates appealed to the post-amble's language of reconciliation to make the case that South Africa had witnessed "nothing less than a miracle".[79] Early in the debate, the NP's Pieter Marais built on the same idea, using reconciliation's religious connotation to rebut the CP's worries over the coming of a new Babel and then contending that it was the Nats who possessed an attitude of "real reconciliation":

We have received a language vineyard. Some of us have worked
too little in it and others not at all. We now have an instrument to
cultivate it with. All that remains is to use it so that we can acquire
that vineyard anew. The owners of that vineyard are not separated by
political or colour bars. Rather, we are linked by unbreakable bonds
of love, loyalty, and faith to something deep inside us which we have
in common, namely our language. Attempts to divide us in the past
failed irrevocably, but unfortunately they have also hurt our language.
Now we are together again and there are many of us. The family is
united. We know the pain of division – the memory of this will remain
– but we now also know the joy of reconciliation.[80]

While the overt metaphor drew from the constitution's recognition of 11
official languages, the subtext of this position was a plea for the growth of
Afrikaans in the midst of a process of reconciliation that had not always
been good to the *taal*. Much more directly, this concern was expressed by
the Freedom Front's Pieter Mulder when he recalled Smuts' advocacy of
conciliation, a programme that was claimed to have set Afrikaners on the
road to a homogenising (English) liberalism. In this light, Mulder contended,
the interim constitution was anything but a beneficial reconciliation to
the degree that its promise of ANC "domination" forsook the path which
"reconciles Afrikaner nationalism with Black liberation".[81] The CP also took
this long view, using echoes of early NGK doctrine to argue repeatedly that
the interim constitution offered a "horizontal reconciliation" which was
an affront to God and thus a calling to struggle in the name of recovering
"vertical" unity.[82]

Declaring that he was both a "Boer and an Afrikaner", the NP's Abraham
Janse van Rensburg responded with a different version of the story: in
the run-up to Union in 1910, "non-whites" had been "sacrificed for the
sake of reconciliation between the two White language groups".[83] Going
further, Dawid de Villiers contended that the CP's nationalistic "fantasy,
insincerity, and inauthenticity" was blind to "the reconciliation which
the new constitution offers South Africa" and could only serve the ends
of intolerance.[84] This offer, however, was characterised in different ways.
While some saw it as the making and marker of a new time, reconciliation
was also defined as that which would follow from the "contract" of the new
constitution, an agreement that required dedicated and disciplined work.
Thus, reconciliation appeared in Parliament's debate as both an ideal and an

ongoing event. Echoing a line of NGK theology, Frederik van Heerden's comments illustrated that the difference between these two interpretations was subtle and not always clear:

> These two groups – the group from the Western cultural sphere and
> the group from the African cultural sphere – are not mixed in the
> constitution. They are merely reconciled. This is important. This gives
> us in South Africa time to prepare everyone spiritually to love, work,
> play and laugh in a totally changed world.[85]

If more than a time to come, what was the precise object of reconciliation and how would it work? Near the very end of Parliament's debate, Nicolaas Koornhof offered a reply that was more specific than most of those offered by his NP colleagues when he argued that reconciliation was an explicit prerequisite to "freedom, peace and tolerance in South Africa". Turning then to its process, he contended that:

> [R]econciliation can never be cheap. A sacrifice is required for it.
> The greatest sacrifice which can be made is to sacrifice everyone's
> self-righteous attitude and self-justifying I.[86]

A rebuttal to the CP's claim that reconciliation was – historically and in the moment – a call to struggle for self-determination, the precision of this claim is noteworthy, especially as it gathered religious and political views of reconciliation and then set them into oppositional relation with the underlying logic of apartheid. More than a once-off act, reconciliation rested on an attitude of self-relinquishment, an *ethos* with which South Africa could "now face its greatest test". For most in the NP, however, this test appeared to demand quite a different sort of opposition – the creation of the unity needed to oppose the ANC in the coming election.

Reconciliation's form, meaning and power was neither singular nor given. At the end of the three days allotted for debate, Roelf Meyer addressed the matter in a telling way when he declared, "The next stage is beginning." The pun was perhaps crucial, an indication that within transition the past was yet everywhere and nowhere: it was time to close history's book and a history-making moment to prop if not pry the book open; progress demanded a refusal to dwell in the past and it was possible only if the country was attuned to history's calling; the bridge between past and future was ready to walk, best burned, and illusory; reconciliation had made new and had only opened the door to a risky process of transition.

What to make of these tensions was well beyond what could be accommodated in Parliament's debate. Nevertheless, these diverging characterisations of the transition and its reconciliation were held and expressed in a single phrase, one that was spoken over and over and over by parliamentarians: "It is not perfect." Referring to the interim constitution, this claim was both an admission of the moment's uncertainty and an important signal that the achievement of reconciliation was not without significant conditions and remainders. Ultimately, it is these announced limitations that mark the significance of Parliament's debate, a discourse and discussion addressed to the real and perceived risks of reconciliation's creation, the transgressions that necessarily followed from its (constitutive) power of invention. Whether for or against the interim constitution, members of Parliament did appear to agree that reconciliation would not come cheap. Its move from potential to actuality, the (re)turn to make new (again) out of violence troubled the comforts of language, revealed a need to question the complex "force" of history, upset taken-for-granted accounts of the past's truth, and laid bare the thin line between productive transition, capitulation, and revolution.

An outgrowth of an (in)sufficiently consensual compromise, reconciliation hinged on a set of works that appeared to entail very difficult if not incommensurable faiths. What *was* the bridge between past and future, and what movement did it allow as it sat on a spirit and philosophy of reconciliation that appeared less to transcend opposition than call it into being in the name of a unity that had more than one face? Was this enabling structure the product of an ahistorical and backroom deal or was it an open call for South Africans to "deal with the past"? This question was not only important inside Parliament. Increasingly, its terms were an urgent problem for those still awaiting access to the halls of government.

3. constituting a vocabulary to deal with the past

Amidst a flurry of farewell speeches, Parliament passed the interim constitution bill by a substantial margin.[87] In the ensuing weeks and just beyond an unexpectedly bloody turn of the year, the question of history's role in the future of reconciliation stood alongside the pressing tasks of designing a fair election and getting hold-outs to come to the party.[88] With the plebiscite fast approaching, the white right and IFP continued to complain of their allergy to change. The severity and nature of the symptoms, however, seemed to vary widely. Claiming definitive constituencies that they could never quite fully produce, the groups issued demands one day and retracted them the next; alliances created early in the week were frequently lucky to survive the weekend.[89] In February, the AVF proclaimed that the antidote to the coming "communist" government was the disruption of the elections and "a little bit of violence to protect ourselves".[90] A week later, opening a debate over amendments to the interim constitution designed partly to alleviate such threats, de Klerk argued that conservative opponents of the transition needed to understand that they had neither "the right to speak on behalf of the Afrikaner people" nor a particularly clear sense of the fact that Parliament was powerless to "change the reality that all South Africans are, inseparably, extremely interdependent upon one another – economically, socially, and constitutionally".[91]

In the preceding year, the MPNP and Parliament's last full debate had both demonstrated and troubled this "symbolic relationship", a bond that de Klerk held out as definitive evidence of a "historic opportunity to achieve peace, reconciliation, and stability in our country".[92] Specifically, the interim constitution was very much the product of negotiations that bracketed history in the name of progress and a process reconciliation in which sufficient consensus referred to the opinions of two parties. These shortcomings were highlighted if not enacted by the post-amble, especially as its call for amnesty set aside the duties of law and gave some credence to the NP's claim that it was time to close the book on the past. Thus, as the CP was warning that the new dispensation was denigrating history's divine calling, another constituency was worrying about whether the country was about to commit a different sort of heresy as it appeared ready to grant a blanket amnesty that was "even more threatening to long term prospects of stability and national reconciliation" than a process that might sow some discord but which would allow South Africans to "actively grapple with their past, for individual rehabilitation, as well as for the (collective) purpose of reconciliation".[93] Was the past to be forgotten? If not, how would citizens find a space to remember that which did not appear to be afforded by amnesty's law? If not precedent, what was to contain and keep collective memory? What was the agenda and the risk attached to the NP's contention in Parliament that it was time to draw a line and move quickly and quietly to the future?

Largely out of public view, the months between the close of the MPNP and the election saw the beginning of an influential debate over how the new South Africa would "deal with the past". Here, I want to trace the appearance of this phrase and its underlying meaning, a synecdoche that would soon become a term of art in the case to create a truth commission.

More precisely, this section examines the direct antecedents, terms, and arguments of a conference that was convened in February of 1994 to address the question of whether and how South Africa needed to discern and redress the historical wounds of apartheid in the name of facilitating a stable transition and ensuring democracy's future health. Convened by a non-governmental organisation called Justice in Transition, a group that was led by Alex Boraine, the conference offered a key reply to the post-amble as well as Parliament's debate. Giving voice and in some sense consolidating a vocabulary that would soon occupy a prominent place in South African politics, delegates at the conference rallied around an interpretation of reconciliation that stood in some contrast to the one offered in the post-amble. Questioning the value of amnesty and its explicit risk of forgetting a past that demanded accountability, the conference proceedings built on an influential view of reconciliation that had been developed several years earlier by Kader Asmal. Calling for words that fulfilled a claimed duty to deal with the past, delegates then professed the need to deter history's repetition and avert the forgetfulness of amnesty. The difficulty, however, was that this position read Asmal's argument through a rather narrow prism, a lens which appeared to presuppose that historical understanding and accountability were best grounded in a liberalist interpretation of human rights, one that sat in some tension with significant threads of South African history.

Convened in Cape Town, the Justice in Transition conference was attended by a number of international figures who were well known for their role in democracy-building, and a variety of South African political activists, academics, and policy-makers, some of whom were soon to receive invitations to sit on the TRC. Perhaps more synthetic than innovative, its agenda to understand "what is desirable and what is possible" in the name of democratic transition was framed both by the post-amble and the debate over amnesty that occurred during the negotiations process but which had been largely excluded from the talks on the grounds that its definitive resolution would either deter the government from handing over power or make the ANC appear soft on human rights protection.[94] In this respect, one of the conference's benefits was to recall this discussion, especially a case that had been made in May of 1992, just as CODESA was hobbling towards breakdown, and which had clearly informed the ANC's response to the reports issued respectively by the Skweyiya and Motsuenyane Commissions.

One of South Africa's foremost philosophers of reconciliation, Kader Asmal is an animated and energetic figure who spent significant time in exile teaching law at the University of Dublin.[95] In the early 1990s, Asmal anticipated an important element of the South African transition when he turned his attention to the question of whether and how the end of apartheid would require South Africa to redress the crimes of apartheid and take steps to "come to terms with its past". In mid-1992, Asmal's most important reply to these issues appeared in his Inaugural Lecture at the University of the Western Cape, an address entitled "Victims, Survivors and Citizens – Human Rights, Reparations, and Reconciliation".

Noting that South Africa sat in a "time of transition from the vile policies of apartheid which have so devastated our country to a rights-based democratic society", Asmal's lecture began by arguing that the success of this movement rested on a "vision of human relations that is the antithesis of the apartheid heritage", an "alternative moral order" that could not be implemented through a "static state-based approach where it is assumed as an article of faith, that restricting the authority of a future state is the best guarantee of individual rights or the only real issue".[96] In positive terms, the need for South Africa to "make good again" (*Weidergutmachung*) required going beyond the strictures of law and redressing the "history of wars of annexation and extermination, slavery and racial discrimination" by recognising and (re)building the communal and collective fabric of society.[97] Beyond the retributive function of law and the liberal procedures of transition, Asmal asked:

> If formal or statutory apartheid has been consigned to the dust bin –
> although there are many limbs of the monster still to be shoved into the
> brimming bin – is it not necessary for our society to come to terms with
> just what that system was in order that we may establish our new order
> on firmer grounds? Is it not necessary to identify how the old order
> continues to manifest itself in our political, economic, and social life?
> Is it not necessary to look at the legacy of apartheid both in its physical
> form and in the hearts and minds of our people?[98]

In a basic way, these queries anticipated the question implicit in the post-amble. According to Asmal, "the formal commitment to constitutionalism" required that the country "close the book on the past" by taking steps to ensure that it "remain open for now". The difficulty, however, was discerning what pages needed to be added in order to understand South Africa's history and how this legacy could serve the ends of nation-building.

To move forward in a productive way, Asmal argued, South Africa needed political and legal remedies that addressed the personal, interpersonal and structural distortions of apartheid.[99] Against the grain, however, he maintained that the appropriate forum for such memory work was not the courtroom: "Our road of change through negotiations is inconsistent with the idea of a Nuremburg-style trial." Moreover, the harm done by apartheid exceeded the law's grasp, requiring not its potential "rope of sand to the poor and dispossessed" but an approach that could "deal with the humiliation, brutality, deprivation, and degradation of the past". Beneath this formulation sat a fundamental dilemma: prosecutions for crimes against humanity risked balkanisation while a formal or informal amnesty legitimised amnesia, a forgetting that the law itself was not well equipped to prevent. Thus, memory needed to be cultivated and contained elsewhere, a point that was made explicit two weeks later when a condensed newspaper version of Asmal's lecture argued that reconciliation would not occur through declarations of law that failed to alter the "Prospero and Caliban relationship" that sat between "victim-survivor and overlord".[100]

For the beginning of the end of apartheid, Asmal's argument was that South Africa needed to embrace a mode of reconciliation that took stock of past crimes, located accountability, and supported the "revival of moral conscience". Neither bracketing nor transcending the past, such a reconciliation entailed more than the creation of "new structures and new arrangements". Rather, he contended that reconciliation entailed significant rhetorical work, an effort that challenged the given terms of history and promoted speech that made the new through a process of "ceaseless debate" about the meaning and value of the past. More precisely, Asmal's inaugural address held that reconciliation's speech-action needed to serve three ends. Initially, reconciliation required a demonstration of apartheid's illegitimacy, a historical investigation that exposed its "life force, assumptions and the old ways", and illumined how the "wreckage of the past" shaped and distorted the "language of our rights discourse".[101] In some sense predicting how the MPNP would unfold, Asmal also argued that reconciliation's potential to enact significant change turned heavily on its capacity to broker "dispute and disputation" that would forge consensus and deter denials about the "evils of apartheid". Finally, he concluded that reconciliation offered the chance for cathartic truth-telling, a process in which South Africans could hear the experiences of fellow citizens, stories that set the stage for the justice of acknowledgement, restitution, and atonement.

Asmal's argument was prescient, particularly as it called for a reconciliation that exposed the past's damage to speech and fostered words that moved accountability beyond the precedents of a legal system which had historically negated its own connection to justice. As well, his position detailed the ambiguous value of amnesty, suggesting that it was equally a pragmatic way of ensuring support for transition, a troublesome exception to the rule of law, and an opportunity to theorise how memory could be cultivated outside the courtroom. While these dilemmas were left aside at the MPNP, the matter continued to provoke discussion in the confines of civil society, a debate that may have only really found political audience after the writing of the post-amble. In this context, worried about the mandate for amnesty and whether it was a troubling echo of the transitional amnesties in Latin and South America that had institutionalised impunity and entrenched precisely the socio-political divisions that democratisation sought to heal, delegates at the Justice in Transition conference sat down to share their "personal accounts" of their "experience under repression" and consider how South Africa might best answer the question of how it was going to "deal with the past".

One of the first South Africans to speak at the meeting was Albie Sachs. A member of the ANC National Executive, former exile, survivor of a car-bombing by state security forces, key player at the MPNP, and currently a Justice on South Africa's Constitutional Court, Sachs offered two stories. The first involved the experience of being asked for forgiveness by an Afrikaner who approached him one night in a Cape Town jazz club. Detailing his discomfort with the request and his inability to engage fully with his unknown interlocutor, Sachs then offered a reflection about his participation in the MPNP and the difficulties that attended working with individuals who likely knew and approved of the plan for "my elimination as Albie Sachs".[102]

Sach's two "parables", as he called them, circled around and expressed the ambiguity that surrounded the end of apartheid. On one side, the anonymous confession and request for forgiveness underscored that the need to address and redress historical oppression was hamstrung by a lack of space and a basic inability for protagonists to find the common ground needed for understanding. On the other, the uncomfortable silences at the MPNP illustrated that progress toward the future came explicitly at the expense of efforts to recognise past suffering and acknowledge the just cause of those who struggled against apartheid. In between, Sachs found the difficult work of repair, an effort with multiple referents and one that could not be reduced to institutional-legal formulas of accountability:

In South Africa, it is not just a matter of dealing with a criminal, aberrant regime that seized power and abused the people. We are dealing with a cruel, unjust system that goes back to colonialism, to slavery, to dispossession, to wars of conquest, and to the whole cultural deprivation and crushing of people. The real reparation we want ties in with the constitution, the vote, with dignity, land, jobs, and education. If we get all those things and there is a sense of forward movement and the creation of a national and real, shared dignity in this country, then I think the pressure simply to punish, to penalise and have commissions of truth becomes much less. Although I strongly support a commission of truth, for all of the reasons that I have given, the danger is that it should never be a substitute for truth in people's lives, for real dignity and the real overcoming of apartheid.[103]

How then to deal with the past? For Sachs, as it came time to speak to the new, the problem was how to reach back in order to find the terms and forge a lexicon that provided meaning to experience and established the basis for shared interaction. Underscored by Adam Michnik's discussion of the moral and political pressures involved in negotiating with those whom "only yesterday you called an oppressor, a murderer or a terrorist", Sach's position set the task of transition as a need to find words in the midst of their apparent limit.[104]

The bulk of the conference was given to those from outside South Africa, many of whom had struggled to craft a voice for history within the context of other political transitions. Together, their positions circled a single theme: South Africa must reckon with the force of history. In detailing this task, speakers consistently medicalised history, describing it as a festering wound that had to be healed in order to prevent (re)infection. Appearing at different sites and showing a variety of forms, the wound encompassed the physical harm inflicted by apartheid, the structural violence and economic exploitation perpetuated by its law, and the psychological damage wrought by its oppression. In all instances, the past was deemed a threat to the health of individual citizens and the body politic. Gross violations of human rights required the recovery of dignity for victims and accountability that would consolidate a long absent rule of law. In the name of transition, South Africa had a duty to make individuals whole again and bring truth to the light of day in the name of securing justice.

For many, this work was threatened by the post-amble's amnesty, the ambiguous wildcard in the transitional deck and a potential affront to norms of international law. Citing the latter's importance, Jose Zalaquett argued that South Africa sat in a difficult position to the degree that its transition could proceed neither from a condition of amnesia nor the will to revenge which would follow from sanctioned forgetting. Several keynote speakers addressed this dilemma, casting it as a problem of how to chart a course between the "ethical requirements" and "political constraints" of transition. Other speakers, however, simply ignored the post-amble and called for a series of prosecutions and trials. Arguing that the task of "building a new democracy" required the "non-discriminatory application of the law", Juan Mendez lobbied for extended prosecutions on the grounds of international law and claimed that along with the need to "respect the plight of victims", the achievement of reconciliation would only follow "after some measure of justice has occurred".[105] Citing the Guatemalan experience with amnesty, Mendez did admit that there were pragmatic limits to prosecution, a concession that led Jose Zalaquett to ask whether appeals to the priority of law had to consider whether justice in transition was not also a function of an amnesty that was conditioned on truth-telling. According to Zalaquett, the discovery and disclosure of the past was a crucial element of dealing with the past, work that laid the ground for an "opening up" that could bridge historical-political divides. Unwilling to forgo the potential benefits of such efforts, he then set the amnesty equation in specific terms:

> Amnesty should possibly serve the ultimate purposes of reparation and prevention; it should be based on the truth, or one cannot really know what the pardon or amnesty is for; there should ideally be an acknowledgement of that truth; and the amnesty must be approved democratically in the sense that it must be the will of the nation to forgive.[106]

Debate over the value of amnesty rested on a difficult puzzle: could norms of justice be presupposed in the midst of transition or did the transitional represent a moment in which the bar had to be (re)defined and (re)set? In other words, it was not clear in early 1994 that it was useful to reject amnesty in favour of a rule of law that enjoyed almost no legitimacy given its role in the definition and enforcement of apartheid. By the same token, a blanket amnesty appeared only to perpetuate law's diremption from justice. Recalling the *Kairos Document,* the problem was partly whether the post-amble's reconciliation was a process or an outcome, something that preceded or followed from the justice that prevented forgetting and located accountability. As the post-amble suggested, the problem of how to deal with the past thus appeared to involve a reconciliation that stood outside the law but worked in its name.

While international delegates debated the existence and shape of a space that could support productive remembrance, some of the South African participants at the conference questioned whether and how well the external formulas fit the domestic bill of particulars. Late in the proceedings, Mary Burton addressed the issue in a succinct way. Addressing the "foreign visitors, some of whom know us well and our experience", she explained:

> I have wanted to call out during the conference: "Yes, but you don't quite know what it's like for us. You don't understand the complexity of the things in which we are involved." I felt that some of our voices had been missing in this discourse. There is the story of the Afrikaner people, their experience in concentration camps and the effect of this on subsequent generations.[107]

With this comment, the former president of the Black Sash was most certainly not affiliating herself with the conservative bombast offered in Parliament several weeks earlier. Rather, the point was that the matter of dealing with the past was not black and white. For those immersed in the South African transition, history had multiple connotations; its dialectic had more than two sides and its force was not a homogenous power.

Returning to the podium, Albie Sachs underscored the point, arguing that South Africa could not tell history to "stop" in order to deal with the "amnesty question". Noting plainly that "there will be an amnesty", he contended that this inevitability would be the context in which the country would have to "deal also with the great humiliations most South Africans have been subjected to by colonialism, racism, and domination". In his terms, the task of transition entailed perhaps less a set of discrete procedures than "one major process".[108] Of this work, Professor Andre du Toit observed that "one hardly knows where to begin", and warned that the country had to keep moving and that "we must use words such as reconciliation, amnesty, and amnesia in their serious senses or not at all".

In the final discussions at the conference, this problem of definition was evident in debate about the post-amble's legal standing – it was deemed "equal in status to other provisions of the constitution" – and how it related to the indemnity legislation that had been used to support the constitutional negotiations.[109] The debate was deepened by discussion over whether mixing theological, political, legal and moral interpretations of reconciliation was the recipe for a healing tonic or a concoction that would allow opponents of transition to cry "witch-hunt". In turn, the ambiguity spurred questions about the merits of a truth commission and how it might work. The dilemmas surrounding the creation of such a body were characterised well by Breyten Breytenbach. In a letter that was ostensibly an apology for his absence, the once imprisoned poet wondered if the call for a truth-seeking commission required "words – teased and cut from emotions" and then urged in the name of gathering transition's energy, "Let the riddles multiply!"

There were riddles to spare. Halfway between the appearance of the post-amble and South Africa's first democratic election, the Justice in Transition conference echoed Parliament's conclusion that the interim constitution's post-amble was not self-interpreting. What's more, the bridge from past to future was not yet built and its construction, let alone traversal, demanded an understanding of South African history that was differently conceptualised, deeply contested, and whose value was radically complicated by a mandate for amnesty that involved making an (unjust) exception to a rule of law that lacked legitimacy in part because it had so long counted on and deployed the power of exception. For those concerned that apartheid's regime of criminals would not be held accountable, amnesty's productive forgetting was small comfort if the pragmatic need for "forgiveness" was not accompanied by a dedicated effort to bring truth to the light of day. At base, the riddle had a simple form: amnesty was inevitable, valuable, and wholly unacceptable. In the midst of a transition, its promise of reconciliation was thus an open and difficult question. In the name of enacting the interim constitution's call for unity in difference, dealing with the past was going to take time and the creation of a space that somehow sat both inside and outside the rule of law.

It was perhaps the questions that mattered more than the answers. In part, this is to say that the Justice in Transition conference was important because it gave explicit voice to problems that had been consistently set aside at the negotiating table in order to "make progress". Too, as the exceptions of the negotiating process were recognised and brought back into the picture, the claimed need to deal with the past stood in contrast to the NP's overall position in Parliament; now was not the time to draw a line, close the book, and move forward. Nor was it a moment to retreat into history's laagers and enclaves. Rather, the task at hand was to acknowledge untold suffering, discern lines of accountability, and take steps to deter history's repetition – all in a manner that did not deepen the already vast divisions in South African society. In this respect, there was then a certain parallel between the rhetorical arc of the conference debate and its counterpart in Parliament. Both events troubled the terms of the post-amble and its promise of reconciliation. At the conference, disturbed by the call for amnesty, delegates expressed significant worry over the impunity that would follow the provision of amnesty and wondered whether the post-amble's legal exception to the rule of law demanded either the use of international tribunals or the creation of an official forum in which to build and sanctify the truth, meaning, and power of that history which amnesty seemed destined to forget. As one commentator put the matter:

> Measures of amnesty can be used in a new society, but if we want to establish the rule of law and have a society in which the dignity of the victims is recognised, then we must take on the task of dealing with the past.[110]

At the end of the conference, there did not appear to be much disagreement with this idea. What is puzzling, however, is that while there was (sufficient?) consensus about the need to deal with the past, very little attention was devoted to theorising the concept's presuppositions. Unspoken at the time, the result of this decision was a riddle heaped upon the riddles already at hand.

What exactly was entailed in "dealing with the past"? As it was employed at the conference, the phrase appeared frequently to imply and assume that history *per se* contained a kind of teleological force, an ability to cycle (inevitably) around and into the present.[111] Described variously, this dynamic was consistently explained in a generic way, grounded much more in the international discourse of human rights than specific analyses of how South African cultures had and continued variously to understand or ascribe power to history. Indeed, the conference proceedings suggest that the claimed need to appreciate a diverse set of historical experiences was routed through a rather monolithic explanation of the historical.

This reduction followed directly from claims about the nature of memory. Repeatedly, arguments about the need to remember as a way to deal with the past were warranted by stock appeals to recovering the identity and protecting the integrity of the modern(ist) liberal political subject. Significantly, these claims about the capacities and inalienable rights of the self-certain subject were not related to but distanced from the communal *ethos* that variously and to different degrees informed Afrikaner nationalism, ANC ideology, and select versions of the African humanism that rested on the idea of ubuntu, which had been given prominent place in the post-amble. As such, the call to remember depended on a liberal ideology that many had questioned if not rejected on the grounds that it was a theoretically inaccurate, socially unproductive and politically untrustworthy account of human subjectivity.[112] In some tension with both Kader Asmal's and Roelf Meyer's previously announced views of reconciliation, the conference's equation of "memory is identity" assumed that recognised diversity was unity and that reconciliation was concerned first and foremost with a self that existed and appeared prior to the collective.

What was the force of history on the South African landscape? Did all South Africans conceive its meaning and power in similar ways? For purposes of transition, did they need to? Would the unity of remembrance come at the expense of diversity? Where did the balance lie? With a promise of dignity, would the recovery of individual identity come at the expense of a sense of self rooted in the communal? What did reconciliation mean under the banner of ubuntu? What subjects were to be the objects of reconciliation? In the context of whether there should be amnesty and how it might be designed, these questions were significant for their suggestion that the stakes of the post-amble had much to do with how to use history and truth-telling *both* to recover the grounds of human *identity* and to promote *identification* between old and divided enemies. With this double agenda, the post-amble's distinction between the duty to remember and the need to forget was very thin. Its terms set a narrow pathway on which there was a need to move and double-back between truth-telling for purposes of recognising experience, upholding dignity, and ensuring accountability, and a process that set aside the historical "causes" and justifications for violence that precluded the formation of mutual identifications that were crucial for political stability.[113] Two months after its announced achievement and advocacy in the interim constitution's post-amble, it appeared that reconciliation was increasingly called to oppose itself in the name of accounting for the cost of its own power to make new.

The "now" was still not yet new. In the MPNP's historic and history-making achievement of reconciliation, the interim constitution's hope for unity in difference held the question of how South Africa was going to deal with its unresolved past. From a post-amble that illustrated the "necessity" of democracy's undemocratic beginning to the debates in Parliament and civil society over whether the country's (re)founding belittled or even lacked a historical foundation, my aim in this chapter has been to consider reconciliation's role in the opening of transition and how this middle time set reconciliation into an opposition with itself. With its middle voice, the post-amble performed reconciliation and also explained the need for its practice, a calling that was justified by a duty to remember and an amnesty that (once again) appeared to bracket the memory of law. In these terms, the post-amble was a challenge and an extension of the MPNP's reconciling logic, a sign that the past could not be bracketed forever and a demand for Parliament to act in a manner that appeared to condone amnesia. Held together, the post-amble's terms thus constituted a productive negativity, an opposition to reconciliation's power to invent the new, a question as to how reconciliation's creation demanded a (re)new(ed) creativity given to gathering the past, assessing its meaning, and using it to fund the interim constitution's promise of justice. Thus, far from transcending apartheid's legacy, the reconciliation achieved at the MPNP kept history in view and then asked after it, a question that began to shed light on the potential cost of the negotiation's success.

The post-amble held the remainder of reconciliation's beginning. Backed by its accomplishment and an appeal for citizens to build a unity in difference, the post-amble contained the opening question of transition, the problem of whether and how South Africa would deal with the past. This question was not easily answered. To reply was to risk violent (re)division in the face of history's perceived desecration or condone the immorality of letting bygones be bygones with an amnesty that threatened to provoke revenge for apartheid's crimes even as it appeased individuals and groups from the old order who held a capacity to disrupt the new government. Evident in Parliament's debate and in the deliberations at the Justice in Transition conference, this dilemma had much to do with identity, the standing of the subject and how the subjects of the new constitution might or might not stand in relation. Put differently, the spirit of transition called for the constitution of individual and collective identity while emphasising that apartheid's violent identitarian logic was precisely why citizens needed to remember the past in the name of creating the identifications of reconciliation. Except insofar as the NP claimed that it would preserve the old while closing the book on the past, this tension went unresolved at Parliament. It also appeared to confound those in civil society who declared that South Africa needed to avert a blanket amnesty in the name of recovering and preserving the memory and hence the identities of those victimised by apartheid-era violence. In short, both forums were bound by the problem of how to explain the need for stable being in the midst of transition's call for becoming. Their common response to this problem was to advocate for the production and expression of words, the development of the "address" heralded in the post-amble as a way to occupy and make within the middle time that challenged and destabilised the grounds of reference, meaning, and value. Taken up in the month's after its writing, the post-amble's reconciliation was an invitation to recollect discourses of history that had been excluded from the MPNP, debate the question of what historical ways and forms of life needed to persist through the transition, and deliberate about how to finesse the line between an amnesty that left voices (and crimes) behind and one that opened a space for those words that could (re)make the connection between law and justice.

In late 1993, South Africa stood before and within an exceptional beginning, one that almost no one predicted and which served notice to the international community that reconciliation was no longer a minor spice in the larger cookbook of transition and democratisation theory. By the same token, it is important to take seriously and reflect on the exception with which reconciliation contributed to the end of statutory apartheid. Used to define and enable the MPNP's constitutive power, the process and goal of reconciliation helped negotiators actualise the potential for a beginning by fostering talk that was bound to neither the rule of law nor the historical justifications for violence that had brought the country to the brink of civil war. When set within the bilateral channel that grew stronger and more exclusive over the course of the MPNP, this taking leave of (legal) precedent and historical necessity opened a time and space to constitute outside the domain of the sovereign. This departure was performed by the post-amble's extra-constitutional voice and acknowledged in its call for forms of reconciliation that could enable law's promise. But the post-amble, along with the debate that it provoked in early 1994, also suggests that reconciliation's rhetorical invention does not come cheap. More precisely, reconciliation's words constituted by exception, by taking exception to the past. Unlike revolution, however, reconciliation was called to face this transgression and account for it. Thus, the post-amble's achievement was tempered if not challenged by a sense of work yet undone – a reconciliation with that history which had been left aside during the constitutional talks in the name of progress. Demonstrated both by those worried about what it meant to cross the interim constitution's bridge of unity in difference and those concerned about the costs of reconciliation's amnesty, reconciliation's words transcended exactly nothing. What they did do was establish the basis and the need for additional talk, speech that could assess, oppose, and then (re)direct the process of making South Africa new.

In the middle time of transition, there was a need to speak (again) about how to create with words and the ways in which speech might turn enmity toward friendship. This need marks the beginning of the Truth and Reconciliation Commission, a body that was *not* mandated or really even imagined within the interim constitution's post-amble. In this regard, the post-amble is far less an expression of the TRC's "founding compromise" or perceived necessity than an argument about the need for South Africa to question how reconciliation's power at the MPNP compromised (on) the necessity of law and history, and the ways in which the forum forgot the degree to which law embodies that memory which constitutes the referent for justice. In a basic opposition to its alleged inspiration, the TRC's beginning is rooted in the post-amble's claim that the MPNP's accomplishment (limit) must be understood in the context of a reconciliation that ended an endless cycle of violence by exception, by both relying on and breaking from a law that was necessarily compromised. Thus, between the insufficiency of compromise and the necessity of its insufficiency, the TRC's beginning lies in the decision to take the post-amble's hermeneutic question seriously and ask whether the enablement of law depended on words dedicated to explaining the past's relationship to the future and enacting a unity in difference that neither repeated history nor deferred justice.

5

the sacrifices of deliberation: making reconciliation's law

Let us not spend a single day in masochistic retroversion.
Constand Viljoen

We sacrifice justice for truth so as to consolidate democracy, to close the chapter of the past, and avoid confrontation.
Kader Asmal

reconciliation begins controversy over the appearance of its sacrifice. By March of 1994, the country was captivated if not consumed by the approaching election. The time to deal with the past was still to come. With an immense task, the TEC struggled to maintain stability while the IEC faced accusations that it was "dangerously behind" in its preparations for the impending vote.[1] Underscored by Carel Boshoff's claim as to how the coming of a new dispensation was a threat to "our (Afrikaner) national life", one that demanded a right to "future self-determination" that would not reflect "those fatal racists ideologies of the twentieth century that was based on chauvinistic expressive escalation of identities or even ethnocentrism which bred discrimination", the white right continued to perform its peculiar interpretation of unity in difference. In early March, General Constand Viljoen announced that he was withdrawing from the political arm of the Freedom Front in order to "concentrate on building and maintaining the armed potential for the Afrikaner Volksfront".[2] Only one week later, citing deep dissatisfaction with the right's violent tactics and lack of discipline, the General resigned from the AVF and pronounced his support for the Freedom Front's participation in the election.[3]

While the liberal media pondered the ambiguities of transition, including the questions of how citizens would navigate between 11 official languages and whether the country's new flag was a "rainbow version of gents y-front underpants", tensions grew as the Goldstone Commission issued a report about the continuing operation of the state's "third force". For some, the validity of the allegation was confirmed by a last minute flood of indemnity applications from state security personnel.[4] The violence did indeed seem to be escalating. In Bophuthatswana, Lucas Mangope continued to reject the IEC's efforts to organise election procedures, a recalcitrance that sparked wholesale strikes and deadly violence between protestors and police. By the end of the month, the homeland was in disarray, occupied by national forces in the wake of a coup and reeling from attacks undertaken by members of the AWB.

While the ballots were being printed and reprinted, the IFP continued to sit on the sidelines. In late March, the level of violence in KwaZulu-Natal led some IEC officials to question whether voting could even occur in the province. A commander of an IFP-aligned self-protection unit conceded that he was preparing troops for the day when the resistance to the ANC had to go underground in order to conduct "Vietnam-style" guerrilla warfare. At the table, talks were hampered by continued accusations about who was responsible for the "blood on the street, blood on the tracks, blood in the fields". In early April, the violence prompted a state of emergency in the region, a measure that was destined to run through the election. An agreement to amend the interim constitution to ensure the position of the Zulu King, Goodwill Zwelithini, counted only as small progress. Inkatha's larger demands, including the postponement of the election until issues of political autonomy were resolved, defied both local and international mediation. Only in the week before the election, faced with increasing isolation, did Buthelezi and his counterparts on the right-wing find cause to participate in the election.[5] Declaring that the "world is watching with fascination", the *Mail and Guardian* editorialised that the historic vote was a crucial test of whether "our country can defy history" and move toward the possibility of "racial reconciliation".[6]

There were kilometre-long queues, mix-ups with ballot papers, pervasive jubilation, and more than a bit of worry. In the end, however, the election on 27 and 28 April 1994 was hailed by South Africa's new President as a "small miracle". The outcome of the voting seemed to confirm Mandela's assessment. In its victory, the ANC failed to receive two-thirds of the vote, a bar that would have allowed it to unilaterally change the constitution; winning 20 per cent, the Nats were disappointed even as they obtained the votes needed to nominate a Deputy President to the Government of National Unity; Inkatha retained control of KwaZulu-Natal. On 2 May, F.W. de Klerk ceded power "not to the majority of the moment, but to the South African people".[7] The ANC took a congruent tack, noting that the election was the "beginning, not the end" and that it was time to make a "better life for all South Africans".[8]

With the announcement of the polling results came a moment to reflect on the past and its uncertain implications for the future. In his autobiography, Mandela recalls being hoarse with a cold on the evening of 2 May, a moment when he felt "overwhelmed with a sense of history" and deeply aware of an obligation to the "sum of patriots who had gone before me".[9] The burden of history and its bearing on the transition appeared clearly in the inaugural address that Mandela delivered in Cape Town.

Speaking on the same Grand Parade where he had addressed thousands on the day of his release from prison, Mandela began by claiming that "our country has arrived at a decision", a point of "ordained" history that would both overcome and make good on the "fateful convergence of the peoples of Africa, Europe and Asia on these shores".[10] Then recalling the ANC's *African's Claims* and *Freedom Charter*, the President declared that the advent of democracy "requires us all to work together to bring an end to division, an end to suspicion and build a nation united in our diversity". Setting this agenda "not as conquerors prescribing to the conquered", he then concluded by claiming that all South African citizens needed to "heal the wounds of the past with the intent of constructing a new order based on justice for all".

At the official inauguration in Pretoria, this keynote was sounded again when Mandela claimed: "The time for the healing of the wounds has come. The moment to bridge the chasms that divide us has come. The time to build is upon us."[11] According to one onlooker, however, the loudest cheer for Mandela followed his declaration, "Laat ons die verlede vergeet! Wat verby is, is verby" (Let's forget the past! What's done is done).[12] While these words were not recorded in later transcripts of the address, they raised a question that was on the minds of many – what (still) needed to be said about the past and what kinds of speech would help South Africans to understand history's relation to the future?

Rooted in specific appeals for reconciliation and reconstruction, the President's suggestion in Cape Town and in Pretoria was that the transition demanded a process of collective law-making, one that would bring the rights and opportunities needed to "bridge the chasms" of historical division. At the speech on the steps of the Union Building, Mandela took some care to argue that such a "just and lasting peace" had much to do with amnesty:

> We have triumphed in the effort to implant hope in the breasts of the millions of our people. We enter into a covenant that we shall build the society in which all South Africans, both black and white, will be able to walk tall, without any fear in their hearts, assured of their inalienable right to human dignity – a rainbow nation at peace with itself and the world. As a token to its commitment to the renewal of our country, the new Interim Government of National Unity will, as a matter of urgency, address the issue of amnesty for various categories of our people who are currently serving terms of imprisonment.[13]

While this assurance seemed directed more toward members of the struggle than those in the previous government, the ANC had made its larger position known two days before the election. Recalling its response to the Motsuenyane Commission's report, the Congress argued that it was committed to a "principle of indemnity" which set in motion a "process of national disclosure of all violations of human rights from all sides". Still unwilling to entertain a blanket amnesty, the ANC maintained that truth-telling was less a "punitive" measure than a necessary pre-condition for "national reconciliation" in the wake of the election.[14]

With the official end of statutory apartheid came a new phase of transition. In it, the ambiguous terms of the post-amble took on new importance. While its mandate for amnesty did not appear to assure indemnity for all applicants, its call for reconciliation did not explicitly suggest that amnesty could be conditioned on the disclosure of past crimes. Recalling the pre-election debate in Parliament and civil society, the question at hand was the degree to which the revelation of history's divisions was necessary for the future's promise of unity and what conditions and procedures were needed to make the past manifest. By what means and to what ends would history appear? In the 18 months after the election, one answer to this question was that South Africa needed to create a "quasi-juridical body" given to promoting that speech which would set the post-amble's language of reconciliation into motion.

The creation of South Africa's TRC was a response to the demands of transition as well as an occasion to think anew about reconciliation's potential power. In this chapter, I am concerned to understand how the Commission took shape in the aftermath of the election and the ways in which its mandate was defined, set into law, and justified to South African citizens, many of whom objected to its proposed work.

Beginning with the new government's opening case for why the country needed to create a forum that could mediate the post-amble's call for amnesty with measures designed to reveal the hidden terms of the past, the chapter turns to the public hearings held in early 1995 at which the TRC's tentative mandate was discussed, contested, and revised. Giving clearer form to the TRC's authorising legislation – the *Promotion of National Unity and Reconciliation Act* (PNUR) – these contentious proceedings saw the TRC defined as a public good, a body that not only needed to conduct its work transparently but one which would promote, hear, and disseminate public speech. Envisaged as a "model in the middle", the TRC's mandate called for it to navigate between the demands of amnesty, the needs of victims, and the work of nation-building with words of testimony and disclosure – speech acts that painted a picture of the past, recognised the experience of those victimised by apartheid, and accounted for the scope and motivation of gross violations of human rights. More precisely, the TRC's claimed value rested on a norm of publicity, a commitment to forms of speech that would constitute and (re)present appearances, the building blocks needed to (re)make the common good and energise collective political life. While celebrated as a means of dealing with the past in a morally acceptable way, this vision of human relationships was also challenged on the grounds that it would violate the rights of apartheid's victims and vilify those who fought in the name of protecting the regime. From early 1995 to mid-1996, the clash between these positions was evident in Parliament's second reading debate over the PNUR bill and the Constitutional Court's rejection of an application that questioned the constitutionality of the TRC's power to grant amnesty to perpetrators of gross violations of human rights. In both venues, the cost of reconciliation was acknowledged by the Commission's advocates but defended as a crucial sacrifice. Reconciliation's constitutive words demanded a willingness (*ethos*) to (fore)give beyond the terms of self-interest in the name of cultivating the grounds for unity in difference.

The TRC's law of reconciliation called for a troubling form of speech, words that appeared to exceed the constitution's protections in the name of composing a sacrifice that would serve the greater good. Within an investigation of the TRC's development, this contention opens a set of doors, none of which I will enter in this chapter. For one, the Commission was one transitional measure among several, a forum that was intended to function alongside efforts to draft South Africa's final constitution and redress apartheid's devastating economic inequality. While the relationship between these events falls outside of what I can address here, it is important to note that the TRC was neither the sole nor perhaps even the most important body in the post-election phase of the transition.[15] Moreover, close study of the TRC's peculiar mandate is an invitation for critique, a nearly irresistible calling to unpack and assess the myriad concepts that were put into play and on display at the Commission's first hearings. Resisting such temptation, this chapter turns instead to the ways in which the Commission's charge to promote reconciliation both answered and deferred the post-amble's hermeneutic question – the problem of how to fashion the potential for human (inter)action in a present that linked past and future. Recalling religious and political interpretations of reconciliation's potential to support dialogue, the beginning of the TRC was neither the first nor the last word of reconciliation. Its creation marked a time in which South Africans were called to define and debate once again the terms of faith needed to sustain the creative works of words.

1. for a model in the middle: speaking to(ward) the act
of reconciliation

The aftermath of the election brought much talk of reconciliation and the beginning of its controversial law-making. In his commentary on Mandela's inauguration, journalist Mark Gevisser observed that the event set a significant precedent to the degree that it "resisted the temptation towards a swaggering liberation dance" in favour of a "tightly managed performance of reconciliation".[16] The same week, Richard Goldstone suggested that while South Africa was unlikely to convene trials for those "guilty of crimes of apartheid", the pain of citizens could not be forgotten if the nation was to move forward. To this end, the judge who did so much to expose the extent of violence in the early 1990s called on the new government to ensure the provision of reparation and urged Parliament to "set up a commission to officially expose the past".[17]

Two weeks later, in his first "state of the nation address", Mandela appeared ready to walk down such a path when he argued that "no more should words like Kaffirs, Hottentots, Coolies, Boy, Girl and Baas be part of our vocabulary" and declared that all citizens had an obligation to struggle against the silences and pains of history in order to "restore the human dignity of each and every South African". Holding that "we must, constrained by and yet regardless of the accumulated effect of our historical burdens, seize the time to define for ourselves what we want to make of our shared destiny", Mandela set the course of government and citizens toward the creation of a "people-centred" society, economic development, and a human rights culture. According to the new President, this work was inseparable from the matter of amnesty:

> In this context, I also need to make the point that the Government will also not delay unduly with regard to attending to the vexed and unresolved issue of an amnesty for criminal activities carried out in furtherance of political objectives. We will attend to this matter in a balanced and dignified way. The nation must come to terms with its past in a spirit of openness and forgiveness and proceed to build the future on the basis of repairing and healing. The burden of the past lies heavily on all of us, including those responsible for inflicting injury and those who suffered. Following the letter and the spirit of the Constitution, we will prepare the legislation which will seek to free the wrongdoers from fear of retribution and blackmail, while acknowledging the injury of those who have been harmed so that the individual wrongs, injuries, fears and hopes affecting individuals are identified and attended to. In the meantime, summoning the full authority of the position we represent, we call on all concerned not to take any steps that might, in any way, impede or compromise the processes of reconciliation which the impending legislation will address.[18]

Behind the scenes, reflection on the post-amble's mandate was provoking debate over whether and how the need for amnesty was a warrant to create the sort of truth commission that had been advocated by the ANC after the Motsuenyane Commision report. According to Dullah Omar, then Minister of Justice, the first "concrete" proposal for such a body came from "Alex Boraine and his organisation, Justice in Transition".[19] In his reflections on the development of the TRC, Boraine details some of this work, including the terms of a letter which he sent to Mandela after the election detailing both the benefits and risks of a commission.[20] As there was some question about whether the equation summed, Omar's recollection was that the motive for a truth commission grew from a number of sources, including "historical wisdom" about the need for South Africa to reflect on its history, and growing concern over whether there were "universal values" that needed to be carried from past to future. Equally important, Omar put it to me that the call for a truth commission was also influenced by the fact that "people do not forget" in South Africa, and by international lessons about the need to create specific procedures designed to heal deep division.[21]

The basic case for a truth commission was developed and made public in the first 100 days of Mandela's administration. Here, I want to consider how the TRC's initial definition called South Africans back to the question of reconciliation's power to make with words. Between May and August 1994, the government gathered the terms of the post-amble, and the debates it had provoked before the election, in order to delineate the need and basic function of a truth commission. Resting heavily on the idea that the interim constitution would not naturally yield a democratic unity in difference and that apartheid's victims could not be ignored, advocates for the Commission argued that its work would give voice to truth, afford opportunities for acknowledgement, and seek disclosure of past crimes in the name of obtaining accountability. In short, the government claimed that the TRC's pursuit of reconciliation was a pragmatic necessity and a moral duty, a task that demanded and provided space for those words that would bridge past and future, heal old wounds, and (re)link the rule of law and justice. With the precise details unexplained and faced with increasing criticism of its proposal, the government extended its case further, arguing that reconciliation's law (for words) was best defined through the collective deliberation to which it was dedicated. Once again before the law, the call for a commission of truth and reconciliation left South Africa to ask after, constitute, and deploy the power of talk.

The subject of debate in Parliament and other ranking political circles, the form, purpose, and justification of the TRC appeared gradually. In the early deliberations, the need for the Commission was pinned to the post-amble's mandate for amnesty. Quickly, this obligation was combined with another, a process of truth-telling and acknowledgement that would help restore apartheid's victims and allow all citizens to learn about and remember the past. According to Johnny de Lange, one of the Commission's key architects, this double approach represented an attempt to craft a "model in the middle", a law that would balance the need for amnesty with justice for victims.[22] By the time that the provisional legislation was tabled in early August, however, it was clear that government's approach was not without significant limitations: "We were not concrete in our thinking," reflected

Omar, when I asked him about the initial case for the Commission. As the moment was one for thinking in "general terms" and "general directions", the early definitions of the Commission's work generated a significant set of puzzles and controversy over the body's potential power.[23]

In the early days of the post-election transition, reconciliation was a priority and an open question. When asked how it shaped both the constitutional talks and the development of the TRC, de Lange contends that, "reconciliation is the bedrock of what we think" and then quickly offers that, "I have not met two people with the same definition of reconciliation." In the three-day parliamentary debate that followed Mandela's state of the nation speech, reconciliation's ambiguous nature and priority was readily evident as Deputy President F.W. de Klerk clashed with Kader Asmal, the new Minister of Water Affairs and Forestry, over whether the nation's aspiration to a unity in difference included a sense of "self-determination" that warranted the protection of minority rights and the creation of a *volkstaat*, or if the process of reconciliation was better given to building a "laager that will be a defence for all our people, without distinction and differentiation".[24]

Among others, this question demonstrated that the transition was not self-executing, a point that Dullah Omar underscored when he took the podium as one of the last speakers in the debate. Warning against the "euphoria of the moment", and "empty rhetoric", Omar argued that "paper equality" had to be turned to "real equality" and that such a transformation would not occur until South Africa was able to "come to terms with its past". Announcing his intention to craft "appropriate legislation which will provide for amnesty", Omar then declared to "those who have fears and who may have perpetrated human rights violations and want to join in reconciliation" that there would be "no Nuremburg-style trials". For "victims and their loved ones", however, the Minister claimed that there would be "no sweeping under the carpet and there will be no suppression of the truth. There will be no amnesty without disclosure."[25] In Omar's terms, dealing with the past involved creating an opportunity for a "clean break", a turn from the past that could only occur if South Africans were afforded a chance to acknowledge the individual and collective damage wrought by apartheid. Between amnesty applicant and victim, there was indeed cause to create a model in the middle.

Just a month after the election, Omar's speech in Parliament served notice that government intended to define and set the "mechanisms, criteria, and procedures" for amnesty within the work of a larger "truth commission". Claiming without explicit evidence that support for the idea "seems

overwhelming", the Minister's justification for such a body rested largely on
its ability to walk a number of fine lines:

> The advantage of a commission, whatever its name – we must avoid
> any connotation which suggests revenge or witch-hunts – is that it can
> facilitate disclosure within a framework that provides amnesty with
> acknowledgement, justice and dignity. Far from being an instrument
> of vengeance or humiliation, it has the advantage of forestalling a
> multiplicity of criminal prosecutions and civil claims. We therefore
> think not just along the lines of a commission, not just of truth, but in
> its totality a commission of truth and reconciliation. As to criteria and
> procedure, legislation would firstly fix clear timeframes within which
> applications for indemnity would have to be submitted. Secondly, there
> should be disclosure and acknowledgement. Thirdly, ordinary crimes
> will not be covered. Fourthly, perpetrators would be indemnified against
> both criminal and civil actions. Fifthly, there should be reparation and
> compensation for victims. In this regard I must say that in my view
> South Africa owes a debt of enormous proportions to victims. There are
> also the families of persons such as Imam Aroon, Steve Biko, Matthew
> Goniwe, David Webster, Anton Lubowski, and many others. Their
> stories and their sufferings must be heard and acknowledged.[26]

Both deferring and answering the question of what it ought to be called,
Omar's position defined the TRC as an appropriate response to the post-
amble, one that could fulfil its mandate for amnesty and make good on its
larger call for citizens to undertake reconciliation. Sitting in his office across
from Parliament in late 2000, Omar deflected much of the credit for this
merger, noting only that if there was "any contribution that I have made", it
was the decision to combine truth and amnesty.[27]

The government's initial call for a truth commission did not proceed
from a clear definition of reconciliation. Was it a process or a goal? Was it
both? Frequently endowed with the pragmatic meaning that it enjoyed at
the MPNP, reconciliation was also interpreted as a "moral duty", a strict
obligation to ensure the respective "disclosure" and "hearing" of amnesty
applicants and victims. In the name of a "spirit of forgiveness" and not the
will to "retribution", the conciliatory function of the proposed commission
was to expose the past and recognise those who suffered during apartheid in a
manner that (re)established their "dignity" and paved the way for "reparation".
In the early going, very few of these key terms or ideas were explained.

Omar's position did not lack critics and competitors. In the same parliamentary debate, F.W. de Klerk argued that a people-centred view of reconciliation risked ignoring that "everything must ultimately be in subjection to God and his commandment", while the IFP's Buthelezi worried about the potential "paternalism" of government reconciliation initiatives and called for decentralised efforts to empower individuals and support community reconstruction.[28] Declaring that the forebears of his Afrikaner constituency "tamed this country", Constand Viljoen applauded Nelson Mandela's "spirit of reconciliation" but warned that a "reconciling" amnesty could not come at the expense of an applicant's dignity.[29]

These remarks were an indication that the debate was just getting started. In the moment, still riding the high of the election, differences over how to pursue and promote reconciliation appeared more as questions than criticisms. Over the next weeks, the queries sharpened into a number of specific controversies. First, the government's announced concern to deal with the past did not include an account of what history needed to be addressed, whether the need was shared equally by all citizens, and if a national truth-telling project held the potential for (re)division, trauma, and resentment. What needed to be remembered and what was best forgotten? Second, the call for reconciliation stood in uncertain relation to the work of reconstruction. While paired in the post-amble, the case for the truth commission had little to say about the redress of apartheid's legacy of economic inequality. How would reconciliation's spirit relate to fulfilling the material needs of the people? Third, the value of reconciliation presupposed an understanding of who or what needed to be reconciled. In the post-amble, amnesty was set out in the name of healing rifts that threatened political (re)integration and the stability of a young democracy. The call for a broader truth commission, however, brought additional dilemmas. Who were the victims and who were the victimisers? Who was neither? How was race to enter into reconciliation's calculus? If victims were defined narrowly, as those individuals who suffered violations of human rights, what would be remembered of the everyday and collective suffering inflicted by apartheid? What did ubuntu mean in the context of the post-amble, particularly with respect to the question of how to define the identity of reconciliation's subjects and objects? Once defined, what was to happen between those called before the TRC? How would it occur? What exactly was to be gained from "disclosure" and "acknowledgement"? What were their curative powers? Finally, government had yet to say much about the power of reconciliation's law. What authority would the TRC enjoy? How would it be related to other government institutions? Did not its legal form portend a judicial process, albeit one that was free to shirk procedural norms of fairness? As a declared alternative to trials, what of those who wanted to seek redress and restitution in the courts?

Many of these questions were not new. In his 27 May speech, Omar acknowledged their urgency, arguing that the ambiguities involved in the soon to be tabled TRC legislation warranted extensive and extended public debate. Calling for commentary and deliberation by members of government, the non-governmental sector, and citizens, Omar emphasised the need to "come up with a proposal which will enable us to take the nation forward with us into the future with reconciliation having taken place". For the sake of transition, he argued, the "terms of justice" had to become "truly accessible to our people".[30] In the ensuing weeks and as government composed the Commission's draft legislation, the basis for such participation was enhanced when Omar offered a somewhat more detailed case for combining amnesty with the larger work of truth-telling.

Included in the proceedings of a second conference convened by Alex Boraine, the Minister's soon to be "stump speech" for the TRC indicated that the Commission would have a limited life span (18 months) and would adhere to "fair procedures" in the name of "investigating and establishing the truth about human rights violations, and their acknowledgement".[31] In the name of building "a human rights culture", Omar contended that truth was the "only moral basis possible" for "coming to terms with the past". Moreover, if truth-telling was to respond to "the demand for justice for victims and facilitate national reconciliation", the process had to be interactive. According to Omar, the Commission was premised on the idea that it was the "victims themselves who must speak. Their voices need to be heard."[32]

With respect to amnesty, matters remained vague. At least in public, government's thinking about who would be eligible for indemnity had not progressed beyond the vague terms of the post-amble. Predictably, this ambiguity brought criticism. In Parliament, the IFP wondered why the TRC legislation was being developed outside the confines of cabinet while NP representatives accused the ANC of fashioning an amnesty process that allowed for self-indemnification and the undue prosecution of apartheid officials. In early August, Johnny de Lange responded to the criticisms and set an important distinction into the mix. Charging that the Commission's critics wanted only to "forgive and forget" the ongoing effects of apartheid's crime against humanity, he contended that the TRC was a "comprehensive, integrated and holistic approach to this vast task of dealing with our past", one that "does not derive its authority from the Constitution nor from any law" but "from our morality, as human beings, as a people who want to heal our nation".[33] Creating a notable distance between the task of the Commission and the work of material reconstruction, de Lange's position recalled the central thrust of the post-amble: the law-making of reconciliation stood before and beneath the constitution's social contract.

There was a need for a law before the law. A week after Mandela devoted a portion of his "100 days" address to reassuring the nation that the Commission would not have "draconian powers" and that it was necessary to deal with the "festering sore" of the past, Omar made an important pitch when he argued that the TRC would help to establish rule of law and re-forge the relationship between law and justice that had been severed by apartheid.[34] In an interview, Omar explained the assumptions behind this position, contending that his job in 1994 was to "give life to the constitution" and that the election had not resolved the "huge legitimacy crisis" stemming from law's historical disconnection from justice.[35] This position was evident in Omar's speech on 26 August. Using Mandela's testimony from the 1962 treason trial to demonstrate the continuing legacy of the old racialised order, the Minster argued that the task of dealing with the past involved not only remaking law but demonstrating its immanent connection to citizens through the creation of formal structures whereby they might shape its terms.[36] In principle, Omar claimed, amnesty was not inconsistent with this work if it was tied to a larger project of truth-telling. Bequeathed by apartheid, the suspect status of precedent demanded an exception to the law, a moment in which its compromised terms were set aside in the name of remembering the past and using its experiences to (re)make the norms of justice that would support transition and sustain democratisation. Before the law, Omar's proposed law of reconciliation was dedicated to the return of its public power.

Inside and outside Parliament, the first months of South Africa's democracy saw the appearance of an evolving case for why the country needed to deal with the past, how a truth commission would serve this end, and the ways that it would energise transition. Rooted in contradictory claims about the nature of history and the relative value of amnesty, this argumentation codified the post-amble's claim that the process of reconciliation demanded the promotion of (public) address between South African citizens. Highlighting its ability to hear and gather truth, one that required testimony from apartheid's victims and disclosure from those seeking amnesty, advocates of the TRC defined reconciliation through speech and claimed that its healing words offered a way to "constitute" dignity and "hold" accountable. Consistent with pre-election discussions, the value of this speech-action was first explained in individual more than communal terms; reconciliation's words would expose the subjection of victims in a manner that returned their identity and standing before the law. In turn, this healed subject would contribute to the development of collective and national life, particularly as its recognition relieved painful paralysis and blunted desires for revenge. For its part, amnesty was defended on the grounds that the testimony of applicants would shed direct light on the past and cultivate an ethic of responsibility that would offset indemnity's risk of silence (forgetting) and impunity.

The initial definition of the TRC was not definitive. While critics held their tongues in the wake of the election, the proposed commission was a site of significant controversy by the time that the draft legislation was presented to Parliament in December 1994. This debate grew directly from the problem of how to interpret the post-amble and operationalise its mandate. From a text that called for a process of reconciliation to underwrite the power of the constitution and support the transition, the architects of the TRC fashioned a case for how amnesty could serve the new nation and why citizens needed to participate in its law-making work. In this sense, the TRC's development was not something that could be "contained" by government. Underscored by increasing disputes over its power, the proposed commission raised questions that not only implicated the public but which appeared to demand extended public deliberation. This need to "democratise the debate" over the TRC and for citizens to "participate in the process of arriving at an acceptable solution" was underscored by Omar on a number of occasions.[37] If it was to be defended through the post-amble's spirit of reconciliation, the Commission could not emerge from an isolated act of law. This did not mean that creating a space for reconciliation required a collective "bear-hugging, kissing and the shedding of tears".[38] Rather, as Kader Asmal pointed out, it was to demonstrate that "too long a sacrifice can make a stone of the heart, [and] we must hold out the opportunity embodied in the fact that our hearts have never turned to stone ...".[39] Between the hard heart and the beautiful soul, the TRC's "model in the middle" demanded that reconciliation's law grow out of the public speech by which it was warranted.

2. composing reconciliation's law of publicity

With legislation tabled, public hearings over the TRC's design and power began just after the turn of the year. Their start was framed by several controversies, including a heated debate in Parliament over whether the Commission would become "an Orwellian parody where the search for truth becomes a bludgeon to beat one party's version of history into the heads of its opponents" or if it was evidence that the "white people of this country should stay on their knees and thank god everyday" for Mandela and his "unflinching sensitivity to reconciliation".[40] In early January, tensions escalated further when Dullah Omar declared that some 3500 applications for indemnity were invalid. Filed mostly by South African Police (SAP) personnel in the days before the election, the applications were rejected on the grounds that they did not specify the activities for which amnesty was sought, an omission that contravened the ANC's position on blanket amnesty. Deemed a "political crisis", the decision provoked accusations that the ANC was favouring its own cadres, undermining the rule of law, and determined to extract retribution from those belonging to the old order.[41] Fed by growing interest in the trials of Eugene de Kock and the individuals accused of the St James Church and Heidelberg Tavern attacks, the dispute underscored a basic lack of agreement over amnesty's purpose and procedure.

Held before the Joint Portfolio Committee on Justice, the hearings over the *Promotion of National Unity and Reconciliation* bill were read by some as a test of government's commitment to transparency. At their commencement, Dullah Omar put the matter plainly when he argued that, "The proceedings in which you are engaged, the hearings which you hold, the debates in which you engage are real, I think that is the essence of the democratic process. We should be able to speak fearlessly about the bill before you and if there [are] areas of the bill which cause concern then these committees must have the right to raise them."[42] While echoed by Alex Boraine, one of the individuals who helped rally NGO participation, the debate was not covered in significant detail by the media, and today the transcripts of the hearings are consigned to a set of dusty boxes in a corner of Parliament's records office. In his consideration of the hearings, Boraine offers a brief account of three submissions to the Committee. The treatment is not especially satisfactory, particularly as it tames the debate and obscures its complexity with respect to the range of issues that were addressed as well as the deep disagreements which appeared over the TRC's value.[43] In fact, Boraine's summary covers over something of the fact that individuals and organisations from all sides of the political spectrum voiced serious objections to the draft legislation.

The public hearings over the TRC reveal a basic controversy over whether the Commission had the "potential to create legitimacy for the democratic process" and if the provision and denial of amnesty would respectively mark a moment of injustice for victims and divisive humiliation for applicants.[44] An indication of how hopes for a model in the middle did not offer clear guidance about how to balance political reality and moral imperative, the proceedings called the meaning of reconciliation into question as well as challenged the TRC's political and ethical presuppositions. Tracing a selection of these arguments and then examining the precise terms of the TRC legislation, my contention here is that the law of reconciliation developed through an evolving case as to how the power of words would help South Africans to understand and perhaps transcend the past. More precisely, the TRC's founding legislation invited, demanded, and created spaces for South Africans to speak in the name of remembrance and use the recollection of historical experience to recover voice and support collective deliberation. Evident in the Portfolio Committee hearings, this rhetorical interpretation of reconciliation was codified in the final version of the TRC legislation, a law that called for testimony and disclosure which would paint a picture of the past, give standing to the historically subjugated, and expose the nature of apartheid-era violence. In all cases, the appearances to be generated by reconciliation's words indicated that the TRC was envisaged as a public good, a transparent and inclusive body whose work was to be guided by a norm of publicity, an expectation that speech would help open democracy's commons and build collective interest from old divisions.

hearing(s) about reconciliation's words

Scheduled to run for three weeks, the Portfolio Committee hearings were framed by the terms of the post-amble and the question of how to interpret its mandate for amnesty. With respect to the latter, the draft PNUR bill specified that amnesty would be given to individuals who fully disclosed the terms of their participation in the commission of gross violations of human rights. Borrowing from the Norgaard principles that had played a significant role in the 1992 *Further Indemnity Act*, the bill also held that applicants would need to demonstrate that their offences were motivated by or "associated with a political objective". If such criteria were met, amnesty would be granted and the applicant would be relieved of any and all criminal and civil liability for their declared offence. What surprised many, however, was the bill's mandate for *in camera* amnesty hearings. Somehow, public disclosure was to occur in secret.

As it presupposed and then built on the post-amble's vision, the PNUR bill's definition of the amnesty process provoked questions about the standing of the post-amble itself and whether it was reasonable to argue that its framers had envisioned an amnesty that was conditioned on truth-telling. Representatives from the SAP argued that it was not and contended that the post-amble's use of the word "shall" constituted an assurance that amnesty would be granted to all applicants. From this perspective, the post-amble was a guarantee, one that covered "all human external activity or lack of activity associated with political objectives and committed in the cause of the conflicts of the past …".[45] Moreover, the SAP maintained that the burden of disclosure was a substantive matter that went well beyond the post-amble's call for the creation of mechanisms, criteria, and procedures.[46]

Drawing out the implications of this argument, the National Party contended in one of its submissions to the Portfolio Committee that the introduction of a "qualified amnesty" was facially unconstitutional, especially as it legitimised unequal treatment between applicants from different sides of the struggle.[47] In response, the Representative for the General Counsel of the Bar maintained that as the post-amble was neither a "substantive text of the constitution" nor "self-executing", it was designed to direct Parliament's approach "generally" and most certainly did not create an "all-embracing right to amnesty or indemnity". Similarly, the submission by the Chief State Law Adviser argued that as amnesty implied indemnity from a *particular* liability, the disclosure of a specific offence was a logical and necessary part of the process.[48] As well, he held that the conditions placed on the provision of amnesty were consistent with the need to "advance the process of reconciliation", especially if amnesty was to remain coupled to its apparent counterpart, reparation.[49] Interesting when set against Maharaj's characterisation of the post-amble, the SAP's rebuttal was that a guaranteed amnesty followed from the fact that "the post-amble to the constitution itself constitutes in its wording, in its spirit coming as it was from representatives of the people from within, itself constitutes the reconciliation that was sought".[50] On this view, with reconciliation achieved, amnesty was merely and only a formality.

Equally contentious was the question of what counted as a politically motivated act and thus who would be eligible for amnesty. Tied to the NP's objections to the Norgaard principles that they had once defended, the SAP maintained that a broad interpretation was vital given that the post-amble did not specify whether offences had to be committed in good faith in order to qualify for amnesty. The TRC's future CEO, Paul van Zyl, disagreed, arguing that a dilution or expansion of the criteria would constitute a breach of international law.[51] Complicated further by a quarrel over the cut-off date for eligible offences, the debate turned to the question of whether it was possible and productive to demand the full disclosure of an act or omission.[52] While relying partly on the Freedom Front's contention that the Afrikaner people did not have a "culture of confession", Constand Viljoen began by questioning the relevance and value of individual disclosure:

> [T]he real reconciliation becomes with the confession and not on
> individual acts, but the confession of wrongs in strategies and the
> confession not by individuals but the confession by the representatives
> of the people saying that I agree that we have gone wrong and the other
> people say we agree we have all gone wrong and then draw the lessons
> from that and that will really bring us to the position of reconciliation.[53]

Preferring statements from commanders not foot soldiers under orders, and admissions of collective responsibility over inquiry into individual acts, Viljoen argued further that the disclosure requirement was counterproductive and potentially divisive, especially as it underestimated the "mutual loyalty" of security personnel and rested on "absolutist" principles that mistook the details for the bigger picture:

> In the end when one after other confessions bring boredom and
> fragmented knowledge of a superficial nature, it may not lead to the
> understanding of the sort one can call truth and it could hardly in my
> view therefore lead to real reconciliation. On the contrary it could lead
> to retaliation.[54]

Within this objection, there was a larger disagreement, one that turned on how to define the meaning of reconciliation. Late in his testimony, the former General claimed that "true reconciliation in this country will be between the Afrikaner people and the black people".[55] To this position, one member of the Portfolio Committee replied that in her view the matter was less about race relations than a "question of reconciliation between democracy and a minority government which imposed its will on the majority of the people".[56] The exchange was a signal, an indication that amnesty's promised contribution to reconciliation presupposed that South Africans had congruent interpretations of the past, the causes of its violence, and the appropriate object of reconciliation.

With the connection between amnesty and reconciliation under close scrutiny, the PNUR bill also raised questions about what and how applicants would need to disclose in order to receive relief from prosecution. For many, however, the prior problem was whether closed door hearings negated the announced value of the entire process. On this score, the voices of victims were the loudest. In letters to the Committee, several groups expressed their dismay at the bill's secrecy clause and argued both that they had a "right to hear these facts at first hand and in every detail" and that only with an open process would the "white community fully understand the pain they inflicted by silently voting for apartheid". While confirming one aspect of Viljoen's view about the process, this position challenged others: individual details mattered; an account of "what happened" was deemed a prerequisite for reconciliation between those on opposite sides of the struggle.[57] Although the need for secrecy was defended on the grounds that it would avoid a witch-hunt and prevent retaliation, Paul van Zyl testified that some 30 NGO's rejected *in camera* hearings on the grounds that they would both impugn the Commission's credibility by contradicting the democratic principles that it claimed to defend and unduly if not unconstitutionally limit the rights of victims.[58]

Whose rights had standing in the reconciliation process? This question figured centrally in the public hearings, especially with respect to the contested procedures for amnesty and controversy over whether it could contribute to a reconstruction of the rule of law. While generally in support of the process, the General Counsel of the Bar argued that any decision to grant amnesty was a "political" decision, one that represented a "socially expedient surrogate for criminal justice and civil claims", and which was facially repugnant to law insofar as it entailed the "ousting of the laws of the land".[59] Moreover, critics from all sides advanced reasons as to why the amnesty process violated the terms of the constitution. While the SAP contended that the PNUR's disclosure requirements violated the terms and the spirit of the post-amble, a representative from Lawyers for Human Rights contended that the provision of amnesty negated "the whole basis of his [victim's] rights", especially as it stripped aggrieved individuals of their constitutional right to pursue criminal and civil relief in the courts. Further, both camps warned that amnesty would lead to impunity, claiming respectively that it was dangerously unhinged from procedural norms of due process and that the very idea of amnesty threatened the law's integrity. Expressed by a number of groups, including Amnesty International, the latter position was extended to the claim that South Africa's resort to amnesty was an affront to international law.[60] Recalling the independence of the MPNP, Dullah Omar's response was that "we are building a future for South Africans" and as "there is a conflict between what the international community is saying and what is in the interests of the people of South Africa then I think that we will have to live with that kind of conflict".[61]

While South Africa's law of reconciliation would come first, Omar's position raised questions about precisely how it would serve the interests of justice. In his testimony before the Committee on 31 January, the Minister made two important arguments in this regard. First, he claimed that the "bill itself has been generally accepted throughout the country" and "the principle of the bill is not questioned by anyone". Second, he contended that "the bill is therefore designed to deal with our past on a morally acceptable basis and make it possible to establish the rule of law. But much more important than that, Mr. Chairperson, to establish the rule of law on the basis of the recognition of human rights and the building of human rights culture in our country." At some level, the former was indefensible and begged the question of what was entailed in the latter. From all sides, there was principled opposition to the proposed TRC. What's more, much of the criticism pointed to the still unresolved question of whether and how to measure the "moral acceptability" of exposing, using, and remembering the past in the name of reconciliation. Against Omar's claim that the past was a wound that would "fester more and more until it explodes", members of the old government charged that the TRC's design meant that it would deal with the past by unfairly distinguishing between "the crimes of the security forces and the crimes committed by members of the liberation movement".[62] However, the fact that the Commission was charged to examine the history of apartheid-era gross human rights violations led others to contend that the TRC's legislation created and legitimised an indefensible "moral equivalence" between those who fought a just struggle and those who supported an unjust regime. While Omar promised fairness and denied making such an equivocation, arguing that the TRC was not intended to deny or overlook apartheid's crime against humanity, the criticism struck deeply and spurred additional questions about the sacrifices that were once again being asked of apartheid's victims. According to government, the Commission's work would allow victims to understand "what has happened" and receive an official acknowledgement – from the "highest authorities of the country" – for their losses.[63]

This then was the constitutive compromise: knowledge and acknowledgement would accrue in exchange for an amnesty that pre-empted the right to legal redress. In the matter of dealing with the past, the bar for moral "acceptability" was a process that allowed victims to recount their experiences, hear details of the crimes to which they had been subjected, and find standing – as citizens – before the law and the nation. In the most philosophically sophisticated testimony heard by the Committee, Andre du Toit contended that this compromise contained its own (moral) logic.[64] More precisely, he set the Commission into a framework of recognition, a process in which the linkage between truth and reconciliation would not yield a traditional satisfaction of justice but an opportunity to (re)constitute the dignity of victims and include their experiences in the annals of "official knowledge". While the precise relation between acknowledgment and recognition was left unspecified, du Toit's testimony made the crucial point that dealing with the past involved choice, decisions about what aspects of history mattered and how they were best brought to light. In his terms, the key difficulty had less to do with the alleged moral equivalence held in the Commission's mandate than whether the TRC could create a "picture of the past" that allowed citizens to understand and also to dispute one another's interpretations of history.[65]

Judging from the debate, such a picture would be difficult to paint. The IFP continued to express its view that a national history-writing exercise would invite endless controversy and diminish the "multi-faceted experience of truth". In the matter of understanding history, Constand Viljoen warned that "what will satisfy the constituency of the ANC on reconciliation will certainly have the opposite effect on my constituency". As the hearings concluded with discussion over whether the legislation was "organisationally weak" with respect to specifics about the form and operation of the TRC, it seemed that Alex Boraine was quite correct when he claimed that the Commission "will necessarily result in controversy" and that the moment was "almost a no win situation".[66] At some level, perhaps, this was the point. For the advocates of the TRC, the need to speak about reconciliation had much to do with the need not to claim victory.

Read closely or from a distance, the public debate over the TRC's founding legislation is frustrating, in part because there is so much clash and partly because there is not enough. Warrants for the various positions advanced were not defended consistently and frequently shared significant ground with their counterparts on the other side of the fence. What exactly happened during the three weeks of hearings? What did all these fast and sometime furious words matter with respect to the development of the TRC? While demonstrating that the TRC's rationale was not self-validating, the hearings also showed that the Commission's work rested on deeply disputed concepts, ones that also sat in an uneasy if not inconsistent relation. For example, the disclosure requirement for amnesty was challenged both by those who did not necessarily want to reveal their crimes and those who believed that truth-telling for indemnity was a denigration if not a violation of international and perhaps domestic law. At the same time, it was precisely an appeal to international jurisprudence that underwrote the case for the Commission to focus on the perpetration and damage caused by gross violations of human rights, an approach which fed the perception that the TRC would enact a horrific moral equivalence. At the end of the hearings, the idea of dealing with the past in a "morally acceptable way" thus seemed to beg the question: What exactly counted as the grounds of morality and justice? In the present, the truth of reconciliation's value rested on a past that had yet to be grasped and overcome, a movement which appeared to involve an unexplained and difficult traverse between individual, collective, and institutional histories.

Set in relation to the disputed terms of the post-amble, the public hearings over the PNUR bill raised and troubled the question of reconciliation's power. How would reconciliation turn between past and future in the name of a present dedicated to transforming enmity to civic friendship? Over the course of the hearings, the unspoken answer to these questions was speech. In the middle of the "model in the middle", the TRC's advocates proposed that South Africans undertake the creation and exchange of reconciliation's words. In their estimation, it was time to perform the power of *disclosure*, undertake *testimony* that expressed the experience of suffering, promote the healing that would follow from *hearing* and *acknowledging* the yet untold history of apartheid, and realise the cathartic and educational benefits of *writing* as full a picture as possible of the past. It was also time for *deliberation* as to when and under what conditions these goods would accrue. Now firmly linked, the need for amnesty and the need to deal with the past was the question of what kinds of speech could yield a transformative remembrance and what sorts of remembrance would support speech's transformations. In close proximity and distinct opposition to the announced achievement of reconciliation at the MPNP, these were now the constitutive questions of reconciliation.

the appearance(s) of reconciliation's law

The near final draft of the *Promotion of National Unity and Reconciliation* bill was tabled in mid-summer. Following the Portfolio Committee hearings, the legislation's revision saw the removal of the secrecy provision for amnesty proceedings and a set of small changes dedicated to tightening the "loose language" that worried a number of legal scholars.[67] Overall, the bill called for the creation of a "juristic person to be known as the Truth and Reconciliation Commission" that would "promote national unity and reconciliation". While the particulars of this mandate remained vague, the legislation charged the TRC's two most powerful committees to facilitate the production and interpretation of rhetorical appearances – forms of testimony and disclosure – that would contribute to the public's ability to understand and redress apartheid-era violence.

The PNUR bill specified that the TRC would be composed of an Amnesty Committee, a Human Rights Violations Committee, and a Reparation and Rehabilitation Committee. Set in a somewhat awkward relationship, with uneven amounts of power, and supported by research and investigative units, the Committees were to be run by commissioners "who are impartial and who do not have a political profile". Authorised to work for 18 months, the legislation charged the Commission to "function without political or other bias or interference and shall unless this Act expressly otherwise provides, be independent and separate from any party, government, administration ...". Alone and yet created by the new state, the TRC was then dedicated to:

(a) establishing as complete a picture as possible of the causes, nature and extent of the gross violations of human rights which were committed during the period from 1 March 1960 to the cut-off date, including the antecedents, circumstances, factors and context of such violations, as well as the perspectives of the victims and the motives and perspectives of the persons responsible for the commission of the violations, by conducting investigations and holding hearings; (b) facilitating the granting of amnesty to persons who make full disclosure of all the relevant facts relating to acts associated with a political objective and comply with the requirements of this Act; (c) establishing and making known the fate or whereabouts of victims and by restoring the human and civil dignity of such victims by granting them an opportunity to relate their own accounts of the violations of which they are the victims, and by recommending reparation measures in respect of them; (d) compiling

a report providing as comprehensive an account as possible of the
activities and findings of the Commission contemplated in paragraphs (a),
(b) and (c), and which contains recommendations of measures to prevent
the future violations of human rights.[68]

This mandate was warranted largely by the post-amble and its assumption
that disclosure and the restoration of dignity were justified respectively by
an amnesty that set understanding over retaliation and a future "founded on
the recognition of human rights". Beyond the post-amble and reflecting the
debate over how to deal with the past that it had provoked, the Commission's
charge to create a "picture" of apartheid-era violence was justified by a short
paragraph that was inserted in the middle of the bill's otherwise faithful
recitation of the post-amble. This supplementary text located reconciliation's
value in its capacity to break the cycle of history's violence:

> [I]t is deemed necessary to establish the truth in relation to past events
> as well as the motives for and circumstances in which gross violations
> of human rights have occurred, and to make the findings known in order
> to prevent a repetition of such acts in future.[69]

Without an explanation for why historical understanding would prevent
conflict, the PNUR bill also glossed over the tension within the TRC's charge
"to promote national unity and reconciliation in a spirit of understanding which
transcends the conflicts and divisions of the past". Specifically, the legislation
offered little clarity as to how the Commission's *promotion* of reconciliation
would proceed in a spirit which *actually* transcended division. While a sign of
a future legitimacy crisis, the mandate's more immediate importance was its
claim that reconciliation was a process dedicated to the creation of appearances.
In its Human Rights Violation Committee (HRVC), for instance, the
Commission was to "restore human and civil dignity" by taking statements
from individuals that had been subjected to gross violations of human rights.
Allowing "victims" to "relate their own accounts of the violations" through
testimony of what was presumed to have not been "known", history would
be heard, presumably without regard to criteria of forensic truth. The victim,
a subject subjected to loss, would find standing with this speech, recovering
human and civil status through the constitutive effect (acknowledgment) of
giving voice in the presence of others. In short, the Committee's work was a
space in which citizens could appear in order to bring their memories to light
and give public form to their own (collective) history.

Coupled with the Commission's task to compile a word "picture", a report that documented the scope, motives, and causes of apartheid-era violence, the appearances constituted by victims were deemed neither transitory nor ephemeral. In the PNUR bill's mandate, they marked the potential for individual and collective political action, particularly as the law presupposed that the expression of experience constituted a basis for that "reconciliation between the people of South Africa" which was set out in the post-amble as a necessary condition for transition. While the legislation did not detail the explicit link between testimony and reconciliation, its underlying logic was not so very far from Desmond Tutu's long-standing claim that reconciliation proceeds through *kenosis*, the healing light of the Word that proceeds against the law in the name of its reconstitution. In slightly more secular terms, the HRVC's proceedings were to compose a scene, a space in a contingent present given to words that would lend if not compose a recognisable form to the past. Granting individuals a presence before others (and the law), the case to hear the testimony of victims blurred the distinction between "being" and "seeming" such that the reality of re-presented experience afforded an opportunity for human beings to establish their dignity and standing as citizens while also constituting the ground for collective action.[70] In transition and faced with deep division, the appearances of reconciliation's words were a making (of) truth, a revelation for the future.[71]

In somewhat different terms, the rhetorical creation of appearances was also a central element of the amnesty process. Drawing from the post-amble's claim that amnesty was a public good, a collective enterprise dedicated to reconciliation and fulfilling the constitution's promise of a unified future, the PNUR bill went further, holding that the amnesty applicants would have to make a "full disclosure of all relevant facts" for those "acts, omissions or offences" that were "proportional" responses to a desired "political objective". While it aimed for public revelation and transparency, this equation was not without ambiguity: What did it mean for a perpetrator to disclose?

By conventional usage, a disclosure opens, exposes or brings something into view. Whether addressed to an event or state of mind, it is something made and performed; a process of declaring or revealing that which has remained secret. Through testimony or writing, it creates an appearance and, in principle, makes this appearance available to an Other. This is not to say that disclosure comes with the guarantee of audience or that it assures the achievement of understanding. Rather, disclosure brings thoughts, ideas, and events to an uncertain readability. It does not ensure meaning or agreement but establishes the referents and creates standing for individuals to formulate and ask questions.[72] In the TRC legislation, however, amnesty's "law of disclosure" was defended as a way for South Africans to "close the book on that past" which thwarted the possibility of reconciliation. Rather than an act of un-closing – the removal of that which encloses an event, state of mind, or action – amnesty applicants would disclose in the name of closure.[73]

Amnesty's closing of the legal book, the invocation of precedent for punishment, was equally a moment of beginning – the dis-completion or dis-internment of history. Bringing (out) the past from its secure (hiding) place, disclosure was to break the ban on speaking of history and contesting its meaning. In positive terms, dis-closure was a means to understand and open debate over the terms and value of what had (not) been.[74] Held out as a therapeutic (healing) endeavour and an invitation to question the past, amnesty's disclosure appeared both for and in distinction to law, a good that remained beyond (before, during and after) the law's finding that the "object" of dis-closure was "deemed not to have taken place". What was to abide in this *place* was the content that corresponded with the post-amble's formal invitation for the public to enter into the authorship/constitution of law.

Beyond what was said (or not said) in the *name* of disclosure or re-presented in order to fill its (undisclosed) requirements, the PNUR bill was a mandate for speech that worked at the limit of law's language. Whether it provided information or elision, amnesty's dis-closure was to call for(th) the expression of experience. This "giving" voice could take shape in testimony that illumined something that was not (publicly) known, or it could indirectly afford recognition and standing to those who (now) want to declare: "We do not yet know what happened or why."[75] In either case, mandatory dis-closure appeared (and created the appearances) to offset amnesty's claimed risk of amnesia. Specifically, it refused the assumption that law was the only available site of memory and held that the testimony of perpetrators could provide *topoi* – materials and space – to both recollect and assess the past from beyond the bounds of precedent. Outside the law, unable either to sit quietly in the dock without fear of self-incrimination or to use the plea of "legal injustice" to trivialise the outcome of a hearing, the PNUR bill's equation of amnesty for disclosure rested heavily on the display, revelation and performance of character (*ethos*). In public, amnesty was to be an exposing experience, one that sought not simply the truth of events but the truth of an individual's motives and perspectives, an interior account of their desires, interests and intentions. In the name of reconciliation, the subject of amnesty stood before

the sovereign law, called to render the self open and vulnerable or stand as a
hypocrite, an embodiment of the disjunction (ruse) between appearing and
being.[76] But this was also amnesty's paradox, the question of whether its law
asked perpetrators to expose their integrity in the name of giving themselves
to a reconciliation that was held up as an alternative to (self) negation.[77]

While limited to the period between 1960 and 1994, the PNUR bill's
call to hear(ings) of the past was a mandate for words that could make the
appearances and expose the subjects of reconciliation. Underwriting this
work was a complex promise of individual and collective unity, a time in
which individuals could establish their differences in a manner that allowed
for the beginning of new relationships, the recognition and peaceful
coexistence envisaged by the post-amble. More concretely, the speech-
action of reconciliation was set out by the law as a public good and a mode
of publicity, a process that implicated all citizens, occurred in an open civic
space, and demonstrated how the people might begin to hear one another
in a manner that allowed them to forge relationships premised on norms of
understanding, reparation, and ubuntu. In some sense, this interpretation of
reconciliation as publicity served to reconcile the post-amble with its pre-
election criticism in Parliament and civil society. With the word, the past
was to be remembered and transcended simultaneously – a beginning that led
some to ask after the cost of reconciliation's (for)giving form.

3. reconciling the difficult sacrifice of a "gift"

The PNUR bill offered an account of what the TRC would look like and
what was likely to appear in its midst. Except for its appeal to the post-
amble, however, the details of the Commission's work remained ambiguous.
What exactly would occur within the TRC's transcending public space and
follow from its commitment to publicity? In mid-1995, the government
attempted to address this question more directly as it began a "campaign
of persuasion" that included the release of a 28-page pamphlet written by
Justice in Transition and published by the Ministry of Justice.[78] Entitled *Truth
and Reconciliation Commission*, the document offered a summary of the PNUR
bill's provisions and prefaced this description with a detailed argument about
the TRC's motivation and value. Claiming that it was "based on the final
clause of the Interim Constitution" and a "necessary exercise to enable South
Africans to come to terms with the past on a morally acceptable basis and
to advance the cause of reconciliation", Dullah Omar's introduction to the
pamphlet offered a deceptively simple rationale for the TRC's creation:

I could have gone to Parliament and produced an amnesty law – but this would have been to ignore the victims of violence entirely. We recognised that we could not forgive perpetrators unless we attempted also to restore the honour and dignity of the victims and give effect to reparation. The question of amnesty must be located in a broader context and the wounds of our people must be recognised. I do not distinguish between ANC wounds, PAC wounds and other wounds – many people are in need of healing, and we need to heal our country if we are to build a nation which will guarantee peace and stability.[79]

Setting Parliament's "moral equivalence" debate into the political context of nation-building, Omar's position (re)named those who had previously been identified as "persons" or "applicants". Now there were victims and perpetrators. Between them, there was a need to restore dignity, provide forgiveness, and undertake reparation. Absent from the post-amble and an idea that had been used inconsistently in the preceding year of debate, save its use within scornful accusations as to how the TRC's critics wanted only to "forgive and forget", Omar's appeal for forgiveness was significant. With it, the Minister's defence of the Commission suggested that its ability to promote reconciliation rested partly on the production of a prior gift, an "unwarranted" exchange in which victims would trade rights for honour and perpetrators would offer truth for a release from punishment. Both efforts appeared to entail significant faith and demand substantial sacrifice.

Moving from Parliament's final debate over the PNUR bill to the Constitutional Court's 1995 finding that amnesty was a justifiable exception to the rights delineated in the interim constitution, my aim here is to examine the debate over whether and how the TRC's public form and function rested on a spirit of sacrifice, a willingness on the part of South Africans to risk if not give up legal rights, historical identity, and a singular commitment to justice in the wake of apartheid. Called for and held by reconciliation's words, this sacrifice entailed setting reconciliation before the law and adopting a character (*ethos*) of productive vulnerability, an attitude of (constitutive) sacrifice that contained the potential for public politics and the grounds of collective judgment.

On 17 May 1995, Parliament convened for the second reading debate of the PNUR bill. In many ways an extension of the Portfolio Committee's public hearings, the outcome of the debate was largely given. The fact that the legislation had the requisite support for passage did not, however, diminish the complexity of the debate or lessen its significance. Read broadly, the proceedings were addressed to the nature of reconciliation and what power the TRC would need in order to enact its promotion. But, recalling Johnny de Lange's observation about the myriad and shifting meanings of reconciliation, the two-day debate demonstrated that these were contentious matters. With disagreement over reconciliation's characteristic process and product came arguments from supporters and critics of the TRC as to whether it would (re)divide or unify South Africans. Indeed, the debate involved a rather vertiginous play of definitions, concepts, and norms. Among some 30 others, reconciliation was cast as a way to open up the past, close the book on history, establish the truth of individual experience, support the catharsis of confession, exorcise evil, account for the nation's collective responsibility, engender ubuntu, revive moral conscience, rejoin law and morality, spur voluntarism, redress motivations for violence, undertake human reconstruction, heal victims, liberate institutions, support transition, and contribute to the development of democracy. With respect to such ends, the TRC was tasked to document but not homogenise truth, perform impartiality, differentiate apartheid's evil from struggle's virtue, set an example for the world, transform individual and collective perceptions, embody the spirit of the post-amble, provoke constructive debate, encourage forgiveness, ensure accountability, restore dignity, foster a culture of human rights, and support nation-building.

In Parliament's debate, reconciliation's unity appears to be composed entirely of its difference (from itself). Nearly every articulated definition of reconciliation was countered by another, one that implied an opposite meaning or issued a significant challenge to the concept's power. At some point, amidst all of the contrary interpretations, it is difficult not to wonder if the deliberations summed to a null. An important reply to this question appeared in the debate's second speech, an address given by the man who perhaps more than anyone has come to embody the character and the sacrifice needed to embrace reconciliation's words. Taking the floor after Dullah Omar's familiar summary of the PNUR bill, Nelson Mandela began the debate with a reflection on the significant power of speech. Claiming that "first and foremost the task of the President is the responsibility to build this nation and to promote the spirit of national reconciliation", Mandela worried about the form of Parliament's discussion over the TRC and its relation to the "fears and concerns of the minorities in this country".[80] Holding that "nation-building must not be a question of rhetoric", the

President urged representatives to reflect on the (rhetorical) questions of how to speak and how to debate in a manner that resisted the urge to "score points" and which took stock of the fact that some members of Parliament did not have "maximum credibility and legitimacy to lead the country".[81] With this (partial) recognition of those from the old order, Mandela then turned to the ANC and delineated its responsibility to debate in a manner that did not foreclose listening:

> [T]he majority party must have understanding, and the humility,
> not to abuse its position, but instead to ensure confidence in the
> minority parties in the country, and to see to it that their views
> are fully accommodated. I also take into account that there are leaders
> on both sides who never make faults; who are sincerely committed to
> nation-building, and want to bring their respective communities to
> a commitment to participate without reservation in the process of
> nation-building and promoting reconciliation. I am concerned that
> some honourable members feel that the cut-off date of 5 December
> 1994 does not accommodate their own people. This is a genuine
> concern which should receive the support of all parties, especially
> the majority party. Our task is to remove the concerns of all national
> groups in this country, and the responsibility for that is that of the
> majority party. As to those who have sacrificed, even lost part of their
> constituencies, we have to reward them for the courageous stand they
> have taken. We have to give them something which they can take to
> their communities.[82]

Addressed partly to the significant dispute over where to draw the line after which political offences would not qualify for amnesty, the President's position directed the debate over the TRC toward the question of how to move between past and future sacrifice, the costs entailed in struggling for liberation, ceding power, and making room in the new South Africa for all citizens. In Mandela's terms, these costs both expressed and constituted (individual and national) character, an *ethos* that the President performed when he admitted to the "many mistakes that we have made in the last twelve months" and closed his speech with an appeal to a "spirit of complete humility, respect and admiration", an attitude that set his own power beneath the work of others and enacted the self-risk needed to undertake the process of reconciliation.

How much sacrifice was necessary, especially from those who had already been forced to give (up) too much? Following the President, Melanie Verwoerd, an ANC representative (and grand-daughter-in-law of the former Prime Minister), offered one reply to this question. Calling on reluctant citizens to recognise that apartheid was not a failed policy but a "life-destroying system", she argued that:

> True reconciliation asks all of us to be honest with ourselves. Long-term reconciliation does not simply ask for a few quick apologies. It calls for a willingness to admit what went wrong in the past. Reconciliation means that sacrifices will have to be made in the process. Of course reconciliation does not mean that we should go on a destructive guilt trip either. We must nurture the creative acceptance of our individual and collective responsibility in order to accept the challenge to attempt to put right what is wrong. The PNUR Bill is indeed a crooked piece of wood from which we hope to obtain a straight plank.[83]

While it invoked Kant, this position spoke more to Hegel's view that reconciliation constitutes and moves within a "middle course of beauty between the extremes". In Parliament, the central question was how the TRC would create and enact this movement. Arguing that "this country needs to open up its discourse" but concerned that the TRC's efforts to understand history's truth would pridefully seek the whole at the cost of its subtle particulars, the IFP's Farouk Cassim claimed that, "This Bill has potential for good but also evil. It is a double-edged and double-sided sword."[84] Echoed by many others in the assembly hall, reconciliation's noble sacrifice was also a risk. Coupled to the question of how reconciliation would work, the precise difference was debated through three lines of argument.

First, MPs argued over whether the PNUR bill sacrificed the rule of law. After a number of speakers claimed that the legislation would demand "major sacrifices" from victims and virtually nothing from perpetrators, the ANC's Devikarani Jana argued that reconciliation would only follow from a gesture that the TRC's legislation did not compel: a "genuine act of repentance in the form of a public apology made to victims and to the nation by the perpetrators".[85] While resisting this call, the Freedom Front's Cornelius Mulder also questioned the fairness of the proposed amnesty process, claiming that its cut-off date and criteria would exclude and alienate a significant percentage of his constituency. From Mulder's perspective, the PNUR bill's offer of a conditional amnesty assured precisely the opposite of what the post-amble had envisioned: "There will be no national unity and reconciliation, but disunity, and unfortunately, possible further conflict."[86] Linked to questions about the actual procedures that would be used to adjudicate amnesty applications, many in Parliament appeared to believe that the bill would serve neither victim nor perpetrator. At some level, reconciliation's sacrifices were held to risk subjection if not subjugation.

Second, the debate involved substantial discussion over whether reconciliation would come at the expense of history and identity. For the NP, the bill's flaw was that it did not recognise the historical symmetry between "the wrong ideology of apartheid" and the liberation struggle's "discredited ideology of communism". This alleged congruence required sacrificing the past to the degree that an historical inquiry rooted in a sense of moral or political differentiation would not help build the future.[87] For MP's representing the PAC, however, the past could not be left behind or equivocated. Willing to "tell our story publicly", Richard Sizani argued that the truth would not appear if the promotion of reconciliation proceeded from an "even-handed doctrine" that set "apartheid's oppressors and its victims on the same pedestal".[88]

While some worried over how history was best read, others voiced concern that the reconciliation would mark the end of their historical traditions and thus the collapse of their identity. Related to Parliament's January 1994 debate over the interim constitution, this issue was at the centre of an exchange between the NP's Frederik van Heerden and two ANC representatives, Jan Momberg and Dirk du Toit. Asking after the future, du Toit defended reconciliation's "new enlightenment" as a way for the Afrikaner to "confirm his political and cultural experience" and make "an absolute break with his sinister past".[89] Going further, du Toit then asked the question that appeared to be a prerequisite for reconciliation:

> Can the Afrikaner sacrifice the comfort and danger of his conventional identity to the extent to which it is not reconcilable with a critical appreciation of his traditions, political history, and culture?[90]

Replying that it was "not enough for the Afrikaner to say he is sorry about apartheid", du Toit claimed that "vicious Afrikaner nationalism is what must be sacrificed", a sacrifice which Momberg held up as the "final liberation of the Afrikaner". At pains to accept this calling, van Heerden accused the "ANC's angel, Minister Omar", of having a "one-sided perception" of history, a view that both ignored how apartheid successfully resisted an "absolutely destructive ideology" and threatened to wipe away the proud history of the Afrikaner.[91] Momberg's interjecting (and later retracted) reply was, "Julle het ons jongmense laat doodmaak op die grens" (You had/let our children be killed on the border), a response that further underscored the problematic relationship between reconciliation, history and sacrifice.[92] For some, dealing with the past in a morally acceptable manner was the basis for a freedom to come. To others, the idea was a sign that the historical roots of identity and culture were on the block as the promise of reconciliation's beginning meant the end of an individual and collective sense of self.

Third, the ambiguous nature of reconciliation brought debate over whether the TRC would serve or sacrifice justice. Linked to disputes about the Commission's relative impartiality and if it was set to replace one exclusive political ideology with another, the issue in some sense was whether Kader Asmal was right when he claimed in the name of ubuntu's generosity that, "[W]e must deliberately sacrifice, as this Bill does, the formal trappings of justice, the courts and the trials, for an even higher Good: Truth."[93] For some of those unwilling to believe with the ACDP's Louis Green that reconciliation's sacrifice was for God, Asmal's position was an indication of how the TRC's mandate sat before the law in a manner that mocked and denigrated its justice. For all its promises to victims, observed Sizani, the bill did not define the idea of truth or how the Commission would uncover and present its terms to the nation. According to Johannes Maree, the truth of the bill was that it was "conceived and born in sin. It was drawn up in one of the suburbs by unknown and secret authors."[94] While this objection may have bordered on the conspiratorial, the underlying point was significant. In the eyes of many, on both sides of the aisle, the TRC's requisite sacrifice constituted a risk to victims and perpetrators alike, a giving (up) in which the power of reconciliation's speech sat perilously close to the loss of words.

When read together, the strands of Parliament's debate set the celebratory and constitutive spirit of reconciliation into a difficult relation with the work needed to render its potential actual. Challenging whether it was enough to say that the TRC would deal with the past in a morally acceptable way, the discussion indicated that reconciliation's virtuous beginning held the risk of undue and indeed an immoral sacrifice, especially for those still struggling to escape apartheid's violence. The character required to perform and accept reconciliation's gift cut (both ways) and demanded as much. Holding the problem of how individuals would (be)come to stand in history and the question of how the nation would cross its defining bridge, the TRC's mandate and justification thus recalled the church's view of reconciliation as well as the controversy that had hamstrung CODESA: at the limit of law, the call for reconciliation assumed that "weakness" could yield strength, in part by asking individuals to give up their (sovereign) rights. As President Mandela signed the PNUR bill at the middle of July, just after the release of a secret report by the Goldstone Commission on the SAP's role in pre-election violence, the merits of such a sacrifice remained uncertain. For his part, Mandela declared that "People and communities all over the country and beyond must begin to organise so that they too can be part of writing the history of our country", and then heralded the Commission's work as an avenue to "truth that can put the past to rest". In several senses, the walk would not begin until reconciliation was called (again) before law.[95]

Over the course of the spring, the country watched as the selection of commissioners raised more than a few hackles and accusations as to how the TRC would never be able to remain impartial. By December, with the appointment process largely complete, Desmond Tutu, the Commission's Chair, gathered his new colleagues in Bishops Court for a photo-op and a short speech in which the Archbishop proclaimed that "the work of our Commission is helping our land and people to achieve a genuine, real and not cheap and spurious reconciliation".[96]

As the 17 commissioners prepared to design and carry out their work, a process that was widely acknowledged to involve "hitting the ground running", a lawsuit was filed by members of the Azanian People's Organisation and three individuals who had lost prominent family members in the struggle against apartheid.[97] In their suit, *AZAPO, Biko, Mxenge and Ribeiro v. the President of the Republic of South Africa, the Government of the Republic of South Africa, the Minister of Justice, the Minister of Safety and Security, and the Chairperson of the Truth and Reconciliation Commission*, the applicants averred that sections of the PNUR Act were unconstitutional insofar as they barred victims of apartheid-era crimes from exercising their "right to have justiciable disputes settled by a court of law". They also claimed that the Act ran contrary to the edicts of international law, and that while amnesty might foreclose the chance for criminal trials, it could not justifiably prevent the initiation of civil claims against perpetrators. In short, the suit challenged the sacrifice called for by the law of reconciliation, questioned how the TRC would be held accountable for its work, and argued that accountability for gross violations of human rights demanded obedience to the rule of law as it followed from the promise of the interim constitution.

The complaint was heard by the Constitutional Court just over a month after Desmond Tutu had opened the first hearing of the Human

Rights Violations Committee in East London. Some two months later, the Constitutional Court returned its judgment. Writing for a nearly unanimous court, Justice Ismael Mohamed's opinion began with a preamble addressed to the context and meaning of the interim constitution's post-amble. Recalling a "debilitating war of internal political dissension and confrontation, massive expressions of labour militancy, perennial student unrest, punishing international economic isolation, widespread dislocation in crucial areas of national endeavour, accelerated levels of armed conflict and a dangerous combination of anxiety, frustration and anger among expanding proportions of the populace", Mohamed claimed that apartheid and the struggle against it had left "the legitimacy of law … deeply wounded as the country haemorrhaged dangerously in the face of this tragic conflict which had begun to traumatise the entire nation".[98] Within this *stasis* appeared the need to "negotiate a different future", a process characterised by a "firm and generous commitment to reconciliation and national unity". Finding that this "fundamental philosophy is eloquently expressed in the epilogue [post-amble] of the constitution", the court's Deputy President set the stage for the court's opinion by claiming that the post-amble has to be "read holistically, particularly as it "expresses an integrated philosophical and jurisprudential approach" to the South African transition.[99]

Mindful of the interim constitution's spirit and letter, the court turned to the merits of the applicant's efforts to "attack the constitutionality" of those provisions of the PNUR Act that allowed the release of successful amnesty applicants from criminal and civil claims at the expense of the constitution's allowance for prosecution and punishment.[100] In obvious sympathy, Mohamed responded by noting that the effects of amnesty "impacts upon very fundamental rights" and agreeing that the provision of amnesty "effectively obliterates such rights". The claimed violation existed. Was it justified? Turning to this question, Mohamed challenged two elements of the applicant's case. First, the suit assumed that the post-amble did not have the same standing as the rest of the interim constitution. Holding against this interpretation on the grounds that the post-amble had "no lesser status", in part because of its mandate for Parliament to act with respect to amnesty, Mohamed turned to the more important problem of whether the Act's limitation of a constitutional right was a permissible "law of general application". According to the court, the PNUR Act's exception to the standing constitutional rights had to be "reasonable and justifiable in an open and democratic society based on freedom and equality" and could not "negate the essential content of the right" that it appeared to suspend.[101] Declining to explain how the court applied this test in light of the Act's acknowledged "obliteration" of victim's rights, Mohamed instead offered what is best read as a soliloquy, a reflection and pronouncement that countered the applicant's appeals for legal consistency with a case for the virtue of reconciliation's inconsistent law. While lengthy, the passage anchored the court's judgment by legitimising amnesty's (un)justified exception:

> Every decent human being must feel grave discomfort in living with
> a consequence which might allow the perpetrators of evil acts to walk
> the streets of this land with impunity, protected in their freedom by an
> amnesty immune from constitutional attack, but the circumstances in
> support of this course require carefully to be appreciated. Most of the
> acts of brutality and torture which have taken place have occurred during
> an era in which neither the laws which permitted the incarceration
> of persons or the investigation of crimes, nor the methods and the
> culture which informed such investigations, were easily open to public
> investigation, verification and correction. Much of what transpired
> in this shameful period is shrouded in secrecy and not easily capable
> of objective demonstration and proof. Loved ones have disappeared,
> sometimes mysteriously and most of them no longer survive to tell their
> tales. Others have had their freedom invaded, their dignity assaulted or
> their reputations tarnished by grossly unfair imputations hurled in the
> fire and the cross-fire of a deep and wounding conflict. The wicked and
> the innocent have often both been victims. Secrecy and authoritarianism
> have concealed the truth in little crevices of obscurity in our history.
> Records are not easily accessible, witnesses are often unknown, dead,
> unavailable or unwilling. All that often effectively remains is the truth
> of wounded memories of loved ones sharing instinctive suspicions, deep
> and traumatising to the survivors but otherwise incapable of translating
> themselves into objective and corroborative evidence which could
> survive the rigours of the law. The Act seeks to address this massive
> problem by encouraging these survivors and the dependants of the
> tortured and the wounded, the maimed and the dead to unburden their
> grief publicly, to receive the collective recognition of a new nation that
> they were wronged, and crucially, to help them to discover what did in
> truth happen to their loved ones, where and under what circumstances
> it did happen, and who was responsible. That truth, which the victims

of repression seek so desperately to know is, in the circumstances, much more likely to be forthcoming if those responsible for such monstrous misdeeds are encouraged to disclose the whole truth with the incentive that they will not receive the punishment which they undoubtedly deserve if they do. Without that incentive there is nothing to encourage such persons to make the disclosures and to reveal the truth which persons in the positions of the applicants so desperately desire. With that incentive, what might unfold are objectives fundamental to the ethos of a new constitutional order. The families of those unlawfully tortured, maimed or traumatised become more empowered to discover the truth, the perpetrators become exposed to opportunities to obtain relief from the burden of a guilt or an anxiety they might be living with for many long years, the country begins the long and necessary process of healing the wounds of the past, transforming anger and grief into a mature understanding and creating the emotional and structural climate essential for the "reconciliation and reconstruction" which informs the very difficult and sometimes painful objectives of the amnesty articulated in the epilogue.

The alternative to the grant of immunity from criminal prosecution of offenders is to keep intact the abstract right to such a prosecution for particular persons without the evidence to sustain the prosecution successfully, to continue to keep the dependants of such victims in many cases substantially ignorant about what precisely happened to their loved ones, to leave their yearning for the truth effectively unassuaged, to perpetuate their legitimate sense of resentment and grief and correspondingly to allow the culprits of such deeds to remain perhaps physically free but inhibited in their capacity to become active, full and creative members of the new order by a menacing combination of confused fear, guilt, uncertainty and sometimes even trepidation. Both the victims and the culprits who walk on the "historic bridge" described by the epilogue will hobble more than walk to the future with heavy and dragged steps delaying and impeding a rapid and enthusiastic transition to the new society at the end of the bridge, which is the vision which informs the epilogue.

Even more crucially, but for a mechanism providing for amnesty, the "historic bridge" itself might never have been erected. For a successfully negotiated transition, the terms of the transition required not only the agreement of those victimised by abuse but also those threatened by the transition to a "democratic society based on freedom and equality". If the Constitution kept alive the prospect of continuous retaliation and revenge, the agreement of those threatened by its implementation might never have been forthcoming, and if it had, the bridge itself would have remained wobbly and insecure, threatened by fear from some and anger from others. It was for this reason that those who negotiated the Constitution made a deliberate choice, preferring understanding over vengeance, reparation over retaliation, ubuntu over victimisation.[102]

In the light of a constitution given for transition, the necessity of law is contingent on the production of truth and the cultivation of that faith needed to create reconciliation's unity in difference. Before the law, amnesty's release of precedent stands in opposition to it, a symbol of why the law did not (yet) have definitive standing or status. Cast as a different form of law by the court, the disclosure of truth in exchange for amnesty (and perhaps reparation) is prior, a means of understanding and repairing the long-standing separation of law and justice, a gap that requires setting aside the rule of law in favour of a spirit given to its reconstruction.[103] Not yet legitimate, the strict application of law only deters the *ethos* of disclosure and discovery, the character that is necessary for reconciliation to move South Africa from past to future. This turn was not a negation of law. Rather, claiming that the necessity of reconciliation demanded "a difficult, sensitive, perhaps even agonising balancing act between the need for justice to victims of past abuse and the need for reconciliation and rapid transition to a new future", Mohamed held that the work of transition was "an exercise of immense difficulty interacting in a vast network of political, emotional, ethical and logistical considerations" and then rejected the applicant's claims on the grounds that the implications of reconciliation were a "calling for a judgement falling substantially within the domain of those entrusted with lawmaking in the era preceding and during the transition period".[104]

Much like the 1993 finding by the Transvaal Court in its review of how "sufficient consensus" was used during the MPNP, Mohamed's opinion set the good faith of reconciliation's words over the juridical enforcement of a (social) contract. More directly, it offered a working explanation of how the TRC would function as a "model in the middle", a body that sat between the language of the post-amble's reconciliation and the need to expand its spirit in the name of giving voice to apartheid's victims. In the Constitutional Court's estimation, this middle was neither an equilibrium nor evidence of (transcending) synthesis. In between victim and perpetrator, individual and nation, and democratisation and justice, reconciliation's performance rested on a norm of publicity that could not escape the terms of its sacrifice: victims would not receive their day in court; legal precedent and rule of law would be set aside in the hopes of finding truth; a future of peace would risk the divisions of history. With words to sustain the faith of beginning, the work of struggle remained. From Mandela's post-election appeals in Parliament to the tenuous logic of the Constitutional Court's judgment, the character of this effort was deemed paramount, a call to embrace and enact a mutual vulnerability, an *ethos* of giving (with) speech that held the potential for South Africans to make the difference of unity.

The development of the TRC was not a sufficient condition to carry South Africa into the transition that followed the election. Its work, however, was frequently defended as necessary. At the TRC's interfaith commissioning service in early February of 1996, Nelson Mandela recalled how "forces locked in apparently irreconcilable conflict found a negotiated path" and then argued that the Commission's work was of "great consequence to the future of our nation". Underscoring the TRC's need to remain independent from "political authority", the President claimed that the participatory nature of the body offered an opportunity to cultivate the grounds for politics. Turning then to the gathered commissioners, he stressed that "your goal is to ensure lasting reconciliation".[105] For a nation that needed to "redeem and reconstruct itself", TRC's charge was thus rendered ambitious and ambiguous. Was Mandela's call to succeed at odds with the PNUR Act's mandate for the TRC to "promote" reconciliation? In the coming 18 months, what was reconciliation to mean? How was it to be pursued? What good would it serve?

From its beginning, the TRC did and did not have control over the answers to these questions. Of and for the public, at least by the law's defining words, the Commission's charge was to facilitate, hear, and record speech given to the expression of experience, truth, and accountability. In this chapter, I have attempted to plot the development and tensions within this work, a reconciliation held in the potential of the word to constitute the appearances needed to understand division, restore dignity, discern cause, and motivate (mutual) acknowledgement. To these ends, the TRC's law of reconciliation both embodied and opposed the post-amble, carrying out its mandate for amnesty and challenging whether such an exception could be justified in the absence of measures for those subject to apartheid's gross violations of human rights. Tailoring reconciliation to the needs of the individual (victim and perpetrator) and casting it as a process of nation-building, the debate over how to define and empower the TRC found resolution and also its limit in reconciliation's constitutive sacrifice: a need to (fore)give at the cost of self; a charge to appear fully without reservation or cover (of law). A delicate "balancing act" that mimicked and resisted the logic of the negotiating table, intent on keeping its faith but unwilling to condone its bracketing of the past, the advent of the TRC offered a potential for beginning that the law could neither define nor contain. For the present, this was the Commission's benefit and its controversial risk.

There was more to say. There was also an opportunity to talk (again) about the power of talk. A logic that had carried throughout, a feature of religious, political and transitional definitions of reconciliation, the creation of the TRC served to radicalise and complicate this meta-discourse. With statutory apartheid ended, South Africa's new beginning offered a moment to question reconciliation's meaning and constitutive power. This was a decisive characteristic of the parliamentary, civil society, and judicial debates over the TRC, the fact that reconciliation rested on concepts – truth-telling, disclosure, acknowledgement, recognition – that appeared to defy definition. In some sense, the tolerance for this ambiguity was admirable, an indication that reconciliation's work had to be made up as it went along. While many critics did accuse the TRC's architects of committing the nation to an unspoken agenda, the Commission's effort to hold open its mandate was an attempt to ensure that the well was not poisoned before it was dug. Put differently, the Commission's task was to unfold reconciliation through its constitutive words, terms that lacked the quality of predestination, the endless potential that had underwritten the violence of apartheid's endless appeal to future salvation. But, the critics also had an important point: the TRC's founding call for speech beckoned sacrifice, one that was not easy to justify and which appeared ready to enact a fundamental injustice.

Behind the TRC was a long history, a history of atrocity and a history of reconciliation itself. Taking the post-amble's question seriously, the PNUR Act put both into play. At neither the beginning nor the end of history, the Commission appeared in and for a middle – a space and movement in which the faith of words was given to the work of building relationships of unity in difference. With respect to the TRC, the struggle for these words and the assessment of their power calls for an inquiry that moves not across ten years but within the fragile lattices that compose moments, a study that takes stock of reconciliation's rhetorical history (making) and moves ever so slightly to the question of how the TRC endeavoured to make history with a rhetorical conception of reconciliation.

epilogue:
the potential of an exceptional beginning

econciliation begins anew within the fleeting aura of the miraculous. Celebrating the end of apartheid's law, Nelson Mandela had declared the transition a "small miracle", a description that was borrowed by more than a few and which subtly but very clearly implied that hard work had also played a vital role in South Africa's nevertheless remarkable beginning.[1] Addressing Parliament, Christiaan Fismer was more direct, arguing that "this miracle did not fall from heaven" but was the result of a multi-faceted negotiated settlement that "set the scene for reconciliation".[2] Just over a month earlier, Desmond Tutu appeared less interested in debating causes and effects when he concluded his first speech to TRC colleagues by noting, "We have seen a miracle unfold before our eyes and the world has marvelled as South Africans, all South Africans, have won this spectacular victory over injustice, oppression, and evil. The miracle must endure."[3]

While many were indeed marvelling, commentators were beginning to wonder and worry over the transition's unexpected consequences. Asking how well citizens were "learning to live with the South African miracle", Graeme Simpson, then a senior director at the Centre for the Study of Violence and Reconciliation, warned against "romanticised" visions of South Africa's turn from apartheid and argued that its success would have much to do with whether "processes of economic and physical reconstruction" could be linked to "reconciliation and democracy-building".[4] Between the material and the symbolic, the bridge was unsteady if even built. In the midst of a miracle, there remained the problem of how to understand, direct, and sustain the power of beginning.

Does the exceptional quality of South Africa's transition represent a "miracle or a mirage"?[5] Reconciliation provokes this question and does not lend an easy answer, particularly as it recalls Hume's claim that, "No testimony is sufficient to establish a miracle", save that which would represent the

283

"mutual destruction of arguments".[6] Confounding reference and upsetting the grounds for analysis, leaving us without the comforts and norms of (law's) words, reconciliation's alleged miracle calls and hands us (over to) a time of "surprise and wonder", a moment in which we struggle both to articulate and to account for the causes of change and the power of creation.

As it plays between the miracle and the mirage, upsetting the stability of the Word in the coming to words, reconciliation's power rests heavily on its potential to make anew. Does the struggle against apartheid and the start of the transition hold the beginning of reconciliation? How has reconciliation helped to compose and constitute South Africa's attempt to begin again? These questions admit to different interpretations. Read one way, they restate part of the NGK's case for separate development: the potential for reconciliation will only be actualised in a time yet to come, a moment for which we must wait, perhaps endlessly. Read another way, they express (or profess) a belief in reconciliation's potential to open a difficult present, the awkward but vital "middle time" of transition. On a third interpretation, the questions hold reconciliation's call to oppose one logic of human relations in the name of (re)turning to another, a potential to move from an identitarian vision of unity *as* difference to the interplay of identifications given to figuring a unity *in* difference.

In reconciliation, there is (just) so much potential: a mode of becoming that may or not come to be; the promise of (re)making not yet fulfilled; a process of beginning that is still if not always in process; a constitutive power that turns back on itself, wary of transcendence, the last(ing) definitive move. In the fragile appearances that characterise its reality, what then do we make of reconciliation's potential? What if anything has reconciliation's potential made? Over the course of this book, I have attempted to demonstrate that these are rhetorical questions. At one level, they invite a consideration of how reconciliation's constitutive words have appeared over time, the ways in which South African institutions, political leaders, and citizens have argued about the meaning of reconciliation in relation to the relative justification for apartheid, the dynamics of "negotiated revolution", and the problem of how a deeply divided society can begin to learn about and deal with the past. At a second level, given that advocacy and criticism of reconciliation appears to envision, perform, and trouble important facets of the South African transition, the question of reconciliation's potential is also the question of how its words have worked to make new, the ways in which the rhetorical performance of reconciliation has opposed historical justifications for violence in the name of opening a time and composing a vocabulary that supported a (re)turn to (civic) friendship. Thus, in closing, I want to reflect on these two registers, the related matters of reconciliation's history and the beginnings sponsored by its speech-action. Returning to the idea of reconciliation's exceptional role in South Africa's move from apartheid, my aim is less to enact the synthetic than underscore the contingent, the fragile quality of reconciliation's historical potential and how its appearance(s) served to express and complicate the history-making play of transition. I also want to suggest that this remarkable turn holds a set of lessons about how we might begin to approach and perhaps assess that controversial commission which laboured under reconciliation's banner.

reconciling (the) works of words

The question is always the same and it is one that I have come to expect: "Did reconciliation work?" It is a query over which one cannot help stumble. Yes, I have learned to reply, it was a practice that both performed and underwrote some of the transition's work. To the ensuing question of what this means, I offer that reconciliation framed a vision of struggle, directed, and complicated negotiations, and provoked debate over how to balance the political necessities of transition with the moral demand to provide justice in the wake of apartheid. Dissatisfied with this apparent "non-answer", my interlocutors frequently press for the definitive, asking for an assessment of whether reconciliation in South Africa has been achieved or the degree to which it was a necessary element of the transition from apartheid. Both questions require a step back, a discussion of whether these questions are coherent, useful, and appropriate. Reconciliation in South Africa is not a single thing or a unified process. The idea of "South African reconciliation" is more trouble than it is worth. Over time and across contexts, reconciliation does not move easily or clearly from its process to product. Its operations appear throughout the transition and with uneven effects, a power that takes pains to resist the logic of cause and effect.

The investigation of reconciliation's history entails an engagement with the non-definitive, a concept and practice that is not simply ambiguous but which strives to change the form and content of human relationships by standing in opposition to the identitarian logic of definition. This quality of reconciliation has led some to conclude that it represents a lack of conflict, a negative interpretation which makes it relatively easy to claim that reconciliation played a prominent role in South Africa's transition.

More sophisticated but no less problematic, others have cast reconciliation as an "essentially contested concept", a view that misunderstands the ways in which appeals for reconciliation worked to contest certain forms of essentialism as well as to cultivate the grounds for action within particular moments of essential(ist) contestation.[7] In short, neither a harmonising absence nor an endless mediation, the question of reconciliation's meaning finds an immanent and yet still only provisional answer when we inquire after its words: the arguments that were advanced about reconciliation's nature, operation, and value; the rules of language that supported such speech; the historical discourses that inaugurated and foreclosed its practice; and the modes of speech that constituted and blurred the difference between reconciliation's subject and object.

Between 1985 and 1995, reconciliation was the topic of significant and widespread talk in South Africa. Both a call to speak and the calling of speech, it was held out as a practice of exchanging words in the name of fostering interaction and composing relationships that do not rest on the necessity of violence. To these ends, reconciliation was defended as a moment in which to break with words, the language of legal and historical precedent that deterred speech, indemnified the state's violence, and unhinged law from its announced commitment to justice. Dedicated to creating the conditions for talking about talk, and cultivating the character (*ethos*) needed for enemies to listen and argue in good faith, calls for reconciliation set language into the motion of speech, a process that involved explicit argumentation about the ways reconciliation worked rhetorically and constituted a basis for creative expression. An occasion and mode of rhetorical invention, reconciliation thus held a constitutive power that called back to the question of its own standing to make anew, the problem of how its beginning (with) words marked a moment of definition that had to be scrutinised if not opposed. Neither a revolution with permanence nor a permanent revolution, reconciliation engendered a struggle for the "wrong state of affairs", a creativity with words that remained attuned to the costs of its own creation.[8]

It is one thing to observe reconciliation's rhetorical form as it appears over the course of a decade. It is quite another to assess the significance of these appearances with respect to their bearing on the terms and development of South Africa's transition from apartheid. As Foucault makes plain in his reflections on the discontinuous operations of discourse, the question of "how" reconciliation works and to what effect does not follow directly from an understanding of its various and variable definitions.[9] If so, a relatively stable vocabulary and evident interest in reconciliation cannot be used to discount the fact that its rhetorical call, interpretation, and practice appears intermittently, changes form, and undertakes a variety of operations over time. So too, it cannot be forgotten that reconciliation's claimed (and actualised) potential to compose appearances is largely directed to the work of relationship-building, the creation of bonds that retain their vitality only as they are not stripped of contingency. In Hans Blumenberg's terms, this means that "*topos* research" into reconciliation's development can only take us so far; with respect to understanding the power of (reconciliation's) beginning, the risk of such an approach is the deployment of a substantive ontology that presupposes reconciliation's conceptual necessity or reads its contribution to transition through the lens of teleology.[10]

In an odd but important way, the dilemmas that attend the assessment of reconciliation are themselves a marker of its significance. As I suggested at the outset, reconciliation's words of beginning blur not only the divide between its theory and practice but also the difference between its characteristic speech acts and the history-making "action that it helps prepare, trigger and enact".[11] More and less than the "fiction" whereby critics set historical acts into words, reconciliation in South Africa has operated as a rhetorical modality of transition. More precisely, its advocacy and practice 1) delineated an occasion for enemies to speak in the midst of violence, 2) underwrote a form of constitutive power in which the terms of historical animosity were fashioned into the basis and enactment of productive (dis)agreement, and 3) supported public controversy over whether the promise of (reconciliation's) law was sufficient to move South Africa from past to future. Considered in turn, these dynamics offer a way to understand the ways in which reconciliation contributed to the transition and how its rhetorical operativity performed the work of beginning.

1. making middle time

More than a plea for dialogue, calls for reconciliation interrupt history's words and open a time to speak. At the limit of speech, in the midst of violence that compromises the word's capacity to support action, the advocacy of reconciliation involves reading the signs of the times and discerning a moment (and need) for choice, a present in which speaking might be given to rendering things otherwise. Cast frequently as a pragmatic and ethical imperative to speak (out), reconciliation's fashioning and announcement of opportunity is especially apparent within the religious debates over how best to struggle against apartheid and the "talks about talks". In each case, re-conciliation illustrated how a *stasis* or "language trouble" was equally a *kairos*, a moment before the end of time in which there remained the potential and need for words. More precisely, calls for reconciliation named a situation of violence. Set in a long line of opposition to apartheid's logic and law, the *Kairos Document*, for example, called on South Africans to name the regime's evil, to tell of "our experience of oppression and tyranny, our experience of conflict, crisis and struggle, our experience of trying to be Christians in this situation". Contrasted with the NGK's case for separate development and building from the premises of Black Theology, the text's redefinition and appeal for reconciliation was composed of argumentation about how to speak of violence in ways that did not replicate or justify its practice. Over the course of 1989, the pleas for reconciliation advanced by F.W. de Klerk and Nelson Mandela were crucial examples of this turn – reciprocated (although not fully believed) signals that each leader viewed the existing situation as untenable. Less the creation of an explicit agreement than the development of a common referent between enemies who claimed to lack a basis for interaction, their respective arguments for reconciliation opened a time and space in which to ask whether (and how) to set aside or bracket the historical causes and commitments that were funding if not fating an endless clash.

Calls for reconciliation consistently announced the potential for transition. Rhetorically, they fashioned an occasion for change, a middle time in which there was an opportunity to oppose the definitive-historical power of language with speech that held a potential to remake the form of human relations. Setting the meaning of the times into flux, questioning what had been, what was, and what could be, reconciliation began as a critique of the power of definition and its capacity to name and codify identity at the expense of identification. Standing between past and future, the interim constitution's post-amble is a remarkable illustration of this turn, an appeal for reconciliation that stands in opposition to apartheid's identitarian law and proceeds in excess of law in general. Holding out a contingent time in which to create the terms of collective (inter)action, reconciliation's potential opened and held a moment in which to recollect, recover, and enact the relational power of speech.

2. constituting a middle voice
Appeals for reconciliation employed speech to create a time for speaking. Opposing a situation of violence with a fragile climate that contained the

basis for talk, reconciliation's announced opportunity framed one of its crucial operations, a process of rhetorical invention that turned justifications for enmity into the potential for productive opposition. As the contours of *stasis* were read and acknowledged to unravel standing rationales for violence, the call for reconciliation revealed that the cost of sovereignty and self-certainty was a shared expense that counted as a reason for dialogue. Such talk had to be built. Thus, the practice of reconciliation endowed speech with a positive content and oriented it to the creation of a constitutive power, a mode of collective action in which each party renounced (at least temporarily) their historical "duty", demonstrated a willingness to talk and listen in good faith, and accepted that there was a difference between violence and heated disagreement about how to define the form and content of transition.

Far less a falling into harmony than a fragile process of entering into argumentation that rendered historical identity and self-interest contingent, reconciliation's generative functions run across and deeply into the negotiated end of apartheid. In church texts, it appears as reconciliation's gift, a prior Word that serves to endow the creativity of human words with the faith needed to enter relationships that defy unilateral control. In related but more secular terms, reconciliation's spirit of interdependence was cultivated repeatedly through appeals to ubuntu and other (perhaps shared) traditions that set the individual subject within the larger play of communal life. At the negotiating table, this constitutive work took more precise form. Following the clashes at CODESA over where to locate the (sovereign) capacity to argue, negotiators prepared for the MPNP by returning to the idea of sufficient consensus. Highlighting its formal-pragmatic quality, they agreed that this mode of decision-making was rooted in the need for a reconciliation that was equally a means of making progress and an outcome of a negotiations process that sat outside and in opposition to the terms of law. In the post-amble, this double interpretation was rendered explicit as reconciliation's constitutive power was first celebrated and then cast as an ongoing event, a process in which the (re)turn of law to justice was a task for all citizens committed to realising that unity in diversity which was held to underpin the work of nation-building.

In South Africa, across a number of contexts and running through religious and political vocabularies that many endeavour to keep separate, reconciliation's constitutive power developed as its practice called for(th) a middle voice, a mode of expression in which performance and production touch, a tropological operation that meta-transitively renders agency relational, without recourse to fixed identity or historical necessity. More precisely, reconciliation explained and enabled a relational form of character, an *ethos* in which the individual and collective subject struggled to constitute *with* the Other. In reconciliation, the long-standing charge against rhetoric – that it allows the weaker to appear the better – counted as something of a virtue; the weaker was the better as the self was "willing" and seen to risk itself in the name of entering into relation. In this way, reconciliation's faith disclosed its attitude toward making and it expressed a desire to "come to terms" between past and future. In this middle, the contingency of identity and the openness of character to the provisionality of definition re-presented the potential to constitute in the present. Neither reversion nor transcendence, reconciliation's speech stood and moved within a constellation of violence, opposition, and understanding.

3. between the appearance(s) of words

More than a hope for words, reconciliation constituted a mode of speaking. For and within the South African transition, operating in a time of flux and dedicated to the creation of bonds that held the promise of a new beginning, this rhetorical power brought a difficult double-bind. With multiple and shifting meanings, setting its own subject and object into motion, and holding precedent at bay, reconciliation's potential provoked practical questions of judgment while appearing to undermine the very basis for their resolution. In an important way, this dynamic is an intrinsic aspect of reconciliation's work. This is to say that one announced goal of reconciliation was the promotion of public life, the opening of deliberative arenas in which it was possible to question reconciliation's value. In the wake of deep division and near civil war, the appearance of this publicity is both evidence of reconciliation's contribution to transition and a moment when reconciliation was turned back on itself in order to assess the value and costs of its potential. More than an unexpected consequence, reconciliation's generative operations motivated struggle, a struggle for recognition in which those asked to engage in reconciliation or gathered (by law) under its banner were called to resolve whether its appearances mattered and if the sacrifices entailed in their production represented an adequate critique of the violence that they aimed to redress. Put differently, the practice and claimed achievement of reconciliation provoked a number of public controversies, most of which were rooted in one of three overlapping questions.

First, did reconciliation's potential demand an unjustified or unjust patience? For advocates of revolution, the English-speaking church's call for reconciliation appeared to portend only incremental change, a reform effort that offered few guarantees about when apartheid would actually be dismantled. Inciting accusations that this was preparation for a sell-out, Nelson Mandela and F.W. de Klerk's appeals for reconciliation were read by some members of their respective constituencies as formless and dangerous promises, visions of a future state that had little to say about whether it would remain in the hands of "criminals" or fall under the control of "terrorists". In the wake of the election, reconciliation's potential at the negotiating table was criticised for not dealing with the past and then criticised again for legitimising the idea of a truth commission, a body that appeared able to strip victims of the justice that was their due. While not always expressed, both objections had much to do with whether reconciliation's potential for unity in difference aimed to recover the standing of the citizen-subject or displace it into a vaguely defined ideal of ubuntu.

Second, did reconciliation's constitutive power (pre)define appropriate norms of expression and thus deter criticism of its process? With significant Christian roots, some argued that reconciliation's conceptual ties to forgiveness and confession rendered it an inappropriate mode of secular politics. More immediate were Inkatha's arguments against sufficient consensus, an objection that alleged the NP and ANC's domination of the negotiations and which raised the larger question of whether reconciliation was a process that could accommodate the voices and needs of more than two parties. In the debate over the TRC, this problem of exclusivity took a different form when groups argued that reconciliation's concern for the future portended the beginning of the end for Afrikaner culture and history. While not a rebuttal precisely, this argument had a counterpart in the claim that reconciliation condoned a damaging and degrading equivalence between the crimes of apartheid and the excesses of struggle. In both positions, reconciliation's power appeared to risk the drawing of a historical line that encouraged talk about some parts of the past while counselling silence about others.

Third, were the symbolic gains of reconciliation coming at the expense of substantive change? Raised explicitly by the *Kairos Document*, this problem also appeared at the end of the MPNP and again after the 1994 election. Wondering whether political power was being traded for the preservation of white control over economic resources, critics appealed to the ANC's *Freedom Charter* and pressed for an account of the precise relationship between the ideas of reconciliation and reconstruction that featured so prominently in the post-amble. From a slightly different perspective, the close of the negotiations and ensuing debate over the need for a truth commission brought questions about how reconciliation would reconstitute the rule of law, especially as it was wed to an amnesty that appeared to risk impunity, set aside the future value of precedent, and contravene international norms about the disposition of crimes against humanity.

Alone or together, the resolution of these questions or an assessment of how they bear on the success of reconciliation is not something that can be taken up here. In many ways, such an effort is beside the point, especially since the disagreements *per se* are a marker of reconciliation's significance in South Africa's turn from apartheid. As it did at the negotiating table, appeals for reconciliation opened opportunities for public discourse, prompted discussion about how to define and cultivate particular public goods, and drew attention to the problem of how a deeply divided society labouring under a legacy of brutal violence, political exclusion, and social-economic inequality could (not) begin to speak about the potential need, form, and rules of collective interaction.

Reconciliation begins: the discernment of a time to speak; the endowment of speech with constitutive power; the capacity to question the cost of speaking's creation. With these rhetorical operations, the concept and practice of reconciliation played an exceptional role in South Africa's transition from apartheid to constitutional democracy. By this I mean that reconciliation appeared within, stood against, and then exceeded the logic of emergency, the state of exception in which historical and juridical law provided itself with the capacity for total violence. More precisely, reconciliation composed an exception to this exception. From the 1985 *Kairos Document* to the 1995 debate over the dangers of amnesty, appeals for reconciliation were arguments about the potential of words; the capacity of leaders and citizens to recover the grounds and generative power of speech in the name of turning law against itself and opening space for collective (inter)action predicated on the need to make South Africa anew. Evident in how delegates at the MPNP used reconciliation to underwrite the sufficient consensus that was required to stand before and (re)make law, this potential for transition resembles what Walter Benjamin described as a "real state of emergency", a kind of weak messianic power that forsakes those forms of revolution which replicate the logic of the old order for a transformative critique of violence that remains conscious of its own danger, the inevitable limit and violence of its speech-action.[12] Indeed, the controversy that followed from the interim constitution's post-amble highlighted this danger as it figured reconciliation's constitutive words as a *pharmakon*, an antidote to South Africa's deep division and a concoction that risked an understanding of the past with the temptations of a future yet to (be)come.[13]

This ambivalence is crucial. Neither a sufficient condition nor outcome of the turn from apartheid, reconciliation's exceptional quality represents less a definitive contribution to South Africa's negotiated revolution than a varied rhetorical performance and norm of rhetorical practice that inaugurated a time of transition and inscribed it with a non-definitive character, a play of unity and difference that endeavoured to render the sovereign (subject) as it was not. This productive opposition is the hinge of reconciliation's power. Occupying a central place in the English-speaking church's rebuttal of apartheid theology, the talks about talks, and the process of constitutional negotiations that extended into the debate over whether to create a truth commission, it betrays how the advocacy and expression of reconciliation's words constituted a politics, a vision of collective life that presupposed and crystallised a faith in the interdependence of human beings. While it may seem ideal if not romantic, this spirit drew much of its power from the all too real threat of civil war, a battle to come at the expense of both past and future and the shadow of which constituted the reason to come to terms. Neither procedure nor system, reconciliation in South Africa was made up as it went along, a fragile (re)turn to the works of words that held the potential for beginnings.

making a present for the future's past

Reconciliation's words were to become more (and perhaps less) than they had been. Nine months after its charge was set into law, the TRC took to the public stage. On 15 April 1996, Archbishop Desmond Tutu opened the first hearings of the TRC's Human Rights Violations Committee with a prayer and then an argument about how the event was designed for "those who would be telling their stories" about the violence of apartheid and dedicated to exposing "the truth of our dark past" in the name of fulfilling the post-amble's call for "national unity and reconciliation". Addressed to a packed crowd in an East London community hall, Tutu's words were themselves an explanation and enactment of reconciliation, a sign of faith in South Africa's capacity to forge a new beginning and a reminder that reconciliation's power did not spring solely from the Commission's undertaking.

In the days that followed, select victims and the family members of those who had suffered gross violations of human rights offered testimony about the terms and meaning of their experiences. Broadcast nationally over television and radio, some of the narratives, along with the TRC's first tentative and awkward steps to create a picture of the past, echoed important aspects of reconciliation's larger history in South Africa. According to Tutu, the Commission's work was a crucial opportunity, a narrow window, a *kairos* in which to begin the work of healing old wounds and moving forward. Evident in its statements and the kinds of questions that its members posed to those who appeared at its first hearings, the Commission was deeply concerned with the problem of how to make with words. In the hearings themselves, the presented stories were cast and interpreted as a means of redressing trauma, exposing truth, reaching collective understanding, providing recognition, and returning dignity. At the same time, the presentations made by victims quickly became an object of concern if not discipline. Were the words working? To what end? As there was not time for a hearing of details, stories soon had to be cut short, altered, and moulded into a form and perhaps even a script that would become more precise as the Commission gathered (methodological) momentum.

Within these emerging limits, the first witnesses set important precedents and reflected on the far from concluded debate over the TRC's creation and potential value. In her testimony, Nyameka Goniwe noted that she "didn't know where to begin, to piece together this story and our story" and voiced scepticism as to whether the Commission could shed any more light on the death of her husband and the other members of the Cradock Four than those previous inquests which had brought only disappointment. On the same day, Beth Savage reflected on the Commission's task, relaying that "I think the idea of speaking out causes healing" and noting that she was willing to "meet that man that threw that grenade in an attitude of forgiveness and hope that he could forgive me too for whatever reason". It would not take long before the Commission would hold up these words as a paradigmatic example of those that it hoped to hear.

Between 1996 and 2003, the TRC carried out its "unique experiment", one that has been widely praised and significantly criticised. Then and now, there remains uncertainty about what was (not) said and (not) heard before the Commission and how these words contributed to the Commission's goals. With several important exceptions, including Antjie Krog's report on the TRC's first years, Philippe Salazar's reading of the amnesty process, and Fiona Ross's study of the testimony that was (and was not) presented to the

HRVC, relatively little attention has been paid to the rhetorical operativity of the speech that was requested and performed in the name of reconciliation. Similarly, the question of how reconciliation was repeatedly defined, contested, and redefined over the course of the TRC's tenure has not been closely scrutinised, particularly as commentators have tended to interpret the meaning of reconciliation through the lens of some of the Commission's other god-terms.

Is reconciliation's (pre-TRC) history relevant to our understanding of the Commission's work and the controversy that it provoked? While a reply to this question rests heavily on extended and immanent study of the TRC's efforts, one that pays particular attention to the ways in which the Commission argued about the nature and performance of reconciliation with public and institutional audiences, I want to close by speculating very briefly about how reconciliation's appearance and practice in the early and middle years of transition may need to figure in the ongoing inquiry into what the TRC endeavoured to accomplish and whether it was able to actualise its vision of a reconciliation that would help South Africa to make a present for the future's past.

Initially, history counsels close attention to how reconciliation was defined within the TRC process. The Commission's legal mandate set reconciliation into a complex field of concepts, defining it through and in relationship to the production of truth, the recovery of human dignity, the accountability wrought by the disclosures of perpetrators, and the need to reconstitute and also displace the terms of individual and collective identity. While this expansive interpretation raises the question of whether the TRC was really all that concerned with reconciliation, it also represents both an extension and a break from the modes of reconciliation that were offered by the church and employed at the constitutional negotiations. On the one hand, the TRC's rendering of reconciliation continued to place a heavy emphasis on its rhetorical quality and power, its potential to explain as well as enact forms of speech that could tropologically turn one kind of human relationship toward another. On the other, the Commission's definition was also an indication that the times had changed and that there was a need to rethink the kinds of conflicts to which reconciliation needed to be directed. In either case, the recollection of reconciliation's historical practice may be a way to better understand controversy over the TRC's definition of reconciliation's "subject", the question of who did and did not "need" to be reconciled and what kinds of work this entailed. Confronted with a concept that had never enjoyed a definitive meaning, the Commission's relative ability to promote reconciliation may have been both supported and confounded by the tension that it encountered between reconciliation's characteristic ambiguity and the need to codify its process and crystallise its product. In turn, this difficulty may open the door to an investigation of an issue that has particular as well as general significance: the question of whether the TRC resolved the meaning of reconciliation by setting it into constellation with the concept of recognition. In other words, the TRC may have resolved the definitional controversy that followed from its mandate by claiming that one rhetorical process of interaction was valuable to the degree that it set the stage for another. The question of which was granted priority, however, remains something of a mystery.[14] Its resolution may demand an inquiry that compares how the TRC spoke of its own purpose with the claims made in Parliament about its political value to the South African public.

Closely related, historical practices of reconciliation both illumine and stress the importance of understanding more about how speech performs reconciliation. With respect to the TRC, this means that there is a need to reflect deeply on the variety of ways in which witnesses spoke before the Commission, contested its discourse norms, and questioned whether the process was more divisive than unifying. Specifically, it may be instructive to discern whether the Commission's view of reconciliation entailed the creation of a productive opposition, or if its hearings placed a premium on mediating disputes, in part through attempts to cast reconciliation as a process of forgiveness. While not exclusive, particularly given the different procedures followed in the Amnesty and Human Rights Violations Committees, the question of how speech yields beginnings may bear directly on the problem of reconciliation's sacrifice: the ways in which its constitutive speech–action calls for the displacement of self-interest; how this gift (or loss) motivates controversy over whether reconciliation degrades the rights afforded by law to (liberal) subjects; and, if unity in difference comes necessarily at the cost of individual and cultural history.

Finally, religious and political calls for reconciliation underscore the need to reflect on the institutionalisation of reconciliation and the legitimacy crises that may follow from it. Just as debates over sufficient consensus were driven by perceptions of exclusion and a sense that reconciliation was being used more to dictate the transition's content than to open channels for its negotiation, the TRC confronted the charge that reconciliation was not a self-evident good and that the Commission had endowed it with a substantive faith. At times declining to engage this issue, citing the dictates of a legal mandate that it had no power to change, the TRC also devoted significant time to justifying the value of its work, an effort that was directed variously to the public, the NGO community, political parties, and other state institutions. This argumentation deserves close scrutiny, particularly as it may illumine a set of announced standards or criteria with which the TRC can be immanently assessed. As important, it may reveal a significant tension between institutional norms of reconciliation and the publicity with which it is justified. In this sense, the TRC's work may show an important resemblance to the calls for reconciliation proffered by the English-speaking churches in the early and mid-1980s.

In the midst of the otherwise troubling film *Long Night's Journey into Day*, there is a poignant moment in which the mother of a former APLA soldier is asked how she feels upon hearing the news that her son has been granted amnesty for a murder committed in the late days of ungovernability. Hinting at the presence of a bad infinity, a movement in which past and future collapse into an indefinite and indeterminate now-time, she replies, "I feel between." The expression is crucial, an indication that within reconciliation's potential to begin the work of becoming new is held the chance that its beginning will not come. Perhaps it is this double quality that (re)presents reconciliation's most important memory, the recollection of the (non)defining contingency that stills history's clamour for progress in the name of entering into relation, an (inter)(ex)change that is never of our own making and which finds the question of the ethical and the political in the transgression of its invention, an offence that calls history back to the stage.

The same point can be made in a different way. In 2001, I asked the TRC's final Chief Executive Officer about how best to assess the definitions and practices of reconciliation in South Africa. Pausing for a moment, he replied, "I cannot give a straight answer" because the matter is "up to history". Will time then (not) tell? As reconciliation's end marks and resembles a beginning, as it asks us to make history and then enter its fold, releasing the capacity for control in the name of constituting relationships, we abide in a middle. In this awkward time and fragile space, reconciliation asks after the faith that may yet abide in the works of words. There is no given reply to the gift of this question and its invitation to set language into play.

Speech about speech gone missing. Words to beckon words. Discourse given to the problem of its own power. For, against, and within history, reconciliation in South Africa is a rhetorical memory made, an active remembering of rhetoric's making, and a remembrance of what rhetoricity may (not) yet make. From the violence of identity's manifold law, the call for reconciliation appeared in a time of shared necessity, a moment in which the paralysis of historical agency prompted the need and desire to speak. With this potential, reconciliation invented. From the opposition between creation and creativity, it both performed and explained the character of speech, a willingness to enter relationships, and an invitation to argue about the ends and means of collective judgment. It, thus, rhetorically (re)constituted the potential for definition, turning the certainty of its violence toward the contingency of its power. Between past and future, this movement spurred and supported deliberation about how best to define and judge the promise of the present. Transcendence is thus the right idea in the wrong way. There is no reconciliation without (self) opposition, a relation that (up)sets the stability of *presence* with the contingency of potential. This is the defining problem. With its words, reconciliation in South Africa inaugurates a dialectic with more than two sides, a power to hold (open) the question of becoming by refusing (but not negating) the endless and silencing despair of emergency. In and for a transition to (be)come, the beginning of reconciliation is the history of an ongoing critique of violence.

notes

introduction

1 For one example, see Desmond Tutu, "Look to the Rock from which you were Hewn," Nelson Mandela Foundation Lecture, 23 November 2004. Also see, Desmond Tutu, *No Future Without Forgiveness* (London: Rider, 1999).

2 Elizabeth Stanley, "Evaluating the Truth and Reconciliation Commission," *Journal of Modern African Studies* 39 (2001), 537.

3 This announced goal appears in the TRC's governing legislation. See Republic of South Africa, *Promotion of National Unity and Reconciliation Act* (No. 34 of 1995).

4 The first to move into the public eye, the Human Rights Violations Committee was tasked to investigate the extent and nature of gross human rights violations between 1960 and 1994 and to hear testimony from their victims, a process that was deemed crucial to restoring "the human and civil dignity" of those subjected to apartheid-era violence. Not unrelated but with significant independence from the rest of the Commission, the Amnesty Committee was mandated to hear and adjudicate amnesty applications from those prepared to make a "full disclosure" of the crimes committed in the name of supporting or ending apartheid, at least insofar as such acts and omissions constituted gross violations of human rights. Less well defined and empowered, the Reparations and Rehabilitation Committee was charged to create recommendations for an effective reparations policy, one that would help "prevent the future violations of human rights" and assist other government bodies dedicated to overcoming apartheid's legacy of material inequality.

5 *Truth and Reconciliation Commission of South Africa Report*. Vol. 1 (Cape Town: Juta, 1999), 49. Hereafter cited as *TRC Final Report*.

6 Quoted in the *TRC Final Report*, Vol. 1, 48. The language is also contained in the post-amble of the 1993 interim constitution of South Africa.

7 Antjie Krog, *Country of My Skull: Guilt, Sorrow and the Limits of Forgiveness in the New South Africa* (New York: Times Books, 1998), 364.

8 Mahmood Mamdani, "A Diminished Truth," in *After the TRC: Reflections on Truth and Reconciliation in South Africa*, eds. Wilmot James and Linda van de Vijver (Cape Town: David Philip, 2000), 60. Also see Mahmood Mamdani, "Reconciliation without Justice," *Southern African Review of Books* 10 (1997): 22–25.

9 Wole Soyinka, *The Burden of Memory, The Muse of Forgiveness* (New York: Oxford University Press, 1999). I have reflected on this debate over the priority of reparation elsewhere. See Erik Doxtader, "The Matter of Words in the Midst of Beginnings: Unraveling the 'Relationship' between Reparations and

Reconciliation," in *To Repair the Irreparable: Reparations and Reconstruction in South Africa*, eds. Erik Doxtader and Charles Villa-Vicencio (Cape Town: David Philip, 2004), 115–48.

10 Anthea Jeffery, *The Truth About the Truth Commission*, (Johannesburg: South African Institute for Race Relations, 1999), 157.

11 For a sense of the range of literature on the TRC, see and compare Kader Asmal, Louise Asmal, and Ronald Roberts, *Reconciliation Through Truth* (Cape Town: David Philip, 1996); Dirkie Smit, "Confession-Guilt-Truth and Forgiveness in the Christian Tradition," in *To Remember and To Heal: Theological and Psychological Reflections on Truth and Reconciliation*, ed. Russel Botman (Cape Town: Human and Rousseau, 1996), 96–117; Njabulo Ndebele, "Memory, Metaphor and the Triumph of Narrative," in *Negotiating the Past: The Making of Memory in South Africa*, ed. Sarah Nuttall (Oxford: Oxford University Press, 1998), 19–28; *Looking Back, Reaching Forward: Reflections on the Truth and Reconciliation Commission of South Africa*, eds. Charles Villa-Vicencio and Wilhelm Verwoerd, (Cape Town: UCT Press, 2000); Andre du Toit, "The Moral Foundations of the South African TRC: Truth as Acknowledgement and Justice as Recognition," in *Truth v. Justice: The Morality of Truth Commissions*, eds. Robert Rotberg and Dennis Thompson (Princeton: Princeton University Press, 2000), 122–40; *Commissioning the Past: Understanding South Africa's Truth and Reconciliation Commission*, eds. Deborah Posel and Graeme Simpson, (Johannesburg: Witwatersrand University Press, 2002); *The Provocations of Amnesty: Memory, Justice and Impunity*, eds. Charles Villa-Vicencio and Erik Doxtader (Cape Town: David Phillip, 2003); Fiona Ross, *Bearing Witness* (Cape Town: Pluto Press, 2003).

12 Johnny de Lange, "The Historical Context, Legal Origins, and Philosophical Foundation of the South African Truth and Reconciliation Commission," in *Looking Back, Reaching Forward*, 14–31.

13 David Mickey Malatsi, *Joint Sitting of Both Houses of Parliament*, 3rd Annual Session–2nd Parliament, 25 February 1999, cols. 117–18.

14 Pumla Gobodo-Madikizela, *A Human Being Died That Night: A Story of Forgiveness* (Cape Town: David Philip, 2003), 148.

15 This conflation has proceeded partly from a view that sets the TRC in isolation from the rest of the transition. Such a relation of distinction is evident in the rather bright line that appears between the vast literatures that address the constitution-making process and the operation of the Commission. At best gesturing to one another, this mutual slight obscures that while the "subject" of reconciliation at the MPNP and the TRC may not have coincided, its "object" was held in common. Compare, for instance, Krog, *Country of My Skull* and Richard Spitz and Matthew Chaskalson, *The Politics of Transition: A Hidden History of South Africa's Negotiated Settlement* (Johannesburg: Witwatersrand University Press, 2000).

16 For a comparative treatment of different truth and reconciliation bodies, see Priscilla Hayner, *Unspeakable Truths: Confronting State Terror and Atrocity* (New York: Routledge, 2001).

17 *TRC Final Report*, Vol. 1, 49–51.

18 I take up the particular variations of this compromise thesis in chapter four, along with discussions of how the idea of ubuntu was used to explain and justify the TRC's work. For an important and broader analysis of the role of compromise

in the transition, see Philippe-Joseph Salazar, "Compromise and Deliberation: A Rhetorical View of South Africa's Democratic Transformation," *Social Science Information* 43 (2004): 145–66.

19 Richard A. Wilson, *The Politics of Truth and Reconciliation in South Africa* (Cambridge: Cambridge University Press, 2001), 99, 97.

20 Quoted in Mark Gevisser, "South Africa's Reconciliation in Motion," *Mail and Guardian* 13–19 May 1994, 9. This comment is not included in the official ANC transcript of Mandela's remarks.

21 John W. de Gruchy, *Reconciliation: Restoring Justice* (Cape Town: David Philip, 2002), 25–26. As de Gruchy suggests, the difficulties are heightened as reconciliation comes loaded with the weight of Christianity and the problem of how to differentiate between a transformative form of love that may well have useful lessons for secular life and a piety that presupposes the facticity of a divine gift.

22 Antjie Krog, "Anticipating a Different Kind of Future," in *Transcending a Century of Injustice*, ed. Charles Villa-Vicencio (Cape Town: Institute for Justice and Reconciliation, 2000), 128.

23 MP Johnny de Lange, Interview with Author, Cape Town, South Africa, 21 June 2000; Theodor Adorno, *Negative Dialectics*, trans. E.B. Ashton (New York: Continuum, 1973), 142.

24 In ancient Greece, for instance, reconciliation was understood as the process of fashioning (civic) friendship from within the midst of discord, a renewal in which the play and exchange of words broke (from) the necessity of law's precedent in order to (re)define the terms and bonds of political order. In the Second Epistle to the Corinthians, Paul claimed that reconciliation's remembrance of faith would bring estranged brothers and sisters into a time in which "The old things [are] passed away; behold! All things have become new!" [This is the literal translation of 2 Corinthians, 5:17, according to Green (*Interlinear Greek-English New Testament*, 3rd Ed., ed. Jay Green (Grand Rapids: Baker Books, 1996)). The *King James Version* of the text inserts "are", an addition that works to resolve the ambiguous sense of agency that appears in the operation of reconciliation].

25 See Erik Doxtader, "Reconciliation – A Rhetorical Concept/ion," The *Quarterly Journal of Speech* 89 (2003): 267–92.

26 G.W.F. Hegel, "The Spirit of Christianity and Its Fate," *On Christianity: Early Theological Writings*, trans. T.M. Knox (New York: Harper, 1948), 182–301.

27 Holding it out as a "rose in the cross of the present", Hegel cast reconciliation as a mode of intersubjective love, a word (*logos*) dedicated to creating and sustaining the "living relation of beings". For a broad, synthetic view of Hegel's notion of reconciliation, see Michael O. Hardimon, *Hegel's Social Philosophy: The Project of Reconciliation* (Cambridge: Cambridge University Press, 1994).

28 Alex Boraine, "A Language of Potential," in *After the TRC: Reflections on Truth and Reconciliation in South Africa*, 80.

29 Aletta Norval, *Deconstructing Apartheid Discourse* (London: Verso, 1996), 2.

30 Reinhart Koselleck, *The Practice of Conceptual History: Timing History and Spacing Concepts* (Palo Alto: Stanford University Press, 2002), 29.

31 Koselleck, *The Practice of Conceptual History*, 25; Hans Blumenberg, *The Legitimacy of the Modern Age*, trans. Robert M. Wallace (Cambridge: MIT Press, 1983), 477.

32 Philippe-Joseph Salazar, *An African Athens: Rhetoric and the Shaping of Democracy in South Africa* (London: Lawrence Erlbaum, 2002).

33 Hannah Arendt, *The Life of the Mind*, (New York: Harcourt Brace Jovanovich, 1978), 34; Hannah Arendt, *On Revolution* (New York: Viking Press, 1965), 175. For a more expansive view, see Thomas Farrell, *Norms of Rhetorical Culture* (New Haven: Yale University Press, 1993).

34 For an important account of how rhetoric may serve to interrupt and displace the experience of time, see Hans Blumenberg, "An Anthropological Approach to the Contemporary Significance of Rhetoric," in *After Philosophy? End or Transformation*, ed. Kenneth Baynes, James Bohman, and Thomas McCarthy, trans. Robert M. Wallace (Cambridge: The MIT Press, 1987), 438.

35 Put this way, the task resembles what some have called a "rhetorical history", a concept that I have considered in relation to one aspect of the South African religious debate over reconciliation. See Erik Doxtader, "In the Name of Reconciliation: The Faith and Works of Counterpublicity," in *Counterpublics and the State*, eds. Robert Asen and Daniel Brower (Albany: SUNY Press, 2001), 59–85.

36 Hans-Georg Gadamer, *Truth and Method*, 2nd ed. (New York: Continuum, 1994).

37 Respectively, see Paul Rabinow, *Anthropos Today: Reflections on Modern Equipment* (Princeton: Princeton University Press, 2003); Michel De Certeau, *The Writing of History*, trans. Tom Conley (New York: Columbia University Press, 1988), 33.

38 Ludwig Wittgenstein, *Philosophical Investigations*, trans. G.E. Anscombe (n.d.), 14–43; Ludwig Wittgenstein, *The Blue and the Brown Books* (New York: Harper Torchbooks, 1960), 25–30.

39 Here, I follow Foucault's sense of problematisation. See Michel Foucault, *The Archaeology of Knowledge*, trans. A.M. Smith (New York: Pantheon, 1972).

chapter 1

1 These elements of a state of emergency are developed more fully in Giorgio Agamben's work on the origins and development of sovereignty. Drawing from Schmitt, Agamben holds that a state of emergency constitutes a zone of indistinction, a relation of the ban that constitutes the conditions for the appearance of the sovereign. (See Giorigio Agamben, *Homo Sacer: Sovereign Power and Bare Life*, trans. Daniel Heller Roazen (Palo Alto: Stanford University Press, 1998), 1–30). Of particular interest, this exception to the law rests on the creation of a potential (*dunamis*) in which the promise of "life to come" justifies the violence of law. There is a substantial literature that addresses this dynamic in the South African context. See Ian Liebenberg, "Government by Illusion: The Legacy and Its Implications," in *The Hidden Hand: Covert Operations in South Africa*, ed. A. Minnear (Pretoria: Human Sciences Research Council, 1994), 25–41; Nicholas Haysom, "International Human Rights Norms and States of Emergency," in *Developments in Emergency Law*, ed. N. Haysom (Johannesburg: Centre for Applied Legal Studies, 1989), 1–24; Geoff Budlender, "Law and Lawlessness in South Africa," *South African Journal on Human Rights* 4 (1992): 139–52.

2 For one account, see Ruth First, *117 Days* (London: Bloomsbury, 1965).

3 The name of the river was the Ncome. Later, the date of the battle was celebrated as the Day of the Vow or the Day of the Covenant. In 1961, the ANC used the

day to announce the formation of its armed branch, Umkhonto we Sizwe. After the 1994 election, 16 December was designated the Day of National Unity and Reconciliation. Thompson offers an important reading of the myth of the battle and how it factored into the rise of Afrikaner nationalism. See Leonard Thompson, *The Political Mythology of Apartheid* (New Haven: Yale University Press, 1985), 144–88.

4   Robert Price, *The Apartheid State in Crisis, 1975–1990* (New York: Oxford University Press, 1991), 191; Tristan Borer, *Challenging the State: Churches as Political Actors in South Africa* (Notre Dame: Notre Dame University Press, 1998), 51.

5   Tom Lodge, *All Here, and Now: Black Politics in South Africa in the 1980s* (Cape Town: David Philip, 1991), 29; South African Institute of Race Relations, *Race Relations Survey 1985* (Pretoria: South African Institute of Race Relations, 1986), 40; For a history of the UDF, see Jeremy Seekings, *The UDF: A History of the United Democratic Front in South Africa, 1983–1991* (London: James Currey, 2000). While hailed by the state as a significant reform, the 1983 Constitution was a lightning rod for opposition as its expansion of political representation in Parliament was limited to the creation of a House of Delegates for those classified as Indian and a House of Representatives for the coloured population.

6   Lodge, *All Here*, 197.

7   South African Institute of Race Relations, *Race Relations Survey 1985*, 421. For a similar but more systematic reading of the period, see Price, *Apartheid State*, 192.

8   For one account of these internal rifts, see Ed Benard and Mwezi Twala, *Mbokodo: Inside MK – Mwezi Twala. A Soldier's Story* (Johannesburg: Jonathan Ball Publishers, 1994).

9   Lodge, *All Here*, 181. John Battersby, "ANC Seeks Revenge for SADF Raid," *Cape Times*, 2 July 1985, 11.

10   P.W. Botha, *Debates of Parliament* (Hansard), 2nd Session–8th Parliament, 19 June 1985, col. 8113.

11   Botha, *Debates*, col. 8105.

12   Anthony Johnson, "HSRC declares apartheid bankrupt," *Cape Times*, 3 July 1985, 1.

13   Editorial, "A Black Perspective," *Cape Times*, 1 July 1985, 10.

14   NA, "UDF men's bodies found," *Cape Times*, 1 July 1985, 1.

15   For an extended treatment of the investigation, see Christopher Nicholson, *Permanent Removal: Who Killed the Cradock Four?* (Johannesburg: Witwatersrand University Press, 2004).

16   Philip Frankel, *An Ordinary Atrocity: Sharpeville and Its Massacre* (Johannesburg: Witwatersrand University Press, 2001).

17   Quoted in South African Institute of Race Relations, *Race Relations Survey 1985*, 456.

18   Kogila Moodley, "African Renaissance and Language Policies in Comparative Perspective," *Politikon* 27 (2000), 3; Liebenberg, "Government by Illusion."

19   Emphasis added. Editorial, "The State of Emergency," *Sechaba*, August 1995, 2.

20   The "Rubicon speech" has been well and thoroughly analysed. For a transcript of the text, see P.W. Botha, "Address by State President P.W. Botha," reprinted in *Adapt or Die: The End of White Politics in South Africa*, ed. Robert Schrire (London: Hurst & Company, 1991), 147–53.

21   Borer, *Challenging the State*, 121.

22   For discussions of South Africa's early colonial history, see T.R.H. Davenport,

South Africa: A Modern History (New York: Macmillan Press, 1977); Hermann Giliomee, *The Afrikaners: Biography of a People* (Cape Town: Tafelberg, 2003); Richard Elphick, *Kraal and Castle: Khoikhoi and the Founding of White South Africa* (Cape Town: Human & Rousseau, 1999); *The Shaping of South African Society, 1652–1840*, eds. Richard Elphick and Hermann Giliomee (Middletown, Conn.: Wesleyan University Press, 1989).

23 Allister Sparks, *The Mind of South Africa* (London: Mandarin, 1991), 30. For a more detailed history of early colonial religion, see Jonathan Gerstner, *The Thousand Generation Covenant: Dutch Reformed Theology and Group Identity in Colonial South Africa, 1652–1814* (Leiden: Brill, 1991).

24 For accounts of the Great Trek, see Giliomee, *The Afrikaners*, 145–70; Thompson, *Political Mythology*, 144–88.

25 Beyond what I can provide here, there is interesting work to be done on the ways in which reconciliation was used in the aftermath of the war and its relationship to controversy over language politics. See, for instance, W.K. Hancock, *Smuts: The Sanguine Years, 1870–1919* (Cambridge: Cambridge University Press, 1962), 230–45; Davenport, *South Africa*,174; Dunbar Moodie, *The Rise of Afrikanerdom: Power, Apartheid and the Afrikaner Civil Religion* (Berkeley: University of California Press, 1975), 73–76; Giliomee, *The Afrikaners*, 357.

26 For an analysis of early debates over the design and implementation of segregation policy, see Saul Dubow, *Racial Segregation and the Origins of Apartheid in South Africa* (New York: St. Martins Press, 1989), 21–74.

27 Dubow, *Racial Segregation*, 28, 131.

28 Susan Ritner, *Salvation through Separation: the Role of the Dutch Reformed Church in South Africa in the Formulation of Afrikaner Race Ideology* (PhD Diss., Columbia University, 1974), 114.

29 Thompson, *Political Mythology*, 5; Dubow, *Racial Segregation*, 177.

30 Aletta Norval, *Deconstructing Apartheid Discourse* (London: Verso, 1996), 30–31. Although the concept of "race" was still quite unstable at the time, Norval claims that the development of this "new subjectivity" had much to do with the work of the *South African Native Affairs Commission*, a body that sought to devise "organisational principles capable of unifying the structure of administration dealing with the African population in order to bring an end to the differential treatment of Africans in the different territories". For an extended treatment of this discourse, see Adam Ashforth, *The Politics of Official Discourse in Twentieth Century South Africa* (New York: Oxford University Press, 1990).

31 Johan Degenaar, "The Myth of the South African Nation," *IDASA Occasional Paper* (Cape Town: IDASA, 1992), 6. For a longer discussion, see Johan Degenaar, "Philosophical Roots of Nationalism," in *Church and Nationalism in South Africa*, ed. Theo Sundermeier (Johannesburg: Ravan Press, 1975), 12–39.

32 Norval, *Deconstructing*, 52.

33 There is an expansive literature on the causes and forms of nationalism. Among others, see Daniel O'Meara, *Volkskapitalisme: Class, Capital and Ideology in the Development of Afrikaner Nationalism, 1934–1948* (Johannesburg: Ravan, 1983); Moodie, *The Rise of Afrikanerdom*; Giliomee, *The Afrikaners*, 447–86; *The Politics of Race, Class and Nationalism in Twentieth Century South Africa*, eds. Shula Marks and Stanley Trapido (London: Longman, 1987); Saul Dubow, "Afrikaner Nationalism,

Apartheid and the Conceptualisation of 'Race'," *Journal of African History* 33 (1992): 20–237; Charles Bloomberg, *Christian Nationalism and the Rise of the Afrikaner Broederbond* (London: Macmillan, 1990).

34 Degenaar, "Myth," 3.

35 Moodie, *The Rise of Afrikanerdom*, 239. For a larger discussion of the language movement, see Isabel Hofmeyr, "Building a Nation from Words: Afrikaans Language, Literature, and Ethnic Identity, 1902–24" in *The Politics of Race*, 95–123.

36 Norval, *Deconstructing*, 16.

37 Quoted in Moodie, *The Rise of Afrikanerdom*, 47.

38 Johann Kinghorn, "Social Cosmology, Religion and Afrikaner Ethnicity," *Journal of Southern African Studies* 20 (1994), 403.

39 Johann Kinghorn, "Modernization and Apartheid: The Afrikaner Churches," in *Christianity in South Africa: A Political Social and Cultural History*, ed. Richard Elphick (Berkeley: University of California Press, 1997), 139; For a report on the matter that received substantial attention, see Carnegie Commission of Investigation on the Poor White Question in South Africa, *The Poor White Problem in South Africa: A Report* (Stellenbosch: Pro-Ecclesia Drukkery, 1932).

40 Moodie argues that Malan conceptualised the dilemmas of poverty, unemployment and urbanisation as the "second Blood River" (Moodie, *The Rise of Afrikanerdom*, 247). The issue was central in 1929 and the so-called "black peril" election (see Dubow, *Racial Segregation*, 142). In his post-apartheid autobiography, F.W. de Klerk did little to back down from the terms of this perceived threat, arguing that nationalism was spurred partly by a fear that "our people would be swamped by the black majority – and that this would inevitably lead to the extinction of our own hard-won right to national self-determination". (F.W. de Klerk, *The Last Trek – A New Beginning, The Autobiography* (New York: Macmillan, 1998), 18).

41 D.F. Malan, quoted in Moodie, *The Rise of Afrikanerdom*, 248.

42 Daniel O'Meara, *Forty Lost Years: The Apartheid State and the Politics of the National Party, 1948–1994* (Johannesburg: Ravan Press, 1996), 41.

43 O'Meara, *Forty Lost Years*, 41.

44 Quoted in Moodie, *The Rise of Afrikanerdom*, 250.

45 O'Meara argues that the concept of apartheid existed largely on paper, a subject of intellectual debate that did little to engage or provoke the "broad mass of Afrikaans speakers". As a slogan, he maintains that apartheid offered voters a way to direct their fear of black urbanisation but did not constitute a coherent system or resolve deep ideological disputes within the National Party, especially the problem of how to square the desire for political segregation with the reality of economic interdependence (O'Meara, *Forty Lost Years*, 41–42, 65). Deborah Posel argues that there was no "grand plan" for apartheid but that it took shape in a series of "uncertainties, conflicts, and failures, and deviations" (Deborah Posel, *The Making of Apartheid, 1948–1961: Conflict and Compromise* (Oxford: Clarendon Press, 1991), 5). Also see *Apartheid's Genesis, 1935–1962*, eds. Philip Bonner, et al. (Johannesburg: Ravan Press, 1993); Harold Wolpe, *Race, Class and the Apartheid State* (London: James Currey, 1988); *Apartheid: A Documentary Study of Modern South Africa*, ed. Edgar Brooks (London: Routledge & Kegan Paul, 1968).

46 Norval, *Deconstructing*, 103; Willem de Klerk quoted in Posel, *The Making of Apartheid*, 2.

47 D.F. Malan, Quoted in O'Meara, *Forty Lost Years*, 67.

48 D. Hobart Houghton, *The Tomlinson Report: A Summary of the Findings and Recommendations of the Tomlinson Commission* (Johannesburg: South African Institute of Race Relations, 1956), 12.

49 Achille Mbembe, "African Modes of Self-Writing," *Public Culture* 14 (2002), 247.

50 For a fuller treatment of this exclusion, see V.A. February, *Mind Your Colour: The "Coloured" Stereotype in South African Literature* (London: Kegan Paul, 1981).

51 Geoffrey Bowker and Susan Star, *Sorting Things Out: Classification and Its Consequences* (Cambridge: MIT Press, 1999), 195–225.

52 Oliver Tambo, "Speech Delivered at Georgetown University," reprinted in *Mandela, Tambo and the African National Congress: The Struggle Against Apartheid, 1948–1990*, ed. Sheridan Johns (New York: Oxford University Press, 1991), 262.

53 Here, the definition of the subject on the grounds of race does not exclude class-based accounts of apartheid's development. Indeed, material questions sat behind the legislation, and the Act itself was clearly a means of designing an economic system that could exploit black labour.

54 Morris Szeftel, "Ethnicity and Democratization in South Africa," *Review of Political Economy* 60 (1994), 193; O'Meara, *Forty Lost Years*, 73.

55 The South African NGK was formed in 1652 in the Cape. The smaller and more conservative NHK (Nederduitsch Hervormde Kerk) was established in the Transvaal in 1855. More conservative still, the GK (Gereformeerde Kerk) practises a strict orthodox Calvinism. Established for those classified as "coloured", the NGSK (Nederduitse Gereformeerde Sendingkerk – Dutch Reformed Missionary Church) was founded in 1881.

56 For a broad outline of this support, see Johann Kinghorn, "The Theology of Separate Equality: A Critical Outline of the DRC's Position on Apartheid," in *Christianity Amidst Apartheid*, ed. Martin Prozesky (New York: St. Martins, 1990), 57–80. For a discussion of South African NGK theology in the late 19th and early 20th centuries, see Gerstner, *The Thousand Generation Covenant*.

57 NGK, General Synod, *Human Relations and the South African Scene in Light of Scripture* (Cape Town: Dutch Reformed Church Publishers, 1974), 5.

58 The relative strength of these influences is a matter of ongoing debate. See Moodie, *The Rise of Afrikanerdom*, 146–74; Andre du Toit, "The Problem of Intellectual History in (post)colonial Societies: The Case of South Africa," *Politikon* 18 (1991): 5–25; Nic Rhoodie, *Apartheid: A Socio-Historical Exposition of the Origin and Development of the Apartheid Idea* (Cape Town: HAUM, 1959). Dubow's work documents the rather uneven development of church policy on race relations, particularly in the period leading up to the Nationalist's victory in 1948 (Dubow, "Afrikaner Nationalism," 211–14, 231).

59 There is a significant literature on the church's role in the development and operation of the state. See Kinghorn, "Modernization and Apartheid," 144. A significant aspect of this involvement, one that was criticised directly in the *Kairos Document*, was the state's appeal to Romans 13 as a way of maintaining that citizens had an obligation to respect and support the edicts of government. See Jan Botha, "Creation of New Meaning: Rhetorical Situations and the Reception of Romans 13:1–7," *Journal of Theology for Southern Africa* 79 (1992): 24–37; John de Gruchy, *The Church in Struggle in South Africa*, (Grand Rapids: Eerdmans, 1986), 218.

60 All citations are drawn from the NGK's official English translation. For background on the NGK's debates over the idea and practice of apartheid, see J.A. Loubser, *The Apartheid Bible: A Critical Review of Racial Theology in South Africa* (Cape Town: Maskew Miller Longman, 1987); Dubow, "Afrikaner Nationalism," 217.

61 NGK, *Human Relations*, 70–71.

62 Christian Council of South Africa, *Race: What does the Bible Say?* (Roodeport: Christian Council of South Africa, 1952), 13. NGK theology is not gender neutral. Here, I will neither correct nor mark such usage. The former strategy (s/he) can degrade the motivation and obscure the evidentiary basis for critique. While popular, the latter approach is a banal compensatory gain that purports to represent individuals who may well not have been represented in the first place. In other words, the approach begs the more basic question of whether the exclusionary language was used historically both to prohibit and to instigate challenges to institutional doctrine and pervasive sexism.

63 Loubser, *Apartheid Bible*, 24.

64 Loubser, *Apartheid Bible*, 60.

65 Opposition to liberal political theory and communism was fierce within the circles that helped forge the terms of Afrikaner nationalism. In 1947, the NGK's report *Kerk en Stad (Church and City)* blamed liberal capitalism and democracy for a variety of social ills, not the least of which being the spiritual and material impoverishment of the people. What's more, the "equalisation" promised by both liberalism and communism encouraged the "admixture of the races", a development that portended a "regress to Babel" and the weakening of obligation to Afrikaner "ideals, language, and religion". Respectively, see Kinghorn, "Social Cosmology," 399; Kinghorn, "Modernization," 140.

66 Bloomberg, *Christian Nationalism*, 16.

67 Loubser, *Apartheid Bible*, 56.

68 Quoted in Kinghorn, "Social Cosmology," 399.

69 NGK, *Human Relations*, 18.

70 There is an ongoing debate over whether and how the NGK misinterpreted Kuyper's theology. For instance, see Herman Giliomee, "The Dutch Reformed Church and Chosen People: The Dynamics of the Rise and Decline of Apartheid," (Unpublished Paper, 2003); G. Schutte, "The Netherlands: Cradle of Apartheid?" *Ethnic and Racial Studies* 10 (1987): 392–414.

71 Kuyper quoted in Loubser, *Apartheid Bible*, 40. Moodie traces the ways in which Kuyper's original set of spheres were challenged and revised in the South African context. He also plots how the spheres idea was contested on the grounds that it compromised the "evangelical" mission of the church and the ways in which the spheres were then altered, connected to the imperatives of nation and people. See Moodie, *The Rise of Afrikanerdom*, 54–70.

72 L.J. du Plessis quoted in Loubser, *Apartheid Bible*, 36.

73 Kinghorn, "Modernization," 142.

74 In their respective analyses, Moodie and Loubser go a step further, arguing that the ordained spheres offered a concrete rationale for apartheid, an explanation of how separate development was used to explain the potential of individual, communal and national life.

75 NGK, *Human Relations*, 65.

76 NGK, *Human Relations*, 32.
77 In the mid-1990s, this distinction was an apparent feature of church submissions to the TRC. See "Faith Communities and Apartheid: The RICSA Report," in *Facing the Truth: South African Faith Communities and the Truth and Reconciliation Commission*, ed. John de Gruchy (Cape Town: David Philip, 1999), 37.
78 NGK, *Human Relations*, 34.
79 NGK, *Human Relations*, 64.
80 NGK, *Human Relations*, 63.
81 de Gruchy, *Church in Struggle*, 203.
82 The phrase is Derrida's. See Jacques Derrida, "From a Restricted to General Economy: A Hegelianism without Reserve," in *Writing and Difference*, trans. Alan Bass (Chicago: University of Chicago Press, 1978), 261.
83 Janet Hodgson, "A Battle for Sacred Power: Christian Beginnings Among the Xhosa," in *Christianity in South Africa*, 68.
84 Cuthbertson quoted in Charles Villa-Vicencio, *Theology and Violence; The South African Debate* (Grand Rapids: Eerdmans, 1988), 21. For a discussion of the English-speaking churches, see James Cochrane, *Servants of Power: The Role of the English-Speaking Churches, 1903–1930* (Johannesburg: Ravan, 1987).
85 John de Gruchy, "Grappling with A Colonial Heritage: The English-Speaking Churches Under Imperialism and Apartheid," in *Christianity in South Africa*, 157.
86 Greg Cuthbertson, ed. *Frontiers of African Christianity: Essays in Honour of Inus Daneel* (Pretoria: University of South Africa, 2003); Allan Anderson, *Zion and Pentecost: The Spirituality and Experience of Pentecostal and Zionist Apostolic Churches in South Africa* (Pretoria: University of South Africa Press, 2000).
87 Johann Kinghorn, "The Churches against Apartheid," in *The Long March: The Story of the Struggle for Liberation in South Africa*, ed. Ian Liebenberg (Pretoria: HAUM, 1994), 149. Indeed, there is a long line of criticism that casts the church's declarations as complicit, paternalistic, and hypocritical. See Peter Walshe, "Christianity and the Anti-Apartheid Struggle: The Prophetic Voice within Divided Churches," in *Christianity in South Africa*, 383–99.
88 Christian Council of South Africa, *Race*, 27.
89 Christian Council of South Africa, *Race*, 19–20.
90 Christian Council of South Africa, *Race*, 28.
91 Majorie Hope and James Young, *The South African Churches in a Revolutionary Situation* (Maryknoll, NY: Orbis, 1981); Patrick Noonan, *They're Burning the Churches* (Bellvue: Jacana, 2003).
92 In this regard, compare de Gruchy, "Grappling," 162 and Kinghorn, "Modernization," 150.
93 *The Cottesloe Consultation*, reprinted in *Apartheid is a Heresy*, eds. John de Gruchy and Charles Villa-Vicencio (Cape Town: David Philip, 1983), 150.
94 *Cottesloe Consultation*, 151.
95 de Gruchy, "Grappling," 162.
96 According to John de Gruchy, this mandated withdrawal was the beginning of the NGK's isolation from the larger South African religious community. See John de Gruchy, "From Cottelsoe to Rustenburg and Beyond," *Journal of Theology for Southern Africa* 74 (1991), 29.
97 In particular, a group of Dutch Reformed theologians issued a volume entitled

Delayed Action! In it, they rejected their church's case for apartheid, an argument which led to calls for their expulsion. See A.S. Geyser, et al, *Delayed Action!* (Pretoria: Craft Press, 1961). In contrast, others were consolidating the NGK's case and aligning it more closely with state policy. See, for instance, A.B. du Preez, *Inside the South African Crucible* (Pretoria: HAUM, 1959).

98   For a history of the Institute, see Peter Walshe, *Church versus State in South Africa* (London: C. Hurst, 1983).

99   Rudolph Meyer and Beyers Naudé, "The Christian Institute of South Africa: A Short History of a Quest for Christian Liberation," in *The Long March*, 165–68. This proved to be an important argument, a signal of an activist commitment in the making, and a form of opposition that would have teeth sufficient enough for the state to harass and then finally ban the Institute in 1977.

100 Appearing at a time when a number of church groups were revising the terms of their opposition to the South African state, the text deserves close scrutiny, particularly for the way in which its opposition to state policy is carried by both a (re)definition and a call for reconciliation. In particular, see Borer's account of the 1968 meeting of the World Council of Churches, a meeting at which delegates rallied against the idea that it was enough for the church to fight apartheid through the occasional release of pastoral letters (Borer, *Challenging*, 153).

101 This position generated substantial debate on the nature of heresy. See Charles Villa-Vicencio, *Civil Disobedience and Beyond: Law, Resistance, and Religion in South Africa* (Grand Rapids: Eerdmans, 1990), 114; John de Gruchy, "Towards a Confessing Church," in *Apartheid is a Heresy*, 81–83.

102 South African Council of Churches, *Message to the People of South Africa*, reprinted in *Apartheid is a Heresy*, 156.

103 SACC, *Message to the People of South Africa*, 158.

104 For a discussion of the state of the ANC in the early 70s, see Stephen Davis, *Apartheid's Rebels: Inside South Africa's Hidden War* (New Haven: Yale University Press, 1987).

105 Such activism demanded "social analysis", a practical hermeneutics that unearthed the hidden experience of suffering and the structural causes of injustice. Then a professor of Religious Studies at the University of Cape Town, Charles Villa-Vicencio argued later that theology needed to address the "present needs of a particular society" and work retroactively to "correct the causes of previous suffering and conflict" (Charles Villa-Vicencio, *A Theology of Reconstruction: Nation-Building and Human Rights* (Cambridge: Cambridge University Press, 1992), 39–41). Also see Villa-Vicencio, *Civil Disobedience*, 140; Borer, *Challenging*, 7; James Cochrane, "War, Remembrance and Reconstruction," *Journal of Theology for Southern Africa* 84 (1993), 26, 39; Peter Walshe, *Prophetic Christianity and the Liberation Movement in South Africa* (Pietermaritzburg: Cluster, 1995), 43–61.

106 Albert Nolan, "Theology in a Prophetic Mode," in *Hammering Swords into Ploughshares: Essays in Honour of Archbishop Mpilo Desmond Tutu*, ed. B. Tlhagale (Johannesburg: Skotaville Publishers, 1986), 138.

107 For a discussion of the Soweto uprising, see P.L. Bonner, *Soweto: A History* (London: Maskew Miller Longman, 1998).

108 Lutheran World Federation, *Southern Africa: Confessional Integrity*, 1977. Reprinted in *Apartheid is a Heresy*, 160–61.

109 Martin Schloemann, "The Special Case for Confessing: Reflections on the Casus Confessionis in the Light of History and Systematic Theology," in *The Debate on Status Confessionis: Studies in Christian Political Theology*, ed. Eckehart Lorennz (Geneva: Lutheran World Federation, 1983), 52.

110 Both, however, were restrictions of freedom, one in the name of creating relations in the midst of *stasis*, the other a form of law that sought *status* through their containment and foreclosure.

111 Schloemann, "The Special Case for Confessing," 66.

112 Schloemann, "The Special Case for Confessing," 130.

113 Schloemann, "The Special Case for Confessing," 125.

114 Schloemann, "The Special Case for Confessing," 88.

115 Schloemann, "The Special Case for Confessing," 35.

116 There is a large literature on the development and varying terms of Black Theology, including the differences between its American and South African forms. For instance, see Itumeleng Mosala, *Biblical Hermeneutics and Black Theology in South Africa* (Grand Rapids: Eerdmans, 1989); *Essays on Black Theology*, ed. Mokgethi Motlhabi (Johannesburg: University Christian Movement, 1973).

117 Nyameko Pityana, "What is Black Consciousness?" in *The Challenge of Black Theology in South Africa*, ed. Basil Moore (Atlanta: John Knox, 1974), 60; Also see Steve Biko, *I Write What I Like: A Selection of His Writings* (London: Bowerdean, 1978); Dwight Hopkins, "Steve Biko, Black Consciousness and Black Theology," in *Bounds of Possibility: The Legacy of Steve Biko and Black Consciousness*, eds. N. Barney Pityana, et al. (Cape Town: David Philip, 1991), 194–200. For a range of essays addressed to the terms and principles of Black Consciousness, see *From Protest to Challenge: A Documentary History of African Politics in South Africa, 1882–1990*, Vol. 5, eds. Thomas Karis and Gwendolen M. Carter. (Bloomington: Indiana University Press), 458–88.

118 Pityana, "Black Consciousness," 60.

119 Pityana, "Black Consciousness," 60–61.

120 Steve Biko, "Black Consciousness and the Quest for a True Humanity," in *Challenge of Black Theology*, 41.

121 Biko, "Quest," 39.

122 Biko, "Quest," 45.

123 For a historical account of this call to critique, see Walshe, "Christianity and the Anti-Apartheid Struggle," 390.

124 Louise Kretzchmar, *The Voice of Black Theology in South Africa* (Johannesburg: Ravan, 1986).

125 See Allan Boesak, *Farewell to Innocence: A Social-Ethical Study of Black Theology and Black Power* (Johannesburg: Ravan Press, 1976), 18, 120.

126 Boesak, *Farewell to Innocence*, 27.

127 Boesak, *Farewell to Innocence*, 75, 106–7.

128 Boesak, *Farewell to Innocence*, 119.

129 Allan Boesak, "He Made Us All, But ...," in *Apartheid is a Heresy*, 3.

130 Boesak, "He Made Us," 4.

131 Nederduitsch Hervormde Kerk, "Statement on the WARC decision," 1982. Reprinted in *Apartheid is a Heresy*, 174.

132 Synod of the Dutch Reformed Mission Church, *Belhar Confession*, 1986. Reprinted

at <www.vgksa.org.za/confessions/belhar_confession.htm> (November 2003).

133 Nederduitse Gereformeerde Sendingkerk, *A Statement on Apartheid and a Confession of Faith*, 1982. Reprinted in *Apartheid is a Heresy*, 175–77.

134 For treatments of ubuntu and its various philosophical, cultural, and political meanings, see Mogobe Ramose, "The Philosophy of Ubuntu and Ubuntu as a Philosophy," in *Philosophy From Africa*, 2nd Ed., eds. P.H. Coetzee and A.P.J. Roux (Oxford: Oxford University Press, 2002), 230–38; Kwasi Wiredu, "Democracy and Consensus in African Traditional Politics: A Plea for Non-party Polity," in *Postcolonial African Philosophy: A Critical Reader*, ed. Emmanuel Chukwudi Eze (London: Blackwell, 1997), 303–12; Augustine Shutte, *Ubuntu: An Ethic for a New South Africa* (Pietermaritzburg: Cluster Publications, 2001); Johann Broodryk, *Ubuntu: Life Lessons From Africa* (Pretoria: Ubuntu School of Philosophy, 2002).

135 Bonganjalo Gobo, "Corporate Personality: Ancient Israel and Africa," in *The Challenge of Black Theology*, 67.

136 Gobo, "Corporate Personality," 69.

137 Desmond Tutu, Interview with Author, Cape Town, 23 August 2001.

138 It has been claimed that Tutu has an "ubuntu theology" of reconciliation. While the claim is a bit thin, see Michael Battle, *Reconciliation: The Ubuntu Theology of Desmond Tutu* (Cleveland: Pilgrim Press, 1997).

139 Philippe Salazar's reading of Tutu's role in the struggle and appearance before the Eloff Commission is essential to understanding the Archbishop's role in the struggle and his understanding of nation-building. See Philippe-Joseph Salazar, *An African Athens: Rhetoric and the Shaping of Democracy in South Africa* (London: Lawrence Erlbaum Associates, 2002), 1–17.

140 Desmond Tutu, "Apartheid is Heresy," in *Apartheid is a Heresy*, 39–47.

141 Tutu, "Apartheid is Heresy," 44.

142 Battle, *Reconciliation*, 42, 59.

143 Desmond Tutu quoted in Battle, *Reconciliation*, 42.

144 Editorial, "Liberation or Reconciliation?" *Pro Veritate* (July 1974), 1.

145 "Liberation or Reconciliation," 1.

146 See Stephen Ellis, "The Historical Significance of South Africa's Third Force," *Journal of Southern African Studies* 24 (June 1998), 269.

147 Borer, *Challenging*, 79; Villa-Vicencio, *Civil Disobedience*, viii.

148 South African Council of Churches, "Prayers for the End to Unjust Rule," *Journal of Theology for Southern Africa* 52 (1985), 56–71.

149 South African Catholic Bishops' Conference, "The Bishops' Statement on the Day of Mourning and Prayer," *Journal of Theology for Southern Africa* 52 (1985), 69.

150 de Gruchy, "Grappling," 169.

151 de Gruchy, "Grappling," 168.

152 Borer, *Challenging*, 183. For extended discussion of this neutral perspective, see Anthony Balcomb, *Third Way Theology: Reconciliation, Revolution and Reform in the South African Churches During the 1980s*, (Pietermaritzburg: Cluster, 1993).

153 Frank Chikane quoted in Villa-Vicencio, *Civil Disobedience*, 100.

154 de Gruchy, *Church in Struggle*, 277.

155 Villa-Vicencio, *Civil Disobedience*, 143.

156 The NIR was launched by African Enterprise, an organisation that some have

characterised as evangelical. Its declared interest was the promotion of a "third way" theology, a position that turned on the question of whether South African churches had an obligation to remain neutral in order to facilitate an end to the conflict between the state and the liberation movements. For the precise terms of the Initiative, see Klaus Nürnberger, *The Cost of Reconciliation in South Africa* (Cape Town: Methodist Publishing House, 1988). The full text of the NIR *Statement of Affirmation* was published in the *Journal of Theology for Southern Africa* 54 (March, 1986).

157 Villa-Vicencio has maintained that the group was concerned to clarify why and how the church could work against a state that had become "an enemy of the common good" (Villa-Vicencio, *Civil Disobedience*, 103). In the end, 156 individuals signed the document. A number of prominent names were missing, including Desmond Tutu's (Borer, *Challenging*, 244). While the South African Council of Churches did not adopt the *Kairos Document*, the organisation lent its public support to its call. For a discussion of the document's background, see Albert Nolan, "Kairos Theology," in *Doing Theology in Context*, eds. John de Gruchy and Charles Villa-Vicencio (Cape Town: David Philip, 1994), 212–18; John de Gruchy, *Democracy and the State – IDASA Occasional Paper #5* (Cape Town: IDASA, nd.), 7.

158 Charles Villa-Vicencio, Interview with Author, Cape Town, October 1999.

159 For the reactions to the *Kairos Document* that followed its publication, see Borer, *Challenging*, 121; "The Kairos Debate," *Journal of Theology in Southern Africa* 55 (1986), 42–57; Peter Beyerhaus, *The Kairos Document: Challenge or Danger to the Church?* (Cape Town: Gospel Defence League, 1987).

160 Bernard Connor, *The Difficult Traverse* (Pietermaritzburg: Cluster, 1998), 74.

161 I have developed this notion of *ethos* elsewhere. See Erik Doxtader, "Characters in the Middle of Public Life: Consensus, Dissent, and *Ethos*," *Philosophy and Rhetoric* 33 (2000): 336–69.

162 Based on a series of seminars delivered at the University of California, Berkeley in the Fall of 1999 and a set of conversations, I am indebted to Giorgio Agamben for his views on *kairos* and the dynamics of messianic time.

163 The key point is not that confession fiats harmony. Rather, it is an opportunity to supplant a desire to negate the Other with the concession that one is bound to one's enemy by an opposition. This acknowledgement of a shared difference is the potential for dialogue, not its culmination. For two very important essays on how the language of confession affords opportunities for individuals to invent the basis for dialogue, see Benjamin Sax, "Active Individuality and the Language of Confession: The Figure of the Beautiful Soul in the *Lehrjahe* and the *Phanomenologie*," *Journal of the History of Philosophy* 21 (1993), 437–66; J.B. Bernstein, "Confession and Forgiveness: Hegel's Poetics of Action," in *Beyond Representation: Philosophy and Poetic Imagination*, ed. Richard Eldridge (Cambridge: Cambridge University Press, 1996), 34–65.

164 NA, "117 More Detained in South Africa," *Cape Times*, 4 January 1986, 3.

165 Agamben, *Homer Sacer*, 17.

166 Lester Ruiz, "Theology, Politics, and the Discourses of Transformation," *Alternatives* 13 (1988), 167.

167 Paul Lederach, quoted in Noel Chicuecue, "Reconciliation: The Role of Truth

Commissions and Alternative Ways of Healing," *Development in Practice* 7 (1997), 484.

168 See Alex Boraine, "A Language of Potential," in *After the TRC: Reflections on Truth and Reconciliation in South Africa*, eds. Wilmot James and Linda van der Vijver (Cape Town: David Philips, 2000), 73–81.

169 Agamben, *Homo Sacer*, 45–46.

chapter 2

1 The NGK's reconsideration of apartheid was presented in a document entitled *Church and Society*. In it, the church retracted much of its position in *Human Relations*, arguing that apartheid "cannot be accepted on Christian-ethical grounds". See NGK, *Church and Society: A Testimony of the Dutch Reformed Church*, October 1986 (Bloemfontein: General Synodical Commission, 1987). For a criticism of the document's reluctant tone, see H.P.P. Lotter, "Some Christian Perceptions of Social Justice in a Transforming South Africa," *Politikon* 19 (1991): 45–65.

2 Editorial, "Political Detainees: Are they Forgotten?" *South African Journal on Human Rights* 4 (1988), vii.

3 Quoted in Anthony Balcomb, *Third Way Theology: Reconciliation, Revolution and Reform in the South African Church in the 1980s* (Pietermaritzburg: Cluster Publications, 1993), 42; F.W. de Klerk, *The Last Trek – A New Beginning* (New York: MacMillan, 1998), 114.

4 Quoted in Deborah Posel, "The Language of Domination, 1978–1983," in *The Politics of Race, Class and Nationalism in Twentieth Century South Africa*, eds. Shula Marks and Stanley Trapido (London: Longman, 1987), 439.

5 African National Congress, "From Ungovernability to People's Power," May 1986. Reprinted at <www.anc.org.za/ancdocs/history/ungovern/html> (March 2002).

6 Steven Friedman, "The Struggle within the Struggle," *Transformation* 3 (1987), 60; Alex Boraine, "Democracy and Government: Towards a People's Struggle," *IDASA Occasional Paper* #3 (nd.), 5.

7 Hermann Giliomee, "Afrikaner Nationalism: 1870–2001," in *A Question of Survival: Conversations with Key South Africans*, ed. Michel Albeldas (Johannesburg: Jonathan Ball, 1987), 16. Also see Hein Marais, *South Africa: Limits to Change – The Political Economy of Transition* (London: Zed Books, 1994), 64.

8 Mike Louw quoted in Hermann Giliomee, "Surrender without Defeat: Afrikaners and the South African Miracle," *Spotlight: South African Institute of Race Relations* (1997), 18.

9 For a comprehensive diagnosis of the situation, see F. van Zyl Slabbert, "The Dynamics of Reform and Revolt in Current South Africa," *Tanner Lectures on Human Values*, Oxford University, 27 October 1987.

10 Barbara Cassin, "Politics of Memory: On Treatments of Hate," *Javnost: The Public* 8 (2001), 11. In the original Greek, *stasis* connotes both the making and outcome of discord. It does not simply mark a moment that calls for but constrains action. Rather, it is a time in which historical justifications for action yield choices that confound their own goals. In *stasis*, the "laws" of human relations are neither negated nor effective.

11 Patti Waldmeir, *Anatomy of a Miracle: The End of Apartheid and the Birth of the New South African Constitution* (New York: WW Norton, 1997), 71.

12   Richard Rosenthal's book details one such set of meetings, an undertaking by
      Rosenthal himself to shuttle between the parties in order to open grounds for talk.
      See Richard Rosenthal, *Mission Improbable: A Piece of the South African Story* (Cape
      Town: David Philip, 1998).
13   In the years since the end of apartheid, numerous theories have been advanced as
      to *why* the civil war in South Africa gave way to a negotiated settlement. A number
      of critics argue that the form of the transition was dictated by the undeniable
      structural failure of apartheid and the early calls by P.W. Botha for the Afrikaner
      to "adapt or die". Closely related is the common view that the end of apartheid
      was spurred by its economic failure, a collapse that left the ruling party bereft of
      legitimacy. International sanctions may have thus played a not insignificant role
      in spurring the transition. Others point out that the ideological underpinning
      of apartheid was inextricably subverted by the end of the Cold War, a moment
      when it became less and less credible for the government to carry on its fight
      against communism. On the other side, there is continued debate over whether
      the pressure of the liberation struggle forced the government's hand or if the ANC
      entered negotiations as mass action took an increasingly undemocratic form. Still
      others point to de Klerk's Damascus experience and Mandela's magnanimity as
      crucial factors in the turn to negotiations. For treatments of the issue, see Adam
      Habib, "South Africa and the Global Order: The Structural Conditioning of
      a Transition to Democracy," *Journal of Contemporary African Studies* 16 (1998):
      95–115; David Ginsburg, "The Democratization of South Africa: Transition
      Theory Tested," *Transformation* 29 (1996): 74–102; Daniel Lieberfeld, "Getting to
      the Negotiating Table: Domestic and International Dynamics," *Politikon* 27 (2000):
      19–36; Allister Sparks, *Tomorrow is Another Country: The Inside Story of South Africa's
      Road to Change* (Chicago: University of Chicago Press, 1995).
14   David Howarth, "Paradigms Gained? A Critique of Theories and Explanations of
      Democratic Transition in South Africa," in *South Africa in Transition*, ed. David
      Howarth (New York: St. Martins, 1998), 205.
15   Roelf Meyer, Interview with Author, Brooklyn, Pretoria, 7 September, 2000.
16   Father Smangaliso Mkhatshwa, Interview with Author, Cape Town, 4 October,
      2000. A few blocks away, on the top floor of an office building that houses the
      F.W. de Klerk Foundation, the former President's ex-Director General and
      speech writer, Dave Steward, skirts the question a bit, detailing the components of
      reconciliation more than its place in South African culture. The answer is related
      to Mkhatshwa's, an argument as to how reconciliation follows from the "imagined
      and real" hurts of the past and entails the "building up of new relationships"
      through an understanding of the "motivation and points of departure of an
      opponent". In these terms, the question of reconciliation is less about it location in
      the past than its ability to shape the future (Dave Steward, Interview with Author,
      Cape Town, 11 September, 2000).
17   Alex Boraine, Interview with Author, Cape Town, 12 July, 2000.
18   Constand Viljoen, Interview with Author, Cape Town, 11 October 2000.
19   Mac Maharaj, Interview with Author, Johannesburg, 16 January, 2001.
20   Antjie Krog, *A Change of Tongue* (Johannesburg: Random House, 2003), 118.
21   South African Information Service, *Progress Through Separate Development* (Pretoria:
      SAG, 1973), 7. For a related and more sophisticated case, one that appeared in

the early 1960s as apartheid was earning condemnation from the UN, see H.
Biermann, ed., *The Case for South Africa as put forth in Public Statements of Eric H.
Louw* (New York: MacFadden Books, 1963).

22 SAG, *Progress*, 30.

23 W.A. de Klerk, *The Puritans in Africa* (London: Rex Collings, 1975), 323.

24 B.J. Vorster, "Speech Delivered at a Rally of the East Rand Rapportryers," in
B.J. Vorster: Selected Speeches (Bloemfontein: Institute for Contemporary History,
1977), 244.

25 Vorster, "East Rand Rapportryers," 246.

26 Vorster, "East Rand Rapportryers," 247.

27 de Klerk, *Puritans*, 323.

28 de Klerk, *Puritans*, 321.

29 de Klerk, *Puritans*, 333.

30 Paul Rich, "Liberalism and Ethnicity in South African Politics, 1921–1948,"
African Studies 35 (1976), 231. For a now classic account of how race and class
intersected in the rise of apartheid, see Harold Wolpe, *Race, Class and the Apartheid
State* (London: James Currey, 1988).

31 Dan O'Meara, *Volkskapitalisme: Class, Capital and Ideology in the Development of
Afrikaner Nationalism, 1934–1948* (Cambridge: Cambridge University Press, 1983),
231. The point is echoed by Andre du Toit's claim that the popular "chosen
people" thesis explains neither the aspirations nor development of nationalism.
See Andre du Toit, "No Chosen People: The Myth of Calvinist Origins of
Afrikaner Nationalism," *American Historical Review* 88 (1983): 920–52.

32 Hermann Giliomee, *The Afrikaners: Biography of a People* (Cape Town: Tafelberg,
2003), 446.

33 Giliomee, *Afrikaners*, 359, 371. Giliomee also notes the influence of scholar and
poet N.P. van Wyk Louw, particularly his concern for "open-ended conversation"
(*oop gesprek*) and criticism that could expose the fluidity of Afrikaner identity.

34 Du Toit, "No Chosen People," 951.

35 This idea appeared in a 1935 issue of *Die Republikein*. Reprinted in Dunbar
Moodie, *The Rise of Afrikanerdom: Power, Apartheid and the Afrikaner Civil Religion*
(Berkeley: University of California Press, 1975), 107. For further discussion on the
debate over who was legitimately an Afrikaner, see Heribert Adam and Hermann
Giliomee, *Ethnic Power Mobilized: Can South Africa Change?* (New Haven: Yale
University Press, 1979), 101.

36 Heribert Adam, "Ethnic vs. Civic Nationalism: South Africa's Non-Racialism in
Comparative Perspective," *South African Sociological Review* 7 (1994), 18.

37 For a detailed account of the perceived risk of communism, see Peter Walshe, *The
Rise of Afrikaner Nationalism in South Africa* (Berkeley: University of California Press,
1971), 287; Moodie, *Rise of Afrikanerdom*, 251.

38 Moodie, *Rise of Afrikanerdom*, 247.

39 South African Department of Information, *Amnesty for Terrorism* (Pretoria:
Simondium Publishers, 1978), 30.

40 Among others, see Giliomee, *Afrikaners*, 404, 468; Adam and Giliomee, *Ethnic
Power*, 27–83; Johan Degenaar, and John Dugard have each addressed the issue in
Jeffrey Butler, et al. eds., *Democratic Liberalism in South Africa: Its History and Prospect*
(Middletown: Wesleyan University Press, 1987); F.A. van Jaarsveld, *The Awakening*

of Afrikaner Nationalism, 1868–1881 (Cape Town: Human and Rousseau, 1961).
41 Adam and Giliomee, *Ethnic Power*, 116.
42 Here, the argument was that separate development allowed for the emergence of political rights within separate population groups as opposed to an outright expression of collective Afrikaner power. See Hermann Giliomee, "Apartheid, Verligtheid, and Liberalism," in *Democratic Liberalism in South Africa*, 365–67.
43 For an interesting discussion of the relationship between the monument and the aspirations of nationalism, see Annie Coombes, *Visual Culture and Public Memory in a Democratic South Africa* (Durham: Duke University Press, 2003), 44–49.
44 Adam and Giliomee, *Ethnic Power*, 119. Evident in the 1938 centenary celebrations of the Great Trek, nationalist doctrine used the past to indemnify a future that obscured the shortfall of the present. On de Klerk's reading, this argument performed a historical shell game, a promise that estranged the Afrikaner from both self and world. In his terms, nationalism's "modes of avoiding the challenge become that of both archaism and futurism: moving at the same time onwards towards a non-attainable future and backwards into a dead past" (de Klerk, *Puritans*, 323). Here, the empirical claim is less significant than the demonstration of how the rationale for nationalism moved between the need to heal and overcome past injuries and the assurance of justice in the future. The link between the two was a sense of sacrifice that legitimised the accumulation and deployment of precisely the sort of institutional power that the calling of nationalism claimed to resist (de Klerk, *Puritans*, 336).
45 Oliver Tambo, "Tribute to the UN Special Committee against Apartheid," 2 April 1973, 1. Reprinted at <www.anc.org.za/ancdocs/history/or/or73-1.html> (March 2003).
46 Oliver Tambo, "Message to the People of South Africa," 26 June 1974. Reprinted at <www.anc.org.za/ancdocs/history/or/or74-1.html> (March 2003).
47 ANC, "Strategy and Tactics of the African National Congress," 25 April 1969, 7. Reprinted at <www.anc.org.za/ancdocs/history/stratact.html> (April 2001).
48 R.O. Ngubengcuka, "The ANC and Nationalism," in *Liberation: A Journal of Democratic Discussion* 22 (1956), 1.
49 Dale McKinley, *The ANC and Liberation Struggle* (London: Pluto Press, 1997).
50 South African Native National Congress, "Resolution against the Natives Land Act 1913 and the Report of the Natives Land Commission," 2 October 1916. Reprinted at <www.anc.org.za> (March 2003). Peter Walshe, *The Rise of African Nationalism in South Africa: The African National Congress, 1912–1952* (London: C. Hurst & Co., 1970), 350; Gail Gerhart, *Black Power in South Africa: The Evolution of an Ideology* (Berkeley: University of California Press, 1978), 46.
51 Zaccheus Mahabane, quoted in Peter Walshe, "Christianity and the Anti-Apartheid Struggle: The Prophetic Voice within Divided Churches," in *Christianity in South Africa: A Political, Social and Cultural History*, ed. Richard Elphick (Berkeley: University of California Press, 1997), 384. The role of Christianity only grew as the Congress matured. In 1952, while endeavouring to find the appropriate and effective terms of struggle, Albert Luthuli, future ANC President and then Chief of the Abase-Makolweni Tribe in the Groutville Mission Reserve – a position that made him a member of the *Native Representative Council* created by the 1936 *Hertzog Bills* – was called to account for his activities in the Congress and

its role in the Defiance Campaign. Rejecting the state's demand that he resign from the ANC, Luthuli was removed as Chief. In an address delivered shortly after his dismissal, he set the aim of the struggle in religious terms, declaring: "It is inevitable that in working for Freedom some individuals and some families must lead and suffer: the Road to Freedom is Via the CROSS. MAYIBUYE! AFRIKA!" (Reprinted in Thomas Karis and Gwendolen Carter, eds., *From Protest to Challenge: A Documentary History of African Politics in South Africa*, Vol. 2 (Stanford: Stanford University Press, 1973), 489. Also see Gerald Pillay, *Voices of Liberation: Albert Luthuli*, Vol. 1 (Pretoria: HSRC Publishers, 1993); Lyn Graybill, *Religion and Resistance in South Africa* (Westport: Praeger, 1995), 29–33). Following Luthuli's claim that he belonged to the ANC "precisely because I am a Christian", the call to remember was some indication that the movement was drawing heavily from the church to build "broader political community". In his work on their historical connection, Peter Walshe claims that the leaders of the movement perceived a convergence between Christian egalitarian and non-racial values, an affinity that the ANC has long acknowledged, particularly in its characterisation of the 1955 *Freedom Charter* as a "document rooted in the great religious concepts revealed to humanity". See Peter Walshe, "South Africa: Prophetic Christianity and the Liberation Movement," *The Journal of Modern Africa Studies* 29 (1991), 30. Also see Cedric Mayson, "Religion and the Freedom Charter," in *ANC Today* 1 (8–14 June, 2001).

52   Walshe, "Christianity and the Anti-Apartheid Struggle," 412; Walshe, *Rise of African Nationalism*, 341.

53   Quoted in Paul Rich, *State Power and Black Politics in South Africa, 1912–1951* (New York: St. Martin's Press, 1996), 98.

54   This vision was also a basic element of the Non-European Unity Movement founded in 1943. For the movement's founding agenda, see "The Ten Point Programme," reprinted in *South Africa's Radical Tradition: A Documentary History*, Vol. 2, ed. Alison Drew (Cape Town: University of Cape Town Press, 1997), 62–63.

55   Gerhart, *Black Power*, 61. Also see Anton Lembede, "Some Basic Principles of African Nationalism," reprinted in Thomas Karis and Gwendolen Carter, eds., *From Protest to Challenge: A Documentary History of African Politics in South Africa*, Vol. 2 (Stanford: Stanford University Press, 1973), 315.

56   Gerhart, *Black Power*, 74.

57   Allison Drew, "Introduction," in *South Africa's Radical Tradition*, 25.

58   Walshe, *Rise of African Nationalism*, 352.

59   African National Congress, *Africans' Claims*, 1943. Reprinted at <www.anc.org.za/ancdocs/history/claims.html> (January 2001); Walshe, *The Rise of African Nationalism*, 353.

60   African National Congress, *ANC Youth League Manifesto*, 1944. Reprinted at <www.anc.org.za/ancdocs/history/ancylman.html> (January 2001).

61   ANC, *Youth League Manifesto*.

62   African National Congress, "ANC Youth League Basic Policy Document," 1948. Reprinted at <www.anc.org.za/ancdocs/history/ancylpol.html> (January 2001).

63   Walshe, *Rise of African Nationalism*, 356.

64   Nelson Mandela, "The Shifting Sands of Illusion," *Liberation* (June 1953).

Reprinted at: <www.anc.org.za/ancdocs/history/mandela/1950s/nm5306/html> (November 2000).

65 For one account of these tensions, see Stephen Ellis and Tsepo Sechaba, *Comrades against Apartheid: The ANC and the South African Communist Party in Exile* (London: James Currey, 1992). In any event, the distrust did not necessarily mean that economic change was incidental to the ANC's struggle but rather that material equality was held to be best achieved through direct action and mass mobilisation aimed at first securing political rights.

66 For a discussion of the rural-urban divide within the Congress, see Colin Bundy, "Land and Liberation: Popular Rural Protest and the National Liberation Movements in South Africa, 1920–1960," in *The Politics of Race, Class, and Nationalism in 20th Century South Africa*, eds. Shula Marks and Stanley Trapido (New York: Longman, 1987), 254–85; Albert Luthuli, "Special Presidential Message," Address to the ANC Annual Conference, 17–18 December 1955, 2. Reprinted at <www.anc.org.za/ancdocs/history/conf/presad44.htm> (November 2003).

67 For particular and general investigations of the significant role that women played in the resistance to apartheid, see Cherryl Walker, *Women and Resistance in South Africa* (Cape Town: David Philip, 1991); Julia Wells, *We Now Demand! The History of Women's Resistance to Pass Laws in South Africa* (Johannesburg: Witwatersrand University Press, 1993); Tom Lodge, *Black Politics in South Africa Since 1945* (Johannesburg: Ravan, 1983), 139–51.

68 For materials on the labour movement, see Jeremy Baskin, *Striking back: A History of Cosatu* (Johannesburg: Ravan Press, 1991); Jon Lewis, *Industrialisation and Trade Union Organisation in South Africa, 1924–55: The Rise and Fall of the South African Trades and Labour Council* (New York: Cambridge University Press, 1984).

69 Jan Liebenberg, "Response to ANC Constitutional Guidelines," *IDASA Occasional Paper #25* (nd.), 3.

70 Kader Asmal, Louise Asmal, and Ronald Roberts, *Reconciliation through Truth* (Cape Town: David Philip, 1996), 113.

71 Charles Villa-Vicencio, *Civil Disobedience and Beyond: Law, Resistance and Religion in South Africa* (Grand Rapids: Eerdmans, 1990), 51.

72 African National Congress, "The Freedom Charter," 26 June 1955. Reprinted at <www.anc.org.za/ancdocs/history/charter.html> (November 2002).

73 Gerhart, *Black Power*, 158. The *Charter* was a basic motivation for the 1958 formation of the Pan Africanist Congress, an organisation led by Robert Sobukwe. At stake in the split was whether and how the ANC could make good on the promise of the *Charter*, taking steps to design a struggle that did actually represent those whom it claimed as constituents. See also McKinley, *ANC and Liberation Struggle*, 21.

74 Nelson Mandela, *Long Walk to Freedom* (London: Abacus, 1994), 251.

75 Mandela, *Long Walk to Freedom*, 270.

76 For a history of MK, see Howard Barrell, *MK: The ANC's Armed Struggle* (London: Penguin, 1990). For a stark account of the organisational difficulties involved in running the MK from outside South Africa, see Ed Benard and Mwezi Twala, *Mbokodo: Inside MK – Mwezi Twala. A Soldier's Story* (Johannesburg: Jonathan Ball Publishers, 1994).

77 African National Congress, "Manifesto of Umkhonto we Sizwe," 16 December 1961. Reprinted at <www.anc.org.za/ancdocs/history/mk/manifesto-mk.html> (February 2002).

78 Albert Luthuli, "Freedom in Our Lifetime: Presidential Address to the 46th Annual Conference of the African National Congress", 14 December 1958, 7. Reprinted at <www.anc.org.za/ancdocs/history/lutuli/lutuli58.html> (February 2002).

79 Nelson and Winnie Mandela, "Racism, Apartheid and A New World Order: Speech In Acceptance of the Third World Prize on Behalf of Nelson and Winnie Mandela," 5 May 1986. Reprinted at <www.anc.org.za/ancdocs/speeches/1980s/or84-4.html> (February 2002).

80 Kenneth Hendrickse quoted in *South Africa's Radical Tradition*, 140.

81 Gerhart, *Black Power*, 100; C.R.D. Halisi, *Black Political Thought in the Making of South African Democracy* (Bloomington: Indiana University Press, 1999), 57.

82 Gerhart, *Black Power*, 64; Walshe, *Rise of African Nationalism*, 355; Halisi, *Black Political Thought*, 59.

83 Quoted in Walshe, *Rise of African Nationalism*, 349. Citing the necessity of an organic communalism, the ANC's case against apartheid was made partly on the grounds of international human rights doctrine, a politics and jurisprudence that laid heavy emphasis on the inalienable rights of individuals. Jakes Gerwel has argued that this position marks an interest in reconciliation.

84 Gerhart calls this dynamic the "struggle within the struggle" (Gerhart, *Black Power*, 81).

85 African National Congress, "Colonialism of a Special Type," March 1987. Reprinted at <www.anc.org.za/ancdocs/history/special.html> (February 2002); also see Wolpe, *Race, Class*, 28–34; Walshe, *Rise of Afrikaner Nationalism*, 305; Heribert Adam and Kogila Moodley, *The Opening of the Apartheid Mind: Options for the New South Africa* (Berkeley: University of California Press, 1993), 18.

86 Quoted in "Joint Sitting of the Executive Committees of the All-African Congress and the African National Congress," 17 April 1949, reprinted in *South Africa's Radical Tradition*, 89.

87 Gerhart, *Black Power*, 99.

88 Hendrik Verwoerd, "Address to the Native Representative Council, 5 December 1950," in *Verwoerd Speaks: Speeches 1948–1966* (Johannesburg: APB Publishers, 1966), 28.

89 Mandela, "The Shifting Sands of Illusion."

90 There is a substantial literature on the problematic status of liberalism in South African politics and culture. In addition to works cited above, see Paul Rich, "Liberalism and Ethnicity in South African Politics, 1921–1948,"*African Studies* 35 (1976): 229–51; Charles Simkins, *Liberalism and the Problem of Power* (Johannesburg: South African Institute of Race Relations, 1986); Jeffrey Butler, "Introduction," in *Democratic Liberalism*, 7–11; *Contending Ideologies in South Africa*, ed. James Leatt (Cape Town: David Philip, 1986), 52–59; Andre Odendaal, "Liberalism and the African National Congress," Paper presented at the Conference on Liberalism in South Africa, Houw Hoek, July 1986.

91 To be very clear, the argument here is not that apartheid wasn't a racist system. Rather, the distinction is that its rationalising doctrine *claimed* that it was not racist,

an argument that convinced very few and which thus led to an endless attempt to muster a position that could convince critics.

92   P.W. Botha, Debates of the House of Assembly (Hansard), 3rd session–8th Parliament, 31 January 1986, col. 14.

93   Nelson and Winnie Mandela (Delivered by Oliver Tambo), "Racism, Apartheid and a New World Order," 5 May 1986. Reprinted at <www.anc.org.za/ancdocs/speeches/1980s/or86-4.html>. (August 2003).

94   Frederick van Zyl Slabbert, "Democracy: A Vision for the Future," *Soweton Quarterly State of the Nation*, Summer 1991, 431.

95   Adam and Moodley, *Opening*, 1.

96   Stanley Uys, "President Dare not Repeat Durban Disaster," *Cape Times*, 3 January 1986, 8.

97   Philip van Niekerk, "Slabbert: I've Lost all Hope," *The Weekly Mail*, 28 February 1986, 1.

98   In 1987, a negotiated settlement was far from fated. During August and September, the *Sunday Times* ran a series of essays in which leading political commentators debated about both the terms of the South African situation and the means by which it might be resolved. Writing in defence of a "third way", Hermann Giliomee argued that "unending strife is a foregone conclusion" unless the contending parties agree on the "very nature of conflict". Responding to Giliomee's view that the contending parties were locked in a "communal conflict" that was less about the racial bifurcation of apartheid than a clash between competing nationalisms, ideologies that each sought to define the terms of national sovereignty, Willem van Vuuren maintained that the proposal to negotiate a "bi-communalism" misunderstood that the NP was trapped in its "selfish political party interests" and blind to the fact that violence was rooted in the "oppression and frustration" generated by a "profoundly undemocratic system" (Hermann Giliomee, "The Third Way," in *Negotiating South Africa's Future*, eds. H. Giliomee and Lawrence Schlemmer (Johannesburg: Southern Book Publishers, 1989 [1987]), 10–13).

99   Winnie Mandela, "Address in Soweto," quoted in *The Guardian*, 15 April 1986, 2.

100 Norman Greenberg, "AWB warns of 'Violence'," *The Weekly Mail*, 2 May 1986, 3.

101 Mobil Oil, "Advertisement – Let's End Violence and Begin a Meaningful Dialogue," *The Weekly Mail*, 2 May 1986, 5.

102 African National Congress, "From Ungovernability to People's Power," 1986, 3. Reprinted at <www.anc.org.za/ancdocs/history/ungovern.html> (February 2002).

103 Anton Harber, "An Invisible Blanket over Unrest Areas," *The Weekly Mail*, 16 May 1986, 11.

104 The Commonwealth Group of Eminent Persons, *Mission to South Africa: The Commonwealth Report* (New York: Penguin, 1986), 99, 38.

105 Commonwealth Group, *Mission to South Africa*, 135.

106 Oliver Tambo, "We have Decided to Liberate Ourselves," Address to the Royal Commonwealth Society, London, 23 June 1986, 4. Reprinted at <www.anc.org.za/ancdocs/history/or/or86-10.html> (February 2002).

107 Tambo, "We have Decided to Liberate Ourselves," 2; Oliver Tambo, "Victory is Within Our Grasp: Statement at the World Conference on Sanctions Against Racist South Africa," Paris, 16 June 1986, 2. Reprinted at <www.anc.org.za/ancdocs/history/or/or86-8.html> (February 2002).

108 Oliver Tambo, "We have Decided to Liberate Ourselves," 5.
109 Pallo Jordan, quoted in Adam and Moodley, *Opening*, 22.
110 Thabo Mbeki quoted in Rosenthal, *Mission Improbable*, 108.
111 African National Congress, "The Illegitimacy of the Apartheid Regime, The Right
     to Struggle Against It, and the Status of the African National Congress," 1987.
     Reprinted at <www.anc.org.za/ancdocs/history/acrime.html> (January 1998).
112 Daniel Lieberfeld, "Getting to the Negotiating Table in South Africa: Domestic
     and International Dynamics," *Politikon* 27 (2000), 31.
113 McKinley, *ANC and Liberation Struggle*, 87.
114 SAG, *Talking with the ANC* (Pretoria: Bureau for Information, 1986), 1.
115 SAG, *Talking with the ANC*, 1.
116 SAG, *Talking with the ANC*, 30.
117 SAG, *Talking with the ANC*, 33.
118 Adam and Moodley, *Opening*, 42. There is a strong temptation to dismiss this
     fear as so much bluff or the warped complaints of the master when faced with
     the end of his power. Perhaps so. But there is substantial evidence that whites
     did fear the advent of majority rule and distrusted the ANC's commitment to
     non-racialism. For survey data about the matter, see Nic Rhoodie, "White South
     African's Expectations Regarding Democratic Nation-Building and Community
     Reconciliation," in *Democratic Nation-Building in South Africa*, ed. Nic Rhoodie
     (Pretoria: HSRC Publishers, 1994), 265.
119 Stoffel van der Merwe, *What About Black People?* (Cape Town: Federal Information
     Service of the National Party, 1985), 15.
120 Compare, for instance, Daniel O'Meara, *Forty Lost Years: The Apartheid State and the
     Politics of the National Party, 1948–1994* (Johannesburg: Ravan Press, 1996); Adam
     Habib, "South Africa and the Global Order: The Structural Conditioning of a
     Transition to Democracy," *Journal of Contemporary African Studies* 16 (1998), 104.
121 Stoffel van der Merwe quoted in Rosenthal, *Mission Improbable*, 125.
122 This was the claim by Gavin Reilly, Chair of Anglo-American. Quoted in Leonard
     Thompson, *The Political Mythology of Apartheid* (New Haven: Yale University Press,
     1985), 85.
123 Rosenthal, *Mission Improbable*, 23. According to Rosenthal, the process was partly
     dedicated to collecting information about the conditions for negotiations and partly
     to do with discerning how the two parties could build the trust needed to talk
     directly (144).
124 Alex Boraine, Interview with Author, Cape Town, 12 July 2000.
125 Frederick van Zyl Slabbert, "Preconditions to Negotiations: Is the Gap Closing?"
     Democracy in Action (1988), 4.
126 African National Congress, "On Negotiations," 9 October 1987. Reprinted at:
     <www.anc.org.za/ancdocs/pr/1980s/pr871009.html> (February 2002).
127 African National Congress, *Discussion Paper on the Issue of Negotiations*, June 16,
     1989. Reprinted at <www.anc.org.za/ancdocs/pr/1989/pr0616.html> (January
     2002).
128 Nelson Mandela, *Long Walk to Freedom*, 523. Fearful that one of the world's most
     famous political prisoners would die in prison, and open to the idea that Mandela
     represented the "moderate" arm of the ANC, Botha offered to release him on the
     condition that he renounce violence. The gesture was refused each time. In 1985,

Mandela's daughter Zindzi read her father's words about the matter, a challenge to Botha to "renounce violence" and "guarantee free political activity so that people may decide who will govern them".

129 Nelson Mandela, *Long Walk to Freedom*, 632.

130 Nelson Mandela, "The Mandela Document: A Document Provided by Nelson Mandela to P.W. Botha before their meeting on 5 July 1989," 1989. Reprinted at <www.anc.org.za/ancdocs/history/mandela/64-90/doc890705.html> (August 1998).

131 Dave Steward, Interview with Author, 11 September 2000.

132 F.W. de Klerk, "Inaugural Address," reprinted in *The Cape Argus*, 20 September 1989, 1.

133 F.W. de Klerk quoted in Tos Wentzel, "In Deadly Earnest," *The Cape Argus*, 17 November 1989, 15.

134 Nelson Mandela, "Document Forwarded to F.W. de Klerk," 12 December 1989. Reprinted at <www.anc.org.za/ancdocs/history/mandela/nm891212.html> (August 1998).

135 de Klerk, *The Last Trek*, 163.

136 F.W. de Klerk, *Debates of Parliament* (Hansard), 2nd Session-9th Parliament, 2 February 1990, cols. 1–18.

137 Willem de Klerk, "The Political Process of Negotiation, 1990–1993," in *Birth of a Constitution*, ed. Bertus de Villiers (Kenwyn: Juta, 1994), 6.

138 Dr Willem Snyman, *Debates of Parliament* (Hansard), 2nd Session-9th Parliament, 5 February 1990, cols. 90.

139 Andries Treurnicht, *Debates of Parliament* (Hansard), 2nd Session-9th Parliament, 5 February 1990, cols. 39–43.

140 Gerrit Viljoen, *Debates of Parliament* (Hansard), 2nd Session-9th Parliament, 5 February 1990, col. 60–70.

141 Roelf Meyer, *Debates of Parliament* (Hansard), 2nd Session-9th Parliament, 5 February 1990, col. 106.

142 Editorial, *The Independent*, 2 March 1990, 16.

143 For a discussion of Afrikaner perceptions of reform proposals, see Kate Manzo, "Afrikaner Fears and the Politics of Despair: Understanding Change in South Africa," *International Studies Quarterly* 36 (1992): 1–24.

144 Nelson Mandela, "Address to Rally in Cape Town on His Release from Prison," 11 February 1990. Reprinted at <www.anc.org.za/ancdocs/history/mandela/1990/release.html> (August 1998).

145 Nelson Mandela, "Address to Rally in Soweto," 13 February 1990. Reprinted at <www.anc.org.za/ancdocs/history/mandela/1990/sp900213.html> (August 1998).

146 Mandela, "Address to Rally in Soweto," 3.

147 A small zine was issued shortly after the release, a compilation of press clippings about the release that did well to map the spirit of the moment. See South African Pressclips, "Mandela Comes Home," 12–15 February 1990.

148 Gaye Davis, "ANC in Secret UK Talks with South Africa," *The Weekly Mail*, 2 March 1990, 1.

149 Waldmeir, *Anatomy of a Miracle*, 158.

150 Steven Friedman, "A 'Social Contract' Should be Achieved," *The Weekly Mail*, 20 April 1990, 12.

151 Gavin Evans, "The Streets are in Flames ... and the ANC Gets Blamed," *The Weekly Mail*, 5 April 1990, 2.

152 Nelson Mandela quoted in Gavin Evans, "Peace on Edge as FW meets Mandela," *The Weekly Mail*, 5 April 1990, 6.

153 Gavin Evans, "A Quick Admission Defuses ANC Torture Claims," *The Weekly Mail*, 5 April 1990, 7.

154 South African Institute of Race Relations, *Race Relations Survey, 1991/92* (Johannesburg: SAIRR, 1992), 455.

155 Gaye Davis, "A Strange Thing Happened in Africa this Week," *The Weekly Mail*, 4 May 1990, 6–7.

156 de Klerk, "The Political Process of Negotiation," 2.

157 Republic of South Africa, *Indemnity Act (No. 35)*, 15 May 1990, 2.

158 Pieter Gous, *Debates of Parliament* (Hansard), 2nd Session-9th Parliament, 7 May 1990, cols. 8154–55.

159 Frank Le Roux, *Debates of Parliament* (Hansard), 2nd Session-9th Parliament, 7 May 1990.

160 Respectively, Willem Botha, *Debates of Parliament* (Hansard), 2nd Session-9th Parliament, 7 May 1990, col. 8174; Jacobus Botha, *Debates of Parliament* (Hansard), 2nd Session-9th Parliament, 7 May 1990, col. 8200.

161 Sheila Camerer, *Debates of Parliament* (Hansard), 2nd Session-9th Parliament, 7 May 1990, col. 8171.

162 M.F. Cassim, *Debates of Parliament* (Hansard), 2nd Session-9th Parliament, 7 May 1990, col. 8124.

163 R.J. Radue, *Debates of Parliament* (Hansard), 2nd Session-9th Parliament, 7 May 1990, col. 8195.

164 Mudene Smuts, *Debates of Parliament* (Hansard), 2nd Session-9th Parliament, 7 May 1990, col. 8204.

165 J.N. Reddy, *Debates of Parliament* (Hansard), 2nd Session-9th Parliament, 7 May 1990, col. 8227.

166 The rules were formalised in early November. This was an important precedent, one that would be used throughout the move from apartheid and which was central in defining how the TRC would come to adjudicate amnesty applications beginning in 1996.

167 F.W. de Klerk, "National Address: Violence is Unacceptable," *The Cape Argus*, 19 December 1990, 19.

168 F.W. de Klerk, "Address Given at the Opening of Parliament," reprinted in *The Cape Argus*, 1 February 1991, 14.

169 African National Congress, National Executive Committee, "Statement of National Executive Committee of the African National Congress," 2 February 1991. Reprinted at <www.anc.org.za/ancdocs/pr.1991/pr0202.html> (March 2002).

170 African National Congress, "Tripartite Meeting ANC-COSATU-SACP," 29 April 1991. Reprinted at <www.anc.org.za/ancdocs/pr/1991/pr0429a.html> (March 2002).

171 Nelson Mandela, "Speech at Pretoria University," 29 April 1991. Reprinted at <www.anc.org.za/ancdocs/history/mandela/1991/sp910429.html> (March 2002).

172 Nelson Mandela, "Speech to May Day Rally," 1 May 1991. Reprinted at <www.anc.org.za/ancdocs/history/mandela/1991/sp910501.html> (March 2002).

173 Gavin Evans, "Mandela Fury," *The Weekly Mail*, 17 May 1991, 1, 3.
174 Philip van Niekerk, "Giving Flesh to the Notion of an Interim Government," *The Weekly Mail*, 9 August 1991, 16.
175 Laurie Nathan, "An Imperfect Bridge: Crossing to Democracy on the Peace Accord," *Track Two*, 2 May 1993, 4.
176 Peter Gastrow, *Bargaining for Peace: South Africa and the National Peace Accord* (Washington D.C.: U.S. Institute for Peace, 1995), 93.

chapter 3

1 Institute for Contextual Theology, *Violence: The New Kairos*, September 1990. Reprinted at <www.anc.org.za/ancdocs/history/transition/kairos.htm> (August 1998).
2 Albie Sachs, "Notes From CODESA," *Mayibuye* (May 1992), 10–11.
3 The literature on the dynamics of the transition is expansive and buttressed by a burgeoning debate over the larger nature of transitional politics and democratisation. For treatments of the latter, see Guillermo O'Donnell, Philippe Plattner, and Larry Diamond, eds., *Transitions from Authoritarian Rule*, Vols. 1–4 (Baltimore: John Hopkins Press, 1986). For work on the field as it pertains to the South African case, see Timothy Sisk, *Democratization in South Africa: The Elusive Social Contract* (Princeton: Princeton University Press, 1995); Nic Rhoodie, ed., *Democratic Nation-Building in South Africa* (Pretoria: HSRC Publishers, 1994); David Ginsburg, "The Democratisation of South Africa: Transition Theory Tested," *Transformation* 29 (1996): 74–102; Heribert Adam and Kogila Moodley, *The Opening of the Apartheid Mind: Options for a New South Africa* (Berkeley: University of California Press, 1983); Willem Van Vuuren, "Transition Politics and the Prospects of Democratic Consolidation in South Africa," *Politikon* 22 (1995), 9; Paul Rich, ed., *The Dynamics of Change in Southern Africa* (New York: MacMillan, 1994).
4 This is an important rift in the field of transition studies. David Howarth and Donald Horowitz, for instance, have each argued that when attempting to assess the mechanics of "a change from one kind of (political) regime to another", appeals to such goods as collective interest, constitutionalism, justice, and natural rights may indicate that theorists have presupposed precisely that which they seek to explain. See David Howarth, "Paradigms Gained? A Critique of Theories and Explanations of Democratic Transitions in South Africa," in *South Africa in Transition*, ed. D. Howarth (New York: St. Martins, 1998), 184; Donald Horowitz, *A Democratic South Africa: Constitutional Engineering in a Divided Society* (Cape Town: Oxford University Press, 1991).
5 This tendency is somewhat apparent in the two best studies of the constitutional negotiations, especially as they reduce the matter of negotiator interaction to a matter of power politics that pays relatively little attention to the question of its form. See Hassen Ebrahim, *Soul of a Nation: Constitution-Making in South Africa* (Cape Town: Oxford University Press, 1998); Richard Spitz and Matthew Chaskalson, *The Politics of Transition: A Hidden History of South Africa's Negotiated Settlement* (Johannesburg: Witwatersrand University Press, 2000).
6 Hannah Arendt, *On Revolution* (London: Pelican, 1963), 142.

7   Kenneth Burke, *A Grammar of Motives* (Berkeley: University of California Press, 1969); Maurice Charland, "Constitutive Rhetoric: The Case of the Peuple Québécois," *Quarterly Journal of Speech* 73: 2 (1987): 133–50.

8   For a brief consideration of this matter in the South African context, see Spitz and Chaskalson, *The Politics of Transition*, 3.

9   Put differently, the deliberative norms that enable constitutive speech have a significant bearing on how and how well constitution-making works over time. For Habermas, this temporal dimension of constitution-making is vital. The communicative principles and methods used to constitute must carry forward, allowing citizens the space and resources to argue about and participate in the ongoing work of constitutional politics. While typically ideal, especially given Habermas's presumptions about the capacity and desirability of intersubjective decision-making, the larger position is useful precisely because it underscores why the form of negotiation politics matters. Thus, the point is much less to determine whether constitutional talks met or deviated from a set of counterfactual conditions than to recognise that the terms and form of such negotiations cannot be divorced from accounts of how transition occurred. See Jürgen Habermas, "Constitutional Democracy – A Paradoxical Combination of Contradictory Principles," Paper presented at the Northwestern School of Law, Chicago, Illinois, 23 October 2000; Jürgen Habermas, *The Inclusion of the Other* (Cambridge: MIT Press, 1998).

10 Fredrick van Zyl Slabbert quoted in Steven Friedman, ed., *The Long Journey: South Africa's Quest for a Negotiated Settlement* (Johannesburg: Ravan, 1993), 174.

11 At CODESA, the issue of sovereignty marked the question of how to move from one form of violence to another. Both Giorgio Agamben and Jacques Derrida have observed that the sovereign is that which endeavours to capture and exceed the given terms of expression, the power of collective action. Writes Agamben, "Language is the sovereign who, in a permanent state of exception, declares that there is nothing outside language and that language is always beyond itself" (Giorigio Agamben, *Homo Sacer: Sovereign Power and Bare Life*, trans. Daniel Heller Roazen (Palo Alto: Stanford University Press, 1998), 21). An exception to itself, abiding in the negative power to "declare" a state of emergency, the sovereign appropriates the grounds and regulates the standing to speak. "In sacrificing meaning," Derrida notes, "sovereignty submerges the possibility of discourse" and that "discourse is thus the loss of sovereignty itself". Between the two, between powerful silence and talk without power, there is potential, a transitional time in which to question what it would mean to invent a beginning (Jacques Derrida, "From Restricted to General Economy: A Hegelianism without Reserve," in *Writing and Difference*, trans. Alan Bass (Chicago: University of Chicago Press, 1978), 261).

12 Gavin Evans, "Stage Set for Serious Horse-Trading," *The Weekly Mail*, 29 November 1991, 5.

13 Steven Friedman, "Negotiating the Status Quo," *The Weekly Mail*, 22 November 1991, 17.

14 Drew Forrest, "Two Days that Stopped a Nation's Heartbeat," *The Weekly Mail*, 8 November 1991, 6.

15 Governed by a plenary body, CODESA's work was divided among five working groups that dealt respectively with issues of: climate creation, constitutional

principles, transitional structures, and reincorporation of the "independent" homelands or TBVC states.

16   The comment was widely reported. See Friedman, *Long Journey*, 25; Doreen Atkinson, "Brokering a Miracle: The Multiparty Negotiating Forum," in *South African Review*, ed. Steven Friedman (Johannesburg: Ravan, 1994), 22.

17   Drew Forrest, "SADF's Hidden Hand in Inkatha," *The Weekly Mail*, 13 December 1991, 1.

18   Friedman, *Long Journey*, 56.

19   NA, "Parliament Could Soon be just Number Two," *The Weekly Mail*, 19 December 1991, 2.

20   Nelson Mandela, "Address to CODESA by Comrade Nelson R. Mandela, President of the ANC," 20 December 1991, 3. Reprinted at <www.anc.org.za/ancdocs.history/Mandela/1991> (October 2002).

21   Lucas Mangope, "Address at the First Plenary Session of CODESA," *Convention for a Democratic South Africa: First Plenary Session* (Johannesburg: CODESA, 1991), 24.

22   Dr F.T. Mdlalose, "Address at the First Plenary Session of CODESA," *Convention for a Democratic South Africa: First Plenary Session* (Johannesburg: CODESA, 1991), 45.

23   Dr Z.J. de Beer, "Address at the First Plenary Session of CODESA," *Convention for a Democratic South Africa: First Plenary Session* (Johannesburg: CODESA, 1991), 33.

24   F.W. de Klerk, "First Address at the First Plenary Session of CODESA," *Convention for a Democratic South Africa: First Plenary Session* (Johannesburg: CODESA, 1991), 132.

25   de Klerk, "First Address," 134.

26   Nelson Mandela, "Second Address at the First Plenary Session of CODESA," *Convention for a Democratic South Africa: First Plenary Session* (Johannesburg: CODESA, 1991), 164.

27   CODESA, "Standing Rules," *Working Documents for CODESA 2, May 15–16, 1992* (Johannesburg: CODESA, 1992), np.

28   Inkatha Freedom Party, "The Removal of Major Obstacles to the Achievement of a Climate Conducive to Peaceful Negotiations: Submission to Working Group 1," January 27, 1991, CODESA Documents, WG1, WG1SC1, January 1992–May 1992, Box 40, Folders 28–49, South African National Archives, Pretoria, South Africa.

29   CODESA, "Minutes of Working Group 1, January 20, 1992, Addendum D," CODESA Documents, WG1, WG1SC1, January 1992–May 1992, Box 39, Folders 1–27, South African National Archives, Pretoria, South Africa.

30   CODESA, "Minutes of Working Group 1, 6 February 1992, Addendum C – Position Paper to be delivered by the Government at WG1," par. 7, CODESA Documents, WG1, WG1SC1, January 1992–May 1992, Box 39, Folders 1–27, South African National Archives, Pretoria, South Africa.

31   This characterisation was made in a submission to the working group. See Lawyers for Human Rights, "Completion of Matters Related to the Release of Political Prisoners – Submission to CODESA Working Group 1," 6 January 1992, CODESA Documents, WG1, WG1SC1, January 1992–May 1992, Box 43, Folders 106–30, South African National Archives, Pretoria, South Africa.

32   There are many ways to explain the events that followed CODESA's tumultuous beginning. A number of political scientists have argued that it was the NP's

continued intransigence at the bargaining table which motivated the ANC
to withdraw from CODESA and undertake protests designed to force the
government's hand. In this turn, some have questioned the ANC's underlying
motives, suggesting that the Congress needed a delay in order to get "ready to
govern". Other analysts have placed more weight on the design of CODESA,
contending that the forum encouraged both sides to employ a "hegemonic model
of bargaining", that encouraged brinkmanship and discouraged efforts to seek the
grounds for compromise (Adam and Moodley, *Opening*, 159). Taking a slightly
longer view, still others have argued that while the breakdown of CODESA may
have been caused by the government's unwillingness to take a stand against political
violence, the resumption of negotiations was motivated by shared fears about
the country's rapidly deteriorating economy. While there is truth in all of these
assessments, significant and specific questions remain: How did the breakdown of
talks follow from the disagreements that appeared during CODESA's first plenary?
Was the breakdown evidence of a *stasis* similar to the one that appeared before the
onset of the talks about talk? How was the breakdown itself an object of discussion,
a problem that motivated parties to reflect explicitly on how they could and ought
to speak with one another? In what ways did this meta-discussion set the stage for
a new round of negotiations? For a treatment of this period, see Steven Friedman
and Doreen Atkinson, eds., *The Small Miracle* (Johannesburg: Ravan Press, 1994).

33   Phillip van Niekerk, "Ring-a-Ring a Rosies: But Will They All Fall Down?"
      The Weekly Mail, 31 January 1992, 15.
34   F.W. de Klerk, "Reconcile Yourselves Once and for All to Change," *Cape Argus*,
      24 January 1992, 12.
35   F.W. de Klerk quoted in Patrick Cull, "FW Promises White Veto," *PE Evening
      Post*, 24 January 1992, 1.
36   "People's Parliament a 'Lesson in Democracy'," *Cape Argus*, 24 January 1992, 12.
37   ANC NEC, "The Response to President de Klerk's Opening Address to
      Parliament," 24 January 1992. Reprinted at <www.anc.org.za/ancdocs/pr/1992/
      pr0214.html>. Also see Mandla Tyla, "Minority Veto," *PE Evening Post*, 24
      January 1992, np.
38   "ANC Position on Minorities Welcomed," *PE Evening Post*, 28 January 1992, np.
39   PAC, "We are Demonstrating Against the Monster Called CODESA," *Cape
      Argus*, 24 January 1992, 13. Also see Maxwell Memadzivhanani, "Why the PAC
      Continues to Fight Against CODESA," *New Nation*, 31 January 1992, 11. Also
      opposed to the process, several right-wing groups undertook to bomb several post
      offices. At a larger level, political violence did seem to be decreasing even as it was
      clear to many that SAG's military intelligence units were continuing to train and
      arm IFP cadres. Drew Forrest, "Inside Inkatha," *The Weekly Mail*, 10 January 1992,
      16–17.
40   Ameen Akhalwaya, "The Past is Still With Us," *The Weekly Mail*, 14 February
      1992, 14.
41   Phillip van Niekerk, "FW's Horror Story: It's Either Me or It's Chaos," *The
      Weekly Mail*, 21 February 1992, 2.
42   Paul Stober, "Quietly CODESA Gets it Together," *The Weekly Mail*, 6 March
      1992, 10.

43 Anthony Johnson, "Whites Close the Door on Apartheid," *Cape Times*, 19 March 1992, 1.

44 Paul Stober, "The Invisible War Criss-Crosses our Land," *The Weekly Mail*, 3 April 1992, 5.

45 NA, "Government and ANC Fail to Agree," *PE Evening Post*, 7 April 1992, np.

46 For accounts of the shifting positions, see Patti Waldmeir, *Anatomy of a Miracle: The End of Apartheid and the Birth of the New South African Constitution* (New York: WW Norton, 1997), 202; Friedman, *Long Journey*, 79–81.

47 Waldmeir, *Anatomy*, 203.

48 Edyth Bulbring, "ANC's Bottom Line," *Sunday Times*, 24 May 1992, np.

49 Phillip van Niekerk, "Standing on the Threshold of a New Era," *The Weekly Mail*, 15 May 1992, 6.

50 Eddie Koch, "Season of Discontent and Negotiations Falter," *Weekly Mail*, 22 May 1992, 1–2.

51 Nelson Mandela, "Intervention of the President of the ANC, Nelson Mandela at the Second Session of CODESA," 16 May 1992. Reprinted at <www.anc.org.za/ancdocs/speeches/1992> (January 2000).

52 Nelson Mandela, "Address by Comrade Nelson R. Mandela to the International Federation of Newspaper Publishers Conference," 26 May 1992. Reprinted at <www.anc.org.za/ancdocs/history/Mandela/1992/> (January 2000).

53 Phillip van Niekerk, "No Gains in Push-me Pull-you CODESA II," *The Weekly Mail*, 22 May 1992, 27.

54 John Hatchard and Peter Slinn, "The Path Towards a New Order in South Africa," *International Relations* 12 (1995), 25.

55 The triple alliance was composed of the ANC, SACP and COSATU. For detailed accounts of the calls for more revolutionary action, see Adam and Moodley, *Opening*, 101.

56 Spitz and Chaskalson, *Hidden*, 27.

57 Nelson Mandela quoted in Waldmeir, *Anatomy*, 206.

58 NA, "ANC Suspends Talks," *Eastern Province Herald*, 22 June 1992, 1.

59 ANC NEC, "Emergency Meeting of the NEC of the ANC," 23 June 1992. Reprinted at <www.anc.org.za/ancdocs/pr/1992/> (October 2001).

60 SAPA, "Time for Cool Heads; Text of Address by F.W. de Klerk," *Cape Argus*, 3 July 1992, np.

61 Nelson Mandela, "Letter to Mr. F.W. de Klerk," 26 June 1992. Reprinted at <www.anc.org.za/ancdocs/history/Mandela/memo920626.htm> (August 1998).

62 Mandela, "Letter to de Klerk."

63 F.W. de Klerk, "Letter to Nelson Mandela," 2 July 1992. Reprinted at <www.anc.org.za/ancdocs/history/transition/lett2july.html> (August 1998).

64 Nelson Mandela, "Response by ANC President, Nelson Mandela, to President de Klerk's Memorandum," 4 July 1992. Reprinted at <www.anc.org.za/ancdocs/history/Mandela/1992/pr920704.html> (August 1998).

65 Nelson Mandela, "Letter to F.W. de Klerk," 9 July 1992. Reprinted at <www.anc.org.za/ancdocs/history/Mandela/fwletter/html> (August 1998).

66 Friedman, *Long Journey*, 143.

67 Patrick Cull, "Historical All-Party Talks to put South Africa's Future in the Balance," *Eastern Province Herald*, 5 March 1993, np.

68 Waldmeir, *Anatomy*, 207.
69 Kader Asmal, "The Constitutional Crossroads," in *The CODESA File*, ed. Fatima Meer (Durban: Madiba Publishers, 1993), 3–4; Atkinson, "Brokering a Miracle," 13; Friedman, *Long Journey*, 154.
70 *Report of the Commission of Enquiry into Complaints by Former African National Congress Prisoners and Detainees* (Bellville: Centre for Development Studies, 1992), 23.
71 Eddie Koch, "Goniwe's Ghost Haunts Cabinet Ministers," *The Weekly Mail*, 21 August 1992, 2.
72 NA, "ANC, Government Mum on Latest Round of Talks," *Eastern Province Herald*, 27 August 1992.
73 ANC, "Statement on the Question of a General Amnesty," 17 August 1992. Reprinted at <www.anc.org.za/ancdocs/pr/1992/pr0817.html> (August 2002).
74 Editorial, "Victims Also Have Rights," *The Weekly Mail*, 14 August 1992.
75 Editorial, "Amnesty or Amnesia?" *The Weekly Mail*, 25 September 1992, 14.
76 Waldmeir, *Anatomy*, 218.
77 "Record of Understanding and Meeting Between the State President of the Republic of South Africa and the President of the African National Congress Held at the World Trade Centre," 26 September 1992. Reprinted at <www.anc.org.za/ancdocs/history/transition/record.html> (August 1998). With respect to the mechanisms for transition, the agreement continued: "The Government and the ANC agreed that during the interim/transitional period there shall be constitutional continuity and no constitutional hiatus. In consideration of this principle, it was further agreed that: the constitution-making body/constituent assembly shall also act as the interim/transitional Parliament; there shall be an interim/transitional government of national unity; the constitution-making body/constituent assembly cum interim/transitional Parliament and the interim/transitional government of national unity shall function within a constitutional framework/transitional constitution which shall provide for national and regional government during the period of transition and shall incorporate guaranteed justiciable fundamental rights and freedoms. The interim/transitional Parliament may function as a one- or two-chambered body."
78 F.W. de Klerk, *The Last Trek – A New Beginning* (New York: MacMillan, 1998), 255. For a nuanced reflection on the effectiveness of the mass action, see Friedman, *Long Journey*, 154.
79 Spitz and Chaskalson, *Hidden*, 30.
80 NA, "Wiping the Slate Clean?" *Negotiation News* (October 1992), 11–12.
81 ANC, "Statement on the Further Indemnity Bill," 6 November 1992. Reprinted at <www.anc.org.za/ancdocs/pr/1992/pr1106a.html> (July 2002). For another criticism of the bill, see N. Kollapen, "Accountability: The Debate in South Africa," *Journal of African Law* 37 (1993), 5.
82 Luwellyn Landers, *Debates of Parliament* (Hansard), 4th Session-9th Parliament, 21 October 1992, col. 12755.
83 Christiaan de Jager, *Debates of Parliament* (Hansard), 4th Session-9th Parliament, 21 October 1992, col. 12769.
84 Jan Momberg, *Debates of Parliament* (Hansard), 4th Session-9th Parliament, 21 October 1992, col. 12783.

85 Joe Slovo, "Negotiations: What Room for Compromise?" *African Communist* 3rd Qtr. (1992), 40.

86 Pallo Jordan, "Committing Suicide by Concession," *The Weekly Mail,* 13 November 1992, 8. For additional commentary on the prevalence of similar views, see Friedman, *Long Journey,* 143.

87 Walter Benjamin, "Critique of Violence," in *Walter Benjamin, Selected Writings, Vol. 1, 1913–1926,* ed. M. Bullock (Cambridge: Harvard University Press, 1996), 244.

88 Delegates to the forum that followed CODESA could never reach consensus on what to call the structure. Archival records show that several options were presented on the initial ballot: CODESA, Negotiating Forum for South Africa (NEFSA), South African Constitutional Forum (SACOF), Democratic Convention of South Africa (DECOSA), and Negotiating South Africa (NEGOSA).

89 ANC NEC, "Statement of the NEC on the Occasion of the 81st Anniversary of the African National Congress," 8 January 1993. Reprinted at <www.anc.org.za/ancdocs/history/jan8-93/.html> (February 2000).

90 F.W. de Klerk, "New Spirit, Greater Realism," *Cape Argus,* 29 January 1993, 12.

91 de Klerk, "New Spirit, Greater Realism," 12.

92 Patrick Cull, "ANC Gives Green Light to Unity," *Eastern Province Herald,* 19 February 1993, 1.

93 Richard Humphries, "Confusion of Options," *Democracy in Action* 6 (October 1992): 14–15; Hein Marais, "A Year of Living Dangerously," *Work In Progress* 85 (December 1992): 15–17.

94 Atkinson, "Brokering," 36. Of those who consider the decision-making procedures employed at the MPNP, Spitz and Chaskalson offer a description of sufficient consensus and its redesign. However, the treatment remains largely descriptive and is tied more to Roger Fisher's claims about his work to introduce the ideas of the Harvard Negotiating Project into the MPNP context. To date, I have found no one in the ANC or NP leadership who recalls Fisher's participation as being influential. See Spitz and Chaskalson, *Hidden,* 59, 419.

95 Patrick Cull, "Historic All-Party Talks to Put SA's Future in Balance," *Eastern Province Herald,* 3 March 1993, 1.

96 Spitz and Chaskalson, *Hidden,* 58.

97 Pravin Gordhan, Statement Delivered at the MPNP Meeting of the Facilitating Committee, 5 March 1993, p. 1, MPNP Files (unsorted), South African National Archives, Pretoria, South Africa.

98 Cyril Ramaphosa, Statement delivered at the MPNP Meeting of the Facilitating Committee, 5 March 1993, p. 4, MPNP Files (unsorted), South African National Archives, Pretoria, South Africa.

99 Pravin Gordhan, Statement to the MPNP Facilitating Committee, pp. 11–12.

100 Cyril Ramaphosa, Statement to the MPNP Facilitating Committee, p. 5.

101 Likely, the speaker was D.S. Rajah. Statement delivered at the MPNP Meeting of the Facilitating Committee, 5 March 1993, p. 7, MPNP Files (unsorted), South African National Archives, Pretoria, South Africa.

102 Benny Alexander, Statement delivered at the MPNP Meeting of the Facilitating Committee, 5 March 1993, p. 13, MPNP Files (unsorted), South African National Archives, Pretoria, South Africa.

103 Rowan Cronje, Statement delivered at the MPNP Meeting of the Facilitating

Committee, 5 March 1993, p. 5, MPNP Files (unsorted), South African National
Archives, Pretoria, South Africa.

104 Desmond Tutu, "His Death Is Our Victory," in *The Rainbow People of God: The Making of a Peaceful Revolution*, ed. John Allen (New York: Doubleday, 1994), 251–54.

105 Editorial, "Rising to Meet the Crisis," *The Weekly Mail*, 16 April 1993, 20. In the weeks following Hani's death, the ANC appeared increasingly to be split over whether to increase the speed of negotiations or chart a more radical path. At the same time, it appeared that the violence that occurred in the aftermath of Hani's death had bolstered the hand of NP conservatives, particularly those that wanted to alter the *Record of Understanding* such that the MPNP would be charged to produce a final constitution. See Spitz and Chaskalson, *Hidden*, 77.

106 The Plenary was composed of party leaders and nine party delegates. The Forum sat four delegates per party while the Negotiating Council was limited to two delegates and two advisors from each party. The Council was the "engine room" of the talks. Between March and November 1993, it met 74 times. The Planning Committee was composed of only 12 individuals and it came to play a key role in the success of the process. Friedman argues that it was the "black box where the process was steered, and crucial agreements reached. An even more closeted centre point was the 'subcommittee', consisting of Fanie van der Merwe of the SAG, Mac Maharaj of the ANC, and Ben Ngubane of the IFP (until it walked out)" (Friedman, *Brokering*, 24).

107 MPNP, Negotiating Council Minutes, Addendum B, Explanatory Memorandum To Be Accepted by All Participants in the Multi-Party Process Relating to Proposals Arising from the Multi-Party Forum Resolution on the Negotiation Process, 13 May 1993, p. 10, MPNP Files (unsorted), South African National Archives, Pretoria, South Africa. For commentary, see Spitz and Chaskalson, *Hidden*, 49. The Technical Committees were Constitutional Issues, Fundamental Rights during Transition, Independent Electoral Commission, Media, Repeal of Existing Legislation, Violence, and Transitional Executive Council.

108 In part, this was done to encourage CODESA-boycotting parties to return to the negotiations. See Atkinson, "Brokering," 23.

109 MPNP, Negotiating Council Minutes, Addendum E, Explanatory Memorandum To Be Accepted by All Participants in the Multi-Party Process Relating to Proposals Arising from the Multi-Party Forum Resolution on the Negotiation Process, 13 May 1993, p. 9, MPNP Files (unsorted), South African National Archives, Pretoria, South Africa.

110 MPNP Negotiating Forum, "Standing Rules of Procedure," in *MPNP – Plenary Session and Documents: Adopted Resolutions of the Multi-Party Negotiating Process* (Kempton Park: MPNP, 13 May 1993), 2.

111 Spitz and Chaskalson, *Hidden*, 37.

112 These issues were reflected in a report to the Negotiating Council from the Technical Committee dated 19 May 1993. The report also took up the issue of whether the problem of having an elected body write the constitution could be overcome by the development of an interim constitution that contained a set of principles that would bind the authors of the final text.

113 MPNP, Minutes of the Negotiating Council, Addendum C, 3 June 1993, p. 22,

MPNP Files (unsorted), South African National Archives, Pretoria, South Africa.

114 KwaZulu Government, The KwaZulu Government Position Statement Delivered by Dr B.S. Ngubane to the Negotiating Council, 15 June 1993, contained in Draft Minutes of the Negotiating Council, Addendum B, 15 June 1993, p. 2, MPNP Files (unsorted), South African National Archives, Pretoria, South Africa.

115 KwaZulu Government, The KwaZulu Government Position Statement Delivered by Dr B.S. Ngubane, p. 3.

116 Walter Felgate, Minutes of the MPNP Negotiating Council, 18 June 1993, np. (partial fax copy), MPNP Files (unsorted), South African National Archives, Pretoria, South Africa.

117 Emphasis added. Pravin Gordhan, Minutes of the MPNP Negotiating Council, 18 June 1993, np. (partial fax copy), MPNP Files (unsorted), South African National Archives, Pretoria, South Africa.

118 Recorded Minutes of the MPNP Ad Hoc Committee on Sufficient Consensus, 24 June 1993, MPNP Files (unsorted), South African National Archives, Pretoria, South Africa.

119 First Report of the MPNP Ad Hoc Committee on Sufficient Consensus, 20 July 1993, p. 5, MPNP Files (unsorted), South African National Archives, Pretoria, South Africa.

120 Cyril Ramaphosa, Minutes of the MPNP Negotiating Forum, 2 July 1993, p. 2, MPNP Files (unsorted), South African National Archives, Pretoria, South Africa.

121 MPNP Negotiating Council Resolution 21: Resolution on Steps to be taken for the Purposes of Establishing a New Constitutional Order Adopted by the Negotiating Council on 30 June 1993, in Adopted Resolutions of the MPNP, March 5 to 17 November 1993, MPNP Files (unsorted), South African National Archives, Pretoria, South Africa.

122 Chief Nota, Minutes of the MPNP Negotiating Forum, 2 July 1993, p. 19, MPNP Files (unsorted), South African National Archives, Pretoria, South Africa.

123 Tom Langley, Minutes of the MPNP Negotiating Forum, 2 July 1993, p. 20, MPNP Files (unsorted), South African National Archives, Pretoria, South Africa.

124 Joe Matthews, Minutes of the MPNP Negotiating Forum, 2 July 1993, p. 23, MPNP Files (unsorted), South African National Archives, Pretoria, South Africa.

125 Mickey Webb, Minutes of the MPNP Negotiating Forum, 2 July 1993, pp. 35–37, MPNP Files (unsorted), South African National Archives, Pretoria, South Africa.

126 Pravin Gordhan, Minutes of the MPNP Negotiating Forum, 2 July 1993, p. 37, MPNP Files (unsorted), South African National Archives, Pretoria, South Africa.

127 Farouk Cassim, Transcript of Video: TVI Agenda, 19 July 1993, p. 4, MPNP Files (unsorted), South African National Archives, Pretoria, South Africa.

128 Government of the Self-Governing Territory of KwaZulu, *Motion of Application*, 28 July 1993, 35–36. This was the first application submitted. It was withdrawn and then resubmitted on 6 August.

129 Pravin Gordhan, "Respondent's Answering Affidavit in the matter of Government of the Self-Governing Territory of KwaZulu vs. Mahlangu and Another," 1 September 1993, 4.

130 Emphasis added. Pravin Gordhan, "Respondent's Answering Affidavit in the matter of Government of the Self-Governing Territory of KwaZulu vs. Mahlangu and Another," 1 September 1993, 5.

131 The respondents also addressed the KZG's particular charge that sufficient
     consensus had been defined and used unfairly, replying that all parties had agreed
     to the rules and that it was clear from the start that they entailed a certain amount
     of discretion. They also suggested that if the applicant's claims were true then the
     rules were void for vagueness and that this would eliminate any existing standing
     to sue.
132 J.P. Eloff, *Government of the Self-Governing Territory of KwaZulu vs. Mahlangu and
     Another*, Transvaal Provincial Division, 1993 (1) South Africa, 635. Here, the
     court was citing dictum in *Estate Breet v. Peri Urban Health Board* 1955 (3) South
     Africa, 523.
133 Eloff, *Government of the Self-Governing Territory*, 636, 638
134 Spitz and Chaskalson, *Hidden*, 41.

chapter 4

1   Nelson Mandela, "Address to the Plenary Session of the Multi-Party Negotiations
     Process," November 17, 1993. Reprinted at <www.anc.org.za/ancdocs/history/
     Mandela/1993/sp931117.html> (September 2002).
2   R.E. Allen, *Plato's Parmenides: Translation and Analysis* (Minneapolis: University of
     Minnesota Press, 1983), 42, 265; Kenneth Burke, *A Grammar of Motives* (Berkeley:
     University of California Press, 1969). Also see Linda M.G. Zerilli, "Castoriadis,
     Arendt and the Problem of the New," *Constellations* 9 (2002): 540–553; Peter
     Osbourne, "Small-Scale Victories, Large-Scale Defeats: Walter Benjamin's Politics
     of Time," in *Destruction and Experience: Walter Benjamin's Philosophy*, eds. Andrew
     Benjamin and Peter Osbourne (Manchester: Clinamen Press, 2000), 80–83.
3   I borrow here from Arendt's discussion of human action and the dynamics of
     its creation. See Hannah Arendt, *The Human Condition* (Chicago: University
     of Chicago Press, 1958).
4   For discussion of this phrase, see Piet Meiring, "The *Baruti* versus the Lawyers:
     The Role of Religion in the TRC Process," in *Looking Back, Reaching Forward:
     Reflections on the Truth and Reconciliation Commission of South Africa*, eds. Charles
     Villa-Vicencio and Wilhelm Verwoerd (Cape Town: University of Cape Town
     Press, 2000), 127. On the appearance and play of questions in transition, see
     Hans-Georg Gadamer, *Truth and Method*, 2nd ed. (New York: Continuum, 1994).
5   P.N. Langa, "Keynote Address," in *Transcending a Century of Injustice*, ed. Charles
     Villa-Vicencio (Cape Town: Institute for Justice and Reconciliation, 2000), 15.
6   This is not a defence of apartheid law. Rather, it is to say that the principle per se
     was an announced feature of the law, even as its practice ran roughshod over such
     a demand.
7   Many of the compromise-driven accounts contend that the Commission was a
     reflection if not outright extension of the "spirit" and "good faith" that supported
     and underwrote the constitutional negotiations. Others, echoing Desmond
     Tutu and the TRC's *Final Report*, hold that the Commission was created as the
     mechanism that would make good on the compromise over amnesty which
     was reached in the MPNP's final days (South African Truth and Reconciliation
     Commission, *Final Report* Vol. 1 (Pretoria: SAG, 1998), 52.) This interpretation is
     tied closely to the necessity hypothesis, one variant of which is that a compromise
     over amnesty was a necessary condition for transition. This is the position defended

by Johnny de Lange, one of the Commission's early architects, when he argues that without the "specific compromise" on amnesty, "there would have been no settlement, no interim constitution, no elections, no democracy, and a possible continuation of the conflicts of the past" (Johnny De Lange, "The Historical Context, Legal Origins, and Philosophical Foundation of the South African Truth and Reconciliation Commission," in *Looking Back, Reaching Forward*, 22). However, there is also a broader interpretation of this claim, one which suggests that the TRC could only emerge from the awkward mechanics of a "colonialism of a special type", the unique premise of the South African struggle, the country's particular style of political transition, and the need to "deal with a past" rife with impunity and the gross violation of human rights. Among others, officials in the Mandela government were notable advocates of this position and used it to ground the "campaign of persuasion" that was undertaken in 1995 to explain the TRC's aim, power, and value.

8   For its part, the compromise thesis acknowledges that the problem, aspiration, and practice of reconciliation were embedded in the constitution-making process. However, its recollection of the negotiations tends toward the ideal if not the romantic, deriving the choice to take the truth's "road to reconciliation" from a "spirit" that does little to account for the fact that the MPNP was intensely bilateral, bitterly contested, surrounded by incredible bloodletting, and dependent on a mode of decision-making that allowed for the deferral of controversial decisions until there was sufficient(ly) (consensual) momentum to carry the day. Good faith entailed much strategy, perhaps a modicum of duplicity, and accusations from every side about who was selling what out to whom. If the amnesty decision was a compromise, it was an exclusive deal, one that was never considered by the larger MPNP. This enabling "side agreement" continues to haunt, especially when one considers both the significant number of PAC cadres who remain in prison and the continuing tension between the IFP, TRC, and ANC. At a larger level, however, the compromise narrative reminds us of an important history but does not contain much room to ask whether the MPNP's constitutive power enacted a compromise that *supported* the TRC's development or if the Commission was a *reaction* to what the compromise left behind. In a similar way, by conflating compromise and the performance of reconciliation at the MPNP, it obscures the possibility that the TRC's creation was motivated by the (unexpected) costs of creating transition. In other words, the TRC's beginning may have rested in the need to begin (again).

In some contrast, necessity-based accounts of the TRC's development tend to be somewhat darker than their counterparts. They hint (without always naming) at something darker, forces in the shadows (of history, politics and logic) that conspired to produce an irresistible need for the Commission. Like certain forms of "democratisation studies", these accounts rest in a kind of historicism, one that in this case fates the initiation of a "history-making" inquiry. More precisely, it is difficult to locate the decisive event(s), especially if one considers the possibility that the often bitter arguments over how to craft the transition had done much to compromise the very concept of necessity. In any case, some skirt this problem by relying on the "no victor" hypothesis, a position that speaks far more to the need for power-sharing than a TRC. Others claim that the Commission was a response to the threat of a coup that was defused by assurances that there would be amnesty. Then and now, this was a matter of (important) appearance, a perception about the conditions needed for stability and legitimacy in the wake of the election. It is a position that would also have to be extended to the problems created by the findings of the Motsuenyane Commission.

9   For works that detail the substantive work at the MPNP, see Hassen Ebrahim, *Soul of a Nation: Constitution-Making in South Africa* (Cape Town: Oxford University Press, 1998); Richard Spitz and Matthew Chaskalson, *The Politics of Transition: A Hidden History of South Africa's Negotiated Settlement* (Johannesburg: Witwatersrand University Press, 2000).

10 SAG, The Repeal of Indemnity Legislation, Submission to the MPNP, 21 July 1993, Submission 1/3/1/4/62, p. 2, MPNP Files (unsorted), South African National Archives, Pretoria, South Africa.

11 ANC, *NEC Response to the Motsuenyane Commission Report* (Johannesburg: ANC, 29 August 1993), 6.

12 SAPA, No title, 31 August 1993. Reprinted at ANC Daily News Briefing Archive <www.anc.org.za/anc/newsbrief/> (September 2002).

13 SAPA, "ANC Report Raises Concerns on Human Rights Abuses Says the Human Rights Commission," 31 August 1993. Reprinted at ANC Daily News Briefing Archive <www.anc.org.za/anc/newsbrief/> (September 2002).

14 SAPA, "Findings of the Commission Showed that Full Indemnity Was Required by the ANC Says Justice Minister Kobie Coetsee," 31 August 1993. Reprinted at ANC Daily News Briefing Archive <www.anc.org.za/anc/newsbrief/> (September 2002). In particular, the ANC's argument against government proposed amnesty was that as the state had neither the "moral authority nor the right to condone unilateral wrong-doing by its agents", its demands for amnesty constituted an affront to those who deserved "acknowledgement and reparations" (ANC, *Response to the Motsuenyane Commission*, 6).

15 See Richard Goldstone, *For Humanity: Reflections of a War Crimes Investigator* (Johannesburg: Witwatersrand University Press, 2000), 40–45.

16 SAPA, "Civil War Would Ensue if the General Elections was Enforced in the OFS Says the CP," 31 August 1993. Reprinted at ANC Daily News Briefing Archive <www.anc.org.za/anc/newsbrief/> (September 2002).

17 SAPA, "The ANC Message is that of Reconciliation Says the ANC President in Cape Town Monday," 13 September 1993. Reprinted at ANC Daily News Briefing Archive <www.anc.org.za/anc/newsbrief/> (September 2002).

18 SAPA, "Passing of TEC Bill Added Proverbial Stick to the Negotiations," 23 September 1993. Reprinted at ANC Daily News Briefing Archive <www. anc.org.za/anc/newsbrief/> (September 2002).

19 SAPA, "Passing of TEC Bill."

20 SAPA, "Compromise by Government and ANC Will Be Needed to Finalise Agreements on Key Issues," 26 October 1993. Reprinted at ANC Daily News Briefing Archive <www.anc.org.za/anc/newsbrief/> (September 2002).

21 SAPA, "AVF Leader says the Negotiations Has Forced the Afrikaner into a Corner," 23 September 1993. Reprinted at ANC Daily News Briefing Archive <www.anc.org.za/anc/newsbrief/> (September 2002).

22 SAPA, "Freedom Alliance Finally Formed by the COSAG Group Members,"

7 October 1993. Reprinted at ANC Daily News Briefing Archive <www.anc.org. za/anc/newsbrief/> (September 2002).

23   SAPA, "The ANC President Warned Rightwingers if they Try to Sabotage the Elections," 7 November 1993. Reprinted at ANC Daily News Briefing Archive <www.anc.org.za/anc/newsbrief/> (September 2002).

24   SAPA, "Political Leaders Should Stop War-Talk and Avoid Armed Conflict," 17 November 1993. Reprinted at ANC Daily News Briefing Archive <www.anc. org.za/anc/newsbrief/> (September 2002).

25   SAPA, "Freedom Alliance Warning on Eve of Plenary," 17 November 1993. Reprinted at ANC Daily News Briefing Archive <www.anc.org.za/anc/ newsbrief/> (September 2002).

26   Spitz and Chaskalson, *The Politics of Transition*, 43; Doreen Atkinson, "Brokering a Miracle: The Multiparty Negotiating Forum," in *South African Review* 7, ed. Steven Friedman (Johannesburg: Ravan, 1994), 35; NA, "Last Minute Trading Clinches the Deal," *The Weekly Mail*, 19 November 1993, 10.

27   Colin Eglin, quoted in "Last Minute Trading Clinches the Deal," 10.

28   SAPA-Reuters, "Curtain on White Rule Finally Brought Down," 17 November 1993. Reprinted at ANC Daily News Briefing Archive <www.anc.org.za/anc/ newsbrief/> (September 2002).

29   For a complete list of the Constitutional Principles, and a discussion of the terms of the constitution and its structuring of government, see Ebrahim, *Soul of a Nation*, 619–27.

30   F.W. de Klerk, *Debates of Parliament* (Hansard), 5th Session-9th Parliament, 22 November 1993, cols. 13795–804.

31   SAPA, " Up to Half the Population of South Africa Do Not Identify with the Agreements Reached Says the CP leader," 17 November 1993. Reprinted at ANC Daily News Briefing Archive <www.anc.org.za/anc/newsbrief/> (September 2002).

32   SAPA, "Acceptance of the Interim Constitution Mark the Beginning of a Violent Take-Over by the Communists Says the AVF leader," 17 November 1993. Reprinted at ANC Daily News Briefing Archive <www.anc.org.za/anc/ newsbrief/> (September 2002).

33   SAPA, "Bophuthatswana Will Decide Its Own Future Says Chief Negotiator," 17 November 1993. Reprinted at ANC Daily News Briefing Archive <www.anc. org.za/anc/newsbrief/> (September 2002).

34   Nelson Mandela, "Statement about the Ultra Right-wing's Threats of Civil War," 26 November 1993. Reprinted at <www.anc.org.za/ancdocs/history/ mandela/1993/pr931126.html> (March 2002).

35   SAPA, "The Freedom Alliance Not Capable of a Sustained Military Threat," 22 November 1993. Reprinted at ANC Daily News Briefing Archive <www.anc. org.za/anc/newsbrief/> (September 2002).

36   "Pigeon-holing" was an explicit practice employed at the MPNP, an approach that saw divisive issues shelved until such time as they could be taken up from a different vantage point. Linked somewhat to the use of sufficient consensus, its underlying goal was to ensure that the negotiations continued to make progress.

37   Philippe Salazar and I have had interesting discussion about what the text is best called. In the literature, there is little agreement on the matter. At the Justice in

Transition conference discussed later in this chapter, the text's appropriate name was debated to non-resolution. One of its authors, Mac Maharaj referred to it consistently as a post-amble, although the South African Constitutional Court has referred to it as an epilogue.

38   At this time, the Inkatha Freedom Party was no longer represented on the Sub-Committee.

39   Mac Maharaj, Interview with Author, Johannesburg, 16 January 2001.

40   F.W. de Klerk also has a vague account of the post-amble's authorship. See F.W. de Klerk, *The Last Trek – A New Beginning* (New York: MacMillan, 1998), 289.

41   Mac Maharaj, Interview with Author, Johannesburg, 16 January 2001.

42   The phrase is Hegel's. See G.W.F. Hegel, *The Philosophy of Right*, trans. T.M. Knox (London: Oxford University Press, 1967), 12.

43   The full text of the interim constitution can be found at <www.oefre.unibe.ch/law/icl/sf10000_.html> (August 2001).

44   This dynamic has an interesting connection with Habermas's recent work on how the project of constitution-making is one that must extend the "founding" moment into the future. In addition to the discussion in the previous chapter, see Jürgen Habermas, *Between Facts and Norms: Contributions to a Discourse Theory of Law and Democracy*, trans. William Rehg (Cambridge: MIT Press, 1996).

45   The idea of a "legal constitutive amnesty" (*rechtskonstituierende Amnestie*) is developed somewhat in *Confronting Past Injustices: Approaches to Amnesty, Punishment, Reparation and Restitution in South Africa and Germany*, eds. M.R. Rwelamira and G. Werle (Durban: Butterworths, 1996), 38–39.

46   I have discussed this relationship elsewhere. See Erik Doxtader, "Easy to Forget or Never (Again) Hard to Remember," in *The Provocations of Amnesty: Memory, Justice and Impunity*, eds. Charles Villa-Vicencio and Erik Doxtader (Cape Town: David Philips, 2003).

47   As du Plessis suggests, this gesture may introduce a humaneness into law, a moment when both its form and content is seen to depend on the interests and actions of those it claims to represent (Lourens Du Plessis, "Observations on Amnesty and Indemnity for Acts Associated With Political Objectives in Light of South Africa's Transitional Constitution," *THRHR* 57 (1994), 481).

48   For discussion of the issue, see Steven Friedman, ed., *The Long Journey: South Africa's Quest for a Negotiated Settlement* (Johannesburg: Ravan Press, 1993), 186. Whatever its form, the question of backlash against the new government by the security forces was tied inextricably to uncertainty and insecurity about the future form and power of security institutions. This included the difficult problem of whether and how to reintegrate MK forces into the SADF. These and related issues were the subject of parallel talks during the MPNP.

49   Constand Viljoen, Interview with Author, Cape Town, 11 October 2000.

50   As Bantu Holomisa wrote to the awards committee, "In the interests of South Africans, whose consciences are revolted at the recent orgy of the violent raid, you are kindly requested to reconsider your decision to award the Nobel Peace Prize to President de Klerk" (quoted in SAPA, "Transkei Leader has Urged the Norwegians to Reconsider Their Awarding the Nobel Prize to de Klerk," 18 October 1993. Reprinted at ANC Daily News Briefing Archive <www.anc.org.za/anc/newsbrief/> (September 2002).) For its part, the right-wing chastised de Klerk for

accepting the award, comparing him to the allegedly duplicitous Jan Smuts.

51 SAPA, "ANC President and de Klerk Call for Reconciliation in South Africa," 9 December 1993. Reprinted at ANC Daily News Briefing Archive (September 2002).

52 SAPA, "Entire South African Government are Political Criminals Says Madiba," 9 December 1993. Reprinted at ANC Daily News Briefing Archive (September 2002).

53 SAPA, "If the ANC Wants War They Would Have It Says AWB Leader," 15 December 1993. Reprinted at ANC Daily News Briefing Archive (September 2002).

54 SAPA, "Afrikaners Will Reaffirm the Vow," 16 December 1993. Reprinted at ANC Daily News Briefing Archive <www.anc.org.za/anc/newsbrief/> (September 2002).

55 Nelson Mandela, "Statement on the Occasion of the 32nd Anniversary of MK," 16 December 1993, 1. Reprinted at <www.anc.org.za/ancdocs/history/ mandela/1993/sp931216.html> (April 2002).

56 Roelf Meyer, *Debates of Parliament* (Hansard), 5th Session-9th Parliament, 17 December 1993, col. 15296.

57 Meyer, cols. 15296–97.

58 Meyer, col. 15297.

59 Daniel du Plessis, *Debates of Parliament* (Hansard), 5th Session-9th Parliament, 17 December 1993, col. 15485.

60 du Plessis, col. 15486.

61 Meyer, col. 15297.

62 Jacobus Beyers, *Debates of Parliament* (Hansard), 5th Session-9th Parliament, 17 December 1993, cols. 15445, 15443.

63 In this argument, Mulder was quoting Smuts. See Pieter Mulder, *Debates of Parliament* (Hansard), 5th Session-9th Parliament, 18 December 1993, col. 15605. A critic of sufficient consensus at the MPNP, Francois Le Roux made the case again in Parliament's debate. See Francois Le Roux, *Debates of Parliament* (Hansard), 5th Session-9th Parliament, 17 December 1993, cols. 15409–12.

64 Wynand van Wyk, *Debates of Parliament* (Hansard), 5th Session-9th Parliament, 17 December 1993, col. 15342; Gerber, *Debates of Parliament* (Hansard), 5th Session-9th Parliament, 17 December 1993, col. 15421.

65 Sheila Camerer, *Debates of Parliament* (Hansard), 5th Session-9th Parliament, 17 December 1993, col. 15375; Ganesan Mari, *Debates of Parliament* (Hansard), 5th Session-9th Parliament, 18 December 1993, col. 15575.

66 Kassavan Padayachy, *Debates of Parliament* (Hansard), 5th Session-9th Parliament, 18 December 1993, col. 15548.

67 Colin Eglin, *Debates of Parliament* (Hansard), 5th Session-9th Parliament, 17 December 1993, col. 15320. For similar characterisations of this transition moment, see the remarks at cols. 15325, 15468, 15529, 15389.

68 Respectively, see Dawid de Villiers, *Debates of Parliament* (Hansard), 5th Session-9th Parliament, 17 December 1993, col. 15364; Christian April, *Debates of Parliament* (Hansard), 5th Session-9th Parliament, 18 December 1993, col. 15520.

69 Dawid de Villiers, *Debates of Parliament* (Hansard), 5th Session-9th Parliament, 17 December 1993, col. 15364; Jacobus Beyers, *Debates of Parliament* (Hansard), 5th

Session-9th Parliament, 17 December 1993, col. 15444; Ismail Richards, *Debates of Parliament* (Hansard), 5th Session-9th Parliament, 17 December 1993, col. 15470. Also see Helenard Hendrickse, *Debates of Parliament* (Hansard), 5th Session-9th Parliament, 17 December 1993, col. 15310.

70   Michael Hendrickse, *Debates of Parliament* (Hansard), 5th Session-9th Parliament, 17 December 1993, col. 15399.

71   Michael Hendrickse, cols. 15399–400.

72   Frederik van Heerden, *Debates of Parliament* (Hansard), 5th Session-9th Parliament, 17 December 1993, col. 13315.

73   Abraham Williams, *Debates of Parliament* (Hansard), 5th Session-9th Parliament, 17 December 1993, cols. 15339–40. The position was echoed by Louis Pienaar's claim that, "We won the revolutionary wars against SWAPO, the ANC and the PAC" (Louis Pienaar, *Debates of Parliament* (Hansard), 5th Session-9th Parliament, 17 December 1993, col. 15346).

74   Jakobus Rabie, *Debates of Parliament* (Hansard), 5th Session-9th Parliament, 17 December 1993, col. 15416.

75   Wynand van Wyk, *Debates of Parliament* (Hansard), 5th Session-9th Parliament, 17 December 1993, col. 15344; Joseph Chiolé, *Debates of Parliament* (Hansard), 5th Session-9th Parliament, 20 December 1993, col. 15729.

76   See, for instance, Louis Stofberg, *Debates of Parliament* (Hansard), 5th Session-9th Parliament, 17 December 1993, col. 15434.

77   The CP's Casper Uys set the argument in the context of the Boer War, arguing that the Afrikaner was again willing to fight. See Casper Uys, *Debates of Parliament* (Hansard), 5th Session-9th Parliament, 18 December 1993, col. 15598.

78   Stephanus Jacobs, *Debates of Parliament* (Hansard), 5th Session-9th Parliament, 18 December 1993, col. 15646.

79   There is an apparent lacuna in the Hansard's attribution of the argument quoted here. In the transcript, the speech is attributed to the Leader of the Official Opposition in the House of Delegates, who in the volume's key is listed as Farouk Cassim, a member of the IFP who argued vehemently at the MPNP against sufficient consensus and spoke against the interim constitution in the Parliament's debate. In any event, the speech appears at col. 15387.

80   Pieter Marais, *Debates of Parliament* (Hansard), 5th Session-9th Parliament, 17 December 1993, col. 15333.

81   Pieter Mulder, *Debates of Parliament* (Hansard), 5th Session-9th Parliament, 18 December 1993, col. 15607.

82   Jan Hoon, *Debates of Parliament* (Hansard), 5th Session-9th Parliament, 18 December 1993, col. 15506.

83   A.P. Janse van Rensburg, *Debates of Parliament* (Hansard), 5th Session-9th Parliament, 17 December 1993, col. 15465.

84   Dawid de Villiers, *Debates of Parliament* (Hansard), 5th Session-9th Parliament, 17 December 1993, col. 15363.

85   Frederik van Heerden, *Debates of Parliament* (Hansard), 5th Session-9th Parliament, 17 December 1993, cols. 15316–17.

86   Nicolaas Jacobus Janse van Rensburg Koornhof, *Debates of Parliament* (Hansard), 5th Session-9th Parliament, 20 December 1993, col. 15675.

87   As reported by SAPA, "South Africa's new interim constitution was passed by

Parliament on Wednesday by 237 votes to 45. The voting on the Bill, which had to be passed by a majority of each of the three houses was: House of Assembly: 132 for, 42 against. House of Representatives: 72 for, 1 against. House of Delegates: 33 for, 2 against" (SAPA, "Constitution-Passed", 22 December 1993. Reprinted at ANC Daily News Briefing Archive <www.anc.org.za/anc/newsbrief/> (September 2002)).

88   In particular, the New Year's Eve bombing of the Heidelberg Tavern in Cape Town was a disturbing reminder of the violence problem.

89   See Bill Sass, "The Might of the Right: The Four Horsemen of the Apocalypse," *African Defence Review*, 1994. Reprinted at <www.iss.co.za/Pubs/ASR/ADR15/Sass.html> (October 2003).

90   NA, "Volksfront Plan to Stop April Election," *Daily Dispatch*, 11 February 1994, 1.

91   F.W. de Klerk, *Debates of Parliament* (Hansard), 5th Session-9th Parliament, 28 February 1994, col. 16324. When the PAC leadership declared a ceasefire in January, many of the cadres were slow if not unwilling to comply. For its part, the IFP stuck to its demand for some kind of independence for the Zulu nation and appeared more than ready to boycott the elections.

92   F.W. de Klerk, col. 16324.

93   Graeme Simpson, "Blanket Amnesty Poses a Threat to Reconciliation," *Business Day*, 22 December 1993. Reprinted at <www.csvr.org.za/articles/artrcgs.htm> (August 2003).

94   Wilmot James, "Comments," in *Dealing with the Past: Truth and Reconciliation in South Africa*, eds. Alex Boraine, Janet Levy and Ronel Scheffer (Cape Town: Institute for Democracy in South Africa, 1994), 133.

95   In particular, see Kader Asmal, Louise Asmal, Ronald Roberts, *Reconciliation through Truth* (Cape Town: David Philip, 1986), 18.

96   Kader Asmal, "Victims, Survivors and Citizens – Human Rights, Reparations, and Reconciliation," Inaugural Lecture, University of the Western Cape, 25 May 1992.

97   Kader Asmal, "Victims, Survivors," 20–21.

98   Asmal, "Victims, Survivors," 8.

99   Asmal, "Victims, Survivors," 8

100 Kader Asmal, "Sins of Apartheid Cannot be Ignored," *Evening Post*, June 8, 1992, np.

101 Asmal, "Victims, Survivors," 9.

102 Albie Sachs, *Dealing with the Past*, 21–22.

103 Sachs, *Dealing with the Past*, 24.

104 Adam Michnik, "Why Deal with the Past?" in *Dealing with the Past*, 16.

105 Juan Mendez, "Prosecution: Who and For What?" in *Dealing with the Past*, 92.

106 Jose Zalaquett, "Why Deal with the Past?" in *Dealing with the Past*, 11.

107 Mary Burton, "South African Response," in *Dealing with the Past*, 121.

108 Sachs, *Dealing with the Past*, 127.

109 Lourens du Plessis, "Legal Analysis," in *Dealing with the Past*, 109–10.

110 Andre du Toit, *Dealing with the Past*, 148.

111 For several differing and provocative accounts of the "force" of history within the South African context, see Anthony Holiday, "Forgiving and Forgetting: The Truth and Reconciliation Commission," in *Negotiating the Past: The Making of Memory in South Africa*, ed. Sarah Nuttall (Cape Town: Oxford University Press,

1998), 43–56; Antjie Krog, *Country of My Skull: Guilt, Sorrow, and the Limits of Forgiveness in the New South Africa* (New York: Random House, 1998).

112 Against this backdrop, it is thus difficult to know what to make of Jose Zalaquett's claim that "A society cannot reconcile itself on the grounds of a divided memory. Since memory is identity, this would result in a divided identity" (Zalaquett, *Dealing with the Past*, 13).

113 Moreover, each "side" of this work is itself unstable. If it is not simply to turn the tables, the cultivation and expression of identity could not come at the expense of the Other. For its part, identification had to be more than an ideal, more than an abstract unity as difference in which there is no room for disagreement or opposition. Looking ahead, the tension between these aims was carried throughout the TRC and is fully evident in its *Final Report*, particularly when one compares the way in which identity is celebrated in the findings of the Human Rights Committee and deeply problematised in the chapter addressed to the amnesty process.

chapter 5

1 Mark Gevisser, "IEC Struggling to be Ready for Vote," *Mail and Guardian*, 11 March 1994, 4.

2 Jan Taljaard, "Viljoen to Hone the Right's Military Might," *Mail and Guardian*, 11 March 1994, 4.

3 Jan Taljaard, "Viljoen Lambasts the Wild Right," *Mail and Guardian*, 18 March 1994, 2.

4 Editorial, "A Change of Underwear," *Mail and Guardian*, 18 March 1994, 16.

5 The reasons for Buthelezi's change of heart remain somewhat unclear. For many on the right, the decision to enter the election followed from the agreement that resulted in the writing of a 34th constitutional principle, one that called for the post-election formation of a council that would undertake negotiations over the viability and potential form of a people's state that would embrace and preserve international norms of minority self-determination. See *The Accord on Afrikaner Self-Determination Between the Freedom Front, the African National Congress and the South African Government/National Party (and Appendix)*, 23 April 1994.

6 Editorial, "Cast Your Vote for Change," *Mail and Guardian*, 22 April 1994, 20.

7 F.W. de Klerk, quoted in Patti Waldmeier, *Anatomy of a Miracle: The End of Apartheid and the Birth of the New South African Constitution* (New York: WW Norton, 1997), 261.

8 ANC, "The Beginning Not the End," 26 April 1994. Reprinted at <www.anc.org.za/ancdocs/pr/1994/pr0426a.html> (August 2003).

9 Nelson Mandela, *Long Walk to Freedom* (New York: Little, Brown and Co., 1994), 744, 749.

10 Nelson Mandela, "Address to the People of Cape Town," 9 May 1994. Reprinted at <www.anc.org.za/ancdocs/history/Mandela/1994/innaugct.html> (April 2003).

11 Nelson Mandela, "Statement of Nelson Mandela at his Inauguration as President of the Democratic Republic of South Africa," 10 May 1994, 2. Reprinted at <www.anc.org.za/ancdocs/history/mandela/1994/inaugpta.html> (April 2003).

12 Quoted in Mark Gevisser, "South Africa's Reconciliation in Motion," *Mail and Guardian*, 13 May 1994, 9.

13 Nelson Mandela, "Statement of Nelson Mandela at his Inauguration."

14 ANC, "Issue of Indemnity for Security Forces Involved in Defending Apartheid," 25 April 1994. Reprinted at <www.anc.org.za/ancdocs/pr/1994/pr0425.html> (April 2003).

15 On this point, one might consider the significance of the constituent assembly and the work that it concluded in 1996.

16 Gevisser, "South Africa's Reconciliation in Motion," 9.

17 Richard Goldstone, "Lest we Forget ... Expose the Crimes of Apartheid," *Mail and Guardian*, 13 May 1994, 19.

18 Nelson Mandela, *Joint Sittings of Both Houses of Parliament*, 1st Session-1st Parliament, 24 May 1994, col. 1–15.

19 Dullah Omar, Interview with Author, 9 November 2000, Cape Town.

20 See Alex Boraine, *A Country Unmasked: Inside South Africa's Truth and Reconciliation Commission* (New York: Oxford University Press, 2001), 30–31.

21 Dullah Omar, Interview with Author, 9 November 2000, Cape Town.

22 Johnny de Lange, Interview with Author, 21 June 2000, Cape Town.

23 Dullah Omar, Interview with Author, 9 November 2000, Cape Town.

24 Kader Asmal, *Debates of the National Assembly* (Hansard), 1st Session-1st Parliament, 25 May 1994, cols. 18, 24.

25 Dullah Omar, *Debates of the National Assembly* (Hansard), 1st Session-1st Parliament, 27 May 1994, col. 188.

26 Dullah Omar, *Debates of the National Assembly* (Hansard), 1st Session-1st Parliament, 27 May 1994, cols. 189–90.

27 Dullah Omar, Interview with Author, 9 November 2000, Cape Town.

28 F.W. de Klerk, *Debates of the National Assembly* (Hansard), 1st Session-1st Parliament, 25 May 1994, cols.15–16; Mangosuthu Buthelezi, *Debates of the National Assembly* (Hansard), 1st Session-1st Parliament, 25 May 1994, cols. 32–33.

29 Constand Viljoen, *Debates of the National Assembly* (Hansard), 1st Session-1st Parliament, 25 May 1994, cols. 43–44.

30 Dullah Omar, *Debates of the National Assembly* (Hansard), 1st Session-1st Parliament, 27 May 1994, cols. 190–91; NA, "Amnesty: Balm or Betrayal?" *Negotiation News*, 15 June 1994, 3.

31 The proceedings of the second Justice in Transition conference were reprinted in Alex Boraine and Janet Levy, eds., *The Healing of a Nation* (Cape Town: Justice in Transition, 1995).

32 Dullah Omar, *The Healing of a Nation*, 2–8. In the winter of 1994, Omar's position appeared in several places. For instance, see "Light in a Dark Place?" *Negotiation News*, 21 July 1994, 12.

33 Johnny de Lange, *Debates of the National Assembly* (Hansard), 1st Session-1st Parliament, 5 August 1994, col. 862.

34 This was a charge levelled by de Klerk. For a reflection of his early view of the Commission, see F.W. de Klerk, *The Last Trek – A New Beginning* (New York: MacMillan, 1998), 369.

35 Dullah Omar, Interview with Author, 9 November 2000, Cape Town.

36 Dullah Omar, *Debates of the National Assembly* (Hansard), 1st Session-1st Parliament, 26 August 1994, cols. 2055–58.

37 Dullah Omar, *Debates of the National Assembly* (Hansard), 1st Session-1st Parliament, 26 August 1994, col. 2069.

38 Father S. Mkhatshwa, *Debates of the National Assembly* (Hansard), 1st Session-1st Parliament, 22 September 1994, col. 3077.
39 Kader Asmal, *Debates of the National Assembly* (Hansard), 1st Session-1st Parliament, 18 October 1994, col. 3190.
40 Respectively, these comments were made in October by F.W. de Klerk and the ANC's Jan Momberg. For an account of the former, see *Healing of a Nation*, xix; also, Jan Momberg, *Debates of the National Assembly* (Hansard), 1st Session-1st Parliament, 18 October 1994, col. 3221.
41 See the debate in *Debates of the National Assembly* (Hansard), 1st Session-1st Parliament, 23 January 1995, cols. 34–73.
42 Dullah Omar, Testimony delivered to Parliament's Joint Committee on Justice with regards to the Promotion of National Unity and Reconciliation Bill, 31 January 1995, p. 54, Archives of Parliament, Cape Town, South Africa.
43 Boraine, *Country Unmasked*, 52–67.
44 Janet Cherry, Testimony delivered to Parliament's Joint Committee on Justice with regards to the Promotion of National Unity and Reconciliation Bill, 7 February 1995, np., Archives of Parliament, Cape Town, South Africa.
45 Adv. Gordhan, Testimony delivered to Parliament's Joint Committee on Justice with regards to the Promotion of National Unity and Reconciliation Bill, 7 February 1995, p. 45, Archives of Parliament, Cape Town, South Africa.
46 Adv. Gordhan, Testimony delivered to Parliament's Joint Committee on Justice, p. 19.
47 National Party, "NP Proposals on Four Contentious Issues," Memorandum re Bill on the Promotion of National Unity and Reconciliation, Position paper submitted to Parliament's Joint Committee on Justice with regards to the Promotion of National Unity and Reconciliation Bill, 28 March 1995, p. 2, Archives of Parliament, Cape Town, South Africa.
48 General Counsel for the Bar, Submission delivered to Parliament's Joint Committee on Justice with regards to the Promotion of National Unity and Reconciliation Bill, 15 February 1995, Archives of Parliament, Cape Town, South Africa.
49 R.P. Rossouw, Submission delivered to Parliament's Joint Committee on Justice with regards to the Promotion of National Unity and Reconciliation Bill, 27 March 1995, np., Archives of Parliament, Cape Town, South Africa.
50 Adv. Gordhan, Testimony delivered to Parliament's Joint Committee on Justice, p. 8.
51 Paul van Zyl, Testimony delivered to Parliament's Joint Committee on Justice with regards to the Promotion of National Unity and Reconciliation Bill, 2 February 1995, np., Archives of Parliament, Cape Town, South Africa.
52 Debate over the cut-off date was particularly important to organisations such as the white right AWB and, on the other side of the spectrum, the PAC. Both organisations had continued campaigns of violence after the close of the MPNP.
53 Constand Viljoen, Unrevised Evidence delivered to Parliament's Joint Committee on Justice with regards to the Promotion of National Unity and Reconciliation Bill, 6 February 1995, p. 16, Archives of Parliament, Cape Town, South Africa.
54 Viljoen, Unrevised Evidence, pp. 5–6.
55 Viljoen, Unrevised Evidence, p. 29.

56   Gandi, Question to Constand Viljoen at Parliament's Joint Committee on Justice with regards to the Promotion of National Unity and Reconciliation Bill, 6 February 1995, p. 35, Archives of Parliament, Cape Town, South Africa.

57   These arguments were advanced in two extended submissions to the Joint Committee. The first is dated 14 February 1995 and signed by the "Women of Port Elizabeth." Second, see "Statement from the Families of Victims of Politically Motivated Violence," Submission to the Joint Committee on Justice on the Promotion of National Unity and Reconciliation Bill, 17 February 1995.

58   Van Zyl, Testimony delivered to Parliament's Joint Committee. This position contrasted directly with that taken by the NP. See National Party, "NP Proposals on Four Contentious Issues."

59   General Counsel to the Bar, Testimony delivered to Parliament's Joint Committee on Justice with regards to the Promotion of National Unity and Reconciliation Bill, 10 February 1995, np., Archives of Parliament, Cape Town, South Africa.

60   Amnesty International, Position paper submitted to Parliament's Joint Committee on Justice with regards to the Promotion of National Unity and Reconciliation Bill, 13 January 1995, p. 2, Archives of Parliament, Cape Town, South Africa. The debate is an extended one, see *The Provocations of Amnesty: Memory, Justice and Impunity*, eds. Charles Villa-Vicencio and Erik Doxtader (Cape Town: David Philip, 2003).

61   Dullah Omar, Testimony delivered to Parliament's Joint Committee on Justice with regards to the Promotion of National Unity and Reconciliation Bill, 31 January 1995, p. 55, Archives of Parliament, Cape Town, South Africa.

62   South African Police, Memorandum and Appendix B – Further Proposals by the SAP on the Truth and Reconciliation Commission submitted to Parliament's Joint Committee on Justice with regards to the Promotion of National Unity and Reconciliation Bill, nd. Also see de Klerk, *Last Trek*, 387.

63   Dullah Omar, Testimony delivered to Parliament's Joint Committee on Justice, 60.

64   Andre du Toit, Testimony delivered to Parliament's Joint Committee on Justice with regards to the Promotion of National Unity and Reconciliation Bill, 6 February 1995, p. 67, Archives of Parliament, Cape Town, South Africa.

65   Andre du Toit, Testimony delivered to Parliament's Joint Committee on Justice, p. 78.

66   Alex Boraine, Testimony delivered to Parliament's Joint Committee on Justice with regards to the Promotion of National Unity and Reconciliation Bill, 10 February 1995, p. 78, Archives of Parliament, Cape Town, South Africa.

67   The text of the PNUR Act is available at: <www.doj.gov.za/trc/legal/act9534. htm>. The question of how the legislation changed from its draft to final form deserves separate study. Several notable changes were introduced into the legislation between the version considered in January 1995 and the one that was passed some seven months later. In particular, the requirements for amnesty underwent significant revision as the framers introduced a proportionality requirement into the criteria for a successful indemnity application.

68   Republic of South Africa, *Promotion of National Unity and Reconciliation Act* (No. 34 of 1995), Chapter 2 (3) (1).

69   Republic of South Africa, *Promotion of National Unity and Reconciliation Act* (No. 34 of 1995), preamble.

70 This discussion relies heavily on Tom Farrell's discussion of rhetoric's constitutive appearances. See Thomas B. Farrell, *Norms of Rhetorical Culture* (New Haven: Yale University Press, 1993), 32. With respect to the function of appearances in the act of testimony, see Shoshana Felman and Dori Laub, *Testimony: Crises of Witnessing in Literature, Psychoanalysis and History* (New York: Routledge, 1992), 85.

71 Here, Martha Nussbaum's discussion proves crucial, particularly as she traces the classical idea of appearance to the dynamics of revelation and truth. See Martha C. Nussbaum, *The Fragility of Goodness: Luck and Ethics in Greek Tragedy and Philosophy* (Cambridge: Cambridge University Press, 1986), 241, 244. With respect to the essential relation between appearance and public life, see Hannah Arendt, *The Human Condition* (Chicago: University of Chicago Press, 1958), 50–51.

72 Hans-Georg Gadamer, *Truth and Method* (New York: Continuum, 1994).

73 Republic of South Africa, *Promotion of National Unity and Reconciliation Act* (No. 34 of 1995), preamble, Chapter 5.

74 Kader Asmal, Louise Asmal, Ronald Roberts, *Reconciliation Through Truth* (Cape Town: David Philip Publishing, 1996), 9.

75 This problem points out the need to conduct a close rhetorical analysis of amnesty testimony, with an eye toward how narrativity yields the grounds for questions.

76 This is not an empirical claim. In practice, the matter has been somewhat different. There is urgent need to consider how the TRC's amnesty process was juridicalised and what implications this had on the meaning of disclosure and the appearances generated by perpetrator testimony. For a more thorough discussion of the importance of character in relation to the work of recognition, see Erik Doxtader, "Characters in the Middle of Public Life: Consensus, Dissent, and *Ethos*," *Philosophy and Rhetoric* 33 (2000): 336–69.

77 In an argument that examines the way in which amnesty blurs the distinction between public and private, Philippe Salazar has considered this dynamic closely. See Philippe-Joseph Salazar, *An African Athens: Rhetoric and the Shaping of Democracy in South Africa* (London: Lawrence Erlbaum, 2002).

78 As far as I know, Wilmot James first coined the apt term "campaign of persuasion" as it applied to the TRC's need to generate support amongst citizens. See Wilmot James, "Coexistence and Community," in *The Healing of a Nation*, 83.

79 *Truth and Reconciliation Commission,* pamphlet published by Justice in Transition, 1995, 3.

80 Nelson Mandela, *Debates of the National Assembly* (Hansard), 2nd Session–1st Parliament, 17 May 1995, col. 1348.

81 Mandela, *Debates,* col. 1349.

82 Mandela, *Debates,* cols. 1349–50.

83 Melanie Verwoerd, *Debates of the National Assembly* (Hansard), 2nd Session–1st Parliament, 17 May 1995, cols. 1402–3.

84 Farouk Cassim, *Debates of the National Assembly* (Hansard), 2nd Session–1st Parliament, 17 May 1995, col. 1406.

85 Devikarani Jana, *Debates of the National Assembly* (Hansard), 2nd Session–1st Parliament, 17 May 1995, col. 1355.

86 Cornelius Mulder, *Debates of the National Assembly* (Hansard), 2nd Session–1st Parliament, 17 May 1995, col. 1373.

87 For an example of this position, see Christiaan Fismer, *Debates of the National Assembly* (Hansard), 2nd Session-1st Parliament, 17 May 1995, cols. 1356–59.

88 Richard Sizani, *Debates of the National Assembly* (Hansard), 2nd Session-1st Parliament, 17 May 1995, col. 1391.

89 Dirk du Toit, *Debates of the National Assembly* (Hansard), 2nd Session-1st Parliament, 17 May 1995, col. 1418.

90 Dirk du Toit, *Debates of the National Assembly* (Hansard), 2nd Session-1st Parliament, 17 May 1995, col. 1418.

91 Frederik van Heerden, *Debates of the National Assembly* (Hansard), 2nd Session-1st Parliament, 17 May 1995, col. 1414.

92 Jan Momberg, *Debates of the National Assembly* (Hansard), 2nd Session-1st Parliament, 17 May 1995, col. 1417.

93 Kader Asmal, *Debates of the National Assembly* (Hansard), 2nd Session-1st Parliament, 17 May 1995, col. 1382.

94 Johannes Maree, *Debates of the National Assembly* (Hansard), 2nd Session-1st Parliament, 17 May 1995, col. 1395.

95 SAPA, "Promotion of National Unity and Reconciliation Bill Becomes Law," 19 July 1995. Reprinted at ANC Daily News Briefing Archive <www.anc.org.za/anc/newsbrief/> (June 2003).

96 Desmond Tutu, "Archbishop Tutu's Address to the First Gathering of the Truth and Reconciliation Commission," 16 December 1995.

97 *AZAPO, Biko, Mxenge, Ribeiro v. The President of the Republic of South Africa, The Government of the Republic of South Africa, The Minister of Justice, The Minister of Safety and Security, The Chairperson of the Truth and Reconciliation Commission*, Case CCT 17/96, par. 60–66. Reprinted at <www.truth.org.za/legal/azapo.html> (March 2003). For commentary on the challenge, see Jeremy Sarkin, "The Trials and Tribulations of South Africa's Truth and Reconciliation Commission," *South African Journal on Human Rights* 12 (1996): 617–40; Peter Parker, "The Politics of Indemnities, Truth Telling and Reconciliation: Ending Apartheid without Forgetting," *Human Rights Law Journal* 17 (April 30, 1996): 1–13.

98 Mohamed, *AZAPO*, par. 1.

99 Mohamed, *AZAPO*, par. 3, 48.

100 Mohamed, *AZAPO*, par. 8.

101 Mohamed, *AZAPO*, par. 10.

102 Mohamed, *AZAPO*, par. 17–19.

103 In the decision, there is an ambiguity over whether amnesty's justification hinges on an assurance of reparation. I have addressed this matter elsewhere. See Erik Doxtader, "The Matter of Words in the Midst of Beginnings: Unravelling the 'Relationship' between Reparations and Reconciliation," in *To Repair the Irreparable: Reparations and Reconstruction in South Africa*, eds. Erik Doxtader and Charles Villa-Vicencio (Cape Town: David Philip, 2004), 115–48.

104 Mohamed, *AZAPO*, par. 21.

105 Nelson Mandela, "Address to the Interfaith Commissioning Service for the Truth and Reconciliation Commission," 13 February 1996, in *Nelson Mandela: From Freedom to the Future: Tributes and Speeches*, ed. Kader Asmal, et al. (Cape Town: Jonathan Ball Publishers, 2003), 130.

epilogue

1   For instance, see Steven Friedman, ed., *The Small Miracle: South Africa's Negotiated Settlement* (Johannesburg: Ravan Press, 1994).

2   Christiaan Fismer, *Debates of the National Assembly* (Hansard), 2nd Session-1st Parliament, 23 January 1995, col. 55.

3   Desmond Tutu, "Archbishop Tutu's Address to the First Gathering of the Truth and Reconciliation Commission," 16 December 1995. Also see, Desmond Tutu, "Let Africa Show the World How to Forgive," 9 November 1999. Reprinted at <www.ncccusa.org/nccat50/daily/1110c.htm> (August 2003).

4   Graeme Simpson, "Learning to Live with the South African 'Miracle'," 1996. Reprinted at <www.csvr.org.za/articles/artdir95.htm>.

5   The question is posed at the beginning of Neville Alexander's important reflection on the South African transition. See Neville Alexander, *An Ordinary Country: Issues in the Transition from Apartheid to Democracy in South Africa* (Pietermaritzburg: University of Natal Press, 2002).

6   David Hume, *Of Miracles* (LaSalle, IL: Open Court, 1985), 32.

7   Elsewhere, I have developed this argument in more detail. See Erik Doxtader, "Reconciliation – A Rhetorical Concept/ion," *Quarterly Journal of Speech* 89 (2003): 267–92.

8   The phrase is Adorno's. See Theodor Adorno, *Negative Dialectics*, trans. E.B. Ashton (Continuum: New York, 1973).

9   Michel Foucault, *The Archeology of Knowledge*, trans. A.M. Sheridan Smith (New York: Pantheon Books, 1972).

10   Hans Blumenberg, *The Legitimacy of the Modern Age*, trans. Robert M. Wallace (Cambridge: MIT Press, 1983).

11   Reinhart Koselleck, *The Practice of Conceptual History: Timing History and Spacing Concepts* (Palo Alto: Stanford University Press, 2002), 25.

12   Walter Benjamin, "On the Concept of History," in *Walter Benjamin: Selected Writings, Vol. 4, 1938–1940*, eds. Howard Eiland and Michael Jennings (Cambridge: Harvard University, 1996), 397.

13   Informing this position is Derrida's consideration of the double and often poisonous quality of *logos*. See Jacques Derrida, *Dissemination*, trans. Barbara Johnson (Chicago: University of Chicago Press, 1981). Also, see Walter Benjamin, "The Critique of Violence," in *Walter Benjamin: Selected Writings, Volume 1, 1913–1926*, ed. Marcus Bullock (Cambridge: Harvard University Press, 1996), 236–52.

14   In a provisional way, I have considered this problem elsewhere. See Erik Doxtader, "The Faith and Struggle of Beginning (with) Words: On the Turn between Reconciliation and Recognition," *Philosophy and Rhetoric* 40 (2007).

bibliography

books, articles, and selected primary documents*

The Accord on Afrikaner Self-Determination between the Freedom Front, the African National Congress and the South African Government/National Party (and Appendix), 23 April 1994.

Adam, Heribert. "Ethnic vs. Civic Nationalism: South Africa's Non-Racialism in Comparative Perspective." *South African Sociological Review* 7 (1994): 15–31.

Adam, Heribert, and Hermann Giliomee. *Ethnic Power Mobilized: Can South Africa Change?* New Haven: Yale University Press, 1979.

Adam, Heribert, and Kogila Moodley. *The Opening of the Apartheid Mind: Options for the New South Africa.* Berkeley: University of California Press, 1993.

Adorno, Theodor. *Negative Dialectics.* Translated by E.B. Ashton. New York: Continuum, 1973.

Agamben, Giorgio. *Homo Sacer: Sovereign Power and Bare Life.* Translated by Daniel Heller Roazen. Palo Alto: Stanford University Press, 1998.

Alexander, Neville. *An Ordinary Country: Issues in the Transition from Apartheid to Democracy in South Africa.* Pietermaritzburg: University of Natal Press, 2002.

Allen, R.E. *Plato's Parmenides: Translation and Analysis.* Minneapolis: University of Minnesota Press, 1983.

Anderson, Allan. *Zion and Pentecost: The Spirituality and Experience of Pentecostal and Zionist Apostolic Churches in South Africa.* Pretoria: University of South Africa Press, 2000.

Arendt, Hannah. *The Human Condition.* Chicago: University of Chicago Press, 1958.

———. *On Revolution.* New York: Viking Press, 1965.

Ashforth, Adam. *The Politics of Official Discourse in Twentieth Century South Africa.* New York: Oxford University Press, 1990.

Asmal, Kader. "Victims, Survivors and Citizens – Human Rights, Reparations, and Reconciliation." Inaugural Lecture, University of the Western Cape, 25 May 1992.

———. "Sins of Apartheid Cannot be Ignored," *Evening Post,* 8 June 1992.

———. "The Constitutional Crossroads." In *The CODESA File,* edited by Fatima Meer, 235–46. Durban: Madiba Publishers, 1993.

Asmal, Kader, Louise Asmal, and Ronald Roberts. *Reconciliation Through Truth.* Cape Town: David Philip, 1996.

*Note: For economy of space, this bibliography does not contain citations for the majority of primary and archival materials used in writing this book. Full references to these resources can be found in the notes that attend each chapter.

Atkinson, Doreen. "Brokering a Miracle: The Multiparty Negotiating Forum." In *South African Review,* edited by Steven Friedman, 13–43. Johannesburg: Ravan Press, 1994.

Balcomb, Anthony. *Third Way Theology: Reconciliation, Revolution and Reform in the South African Churches during the 1980s.* Pietermaritzburg: Cluster, 1993.

Barrell, Howard. *MK: The ANC's Armed Struggle.* London: Penguin, 1990.

Baskin, Jeremy. *Striking back: A History of Cosatu.* Johannesburg: Ravan Press, 1991.

Battle, Michael. *Reconciliation: The Ubuntu Theology of Desmond Tutu.* Cleveland: Pilgrim Press, 1997.

Benard, Ed, and Mwezi Twala. *Mbokodo: Inside MK-Mwezi Twala – A Soldier's Story.* Johannesburg: Jonathan Ball Publishers, 1994.

Benjamin, Walter. "The Critique of Violence." In *Walter Benjamin: Selected Writings, Volume 1, 1913–1926,* edited by Marcus Bullock, 236–52. Cambridge: Harvard University Press, 1996.

———. "On the Concept of History." In *Walter Benjamin: Selected Writings, Vol. 4, 1938–1940,* edited by Howard Eiland and Michael Jennings, 389–400. Cambridge: Harvard University Press, 1996.

———. "On Language as Such and on the Language of Man." In *Walter Benjamin: Selected Writings, Volume 1, 1913–1926,* edited by Marcus Bullock, 62–74. Cambridge: Harvard University Press, 1996.

Bernstein, J.B. "Confession and Forgiveness: Hegel's Poetics of Action." In *Beyond Representation: Philosophy and Poetic Imagination,* edited by Richard Eldridge, 34–65. Cambridge: Cambridge University Press, 1996.

Beyerhaus, Peter. *The Kairos Document: Challenge or Danger to the Church?* Cape Town: Gospel Defence League, 1987.

Biermann, H., ed. *The Case for South Africa as put forth in Public Statements of Eric H. Louw.* New York: MacFadden Books, 1963.

Biko, Steve. *I Write What I Like: A Selection of His Writings.* London: Bowerdean, 1978.

Bloomberg, Charles. *Christian Nationalism and the Rise of the Afrikaner Broederbond.* London: Macmillan, 1990.

Blumenberg, Hans. *The Legitimacy of the Modern Age.* Translated by Robert M. Wallace. Cambridge: MIT Press, 1983.

———. "An Anthropological Approach to the Contemporary Significance of Rhetoric." In *After Philosophy? End or Transformation,* edited by Kenneth Baynes, James Bohman, and Thomas McCarthy, translated by Robert M. Wallace, 429–458. Cambridge: MIT Press, 1987.

Boesak, Allan. *Farewell to Innocence: A Social-Ethical Study of Black Theology and Black Power.* Johannesburg: Ravan Press, 1976.

Bonner, P.L. *Soweto: A History.* Cape Town: Maskew Miller Longman, 1998.

———, ed. *Apartheid's Genesis, 1935–1962.* Johannesburg: Ravan Press, 1993.

Boraine, Alex. "Democracy and Government: Towards a People's Struggle." *IDASA Occasional Paper* #3 (nd).

———. Alex Boraine, "A Language of Potential." In *After the TRC: Reflections on Truth and Reconciliation in South Africa,* edited by Wilmot James and Linda van der Vijver, 73–80. Cape Town: David Philip, 2000.

———. *A Country Unmasked: Inside South Africa's Truth and Reconciliation Commission.* New York: Oxford University Press, 2001.

Boraine, Alex, Janet Levy and Ronel Scheffer, eds. *Dealing with the Past: Truth and Reconciliation in South Africa*. Cape Town: Institute for Democracy in South Africa, 1994.

Boraine, Alex, and Janet Levy, eds. *The Healing of a Nation*. Cape Town: Justice in Transition, 1995.

Borer, Tristan. *Challenging the State: Churches as Political Actors in South Africa*. Notre Dame: Notre Dame University Press, 1998.

Botha, Jan. "Creation of New Meaning: Rhetorical Situations and the Reception of Romans 13:1–7." *Journal of Theology for Southern Africa* 79 (1992): 24–37.

Botha, P.W. "Address by State President PW Botha, 5 August 1985." In *Adapt or Die: The End of White Politics in South Africa*, edited by Robert Schrire, 147–59. London: Hurst & Co., 1985.

Bowker, Geoffrey, and Susan Star. *Sorting Things Out: Classification and Its Consequences*. Cambridge: MIT Press, 1999.

Broodryk, Johann. *Ubuntu: Life Lessons From Africa*. Pretoria: Ubuntu School of Philosophy, 2002.

Brooks, Edgar, ed. *Apartheid: A Documentary Study of Modern South Africa*. London: Routledge & Kegan Paul, 1968.

Budlender, Geoff. "Law and Lawlessness in South Africa." *South African Journal on Human Rights* 4 (1992).

Bundy, Colin. "Land and Liberation: Popular Rural Protest and the National Liberation Movements in South Africa, 1920–1960." In *The Politics of Race, Class, and Nationalism in 20th Century South Africa*, edited by Shula Marks and Stanley Trapido, 254–85. New York: Longman, 1987.

Burke, Kenneth. *A Grammar of Motives*. Berkeley: University of California Press, 1969.

Butler, Jeffrey, ed. *Democratic Liberalism in South Africa: Its History and Prospect*. Middletown: Wesleyan University Press, 1987.

Butler, Judith. *Giving an Account of Oneself*. New York: Fordham University Press, 2005.

Carnegie Commission of Investigation on the Poor White Question in South Africa. *The Poor White Problem in South Africa: A Report*. Stellenbosch: Pro-ecclesia-drukkery, 1932.

Cassin, Barbara. "Politics of Memory: On Treatments of Hate." *Javnost: The Public* 8 (2001): 9–22.

Charland, Maurice. "Constitutive Rhetoric: The Case of the Peuple Québécois." *Quarterly Journal of Speech* 73 (1987): 133–50.

Christian Council of South Africa. *Race: What does the Bible Say?* Roodeport: Christian Council of South Africa, 1952.

Chicuecue, Noel. "Reconciliation; The Role of Truth Commissions and Alternative Ways of Healing." *Development in Practice* 7 (1997).

Cochrane, James. *Servants of Power: The Role of the English-Speaking Churches, 1903–1930*. Johannesburg: Ravan Press, 1987.

———. "War, Remembrance and Reconstruction." *Journal of Theology for Southern Africa* 84 (1993): 25–40.

———. John de Gruchy, and Stephen Martin, eds. *Facing the Truth: South African Faith Communities and the Truth and Reconciliation Commission*. Cape Town: David Philip, 1999.

CODESA. *Convention for a Democratic South Africa: First Plenary Session.* Johannesburg: CODESA, 1991.

CODESA. *Working Documents for CODESA 2, May 15–16, 1992.* Johannesburg: CODESA, 1992.

The Commonwealth Group of Eminent Persons. *Mission to South Africa: The Commonwealth Report.* New York: Penguin, 1986.

Connor, Bernard. *The Difficult Traverse.* Pietermaritzburg: Cluster, 1998.

Constitutional Court of South Africa. Judgment in re AZAPO, Biko, Mxenge, Ribeiro v. The President of South Africa, The Government of South Africa, The Minister of Justice, The Minister of Safety and Security, The Chairperson of the Truth and Reconciliation Commission. Case CCT 17/96.

Coombes, Annie. *Visual Culture and Public Memory in a Democratic South Africa.* Durham: Duke University Press, 2003.

Cuthbertson, Greg, ed. *Frontiers of African Christianity: Essays in Honour of Inus Daneel.* Pretoria: University of South Africa, 2003.

Davenport, T.R.H. *South Africa: A Modern History.* New York: Macmillan Press, 1977.

Davis, Stephen. *Apartheid's Rebels: Inside South Africa's Hidden War.* New Haven: Yale University Press, 1987.

de Certeau, Michel. *The Writing of History,* translated by Tom Conley. New York: Columbia University Press, 1988.

de Gruchy, John. *The Church in Struggle in South Africa.* Grand Rapids: Eerdmans, 1986.

_____ . "From Cottesloe to Rustenburg and Beyond." *Journal of Theology for Southern Africa* 74 (1991): 21–34.

_____ . *Reconciliation: Restoring Justice.* Cape Town: David Philip, 2002.

de Gruchy, John, and Charles Villa-Vicencio, eds. *Apartheid is a Heresy.* Cape Town: David Philip, 1983.

de Klerk, F.W. "Inaugural Address." Reprinted in *The Cape Argus,* 20 September 1989.

_____ . "National Address: Violence is Unacceptable." *The Cape Argus,* 19 December 1990.

_____ . *The Last Trek – A New Beginning, The Autobiography.* New York: Macmillan, 1998.

de Klerk, W.A. *The Puritans in Africa.* London: Rex Collings, 1975.

de Klerk, Willem. "The Political Process of Negotiation, 1990–1993." In *Birth of a Constitution,* edited by Bertus de Villiers, 1–11. Kenwyn: Juta, 1994.

de Lange, Johnny. "The Historical Context, Legal Origins, and Philosophical Foundation of the South African Truth and Reconciliation Commission." In *Looking Back, Reaching Forward: Reflections on the Truth and Reconciliation Commission of South Africa,* edited by Charles Villa-Vicencio and Wilhelm Verwoerd, 14–31. Cape Town: University of Cape Town Press, 2000.

Degennar, Johan. "Philosophical Roots of Nationalism." In *Church and Nationalism in South Africa,* edited by Theo Sundermeier. Johannesburg: Ravan Press, 1975.

_____ . "The Myth of the South African Nation." *IDASA Occasional Paper.* 1992.

Derrida, Jacques. *Writing and Difference.* Translated by Alan Bass. Chicago: University of Chicago Press, 1978.

_____ . *Dissemination.* Translated by Barbara Johnson. Chicago: University of Chicago Press, 1981.

_____ . "The Laws of Reflection: Nelson Mandela, In Admiration." In *For Nelson*

Mandela, edited by Jacques Derrida and Mutapha Tlili, 13–42. New York: Holt, 1987.

_____ . *On the Name.* Translated by David Wood. Palo Alto: Stanford University Press, 1995.

Doxtader, Erik. "Characters in the Middle of Public Life: Consensus, Dissent, and *Ethos.*" *Philosophy and Rhetoric* 33 (2000): 336–69.

_____ . "Reconciliation – A Rhetorical Concept/ion." *Quarterly Journal of Speech* 89 (2003): 267–292.

_____ . "Easy to Forget or Never (Again) Hard to Remember." In *The Provocations of Amnesty: Memory, Justice and Impunity,* edited by Charles Villa-Vicencio and Erik Doxtader, 121–55. Cape Town: David Philip, 2003.

_____ . "The Matter of Words in the Midst of Beginnings: Unraveling the 'Relationship' between Reparations and Reconciliation." In *To Repair the Irreparable: Reparations and Reconstruction in South Africa,* edited by Erik Doxtader and Charles Villa-Vicencio, 115–148. Cape Town: David Philip, 2004

_____ . "The Faith and Struggle of Beginning (with) Words: On the turn between Reconciliation and Recognition." *Philosophy and Rhetoric* 40 (2007): 119–46.

Drew, Allison, ed. *South Africa's Radical Tradition: A Documentary History, Volume 2.* Cape Town: University of Cape Town Press, 1997.

Dubow, Saul. *Racial Segregation and the Origins of Apartheid in South Africa.* New York: St. Martins Press, 1989.

_____ . "Afrikaner Nationalism, Apartheid and the Conceptualization of 'Race'." *Journal of African History* 33 (1992): 209–237.

du Plessis, Lourens. "Observations on Amnesty and Indemnity for Acts Associated With Political Objectives in Light of South Africa's Transitional Constitution." *THRHR* 57 (1994): 950-81.

du Preez, A.B. *Inside the South African Crucible.* Pretoria: HAUM, 1959.

du Toit, Andre. "No Chosen People: The Myth of Calvinist Origins of Afrikaner Nationalism." *American Historical Review* 88 (1983): 920–52.

_____ . "The Problem of Intellectual History in (post)colonial Societies: The Case of South Africa." *Politikon* 18 (1991): 5–25.

_____ . "The Moral Foundations of the South African TRC: Truth as Acknowledgement and Justice as Recognition." In *Truth v. Justice: The Morality of Truth Commissions,* edited by Robert Rotberg and Dennis Thompson, 122–40. Princeton: Princeton University Press, 2000.

Ebrahim, Hassen. *Soul of a Nation: Constitution-Making in South Africa.* Cape Town: Oxford University Press, 1998.

Ellis, Stephen. "The Historical Significance of South Africa's Third Force." *Journal of Southern African Studies* 24 (June 1998): 261–99.

Ellis, Stephen, and Tsepo Sechaba. *Comrades against Apartheid: the ANC and the South African Communist Party in Exile.* London: James Currey, 1992.

Eloff, J.P. *Judgment in Government of the Self-Governing Territory of KwaZulu vs. Mahlangu and Another.* Transvaal Provincial Division, 1993 (1) South Africa 635.

Elphick, Richard. *Kraal and Castle: Khoikhoi and the Founding of White South Africa.* Cape Town: Human & Rousseau, 1999.

Elphick, Richard, and Hermann Giliomee, eds. *The Shaping of South African Society, 1652–1840.* Middletown: Wesleyan University Press, 1989.

Farred, Grant. "The Black Intellectual's Work is Never Done: A Critique of the Discourse of Reconciliation in South Africa." *Postcolonial Studies* 7 (2004).

Farrell, Thomas. *Norms of Rhetorical Culture.* New Haven: Yale University Press, 1993.

February, V.A. *Mind Your Colour: The "Coloured" Stereotype in South African Literature.* London: Kegan Paul, 1981.

First, Ruth. *117 Days.* London: Bloomsbury, 1989.

Foucault, Michel. *The Archaeology of Knowledge.* Translated by A.M. Smith. New York: Pantheon, 1972.

Frankel, Philip. *An Ordinary Atrocity: Sharpeville and Its Massacre.* Johannesburg: Witwatersrand University Press, 2001.

Friedman, Steven. "The Struggle within the Struggle," *Transformation* 3 (1987): 58–70.

____ , ed. *The Long Journey: South Africa's Quest for a Negotiated Settlement.* Johannesburg: Ravan Press, 1993.

____ , ed. *The Small Miracle: South Africa's Negotiated Settlement.* Johannesburg: Ravan Press, 1994.

Gadamer, Hans-Georg. *Truth and Method.* New York: Continuum, 1994.

Gastrow, Peter. *Bargaining for Peace: South Africa and the National Peace Accord.* Washington D.C.: U.S. Institute for Peace, 1995.

Gerhart, Gail. *Black Power in South Africa: The Evolution of an Ideology.* Berkeley: University of California Press, 1978.

Gerstner, Jonathan. *The Thousand Generation Covenant: Dutch Reformed Theology and Group Identity in Colonial South Africa, 1652–1814.* Leiden: Brill, 1991.

Geyser, A.S. *Delayed Action!* Pretoria: Craft Press, 1961.

Giliomee, Hermann. "Afrikaner Nationalism: 1870–2001." In *A Question of Survival: Conversations with Key South Africans,* edited by Michel Albeldas, 3–20. Johannesburg: Jonathan Ball, 1987.

____ . "Apartheid, Verligtheid, and Liberalism," in *Democratic Liberalism in South Africa,* edited by Jeffrey Butler, 363-83. Middletown: Wesleyan University Press, 1987.

____ . "The Third Way." In *Negotiating South Africa's Future,* edited by H. Giliomee and L. Schlemmer, 10–13. Johannesburg: Southern Book Publishers, 1989.

____ . "Surrender without Defeat: Afrikaners and the South African Miracle." *Spotlight: South African Institute of Race Relations* (1997): 1–30.

____ . *The Afrikaners: Biography of a People.* Cape Town: Tafelberg, 2003.

____ . "The Dutch Reformed Church and Chosen People: The Dynamics of the Rise and Decline of Apartheid." Unpublished Paper, 2003.

Ginsburg, David. "The Democratization of South Africa: Transition Theory Tested." *Transformation* 29 (1996): 74–102.

Gobo, Bonganjalo. "Corporate Personality: Ancient Israel and Africa." In *The Challenge of Black Theology,* edited by Basil Moore, 65–73. Atlanta: John Knox, 1974.

Gobodo-Madikizela, Pumla. *A Human Being Died That Night: A Story of Forgiveness.* Cape Town: David Philip, 2003.

Goldstone, Richard. *For Humanity: Reflections of a War Crimes Investigator.* Johannesburg: Witwatersrand University Press, 2000.

Gordhan, Pravin. "Respondent's Answering Affidavit in the matter of Government of the Self-Governing Territory of KwaZulu vs. Mahlangu and Another," 1 September 1993.

Government of South Africa. *Talking with the ANC*. Pretoria: Bureau for Information, 1986.

Government of South Africa, Department of Information. *Amnesty for Terrorism*. Pretoria: Simondium Publishers, 1978.

Government of South Africa, Information Service. *Progress Through Separate Development*. Pretoria: SAG, 1973.

Government of the Self-Governing Territory of KwaZulu. *Motion of Application*, 28 July 1993, 35–6.

Graybill, Lyn. *Religion and Resistance in South Africa*. Westport: Praeger, 1995.

Habermas, Jürgen. *Between Facts and Norms: Contributions to a Discourse Theory of Law and Democracy*. Translated by William Rehg. Cambridge: MIT Press, 1996.

_____ . *The Inclusion of the Other*. Edited by Ciaran Cronin and Pablo De Greiff. Cambridge: MIT Press, 1998.

_____ . "Constitutional Democracy – A Paradoxical Combination of Contradictory Principles," Paper presented at the Northwestern School of Law, Chicago, Illinois, 23 October 2000.

Habib, Adam. "South Africa and the Global Order: The Structural Conditioning of a Transition to Democracy." *Journal of Contemporary African Studies* 16 (1998): 95–115.

Halisi, C.R.D. *Black Political Thought in the Making of South African Democracy*. Bloomington: Indiana University Press, 1999.

Hancock, W.K. *Smuts: The Sanguine Years, 1870–1919*. Cambridge: Cambridge University Press, 1962.

Hardimon, Michael. *Hegel's Social Philosophy: The Project of Reconciliation*. Cambridge: Cambridge University Press, 1994.

Hatchard, John, and Peter Slinn. "The Path Towards a New Order in South Africa." *International Relations* 12 (1995): 1–26.

Hayner, Priscilla. *Unspeakable Truths: Confronting State Terror and Atrocity*. New York: Routledge, 2001.

Haysom, Nicholas. "International Human Rights Norms and States of Emergency." In *Developments in Emergency Law*, edited by N. Haysom, 1–24. Johannesburg: Centre for Applied Legal Studies, 1989.

Hegel, G.W.F. "The Spirit of Christianity and Its Fate," In *On Christianity: Early Theological Writings,* trans. T.M. Knox, 182–301. New York: Harper, 1948.

_____ . *The Philosophy of Right*. Translated by T.M. Knox. London: Oxford University Press, 1967.

Hofmeyr, Isabel. "Building a Nation from Words: Afrikaans Language, Literature, and Ethnic Identity, 1902–24." In *The Politics of Race, Class and Nationalism in Twentieth Century South Africa*, edited by Shula Marks and Stanley Trapido, 95–123. London: Longman, 1987.

Holiday, Anthony. "Forgiving and Forgetting: The Truth and Reconciliation Commission." In *Negotiating the Past: Making Memory in South Africa*, edited by Sarah Nuttall, 43–56. Cape Town: Oxford University Press, 1998.

Hope, Majorie, and James Young. *The South African Churches in a Revolutionary Situation*. Maryknoll, NY: Orbis, 1981.

Hopkins, Dwight. "Steve Biko, Black Consciousness and Black Theology." In *Bounds of Possibility: The Legacy of Steve Biko and Black Consciousness*, edited by N. Barney Pityana, 194–200. Cape Town: David Philip, 1991.

Horowitz, Donald. *A Democratic South Africa: Constitutional Engineering in a Divided Society*. Cape Town: Oxford University Press, 1991.

Houghton, D. Hobart. *The Tomlinson Report: A Summary of the Findings and Recommendations of the Tomlinson Commission*. Johannesburg: South African Institute of Race Relations, 1956.

Howarth, David. "Paradigms Gained? A Critique of Theories and Explanations of Democratic Transition in South Africa." In *South Africa in Transition,* edited by David Howarth, 184–214. New York: St. Martins, 1998.

Hume, David. *Of Miracles*. LaSalle, IL: Open Court, 1985.

Institute for Contextual Theology. *Violence: The New Kairos*. Johannesburg: ICT, 1990.

Jeffery, Anthea. *The Truth About the Truth Commission*. Johannesburg: South African Institute for Race Relations, 1999.

Johns, Sheridan, ed. *Mandela, Tambo and the African National Congress: The Struggle Against Apartheid, 1948–1990*. New York: Oxford University Press, 1991.

Justice in Transition. *Truth and Reconciliation Commission* (Public Pamphlet). Cape Town: Justice in Transition, 1995.

"The Kairos Debate," *Journal of Theology in Southern Africa* 55 (1986): 42–57.

Karis, Thomas, and Gwendolen M. Carter, eds. *From Protest to Challenge: A Documentary History of African Politics in South Africa, Volume 2*. Stanford: Stanford University Press, 1973.

_____ . *From Protest to Challenge: A Documentary History of African Politics in South Africa, 1882–1990, Volume 5*. Bloomington: Indiana University Press, 1997.

Kinghorn, Johann." The Theology of Separate Equality: A Critical Outline of the DRC's Position on Apartheid." In *Christianity Amidst Apartheid*, edited by Martin Prozesky. New York: St. Martins, 1990.

_____ . "Social Cosmology, Religion and Afrikaner Ethnicity." *Journal of Southern African Studies* 20 (1994): 393–404.

_____ . "The Churches against Apartheid." In *The Long March: The Story of the Struggle for Liberation in South Africa*, edited by Ian Liebenberg, 149–53. Pretoria: HAUM, 1994.

_____ . "Modernization and Apartheid: The Afrikaner Churches." In *Christianity in South Africa: A Political Social and Cultural History*, edited by Richard Elphick, 135–54. Berkeley: University of California Press, 1997.

Kollapen, N. "Accountability: The Debate in South Africa." *Journal of African Law* 37 (1993): 1–9.

Koselleck, Reinhart. *The Practice of Conceptual History: Timing History and Spacing Concepts*. Palo Alto: Stanford University Press, 2002.

Kretzchmar, Louise. *The Voice of Black Theology in South Africa*. Johannesburg: Ravan Press, 1986.

Krog, Antjie. *Country of My Skull: Guilt, Sorrow and the Limits of Forgiveness in the New South Africa*. New York: Times Books, 1998.

_____ . *A Change of Tongue*. Johannesburg: Random House, 2003.

Leatt, James, ed. *Contending Ideologies in South Africa*. Cape Town: David Philip, 1986.

Lewis, Gavin. *Between the Wire and the Wall: A History of South African "Coloured" Politics*. New York: St. Martins, 1987.

Lewis, Jon. *Industrialisation and Trade Union Organisation in South Africa, 1924–55: The Rise and Fall of the South African Trades and Labour Council*. New York: Cambridge University Press, 1984.

Liebenberg, Ian. "Response to ANC Constitutional Guidelines." *IDASA Occasional Paper #25* (nd).

_____. "Government by Illusion: The Legacy and Its Implications." In *The Hidden Hand: Covert Operations in South Africa*, edited by A. Minnear, 25–41.Pretoria: Human Sciences Research Council, 1994.

Lieberfeld, Daniel. "Getting to the Negotiating Table: Domestic and International Dynamics." *Politikon* 27 (2000): 19–36.

Lodge, Tom. *Black Politics in South Africa since 1945*. New York: Longman, 1983.

_____. *All Here, and Now: Black Politics in South Africa in the 1980s*. Cape Town: David Philip, 1991.

Lotter, H.P.P. "Some Christian Perceptions of Social Justice in a Transforming South Africa." *Politikon* 19 (1991): 45–65.

Loubser, J.A. *The Apartheid Bible: A Critical Review of Racial Theology in South Africa*. Cape Town: Maskew Miller Longman, 1987.

Lutheran World Federation. *Southern Africa: Confessional Integrity*, 1977.

Luthuli, Albert "Special Presidential Message – Address to the ANC Annual Conference," 17–18 December 1955.

_____. "Freedom in Our Lifetime: Presidential Address to the 46th Annual Conference of the African National Congress," 14 December 1958.

Magubane, Bernard Makhoseze. *The Political Economy of Race and Class in South Africa*. New York: Monthly Review Press, 1979.

Mamdani, Mahmood. "A Diminished Truth." In *After the TRC: Reflections on Truth and Reconciliation in South Africa*, edited by Wilmot James and Linda van de Vijver, 58–61. Cape Town: David Philip, 2000.

Mandela, Nelson. "The Shifting Sands of Illusion." *Liberation* (June 1953).

_____. "The Mandela Document: A Document Provided by Nelson Mandela to P.W. Botha before their meeting on 5 July 1989," 1989.

_____. "Document Forwarded to F.W. de Klerk," 12 December 1989.

_____. "Address to Rally In Cape Town on his Release from Prison," 11 February 1990.

_____. "Address to Rally in Soweto," 13 February 1990.

_____. "Speech at Pretoria University," 29 April 1991.

_____. "Speech to May Day Rally," 1 May 1991.

_____. "Address to CODESA by Comrade Nelson R. Mandela, President of the ANC," 20 December 1991,

_____. "Intervention of the President of the ANC, Nelson Mandela at the Second Session of CODESA," 16 May 1992.

_____. "Address by Comrade Nelson R. Mandela to the International Federation of Newspaper Publishers Conference," 26 May 1992.

_____. "Letter to Mr. F.W. de Klerk," 26 June 1992.

_____. "Response by ANC President, Nelson Mandela, to President de Klerk's Memorandum," 4 July 1992.

_____. "Letter to F.W. de Klerk," 9 July 1992.

_____. "Address to the Plenary Session of the Multi-Party Negotiations Process," November 17, 1993.

_____. "Statement about the Ultra Right-wing's Threats of Civil War," 26 November 1993.

_____. "Statement on the Occasion of the 32nd Anniversary of MK," 16 December 1993.

_____ . *Long Walk to Freedom.* London: Abacus, 1994.

_____ . "Address to the People of Cape Town," 9 May 1994.

_____ . "Statement of Nelson Mandela at his Inauguration as President of the Democratic Republic of South Africa," 10 May 1994.

_____ . "Address to the Interfaith Commissioning Service for the Truth and Reconciliation Commission, 13 February 1996." In *Nelson Mandela: From Freedom to the Future: Tributes and Speeches*, edited by Kader Asmal, et al. Cape Town: Jonathan Ball Publishers, 2003.

Mandela, Nelson, and Winnie Mandela (Delivered by Oliver Tambo). "Racism, Apartheid and a New World Order," 5 May 1986.

Manzo, Kate. "Afrikaner Fears and the Politics of Despair: Understanding Change in South Africa." *International Studies Quarterly* 36 (1992): 1–24.

Marais, Hein. *South Africa: Limits to Change – The Political Economy of Transition.* London: Zed Books, 1994.

Marks, Shula, and Stanley Trapido, eds. *The Politics of Race, Class and Nationalism in Twentieth Century South Africa.* London: Longman, 1987.

Mayson, Cedric. "Religion and the Freedom Charter." *ANC Today* 1 (8–14 June 2001).

Mbembe, Achille. "African Modes of Self-Writing." *Public Culture* 14 (2002): 239–73.

McKinley, Dale. *The ANC and Liberation Struggle.* London: Pluto Press, 1997.

Meiring, Piet. "The *Baruti* versus the Lawyers: The Role of Religion in the TRC Process." In *Looking Back, Reaching Forward: Reflections on the Truth and Reconciliation Commission of South Africa*, edited by Charles Villa-Vicencio and Wilhelm Verwoerd, 123–33. Cape Town: University of Cape Town Press, 2000.

Moodie, Dunbar. *The Rise of Afrikanerdom: Power, Apartheid and the Afrikaner Civil Religion.* Berkeley: University of California Press, 1975.

Moodley, Kogila. "African Renaissance and Language Policies in Comparative Perspective." *Politikon* 27 (2000): 103–15.

Mosala, Itumeleng. "The Meaning of Reconciliation: A Black Perspective." *Journal of Theology for Southern Africa* 59 (1987): 19–25.

_____ . *Biblical Hermeneutics and Black Theology in South Africa.* Grand Rapids: Eerdmans, 1989.

Motlhabi, Mokgethi, ed. *Essays on Black Theology.* Johannesburg University Christian Movement, 1973.

MPNP. *MPNP – Plenary Session and Documents: Adopted Resolutions of the Multi-Party Negotiating Process.* Kempton Park: MPNP, 13 May 1993.

Nathan, Laurie. "An Imperfect Bridge: Crossing to Democracy on the Peace Accord." *Track Two* (2 May 1993): 1–5.

Ndebele, Njabulo. "Memory, Metaphor and the Triumph of Narrative." In *Negotiating the Past: The Making of Memory in South Africa*, edited by Sarah Nuttall, 19–28. Oxford: Oxford University Press, 1998.

NGK, General Synod. *Human Relations and the South African Scene in Light of Scripture.* Cape Town: Dutch Reformed Church Publishers, 1974.

NGK. *Church and Society: A Testimony of the Dutch Reformed Church.* Bloemfontein: General Synodical Commission, 1987.

Ngubengcuka, R.O. "The ANC and Nationalism." *Liberation: a Journal of Democratic Discussion* 22 (1956).

Nicholson, Christopher. *Permanent Removal: Who Killed the Cradock Four?* Johannesburg: Witwatersrand University Press, 2004.

Nolan, Albert. "Theology in a Prophetic Mode." In *Hammering Swords into Ploughshares: Essays in Honour of Archbishop Mpilo Desmond Tutu,* edited by B. Tlhagale, 132–40. Johannesburg: Skotaville Publishers, 1986.

_____ . "*Kairos* Theology," in *Doing Theology in Context,* edited by John de Gruchy and Charles Villa-Vicencio, 212–218. Cape Town: David Philip, 1994.

Noonan, Patrick. *They're Burning the Churches.* Bellvue: Jacana, 2003.

Norval, Aletta. *Deconstructing Apartheid Discourse.* London: Verso, 1996.

Nurnberger, Klaus. *The Cost of Reconciliation in South Africa.* Cape Town: Methodist Publishing House, 1988.

Nussbaum, Martha C. *The Fragility of Goodness: Luck and Ethics in Greek Tragedy and Philosophy.* Cambridge: Cambridge University Press, 1986.

Odendaal, Andre. "Liberalism and the African National Congress." Paper presented at the Conference on Liberalism in South Africa, Houw Hoek, July 1986.

O'Donnell, Guillermo, Philippe C. Schmitter, and Laurence Whitehead, eds. *Transitions from Authoritarian Rule, Vols. 1–4.* Baltimore: Johns Hopkins University Press, 1986.

O'Meara, Dan. *Volkskapitalisme: Class, Capital and Ideology in the Development of Afrikaner Nationalism, 1934–1948.* Johannesburg: Ravan Press, 1983.

_____ . *Forty Lost Years: The Apartheid State and the Politics of the National Party, 1948–1994.* Johannesburg: Ravan Press, 1996.

Osborne, Peter. "Small-scale Victories, Large Scale Defeats: Walter Benjamin's Politics of Time." In *Destruction and Experience: Walter Benjamin's Philosophy,* edited by Andrew Benjamin and Peter Osborne, 57–109. Manchester: Clinamen Press, 2000.

Parker, Peter. "The Politics of Indemnities, Truth Telling and Reconciliation: Ending Apartheid without Forgetting." *Human Rights Law Journal* 17 (April 30, 1996): 1–13.

Pillay, Gerald. *Voices of Liberation: Albert Luthuli, Volume 1.* Pretoria: HSRC Publishers, 1993.

Pityana, Nyameko. "What is Black Consciousness?" In *The Challenge of Black Theology in South Africa,* edited by Basil Moore, 58–63. Atlanta: John Knox, 1974.

Posel, Deborah. "The Language of Domination, 1978–1983." In *The Politics of Race, Class and Nationalism in Twentieth Century South Africa,* edited by Shula Marks and Stanley Trapido, 419–443. London: Longman, 1987.

_____ . *The Making of Apartheid, 1948–1961: Conflict and Compromise.* Oxford: Clarendon Press, 1991.

Posel, Deborah, and Graeme Simpson, eds. *Commissioning the Past: Understanding South Africa's Truth and Reconciliation Commission.* Johannesburg: Witwatersrand University Press, 2002.

Price, Robert. *The Apartheid State in Crisis, 1975–1990.* New York: Oxford University Press, 1991.

Rabinow, Paul. *Anthropos Today: Reflections on Modern Equipment.* Princeton: Princeton University Press, 2003.

Ramose, Mogobe. "The Philosophy of Ubuntu and Ubuntu as a Philosophy." In *Philosophy From Africa,* edited by P.H. Coetzee and A.P.J. Roux, 230–30. Oxford: Oxford University Press, 2002.

Record of Understanding and Meeting Between the State President of the Republic of

South Africa and the President of the African National Congress Held at the World
Trade Centre, 26 September 1992.

*Report of the Commission of Enquiry into Complaints by Former African National Congress
Prisoners and Detainees.* Bellville: Centre for Development Studies, 1992.

Republic of South Africa. *Indemnity Act* (No. 35), 15 May 1990.

Republic of South Africa. *Promotion of National Unity and Reconciliation Act* (No. 34
of 1995).

Rhoodie, Nic. *Apartheid: A Socio-Historical Exposition of the Origin and Development of the
Apartheid Idea.* Cape Town: H.A.U.M., 1959.

_____ . "White South African's Expectations Regarding Democratic Nation-Building
and Community Reconciliation." In *Democratic Nation-building in South Africa,* edited
by Nic Rhoodie, 257–73. Pretoria: HSRC Publishers, 1994.

Rich, Paul. "Liberalism and Ethnicity in South African Politics, 1921–1948." *African
Studies* 35 (1976).

_____ . *State Power and Black Politics in South Africa, 1912–1951.* New York: St. Martins
Press, 1996.

_____ , ed. *The Dynamics of Change in Southern Africa.* London: St. Martins, 1996.

Ritner, Susan. *Salvation through Separation: the Role of the Dutch Reformed Church in South
Africa in the Formulation of Afrikaner Race Ideology.* Ph.D. Dissertation, Columbia
University, 1974.

Rosenthal, Richard. *Mission Improbable: A Piece of the South African Story.* Cape Town:
David Philip, 1998.

Ross, Fiona. *Bearing Witness.* Cape Town: Pluto Press, 2003.

Ruiz, Lester. "Theology, Politics, and the Discourses of Transformation." *Alternatives* 13
(1988): 155–76.

Rwelamira, M.R., and G. Werle, eds. *Confronting Past Injustices: Approaches to Amnesty,
Punishment, Reparation and Restitution in South Africa and Germany.* Durban:
Butterworths, 1996.

Sachs, Albie. "Notes From CODESA." *Mayibuye* (May 1992).

Salazar, Philippe-Joseph. *An African Athens: Rhetoric and the Shaping of Democracy in South
Africa.* London: Lawrence Erlbaum, 2002.

_____ . "Compromise and Deliberation: A Rhetorical View of South Africa's Democratic
Transformation." *Social Science Information* 43 (2004): 145–66.

Sarkin, Jeremy. "The Trials and Tribulations of South Africa's Truth and Reconciliation
Commission." *South African Journal on Human Rights* 12 (1996): 617–640.

Sax, Benjamin. "Active Individuality and the Language of Confession: The Figure
of the Beautiful Soul in the *Lehrjahre* and the *Phänomenologie.*" *Journal of the History
of Philosophy* 21 (1993): 437–466.

Schloemann, Martin. "The Special Case for Confessing: Reflections on the Casus
Confessionis in the Light of History and Systematic Theology." In *The Debate on
Status Confessionis: Studies in Christian Political Theology,* edited by Eckehart Lorennz,
47–94. Geneva: Lutheran World Federation, 1983.

Schrire, Robert, ed. *Adapt or Die: The End of White Politics in South Africa.* London:
Hurst & Company, 1991.

Seekings, Jeremy. *The UDF: A History of the United Democratic Front in South Africa,
1983–1991.* London: James Currey, 2000.

Simkins, Charles. *Liberalism and the Problem of Power.* Johannesburg: South African Institute of Race Relations, 1986.

Sisk, Timothy. *Democratization in South Africa: The Elusive Social Contract.* Princeton: Princeton University Press, 1995.

Slovo, Joe. "Negotiations: What Room for Compromise?" *African Communist* 3rd Qtr. (1992).

Smit, Dirkie. "Confession-Guilt-Truth and Forgiveness in the Christian Tradition." In *To Remember and To Heal: Theological and Psychological Reflections on Truth and Reconciliation,* edited by Russell Botman, 96–117. Cape Town: Human and Rousseau, 1996.

South African Catholic Bishops' Conference. "The Bishops' Statement on the Day of Mourning and Prayer." *Journal of Theology for Southern Africa* 52 (1985).

South African Council of Churches. "Prayers for the End to Unjust Rule." *Journal of Theology for Southern Africa* 52 (1985), 56–71.

South African Institute of Race Relations, *Race Relations Survey 1985.* Pretoria: South African Institute of Race Relations, 1986.

_____ . *Race Relations Survey, 1991/92.* Johannesburg: SAIRR, 1992.

South African Pressclips. *Mandela Comes Home.* Cape Town: South Africa Pressclips, 1990.

Soyinka, Wole. *The Burden of Memory, The Muse of Forgiveness.* New York: Oxford University Press, 1999.

Sparks, Allister. *The Mind of South Africa.* London: Mandarin, 1991.

_____ . *Tomorrow is Another Country: The Inside Story of South Africa's Road to Change.* Chicago: University of Chicago Press, 1995.

Spitz, Richard, and Matthew Chaskalson. *The Politics of Transition: A Hidden History of South Africa's Negotiated Settlement.* Johannesburg: Witwatersrand University Press, 2000.

Stanley, Elizabeth. "Evaluating the Truth and Reconciliation Commission." *Journal of Modern African Studies* 39 (2001): 525–46.

Szeftel, Morris. "Ethnicity and Democratization in South Africa," *Review of Political Economy* 60 (1994).

Tambo, Oliver. "Tribute to the UN Special Committee against Apartheid," 2 April 1973.

_____ . "Message to the People of South Africa," 26 June 1974.

_____ . "Victory is Within Our Grasp: Statement at the World Conference on Sanctions Against Racist South Africa," Paris, 16 June 1986.

_____ . "We have Decided to Liberate Ourselves – Address to the Royal Commonwealth Society," London, 23 June 1986.

Thompson, Leonard. *The Political Mythology of Apartheid.* New Haven: Yale University Press, 1985.

_____ . *A History of South Africa.* New Haven: Yale University Press, 1995.

Truth and Reconciliation Commission of South Africa. *Truth and Reconciliation Commission Final Report.* 7 Vols. Pretoria: Republic of South Africa, 1998/2003.

Tutu, Desmond. "Apartheid is Heresy." In *Apartheid is a Heresy,* edited by John de Gruchy and Charles Villa-Vicencio, 39–47. Grand Rapids: Eerdmans, 1983.

_____ . *Hope and Suffering: Sermons and Speeches.* Johannesburg: Skotaville, 1983.

_____ . "His Death Is Our Victory." In *The Rainbow People of God: The Making of a Peaceful Revolution,* edited by John Allen. New York: Doubleday, 1994.

_____ . "Archbishop Tutu's Address to the First Gathering of the Truth and Reconciliation Commission," 16 December 1995.

_____ . *No Future Without Forgiveness.* London: Rider, 1999.

Van der Merwe, Stoffel. *What About Black People?* Cape Town: Federal Information Service of the National Party, 1985.

Van Jaarsveld, F.A. *The Awakening of Afrikaner Nationalism, 1868–1881.* Cape Town: Human and Rousseau, 1961.

Van Vuuren, Willem. "Transition Politics and the Prospects of Democratic Consolidation in South Africa." *Politikon* 22 (1995): 5–23.

Van Zyl Slabbert, Frederick. "The Dynamics of Reform and Revolt in Current South Africa." *Tanner Lectures on Human Values.* Oxford University, 27 October 1987.

_____ . "Preconditions to Negotiations: Is the Gap Closing?" *Democracy in Action* (1988): 4.

_____ . "Democracy: A Vision for the Future." *Sowetan Quarterly State of the Nation* (Summer 1991): 4–6.

Verwoerd, Hendrik. "Address to the Native Representative Council, 5 December 1950." In *Verwoerd Speaks: Speeches 1948–1966.* Johannesburg: APB Publishers, 1966.

Villa-Vicencio, Charles. *Theology and Violence: The South African Debate.* Grand Rapids: Eerdmans, 1988.

_____ . *Civil Disobedience and Beyond: Law, Resistance, and Religion in South Africa.* Grand Rapids: Eerdmans, 1990.

_____ . *A Theology of Reconstruction: Nation-Building and Human Rights.* Cambridge: Cambridge University Press, 1992.

_____ , ed. *Transcending a Century of Injustice.* Cape Town: Institute for Justice and Reconciliation, 2000.

Villa-Vicencio, Charles, and Wilhelm Verwoerd, eds. *Looking Back, Reaching Forward: Reflections on the Truth and Reconciliation Commission of South Africa.* Cape Town: UCT Press, 2000.

Villa-Vicencio, Charles, and Erik Doxtader, eds. *The Provocations of Amnesty: Memory, Justice and Impunity.* Cape Town: David Phillip, 2003.

Vorster, B.J. "Speech Delivered at a Rally of the East Rand Rapportryers." In *B.J. Vorster: Selected Speeches.* Bloemfontein: Institute for Contemporary History, 1977.

Waldmeir, Patti. *Anatomy of a Miracle: The End of Apartheid and the Birth of the New South African Constitution.* New York: WW Norton, 1997.

Walker, Cheryl. *Women and Resistance in South Africa.* Cape Town: David Philip, 1991.

Walshe, Peter. *The Rise of African Nationalism in South Africa: The African National Congress, 1912–1952.* London: C. Hurst & Co., 1970.

_____ . *The Rise of Afrikaner Nationalism in South Africa.* Berkeley: University of California Press, 1971.

_____ . *Church versus State in South Africa.* London: C. Hurst, 1983.

_____ . *Prophetic Christianity and the Liberation Movement in South Africa.* Pietermaritzburg: Cluster, 1995.

_____ . "Christianity and the Anti-Apartheid Struggle: The Prophetic Voice within Divided Churches." In *Christianity in South Africa: A Political, Social and Cultural History,* edited by Richard Elphick, 383–399. Berkeley: University of California Press, 1997.

Wells, Julia. *We Now Demand! The History of Women's Resistance to Pass Laws in South Africa*. Johannesburg: Witwatersrand University Press, 1993.

Welsh, Franke. *South Africa: A Narrative History*. New York: Kodansha International, 1999.

Wilson, Richard A. *The Politics of Truth and Reconciliation in South Africa*. Cambridge: Cambridge University Press, 2001.

Wiredu, Kwasi. "Democracy and Consensus in African Traditional Politics: A Plea for Non-party Polity." In *Postcolonial African Philosophy: A Critical Reader*, edited by Emmanuel Chukwudi Eze, 303–12. London: Blackwell, 1997.

Wittgenstein, Ludwig. *The Blue and the Brown Books*. New York: Harper Torchbooks, 1960.

Wolpe, Harold. *Race, Class and the Apartheid State*. London: James Currey, 1988.

south african archives and archival collections

african national congress – documents, speeches and press releases
African National Congress Online Library. URL: <www.anc.org.za>.
ANC Archive, Fort Hare University.
Mayibuye Centre, University of the Western Cape.

convention for a democratic south africa (CODESA) – speeches, minutes, records
CODESA Documents. South African National Archives, Pretoria, South Africa.
Government Documents Library, University of Cape Town.

multi-party negotiating process (MPNP) – speeches, meeting minutes, working documents, submissions
MPNP Ad Hoc Committee on Sufficient Consensus. MPNP Files (unsorted). South African National Archives, Pretoria, South Africa.
MPNP Facilitating Committee Minutes. MPNP Files (unsorted). South African National Archives, Pretoria, South Africa.
MPNP Negotiating Forum Records. MPNP Files (unsorted). South African National Archives, Pretoria, South Africa.
MPNP Negotiating Council Minutes. MPNP Files (unsorted). South African National Archives, Pretoria, South Africa.
MPNP Negotiating Council Resolutions. Adopted Resolutions of the MPNP, 5 March to 17 November 1993. MPNP Files (unsorted), South African National Archives, Pretoria, South Africa.

south african parliament – debates and legislation
Debates of Parliament (Hansard).
Debates of the National Assembly (Hansard).
Joint Sittings of Both Houses of Parliament (Hansard).
Government Gazette.

promotion of national unity and reconciliation bill – testimony and submissions

African Studies Library, University of Cape Town.
Materials delivered to Parliament's Joint Committee on Justice with regards to the Promotion of National Unity and Reconciliation Bill. Unsorted Files. Archives of Parliament, Cape Town, South Africa.

south african newspapers and popular media collections

ANC Daily News Briefing Archive (digital).
Business Day.
Cape Times (print and digital).
Cape Argus (print and digital).
Drum.
Eastern Province Herald.
Mail & Guardian (print and digital).
New Nation.
PE *Evening Post* (digital).
Sechaba.
South African Press Association (digital).
Sunday Independent.
The Sowetan.
The Weekly Mail.

author's interviews

Asmal, Kader. Cape Town, 15 August 2002.
Bizos, George. Johannesburg, 1 March 2001.
Boraine, Alex. Cape Town, 12 July 2000.
Burton, Mary. Cape Town, 13 March 2001.
Cheadle, Halton. Cape Town, 22 August 2000.
Coetzee, Martin. Cape Town, 20 February 2001.
Corder, Hugh. Cape Town, 12 April 2000.
de Lange, Johnny. Cape Town, 20 and 21 June 2000.
Maharaj, Mac. Johannesburg, 16 January 2001.
Meyer, Roelf. Brooklyn, Pretoria, 7 September 2000.
Mkhatshwa, Smangaliso. Cape Town, 4 October 2000.
Nathan, Laurie, 16 August 2001.
Omar, Dullah. Cape Town, 9 November 2000.
Rosenthal, Richard. Cape Town, 14 September 2000.
Steward, Dave. Cape Town, 11 September 2000.
Tutu, Desmond. Cape Town, 23 August 2001.
Viljoen, Constand. Cape Town, 11 October 2000.
Villa-Vicencio, Charles. Cape Town, October 1999.

index

AAC 107

Adam, Heribert

Adorno, Theodor 12, 15

African Independent
Churches 59

Afrikaans language movement
46, 82, 97, 98, 225

Afrikaner nationalism 45, 46,
59, 92, 94, 96, 98–101, 104,
107–110
organising myths 97
Volksfront 242
volkstaat 204, 207–208, 213
youth 95, 99, 108

Agamben, Giorgio 81, 140

Alexander, Benny 180

amnesty 10, 22, 23, 133,
169–174, 201–202, 214–215,
216–217, 228–229, 231–232,
233–236, 239–241, 245–246,
249, 252
conditional 272
disclosure 267
NEC refusal 206
TRC 253, 255–262
violating constitution,
human rights 260, 275–276

ANC 27, 45, 111, 114–115,
117–118, 130, 103, 107–109,
168, 211, 212, 223, 244–246
African's Claims in South
Africa 101–102, 244
ANC's Defiance
Campaign 103
ANCYL 101–102
Basic Document 102–103
Bill of Rights 176–177
Campaign for Peace and

Democracy and mass
action 168
collective identification 109
Congress Alliance 104, 107
Harare Declaration 120
Kabwe Conference 111
MK 64, 105, 88–89, 111,
115, 134, 139, 162, 219
Motsuenyane Commission
204, 216, 229, 245
nationalism 92, 94, 99, 100,
104, 108–110
non-racialism 93, 101, 109,
136, 176
Sechaba 39, 113
suspended negotiations 164
tension with UDF 129
withdrawal from National
Peace Accord 163

Anti-Communism Act see
Suppression of Communism
Act 98, 104

apartheid, violence of 58
four pillars of 47, 113
Groote Schuur Minute 131
identitarian logic (of
apartheid) 21, 42, 48, 50, 55,
58, 62, 63, 70, 82, 96, 239,
284–285
Pretoria Minute 134
see also separate development

Arendt, Hannah 15

Asmal, Kader 9, 23, 14, 23, 163,
198, 229–231, 250, 255, 274

AVF 183, 228

AVU 172

AWB 112, 188, 243

AZAPO 146–7

AZAPO, Biko, Ribeiro vs
Pres. of SA et al 275–80

Barthes, Roland 66

Belhar Confession 69, 70

Benjamin, Walter xi, 175, 292

Biko, Steve 67, 68

Bisho 174

Black Nationalism 68

Black Theology (and BCM)
58, 64, 67, 68, 70, 71, 72, 78,
82, 288

Blackburn, Molly, 37

Blumenberg, Hans 15, 287

Boesak, Allan 68, 69

Bonhoeffer, Dietrich 66

Boipatong 174

Bonganjalo, Goba 70

Boraine, Alex 13, 93, 116, 229,
248, 256, 262

Botha, P.W. 14, 35, 38, 86, 87,
110, 112, 117, 119, 121

Breytenbach, Breyten 236

Broederbond 88

Burke, Kenneth 200

Burton, Mary 123

Buthelezi, Manas 71

Buthelezi, Mangosuthu 147,
243, 252

Calata, Fort 38

Camus, Albert 2

Cassim, Farouk 132, 190–191,
272

Cassin, Barbara 87

CCB 130, 145

Chikane, Frank 75

Chiole, Joseph 223

Christian Institute 61, 62, 65

CODESA xiii, 8, 16, 22,

140–141, 143–148, 157, 159,
161–162, 173–178, 182–183,
190, 195, 197–198, 229, 275
CODESA II 162–163
Declaration of Intent 146,
148–155
Coetsee, Kobie 119, 121, 132,
169, 205
Confession of Faith (WARC)
69, 70
Congress of South African
Students 40
Consensus 192–193
Constitution
legitimacy of state
involvement 150
negotiations 141–143
transition 188
writing of 135, 183
see also interim constitution
*Constitution of the Republic of
South Africa Bill* 218
COSATU 37
CP 88, 147, 221, 223–224
Cradock Four, 36, 38, 75,
169, 294
Cronje, Rowan 181, 210
Cuthbertson, Craig 58
Dakar, 1987 meeting
in 116–117
De Beer, Zach 149
De Gruchy, John 12, 75
De Jager, Christiaan 172
de Klerk, F.W. 86, 89,
111–123, 131,135, 138, 147,
150, 159, 162, 170–171,
173, 177, 206, 209–210,
218, 228, 244, 250, 252, 288
at CODESA 150
election 121–22
February 2 1990 speech 123
re indemnity 131–32
referendum 161–62
relations with ANC 128–29,
164–67, 170
view of reconciliation
122,126
view of transition 128
De Klerk, W.A. 47, 96, 157, 209
De Kock, Eugene 73, 173, 256

De Lange, Johnny 8, 249–250,
253
De Villiers, Dawid 225
Degenaar, Johan 45
Du Plessis, Daniel 219–220
Du Toit, Andre 97, 235, 273
Du Toit, Dirk 273
Du Toit, S.J. 51
Dubow, Saul 44
Dutch Reformed Church
see NGK
Eglin, Colin 180, 221
English-speaking churches 21,
41, 58, 72, 91, 293, 297
EPG 113
Fanon, Frantz xii
Felgate, Walter 185
Fismer, Christiaan 283
Foucault, Michel 287
Freedom Alliance 207, 208,
210–211
Freedom Charter 37, 104, 107,
176, 208, 213, 244, 292
Friedman, Steven 129, 135
Further Indemnity Act 22, 171,
173, 174, 176, 197, 204, 257
see also indemnity
Gadamer, Hans-Georg 17
Garvey, Marcus 102
Gerhart, Gail 101, 107
Gevisser, Mark 247
Giliomee, Hermann 97
Goldstone Commission 137,
169, 206, 243, 275
Goldstone, Richard 247
Goniwe, Matthew 38, 169
Goniwe, Nyameka x, 294
good faith 24, 111, 125, 126,
128, 135, 137, 139, 141,
194, 289
see also reconciliation
Gordhan, Pravin 178–180,
185, 187, 189–190
Gordimer, Nadine 199
Gous, Pieter 132
Green, Louis 274
Group Areas Act 49
Habermas, Jürgen 142
Hani, Chris 140, 163, 181
Harms Commission 130

Hartzenberg, Ferdie 209–210,
220
Haysom, Nicholas 39
Hegel, G.W. F. x, 13, 83, 92
Hendrickse, Michael 222
Hertzog Bills 100
Holomisa, General Bantu 205
Horowitz, Donald 141
Howarth, David 141
HRVC 266, 295
Hume, David 284
IDASA 116
identity and community
108–109
and memory 238
IEC 242, 243
IFP 129, 137, 147, 190, 191,
243
Indemnity Act 127, 131,132, 133,
134, 139
indemnity 131–135, 170–172,
203, 211, 243, 253, 257–258,
277
see also amnesty
Inkatha Freedom Party 147,
243
interim constitution 201 203,
209–211, 217–218, 221–222,
224, 227–228, 243, 268
as law of faith 216
see also post-amble
interim government 135, 137,
148, 160, 161–162, 177, 191,
199, 245
Internal Security Act 73
Jacobs, Fanie 189
Jacos, Stephanus 224
Jeffery, Anthea, 7
Jordan, Pallo 114, 164, 173
Justice in Transition 229,
236, 248
kairos 64, 65, 76, 78, 92, 140,
288, 294
Kairos Document 40–42, 57,
73–74, 76–82, 84, 89, 108,
197, 288, 291–292
Kinghorn, Johann 52
Koornhof, Nicolaas 226
Koselleck, Reinhart 15
Krog, Antjie 6, 12, 94, 295

Kuyper, Abraham 52, 59, 62
Kwandebele Nine 36
KZG 191
Landers, Luwellyn 172
Langley, Tom 189
language *see* rhetoric
Lapsley, Michael 130
Le Grange, Louis 113
Le Roux, Frank 132, 133, 189
Lekota, Mosiuoa 129
Lembede, Anton 100, 102, 106, 109
Liberal Party 109
Liberalism 106, 107
Lutheran World Federation 65–66
Luthuli, Albert 103, 106
Maduna, Penuell 129
Maharaj, Mac xiii, 93, 134, 212
Malan, Daniel 46, 48, 56, 98, 224
Mamdani, Mahmood 7
Mandela, Nelson 2, 5, 6, 11, 13, 18, 21, 37, 88, 89, 103–105, 108, 111, 113, 119, 122, 126, 130, 136, 137, 138, 164, 174, 200, 208, 244, 280, 288
early work 103
election and inauguration 243–45
100 days address 254
CODESA 148–150
constitution 210
miracle of transition 283
Nobel Peace Prize 218
power of speech 270–271
productive opposition 163
Programme of Action 103
reconciliation 165–167
release and world tour 127–129
state of the nation address 247–248
Unesco Peace Prize 160
Mangope, Lucas 148, 243
Manual, Trevor 199
Marais, Pieter 224
Maree, Johannes 274
Matthews, Joe 106
Mbeki, Thabo 114, 130, 212

Mbembe, Achille 49
Mda, A.P. 106
Mdlalose, Frank 140, 149
Mendez, Juan 234
Meyer, Roelf 93 124, 168, 199, 219, 221, 226, 238
Mhlaui, Sicelo 38
Michnik, Adam 233
Mixed Marriages Act 112
Mkhatshwa, Smangaliso 93
Mkhonto, Sparrow 38
Mohamed, Justice Ismail 151, 209, 276–280
Momberg, Jan 172, 273
Moodie, Dunbar 46, 96
Moodley, Kogila 111
Morkel, Gerald 222
MPNP 144, 175, 176, 178, 181, 182, 185, 190–192, 194, 196, 198–199, 201–203, 208, 211, 216, 224, 228, 232, 261, 292
see also Sufficient Consensus
Mulder, Cornelius 220, 272
Mulder, Pieter 225
Nathan, Laurie 40, 137
National Peace Accord 137, 146, 205
Native Bills 44, 45
Native Land Act 45, 100
Natives Representation Council 101
Naudé, Beyers 61
NEC 86, 205
NGK 40, 41, 43–44, 49–53, 55–57, 59, 61, 64, 69, 82, 85, 88, 100, 135, 224–226, 288
Human Relations and the South African Scene in Light of Scripture 50–57, 95
Ngubane, Ben 184
NHK 69
Niehaus, Carl 177
Nietverdient Ten 36
NIR church divisions 75–76
Nolan, Albert 65
Norgaard principles 134
Norwal, Aletta 45, 55
NP 88, 111, 135
OAU 120

Omar, Dullah 14, 248, 250–254, 256, 261, 268–270
O'Meara, Daniel 96
Oosthuizen, Abrie 206
PAC 60, 104, 146, 203, 273
Padayachy, Kassavan 221
Peterson, Hector 65
Pityana, Nyameko 67
Population Registration Act 43, 48, 49, 50, 55, 56, 59
Post-amble [epilogue] of 1993 interim constitution xiii, 9, 22, 201, 211, 213–217, 237, 241, 255, 265, 276
see also interim constitution
Promotion of National Unity and Reconciliation Act 18, 23, 246, 256–258, 260, 263–265, 266–269, 272, 273–274, 275–276, 280
Public Safety Amendment Bill 113
Rabie, Jakobus 223
Rabinow, Paul 17
Radue, Raymond 133
Ramaphosa, Cyril 147, 168, 178–180, 212
reconciliation, concept in relation to
accountability 255
ambiguity 12
amnesty 10, 22, 133, 215
as becoming 284, 297
as critique of violence 19, 292, 298
as *pharmakon* 293
basis for speech 111
catharsis 231
Christianity, liberation 71
collective action 4, 80, 289
collective deliberation 257, 292
collective interaction 70
commonality 21, 22
communication 14
compromise 9
compromise and consensus 93
conditions for speech 120
confession and repentance 165

constitutive opposition 198
constitutive power 19, 22,
91, 142, 289, 292
contract of constitution 225
controversies and questions
291
dignity 255
disclosure 263
Dutch Reformed Church 2
essentialism 286
exchange: rights for honor,
truth for amnesty 269, 279
faith 35, 84, 174, 247, 269
forgiveness x
Hegel, G.W.F. 13
identity 70
justice 197, 241
kairos ('extraordinary time')
21, 72, 83, 84
kenosis 266
law of faith 216
legislation 23, 24
logical operation 120
Mandela, Nelson 2, 14, 122,
165, 167, 174, 270
messianic potential 62, 292
meta-discourse (talk about
talk) 18, 84, 85, 112, 134,
137, 138, 139, 140, 143, 178,
286, 293
middle voice 20, 23 course
272, 279
time 287–289, 297
mode of opposition 74
MPNP and TRC
interpretations 203
naming 78, 80, 81
negotiation politics 116
NGK's early view 52–55
not claiming victory 262
people-centred view 252
personal guilt 77
post-amble 212
potential (*dunamis*) xi, 13,
14, 36
power of speech 12, 13,
249, 257
prior to TRC 8, 10
productive disagreement 287

productive negativity
214, 239
productive opposition 84,
110, 139, 163, 176, 195, 289,
293, 296
productive vulnerability 269,
280
public discourse 292
reconstruction 252
representation 19
rhetorical nature x, 4, 15, 16,
17, 20, 80, 81, 84, 91, 139,
142, 144, 231, 240, 264, 271,
283–285, 286–287, 289–290,
292–293, 295–296, 298
risk of passivity 108
sacrifice of self-certainty 1,
20, 22, 24, 63, 112, 126, 167,
226, 242, 269, 271–273, 273,
281, 289, 296–298
separate development 49
speech (action) 3, 14, 81,
187, 231, 246, 255, 285–286,
287, 293, 296
subject and object
of discourse 18
sufficient consensus 20,
22, 147
time and stasis 20
transition 19, 239, 293
truth-telling 245, 258
ubuntu 71
unity in difference 13, 14,
20, 63, 70, 84, 279, 293
victims and perpetrators 269
vs state of emergency
285–292
wholeness in life 69
willingness to stand in
contradiction 159
see also unity in difference
Record of Understanding
170–171, 174
Reddy, Jagaram 133
Reparation 115
rhetoric
as naming 78–83
constitution 142
element of nationalism 108
form of study 4, 15, 17

historical inquiry 4, 16, 81
invention 80
speech acts 126
see also reconciliation
Rich, Paul 96
Ross, Fiona 295
Rousseau, Jean-Jacques 199
Sachs, Albie 232, 235
SACP 103, 107, 173, 256
SAG *Progress through Separate
Development* 94
Talking with the ANC 115
*Truth and Reconciliation
Commission* 268
Salazar, Philippe-Joseph 15, 295
SAP 275
Savage, Beth 194
Schloemann, Martin 65–66
separate development
Christian nationalism 95–96,
107, 110
Christianity 43
criticism by *Cottesloe
Statement* 60–64
logic of the ban 82
national differentiation 47
NGK 50–54
NHK 69
'parallel logic' 53, 55
preparation for
reconciliation 50
unity and diversity 54–60
see also apartheid
see also SAG
Sharpeville massacre 40, 60,
104
Sisulu, Walter 104
Sizani, Richard 273–274
Skweyiya Commission 168,
229
Slovo, Joe 173, 185, 189, 212
Smuts, Jan 1, 2, 102
Smuts, Mudene 133
South Africa Act 44
South African Council of
Churches SACC 59
A Call to Prayer for the End
to Unjust Rule 74
Cottesloe Statement 60, 61, 63,
64, 75

Message to the People of South Africa 61–65, 67, 69
South African Native National Congress 100
South African Students' Organisation 67
sovereignty 145, 167
Soyinka, Wole 7
St James Church massacre 203
stasis, public 'language trouble' 87, 88, 91,92, 111–112, 125–126, 127, 138, 141, 156–158, 174, 276, 288–289
state of emergency 39, 40, 60, 66, 73, 75, 83, 86, 92, 113, 243
    as potential for 292
    see also reconciliation
status confessionis 65–66, 69, 70, 76
Steward, Dave 14, 121
Steyn, Pierre 210
Storey, Peter, 74
sufficient consensus 20, 22, 140, 143, 144, 147, 154, 175, 178–81, 183, 185–186, 188, 190, 194–197, 207, 212, 216, 289, 292, 296
    see also MPNP
    see also CODESA
Suppression of Communism Act 98, 104
talks about talks 110–125
    see also reconciliation
Tambo, Oliver 49, 99, 105, 110, 114, 129, 182
TEC 206, 242
Terreblanche, Eugene 112, 208, 219
third force 73, 130, 141, 145, 173, 243
Tomlinson Report 48
Total Strategy 86, 87, 125
transition 5, 19, 22, 80, 111, 148, 151–152, 159, 161, 166, 174–177, 188, 190, 194, 198–202, 217–218, 222, 226–227, 229, 233, 239, 241,

244–245, 278–279, 288, 292, 297
TRC ix, 5, 202–203
    aims of 264
    authorising legislation 246, 253, 257
    AZAPO lawsuit 275
    birth in compromise 9
    central aims 6
    collective vs individual responsibility 259
    concept of truth commission 23, 163, 170, 205, 211, 233, 248–249
    counterpart to negotiations 9
    criticism of 7, 8
    defining laws 8
    design and power 256
    disclosure & accountability 249–252, 278
    disclosure requirement 263–265
    Final Report 7, 8
    independent from political authority 280–290
    law of publicity 256–257, 290
    lifespan 253, 254
    model in the middle 23, 279
    model in the middle 246, 247–248
    post-amble 9
    relation to justice and sacrifice 274, 281
    repentance 272
Treurnicht, Andries 124
Tutu, Desmond x, 5, 40, 58, 71, 128, 181, 266, 275, 293
ubuntu 9, 58, 65, 70, 71, 72, 79, 80, 94, 213, 219, 238, 252, 268, 270, 274, 289, 293
UDF 37, 129, 279
unity in difference ix, 24, 41, 42, 49, 54–57, 59, 99, 70, 84, 94, 99, 110, 139, 144, 197, 201, 208, 216, 236, 238, 239, 241–242, 250, 284, 289, 296

vs unity *as* difference 82
    see also reconciliation
Uys, Stanley 112
Van der Merwe, Fanie 212
Van der Merwe, Stoffel 116
Van Der Westhuizen, 'Joffel' 208
Van der Westhuizen, H.M. 47
Van Eck, Jan 210
Van Heerden, Frederik 222, 226, 273
Van Rensberg, Abraham Janse 225
Van Wyk Louw, N.P. 224
Van Wyk, Wynand 223
Van Zyl Slabbert, Frederik 39, 111, 112, 116, 117, 144
Van Zyl, Paul 259
Vance, Cyrus 168
Verwoerd, Hendrik 61, 104, 107
Verwoerd, Melanie 272
Viljoen, Constand 93, 210, 216, 218, 252, 259, 262
Viljoen, Gerrit 124, 148, 207
Villa-Vicencio, Charles 75, 79
Violence 86, 110,114–115, 119, 120
    church resistance 74
    critique of 290, 293
    Goldstone Commission 137
    reduction 168, 223, 285
Violence: The New Kairos 140
Vorster, B.J. 95–96, 99, 108
Vorster, J.D. 51–52, 56
WARC 69
Webb, Mickey 189
Wessels, Leon 185
Western Province Council of Churches 74
White, Hayden, 15
Williams, Abraham 222
Wilson, Richard 10
Wittgenstein, Ludwig 19
Zalaquett, Jose 234
Zuma, Jacob 129
Zwelithini, King Goodwill 147, 243